P9-DMT-735

THE BEST OF
FOOD&WINE
1989 COLLECTION

American Express
Publishing Corporation
New York

Cover: Boardwalk Buttercrunch Cake (p. 171).

THE BEST OF FOOD & WINE/1989 COLLECTION
Publisher: Claire Gruppo
Editorial Director: Susan Crandell
Editor/Designer: Kate Slate
Art Director: Elizabeth G. Woodson
Managing Editor: Victoria Smith Walsh
Illustrator: Hong Chow

Published by American Express Publishing Corporation
1120 Avenue of the Americas, New York, New York 10036

Manufactured in the United States of America

ISBN 0-916103-08-0

TABLE OF CONTENTS

FOREWORD

We invite you to savor another edition of *The Best of Food & Wine*, a collection of fine recipes that have appeared in the pages of *Food & Wine* magazine. They reflect the same precision and high style you will find in every issue of the magazine. This special collection also echoes our belief that in this frenetic modern age, the kitchen has once again become the focal point of the house. It is the one place where busy friends and family pause and gather to cook and celebrate. And so we present great recipes that you know you can count on, plus menu suggestions to help you plan a major celebration or to pull together an impromptu dinner with finesse. (Look for shaded boxes in all of the entrée chapters; they offer menu recommendations for deliciously tempting meals to fit any occasion, from simple-and-satisfying to showstopper.)

As time becomes more and more precious, you want to make every minute count. And that is why we give you the assurance that every one of the over 450 recipes in this volume will work in your kitchen with minimum fuss and maximum taste. Test kitchen director Diana Sturgis and Marcia Kiesel, the associate director, oversee the testing—and often retesting—of every recipe in *Food & Wine.* They work on home equipment to try out and to translate each recipe, simplifying and refining techniques along the way, and making sure that there is always a big payoff in taste and appeal for cook and guests alike.

This book is filled with inspiration—for an eye-opening breakfast with your family, a quick, low-cal lunch for yourself, a leisurely late-night supper with friends or a gala holiday dinner. It will suit your many moods, from country casual to up-to-the-minute sophisticated, from American regional to international. *The Best of Food & Wine* is for all of us who are passionate about living well.

Ila Stanger

Ila Stanger
Editor-in-Chief

FOOD & WINE'S VINTAGE RATINGS 1977-1987

COMPILED BY ELIN McCOY & JOHN FREDERICK WALKER

	1977	1978	1979	1980	1981
Red Bordeaux	4 Lightweight, lacks fruit. Now or never.	8 Rich, full, good depth. Start drinking.	8 Fruity & well-balanced. Start drinking.	5 Small-scale, lightweight, pleasant. Drink up.	7½ Full, attractive wines. Start tasting.
Sauternes	3 Very weak. Avoid.	5 Big, but lacks typical richness. Drink up.	6 Light but has character. Drink up.	7 Attractive, small-scale. Start drinking.	7½ Well-balanced wines. Start drinking.
Red Burgundy	4 Light, thin, uneven. Avoid.	8 Outstanding; excellent balance. Drink now.	6 Soft, supple, appealing. Drink now.	6 Mostly light wines. Drink now.	5½ Variable vintage. Most early maturing.
White Burgundy	5 Light, lean, acidic. Drink up.	9 Superb; well-balanced. Drink now.	7 Attractive, fruity wines. Drink now.	5 Variable; the best are attractive. Drink now.	8 Attractive wines. Drink now.
Napa/Sonoma Cabernet Sauvignon	7½ Variable. Some well-balanced wines. Drink now.	8 Full, rich, soft. Drink now.	7 Uneven quality; some very good. Start drinking.	8 Powerful, tannic. Start drinking.	8 Variable. Many attractive. Drink now.
Napa/Sonoma Chardonnay	7 Uneven, fading. Drink up.	8 Powerful, ripe wines. Fading. Drink up.	8 Rich, intense, fading. Drink up.	9 Balanced but fading. Drink up.	7 Soft, ripe wines. Drink up.
Barolo & Barbaresco	4 Light, thin wines. Now or never.	9 Classic, concentrated & tannic. Start sampling.	8 Elegant, well-balanced wines. Start drinking.	6 Uneven. Best are well-balanced, attractive. Drink now.	7 Firm, solid wines. Start sampling.
Chianti	7 Good to very good; firm, stylish. Drink up.	8½ Exceptional; solid, tannic. Drink now.	7 Attractive, ripe wines. Drink up.	6 Uneven; best are small-scale. Drink up.	7 Good, firm wines. Drink up
Germany	6 Lightweight, crisp. Drink up.	6 Lightweight, crisp. Drink up.	7 Good quality & balance. Drink up.	5 Light & lean. Drink up.	7 Well-balanced, attractive. Drink up.
Vintage Porto	9½ Superlative; ripe & dense. Wait 6-8 years.	5 Not generally declared. Rich, soft. Try now.	No vintage declared.	7 Light but promising. Sample in 2-6 years.	No vintage declared.

The following ratings and comments reflect a variety of opinions, including our own, on the quality and character of various categories of wines from recent vintages. The ratings—0 for the worst, 10 for the best—are averages, and better or worse wine than indicated can be found in each vintage. Assessments of the most current vintages are more predictive and hence less exact than those of older vintages.

Scores are based on a wine's quality at maturity. A lower-rated but mature wine will often be superior to a higher-rated but immature wine. When-to-drink advice is based on how such wines seemed to be developing in mid-1988, and presumes good storage. The earliest date suggested for consumption applies to the lesser wines of the vintage, which will mature faster than the finest examples of the year.

1982	1983	1984	1985	1986	1987
9½ Rich, massive. Sample now or wait 5 years.	8 Firm, powerful. Try in 3 years.	6 Small-scale, firm. Wait 3 years.	8½ Soft, delicious, elegant. Try in 3 years	8 Mixed vintage. Some classic tannic wines. Try in 6 years.	6 Flavorsome but lightweight. Wait 5 years.
7 Variable. Best are big, powerful wines. Start drinking.	9 Very promising, rich, classic wines. Sample now.	6 Moderate quality. Some good. Drink now.	7½ Good quality. Sample now.	8½ Luscious & rich. Sample now.	6 Not promising; small crop, few good wines.
7 Big, soft wines. Drink now.	9 Some very good, powerful wines. Start sampling.	7 Variable quality. Sample now.	9½ Glorious, rich and round. Wait 2 years.	7 Variable; mostly light, soft wines. Sample now.	7 Promising, stylish lighter wines. Sample now.
8½ Excellent. Big, rich wines. Drink now.	8 Good, rich wines. Start drinking.	7 Some fine. Start drinking.	8 Big but soft. Start sampling.	8½ Crisp, balanced, classic. Start sampling.	7 Light, round, soft. For early drinking.
7½ Lighter style; some attractive. Drink now.	7 Good, but not great. Start drinking.	8 Big, soft, powerful. Try in 2 years.	9 Brilliant, deep and elegant. Wait 4 years.	8 Deep, full and promising. Wait 5 years.	8 Dark, fruity, promising. Wait 5 years.
7½ Many light, some excellent. Drink up.	7 Good moderate year. Drink now.	7 Good full wines. Start drinking.	8 Lovely, balanced. Start sampling.	9 Crisp, leaner style. Start sampling.	8 Elegant and crisp. Start sampling.
8½ Big, powerful wines; very promising. Wait 1-4 years.	7½ Promising vintage. Wait 1-2 years.	5½ Light, variable. For early drinking.	9 Splendid, rich. Wait 4 years.	8 Well-balanced and promising. Wait 5 years.	8 Round, rich, balanced. Wait 5 years.
7½ Attractive but early maturing. Drink now.	7 Attractive, early maturing. Drink now.	5 Spotty. Drink up.	9½ Wonderful. Start sampling.	8 Fine quality; promising. Wait 1 year.	7 Average quality. Start sampling.
7 Soft, fruity. Drink up.	9 Excellent year. Marvelous late-harvest wines. Drink now.	7 Pleasant. Drink now.	8½ Excellent. Start sampling.	6 Light wines for early consumption.	7 Mostly average, some fine. Start sampling.
7 Soft, well-balanced. Sample in 4-7 years.	8 Firm, solid wines. Sample in 5-10 years.	No vintage declared.	9 Marvelous, deep and fruity. Wait 10-12 years	——	——

APPETIZERS

GUACAMOLE

The best guacamole is the simplest and the freshest, made with flavorful avocados (the wrinkled, black-skinned Hass variety or a near relative), ripe tomatoes, fresh jalapeños or serrano chiles, a bit of onion, salt and—in my house at least—a generous amount of fresh coriander. To my taste, other obfuscations often tossed in—lime juice, garlic, cumin, cottage cheese, mayonnaise, sour cream—complicate without contributing.

The version below was inspired by the guacamole served at Manhattan's Rosa Mexicano restaurant, where the waiters prepare it tableside. I had some fresh marjoram on hand, and since its pungent taste is almost as southwestern to my palate as coriander, I decided to combine the two. The result is chunky and assertive, indeed, more an avocado and tomato salad than a dip or sauce. It is perhaps best appreciated alongside smoky grilled meats or rolled into tortillas with fajitas. If you don't have any fresh marjoram or oregano on hand, don't use dried; just increase the coriander if you like.

6 to 8 Servings

¼ cup minced yellow onion
¾ cup coarsely chopped fresh coriander, stems included
2 tablespoons chopped fresh marjoram or oregano
1 to 1½ jalapeño peppers, to taste, stemmed
1 teaspoon salt
4 ripe but firm Hass avocados
2 large ripe tomatoes, seeded and cut into ¾-inch chunks
⅓ cup finely diced red onion

1. In a food processor or blender, combine the yellow onion, coriander, marjoram, jalapeños and salt. Process until smooth, about 30 seconds.

2. Halve and pit the avocados. Using the dull side of a knife, deeply score the flesh into ¾-inch chunks. Scoop the chunks out of the skins into a medium bowl.

3. Add the pureed herb mixture, the tomatoes and the red onion to the bowl and toss gently until just combined. (*The recipe can be prepared up to 1 hour ahead. Cover tightly with plastic wrap and let stand at room temperature.*)

—Michael McLaughlin

• • •

GRAND AIOLI

Here aioli gives its name to the pungent garlic mayonnaise as well as to the Provençal dish in which the mayonnaise stars. My favorite aioli is served on Friday afternoons at Le Bistro du Paradou in Le Paradou, not far from Les Baux-de-Provence. There, the stone mortar filled with fragrant aioli is placed in the center of the table, alongside a platter that includes hard-cooked eggs, boiled potatoes, salt cod and local land snails known as *petit gris*. There is no limit to the variety of cooked or raw vegetables that can be included in a *grand aïoli*, which in Provence is often also called an *aïoli monstre*. Since this dish includes so many ingredients and takes a bit of time to prepare, it works best for a crowd.

🍷 Serve either a Côtes de Provence white or rosé.

12 to 16 Servings

Aioli (p. 254), recipe tripled
2 pounds salt cod
2 pounds small potatoes
1 pound thin green beans
1 pound medium carrots
1 head of cauliflower, cut into florets
1 pound medium beets
8 hard-cooked eggs

1. One to two days before preparing the Aioli, depending on the saltiness of the fish, soak the salt cod in a large bowl of cold water. Change the water 3 or 4 times during the soaking period to remove excess salt. Drain and rinse the fish.

2. Put the cod in a large saucepan. Add fresh cold water to cover and bring just to a simmer over moderate heat. Immediately remove the pan from the heat. Cover and let stand for at least 15 minutes. Drain well. Scrape off any fatty skin and remove any bones. Tear the fish into large pieces.

3. Steam or boil the vegetables separately until tender, about 20 minutes for the potatoes, 4 minutes for the beans, 20 minutes for the carrots, 7 minutes for the cauliflower and 40 minutes for the beets.

4. Let cool, then peel the beets. Halve the beets, carrots and eggs. Arrange the vegetables on a large heated platter, along with the cod and eggs. Pass the Aioli separately.

—Patricia Wells

• • •

ANCHOIADE

This delicious anchovy, garlic and olive oil spread, also known as *quichét*, is served on tiny toast rounds with drinks at Chez Gilbert, a Provençal bistro set along the sun-kissed port of Cassis. I love the surprising taste of vinegar, which pairs well with the salty hit of anchovy and the pungency of garlic. I find that anchovy fillets packed in olive oil work best here. Anchovies tend to be too salty for American tastes, so they've been soaked before using, but this is an optional step.

🍷 Serve this spread with a chilled rosé, such as Domaine Tempier Bandol.

6 to 8 Servings

16 slices of long, narrow French bread, cut ½ inch thick
2 cans (2 ounces each) flat anchovy fillets in olive oil, drained, oil reserved
2½ teaspoons red wine vinegar
4 garlic cloves, coarsely chopped
⅓ cup chopped parsley

1. Preheat the broiler. Arrange the bread slices on a baking sheet and broil about 4 inches from the heat, turning once, until browned on both sides, about 1½ minutes. Keep the broiler on.

2. In a small bowl, cover the anchovies with 1 cup of cold water. Soak for 10 minutes. Drain the anchovies and pat dry on paper towels.

3. Finely chop the anchovies with their reserved oil. Add the vinegar, garlic and parsley and chop together; the mixture should be rather coarse.

4. Spread the *anchoïade* over the toasts and broil for about 1 minute, just until warm. Serve immediately.

—*Patricia Wells*

• • •

TAPENADE

Unlike most tapenades, which are blended to a puree, this version of the Provençal black olive, caper, anchovy and herb spread is only very lightly mixed in a food processor until chunky. At the homey, museumlike Marseilles restaurant, Maurice Brun, it is served as a separate course to be eaten with a fork, not spread on bread.

If your olives are very salty, you may want to rinse or soak them before assembling the tapenade.

🍷 As a change of pace, try this with the sparkling Clairette de Die Tradition.

Makes About 1 Cup

2 tablespoons drained capers
4 flat anchovy fillets
2 tablespoons extra-virgin olive oil
1 teaspoon chopped fresh thyme
1 tablespoon amber rum
2 cups (8 ounces) oil-cured black olives, preferably from Nyons, pitted

In a food processor, combine the capers, anchovies, olive oil, thyme and rum. Process until just blended. Add the olives and turn the machine on and off about 10 times, until the tapenade is blended but still quite coarse.

—*Patricia Wells*

• • •

SALMON RILLETTES

This elegant salmon pâté is from The Four Seasons restaurant in New York.

8 to 10 Servings

Quick Court Bouillon (recipe follows)
¾ pound fresh salmon steak, cut 1¼ inches thick
¾ pound Scotch smoked salmon, diced
2 sticks (8 ounces) unsalted butter
Pinch of cayenne pepper
1 jar (4 ounces) salmon caviar

1. In a skillet, bring the Court Bouillon to a boil over moderately high heat. Reduce the heat to a simmer and add the salmon steak; cover and poach, turning once, until just slightly translucent in the center, about 5 minutes. Remove the salmon to a bowl and let cool. Using your hands, flake the salmon, discarding the skin and bones.

2. In a food processor, blend the diced smoked salmon with the butter and cayenne until smooth, about 1 minute.

3. Add the flaked fresh salmon and turn the machine quickly on and off 2 or 3 times, until the mixture is blended but still coarse.

4. Transfer to a medium bowl and fold in the salmon caviar. Serve at room temperature, accompanied with toast points or crusty French bread.

—*The Four Seasons, New York City*

• • •

QUICK COURT BOUILLON

Makes About 1½ Cups

½ cup dry white wine
1 carrot, cut into ¼-inch dice
1 celery rib, cut into ¼-inch dice
½ small onion, coarsely chopped
3 or 4 sprigs of parsley
Pinch of tarragon
12 peppercorns, crushed

In a small saucepan, combine the wine, carrot, celery, onion, parsley, tarragon and peppercorns with 1 cup of water. Bring to a boil, then reduce the heat and simmer for 5 minutes. Strain.

—*The Four Seasons, New York City*

• • •

COUNTRY-STYLE PATE

This traditional pâté improves as it stands. It should be refrigerated for up to three days before serving.

10 to 12 Servings

1 pound chicken livers, halved and trimmed
⅓ cup Cognac or brandy
1 pound ground beef chuck
1 pound ground pork shoulder
¼ pound fresh pork fat, finely diced
½ cup fresh bread crumbs
1 tablespoon salt

2 teaspoons freshly ground pepper
½ teaspoon allspice
2 tablespoons unsalted butter
¼ pound mushrooms, chopped
2 eggs
1 tablespoon plus 1 teaspoon tarragon
1 garlic clove, minced
14 thin slices of bacon (about ½ pound)

1. Pick out half of the chicken livers, choosing the plumpest and most perfect. Soak them in the Cognac in a small bowl for 30 minutes. Drain the livers, reserving the Cognac.

2. In a large bowl, combine the beef, pork, pork fat, bread crumbs, salt, pepper and allspice. Mix well.

3. In a large skillet, melt 1 tablespoon of the butter over high heat. When the foam subsides, add the marinated chicken livers and sauté, turning once, for about 30 seconds on each side, or until lightly browned around the edges. Transfer to a plate and set aside.

4. Melt the remaining 1 tablespoon butter in the skillet. Add the mushrooms and sauté over high heat until they are browned, about 5 minutes. Scrape them into the bowl of meats.

5. In a blender or food processor, puree the remaining raw chicken livers with the eggs, tarragon, garlic and reserved brandy. Add to the meat mixture and mix until well blended.

6. Preheat the oven to 375°.

7. Line a 9-cup (11½-by-4-inch) terrine with crosswise strips of bacon; line the ends of the terrine with lengthwise strips of bacon, allowing the ends to overhang. Evenly spread half the filling in the mold. Arrange the sautéed chicken livers in a row down the center and top with the remaining meat mixture. Smooth the top and fold the bacon ends over the mixture. Cover the terrine tightly with foil and place in a large roasting pan in the oven. Add enough warm water to the pan to reach halfway up the sides of the terrine.

8. Bake for 1½ hours. Using a bulb baster, remove any melted fat from the top of the meat loaf. Carefully transfer the terrine to a baking sheet or larger pan. Cut out a piece of cardboard to fit inside the terrine, cover it with foil and place it on top of the meat. Weigh down with about 5 pounds of weights or heavy cans. Let cool, then refrigerate, still weighted, overnight. Unmold the pâté before serving if desired.

—Diana Sturgis

• • •

SPICY TEA EGGS

In this classic Chinese recipe, the tea imparts flavor and color to the hard-cooked eggs. To keep the eggs moist, peel them just before serving.

12 Servings

1 piece of dried orange peel*
12 eggs, at room temperature
¼ cup Chinese Keemun black tea leaves
¼ cup dark soy sauce*
2 whole star anise pods*
1 tablespoon Szechuan peppercorns*
2 tablespoons sugar
1 tablespoon coarse (kosher) salt
****Available at Oriental markets***

1. Soak the dried orange peel in warm water to cover until softened, about 30 minutes. Drain the peel and scrape it with a knife to remove any white pith.

2. Meanwhile, put the eggs in a large saucepan with cold water to cover. Bring to a simmer over moderate heat. Reduce the heat and simmer for 15 minutes. Remove the eggs, reserving the water. Immediately cool the eggs under cold running water for 5 minutes. Gently tap the eggs all over with the back of a spoon to crack the shells (do not remove the shells).

3. Bring the reserved water to a boil. Stir in the softened orange peel, tea leaves, soy sauce, star anise, Szechuan peppercorns, sugar and salt. Add the eggs; if there isn't enough liquid to cover the eggs, add more water.

4. Gently simmer the eggs until the shells are a rich brown color, about 1 hour. Remove the pan from the heat. Leave the eggs in the liquid for at least 1 hour or refrigerate overnight. Peel the eggs and serve whole, halved or quartered, at room temperature.

—Ceri E. Hadda

• • •

PROSCIUTTO-WRAPPED HEARTS OF PALM

These tasty, bite-size hors d'oeuvres can be prepared the night before.

8 Servings

¼ cup white wine vinegar
½ cup extra-virgin olive oil
4 sprigs of fresh thyme or ½ teaspoon dried
¼ teaspoon freshly ground pepper
2 cans (14 ounces each) hearts of palm, drained and rinsed
½ pound thinly sliced prosciutto, halved lengthwise
2 bunches of arugula, large stems removed

1. In a nonreactive bowl, combine the vinegar, oil, thyme and pepper.

2. Cut the hearts of palm in half crosswise. (If some are very thick, halve them lengthwise first. Use only the tender stalks.) Wrap each piece in a slice of prosciutto and secure with a toothpick. Place the hearts of palm in the marinade, cover with plastic wrap and refrigerate for 3 hours or overnight.

3. Remove the prosciutto-wrapped hearts of palm from the marinade. Place the arugula leaves on a serving platter and arrange the wrapped hearts of palm on top. Sprinkle with a grinding of pepper and serve at room temperature.

—James W. Brown, Jr.

• • •

RUTH'S HERBED OYSTER CANAPES

Test Kitchen Associate Mimi Brodeur's mother always serves these herbed oysters in a chafing dish accompanied with slices of baguette to sop up the marinade. 🍷 Oysters need the contrast of a wine with considerable acidity. Pick a crisp California sparkling wine, such as 1983 Iron Horse Brut.

8 Servings

2 dozen freshly shucked oysters, 1/4 cup liquor reserved
2 tablespoons Pernod
8 sprigs of fresh thyme or 1 teaspoon dried
4 large garlic cloves, minced
2 tablespoons Champagne vinegar or white wine vinegar
2 tablespoons fresh lemon juice
1/3 cup extra-virgin olive oil
2 tablespoons chopped chives
2 tablespoons chopped Italian flat-leaf parsley
1/4 teaspoon salt
1/4 teaspoon freshly ground pepper
1 long narrow loaf of French bread, sliced 1/4 inch thick
2 tablespoons unsalted butter, melted

1. In a shallow nonreactive baking dish, spread the oysters in a single layer. Add the oyster liquor, Pernod, thyme, garlic, vinegar, lemon juice, olive oil, chives, parsley, salt and pepper. Cover and marinate in the refrigerator for 3 hours or overnight. Let return to room temperature before broiling.

2. Preheat the oven to 400°.

3. Brush one side of each bread slice with the butter and arrange them on a baking sheet. Bake for 10 minutes, or until golden brown. Turn the croutons over and bake until lightly toasted, about 2 minutes longer.

4. Preheat the broiler.

5. Broil the oysters in the baking dish 3 to 4 inches from the heat until their edges begin to curl, about 1 minute. With a slotted spoon set the oysters on the croutons and arrange on a serving platter. Serve hot.

—Ruth Brodeur

• • •

CROSTINI WITH PEA PUREE

The combination of flavors in this appetizer is pure Florentine, and here I've given the traditional Italian Easter dish of whole peas an entirely new treatment.

6 Servings

5 ounces pancetta, thinly sliced
4 garlic cloves
1/4 cup plus 2 tablespoons olive oil
1/4 pound fresh peas or 1 package (10 ounces) frozen peas
1/4 cup chopped parsley
1/4 teaspoon salt
1/4 teaspoon freshly ground pepper
18 slices of Italian bread, cut 3/8 inch thick

1. Finely chop enough of the pancetta to yield ½ cup. In a large skillet, cook the chopped pancetta over moderate heat until crisp, about 5 minutes. Drain on paper towels and set aside.

2. In a food processor, puree the remaining pancetta with 3 of the garlic cloves. Scrape the puree into a large skillet, add 2 tablespoons of the olive oil and cook over moderately low heat until the garlic is just golden, about 4 minutes. Add the fresh peas, 2 tablespoons of the parsley, the salt, pepper and ¼ cup of water. Cook until the peas are completely tender, 15 to 20 minutes. If using frozen peas, omit the water and cook for only 10 minutes.

3. In a food processor, puree the cooked peas until smooth. Strain to remove the skins. Add 1 tablespoon of the olive oil and the remaining 2 tablespoons parsley and mix to blend well.

4. Preheat the oven to 400°.

5. Bake the bread slices directly on the oven rack until lightly toasted, about 4 minutes. Cut the remaining garlic clove in half and rub over one side of the toast slices. Brush the garlic-rubbed sides with the remaining 3 tablespoons olive oil. Spread 1 scant tablespoon of the pea puree over each toast slice and sprinkle with the reserved crisp pancetta.

—Nancy Verde Barr

• • •

EGGPLANT COOKIES WITH GOAT CHEESE AND TOMATO-BASIL SAUCE

Robert McGrath's savory eggplant rounds can be served as an appetizer or as an accompaniment to a main course.

—4 Servings—

6 tablespoons plus 2 teaspoons olive oil
1 large garlic clove, minced
1 small shallot, minced
1 tablespoon tequila, preferably golden
1½ tablespoons dry red wine
2 large tomatoes—peeled, seeded and chopped
Pinch of salt and freshly ground pepper
2 tablespoons julienned fresh basil
½ cup all-purpose flour, sifted
1 egg, lightly beaten
½ cup fresh bread crumbs
2 long, narrow Oriental eggplants, peeled and cut into ½-inch rounds
4 ounces cylindrical goat cheese, cut into 12 rounds

1. In a medium saucepan, heat 2 teaspoons of the oil. Add the garlic and shallot and cook over moderate heat, stirring, until softened but not browned, about 1 minute. Add the tequila and red wine and cook until almost completely absorbed, about 1 minute. Stir in the tomatoes, salt and pepper and cook until slightly thickened, about 5 minutes. Stir in the basil and keep warm.

2. Put the flour, egg and bread crumbs in 3 separate shallow bowls. Dip the eggplant rounds in the flour until completely coated. Next, coat with the egg and then roll in the bread crumbs.

3. In a large heavy skillet, heat 2 tablespoons of the olive oil over moderately high heat. Add one-third of the eggplant slices and sauté, turning once, until crisp and golden brown, about 4 minutes on each side. Drain on paper towels. Repeat 2 more times with the remaining oil and eggplant.

4. Sandwich 1 slice of the goast cheese in between 2 slices of hot fried eggplant. Spoon the tomato-basil sauce onto 4 heated plates and arrange 3 eggplant "cookies" on each one. Serve warm.

—Robert McGrath,
Four Seasons Hotel, Dallas

• • •

WALNUT-STUFFED BRIE

Choose the best Brie you can find. It should be ripe but should not smell of ammonia. The rind should have some light brown striations, and the cheese should be no harder than a grapefruit even when cold.

—24 to 30 Servings—

8½-inch wheel of Brie (2 pounds), well chilled
½ pound mascarpone cheese
¾ cup finely chopped toasted walnuts

1. Using a large knife, split the Brie in half horizontally. In a small bowl, blend the mascarpone and chopped walnuts. Spread this mixture in an even layer, to about ¼ inch from the edge, over the cut side of the bottom half of the Brie. Set the top of the Brie in place and press gently to sandwich the layers. If any filling squeezes out, use a narrow spatula to smooth it into place.

2. Wrap the Brie in plastic wrap. If you've saved the wooden container it came in, set it back in the container. Refrigerate for 4 days to allow the flavors to develop. Let stand at room temperature for at least 3 hours before serving.

—Susan Wyler

• • •

SPINACH-STUFFED MUSHROOMS WITH CHEDDAR AND CHERVIL

These chervil-flavored mushrooms make wonderful appetizers or hors d'oeuvres.

—4 to 6 Servings—

2 tablespoons unsalted butter
1 small onion, chopped
1½ cups chopped cooked fresh spinach or 2 packages (10 ounces each) frozen chopped spinach leaves, thawed
½ cup heavy cream
½ cup plus 1 tablespoon chopped fresh chervil
¾ teaspoon salt
¼ teaspoon freshly ground pepper
½ teaspoon fresh lemon juice
¾ cup grated mild Cheddar cheese
1 tablespoon olive oil
2 pounds medium to large fresh white mushroom caps, stems removed

1. Preheat the oven to 500°. In a medium saucepan, melt the butter over moderate heat. Add the onion and cook over low heat until soft, about 10 minutes.

2. Add the spinach. Increase the heat to high and stir in the cream. Cook, stirring, until the cream is very thick,

about 3 minutes. Remove the mixture from the heat and stir in ¼ cup of the chervil, the salt, pepper, lemon juice and ⅓ cup of the grated Cheddar cheese. Set aside.

3. In a large skillet, heat the olive oil over high heat. Add the mushroom caps and 1 tablespoon of water. Cover and cook over high heat until the mushrooms are tender and glazed, about 4 minutes.

4. Using a slotted spoon, transfer the mushrooms to a baking sheet, hollow-side up. Divide the spinach mixture evenly among the mushroom caps, filling them generously. Top with the remaining grated Cheddar and bake until the mushrooms are heated through and the cheese is melted, about 5 minutes. Arrange the stuffed mushrooms on a serving dish. Sprinkle with the remaining chopped chervil and serve at once.

—Marcia Kiesel

• • •

VEGETARIAN SPRING ROLL

The spring roll is a delicate preparation, quite different from the egg roll that evolved from it. In Canton and Shanghai, it is traditionally made with vegetables combined either with pork or shrimp. This all-vegetable roll is Chinese in feeling, but with a fresh and different taste. (These can be frozen after they have been lightly browned. To cook: defrost, let come to room temperature and dry off any moisture with paper towels. Deep-fry until golden brown.)

Makes 18

10 dried Chinese black mushrooms
1½ tablespoons oyster sauce*
1½ teaspoons mushroom soy sauce*
1 teaspoon dry sherry
1 teaspoon distilled white vinegar
1 teaspoon Oriental sesame oil
1 teaspoon sugar
½ teaspoon salt
Pinch of freshly ground white pepper
1 tablespoon cornstarch
5 cups peanut oil
1 bunch of scallions, quartered lengthwise and cut into 1½-inch pieces
1 large Chinese celery cabbage (about 1½ pounds), stalks quartered lengthwise and cut into ¼-inch slices
18 egg roll skins (in plastic bags)
2 eggs, lightly beaten
Sweet and Sour Sauce (p. 255) or Chili Soy Sauce (p. 255)
****Available at Oriental markets***

1. Put the mushrooms in a small bowl, add hot water to cover and soak until softened, about 30 minutes. Rinse the mushrooms and squeeze dry. Discard the stems; slice the caps thinly.

2. In a small bowl, stir together the oyster sauce, soy sauce, sherry, vinegar, sesame oil, sugar, salt, white pepper, cornstarch and 1½ tablespoons of water. Set the sauce aside.

3. Heat a wok over high heat for 30 seconds. Add 2½ tablespoons of the peanut oil, stirring with a Chinese metal spatula to coat the sides of the wok. As soon as a wisp of white smoke appears, add the mushrooms and scallions and stir-fry for 45 seconds. Add the celery cabbage and stir-fry until wilted, about 2 minutes.

4. Make a well in the center of the vegetables. Stir the reserved sauce and pour it into the well. Toss and stir to thoroughly combine all the ingredients. Cook over moderate heat, stirring until the sauce thickens, about 1 minute. Remove from the heat and transfer the filling to a shallow dish. Let cool to room temperature, then cover and refrigerate for at least 8 hours or overnight.

5. One at a time, lay an egg roll skin on a flat surface with a corner facing you. Place 2 tablespoons of the filling across the bottom third of the wrapper. Brush the beaten egg around the edges of the entire wrapper. Fold up the bottom corner and roll once. Then fold in both sides and roll up all the way. Press the end to seal tightly. Repeat with the remaining wrappings and filling.

6. In a large saucepan or deep-fryer, heat the remaining peanut oil to 350°. Deep-fry the spring rolls in batches without crowding, turning frequently, until golden brown, 3 to 5 minutes. Drain on paper towels and serve with Sweet and Sour Sauce and/or Chili Soy Sauce for dipping.

—Eileen Yin-Fei Lo

• • •

SURPRISE PACKAGES

These hors d'oeuvres can be frozen after frying, but if you plan to do so, cook them only half the specified time, or until they are light brown. To serve, defrost and let return to room temperature before deep-frying in 340° oil until golden brown, 2 to 2½ minutes.

Makes 2 Dozen

4 cups chicken stock or canned broth
1 pound of well-trimmed filet mignon, cut along the grain into strips 2 inches long and ½ inch wide
3 scallions, white part quartered lengthwise, white and green cut into 1½-inch pieces

1½ tablespoons finely shredded fresh ginger
24 sun-dried tomatoes packed in olive oil, cut lengthwise into 4 strips each
½ teaspoon salt
6 egg roll skins
1 quart peanut oil, for deep-frying

1. In a medium saucepan, bring the chicken stock to a boil over high heat. Add the beef strips, cook for 30 seconds and remove from the heat. Cover the pan and let stand for 1 minute. Strain immediately (reserve the stock for another use if you like) and let the beef cool to room temperature.

2. In a medium bowl, combine the beef, scallions, ginger, sun-dried tomatoes and salt. Toss to mix well.

3. To form the surprise packages, cut each egg roll skin into 4 equal squares. Place 1 piece of beef, 4 pieces of scallion, several shreds of ginger and 4 strips of sun-dried tomato in the center of each wrapper. Moisten the 2 edges of the wrapper that run in the same direction as the beef. Pick up the 2 edges and squeeze between your thumb and index finger to seal; fold the seam down to tighten into a cylinder. The package will resemble a log with both ends open. Twist each end gently but firmly to seal completely in a firecracker shape.

4. Heat a wok over high heat for 30 seconds. Add the peanut oil and heat to 350°. In small batches without crowding, slide the packages into the hot oil and fry, turning frequently, until crisp and golden brown all over, 4 to 5 minutes. Remove with a slotted spoon, drain on paper towels and serve hot.

—Eileen Yin-Fei Lo

• • •

RICE PAPER SHRIMP ROLLS

🍷 These savory canapés, accented with scallions and sun-dried tomatoes, need a crisp and assertive white, such as an Iron Horse sparkling wine from California.

Makes 16

½ pound medium shrimp, shelled and deveined
1 tablespoon olive oil
2 tablespoons (loosely packed) fresh tarragon or 1 teaspoon dried
2 tablespoons chopped scallion greens
2 tablespoons chopped sun-dried tomatoes
⅛ teaspoon freshly ground pepper
16 rice paper rounds, 6 inches in diameter (I use Banh Trang brand)*
3 cups peanut oil, for deep-frying
****Available at Oriental markets***

1. In a bowl, toss the shrimp with the olive oil, tarragon, scallions, sun-dried tomatoes and pepper. Cover and refrigerate for at least 1 hour, or overnight.

2. Fill a medium bowl with warm water. Dip a rice paper round in the water until slightly softened, crinkly and translucent, 5 to 10 seconds. Remove and drain briefly on a kitchen towel.

3. Place 1 shrimp and some of the marinating mixture along the lower edge of the rice paper, about 1 inch from the edge. Fold the bottom of the rice paper snugly over the shrimp and fold in both sides. Roll up into a compact cylinder about 3 inches long. Set on a plate and repeat with the remaining shrimp, marinade and rice paper. (*The shrimp rolls can be made ahead to this point, covered with plastic wrap and refrigerated for up to 4 hours or frozen for up to 1 month.*)

4. In a wok or large heavy saucepan, heat the peanut oil to 385°. Fry the shrimp rolls, in batches of 3 or 4, until lightly browned, 2 to 3 minutes. Drain on paper towels. Serve hot.

—Ken Hom

• • •

SOUTHWEST WON TONS

Be sure to buy fresh water dumpling skins from the refrigerator case at the market. They come in different thicknesses. Thinner is better, even though they are a bit more difficult to work with. The skins can be frozen.

The finished won tons can be frozen *after* cooking, but fry them only to a light brown. Let cool, then wrap in plastic and foil and freeze. To serve, defrost and deep-fry until golden brown.

🍷 A rich beer, such as Samuel Adams or Anchor Steam, would cool the palate between bites of this spicy hors d'oeuvre.

Makes 40

¼ pound mild chorizo sausage, cut into ⅛-inch dice
1 cup grated Monterey Jack cheese (about 4 ounces)
3 tablespoons thinly sliced scallion green
1 tablespoon chopped fresh coriander
1¼ teaspoons minced and seeded jalapeño pepper
¼ cup finely diced jicama
40 round water dumpling skins
1 quart peanut oil, for deep-frying
Southwest Salsa (p. 257)

1. In an electric mixer, place the sausage, cheese, scallion green, coriander, jalapeño and jicama. Mix on medium speed for 3 minutes, until the mixture forms a paste. Alternatively, combine the ingredients in a large bowl and mix with your hand, slapping the filling against the side of the bowl until well blended and thickened. Transfer to a shallow dish.

2. Cover the dumpling skins with a damp cloth to keep them soft. Remove one by one to work. To assemble each won ton, place a dumpling skin in one hand. Place 1 teaspoon filling in the center of the dumpling skin and flatten slightly with a blunt knife. Wet the won ton skin all around from the edge to the filling.

3. Fold into a half-moon shape. Squeeze around the edges to seal. Dampen one corner of the half-moon, then gently pull the two corners together and squeeze the ends together to seal. Repeat with the remaining dumpling skins and filling.

4. Heat a wok over high heat for 30 seconds. Add the peanut oil and heat to 350°. Fry the won tons in batches without crowding, turning several times, until golden brown all over, 2 to 3 minutes. Remove with a slotted spoon and drain briefly on paper towels. Serve hot with the Southwest Salsa.

—*Eileen Yin-Fei Lo*

• • •

POT STICKERS

It is believed that these dumplings originated in Shanghai, where they are referred to as *wor tip*, two words that mean "pot" and "stick." They have come, therefore, to be called "pot stickers" and are as popular in the south of China as they are in Peking.

Makes About 4 Dozen

1 medium head of bok choy (about 1½ pounds)
1½ teaspoons salt
½ teaspoon baking soda
1 pound lean ground pork
½ cup thinly sliced scallions
1 egg, lightly beaten
2 tablespoons cornstarch
1 tablespoon Oriental sesame oil
2 teaspoons sugar
2 teaspoons grated fresh ginger
2 teaspoons dry white wine
1½ teaspoons light soy sauce
Pinch of freshly ground white pepper
50 round water dumpling wrappers, preferably Twin Dragon*
½ cup plus 1 tablespoon peanut oil
Soy Sesame Sauce (p. 255)
****Available in the freezer section of Oriental markets and some supermarkets***

1. Separate the leaves from the stalks of the bok choy. Wash and dry thoroughly. Cut enough of the stalks into ¼-by-½-inch slices to measure 1 cup. Shred enough of the leaves to measure 1½ cups firmly packed.

2. In a large saucepan, bring 4 cups of water to a boil with ½ teaspoon of the salt and the baking soda. Add the bok choy stalks and leaves and blanch for 1 minute. Drain immediately and rinse under cold running water; drain well. Squeeze in a kitchen towel to remove excess water.

3. In a large bowl, combine the bok choy, pork, scallions, egg, cornstarch, sesame oil, sugar, ginger, wine, soy sauce, white pepper and remaining 1 teaspoon salt. Mix well in one direction with chopsticks or a large spoon until thoroughly blended. Refrigerate the filling uncovered for 3 to 4 hours, or covered overnight.

4. To form each pot sticker, spread about 1½ teaspoons of the filling down the center of a round wrapper. Wet the edge of the wrapper with water. Close into a half-moon shape and then pleat the wrapper to seal it. Pinch the pleating to seal firmly. Press one side of the dumpling against the fleshy part of your hand at the base of the thumb to create the classic curved pot sticker shape. Repeat until all the dumplings are made. *(The dumplings can be prepared ahead to this point and frozen up to 2 months in advance. Thaw before proceeding.)*

5. To fry each batch of dumplings, heat 3 tablespoons of the peanut oil in a large skillet, preferably cast iron, over high heat until the first wisp of smoke appears. Arrange 3 rows of dumplings in the skillet, 5 or 6 to a row; they should be touching lightly. Cook for 3 minutes. Pour ½ cup of cold water into the skillet, cover, reduce the heat to moderate and cook until all of the water has evaporated, about 5 minutes.

6. Reduce the heat to low and continue to cook, rotating the pan to distribute the heat evenly, until the dumplings are golden brown on the bottom and somewhat translucent on top, 1 to 2 minutes longer. Remove the dumplings from the skillet and drain on paper towels. Repeat twice with the remaining oil and dumplings. Serve hot with Soy Sesame Sauce.

—*Eileen Yin-Fei Lo*

• • •

FLOWER DUMPLINGS

This is an adaptation of a traditional Chinese dim sum, *siu mai*, which has a shape quite similar to the bud of a flower. In Canton these are traditionally made with a filling of pork, shrimp and mushrooms, but I like the color and taste of chicken and vegetables. Serve with Soy Sesame Sauce.

The dumplings can be frozen for 6 to 8 weeks before or after steaming. To serve, defrost, allow to come to room temperature and steam for 3 to 5 minutes to reheat or 8 to 10 minutes to cook.

Makes 2 Dozen

½ pound skinless, boneless chicken, chopped to a paste
¼ cup finely diced jicama
¼ cup finely diced carrot
⅓ cup thinly sliced scallions
¾ teaspoon grated fresh ginger
1 egg white, lightly beaten
1½ tablespoons peanut oil
1½ teaspoons Oriental sesame oil
1 teaspoon dry white wine
1 teaspoon soy sauce
¾ teaspoon salt
1¾ teaspoons sugar
2 tablespoons cornstarch
Pinch of freshly ground white pepper
24 won ton wrappers
Soy Sesame Sauce (p. 255)

1. In an electric mixer, combine all of the ingredients except the won ton wrappers and mix on low speed until the consistency is smooth and even, about 3 minutes. Alternatively, combine the ingredients in a large bowl and mix and knead with your hand, slapping the mixture against the side of the bowl until it is well blended and stiffened. Refrigerate until the flavors blend and the mixture is firm, about 4 hours, or overnight.

2. Using kitchen shears, cut the won ton wrappers into rounds, 2¾ inches in diameter. Keep covered with a damp towel; pull them out as needed.

3. To form each flower dumpling, hold a won ton wrapper in your hand and scoop about 1 tablespoon filling into the middle. Holding down the filling with the tip of a small blunt knife, gently squeeze the dumpling in your fist to form a bud-like shape, gradually twisting the dumpling as you squeeze.

4. Remove the knife and squeeze the top of the dumpling to create a tighter neck. Pack down the filling with the knife even with the edge of the wrapper so there are no air bubbles. Tap the dumpling lightly on the work surface to flatten the bottom so that it will stand upright in the steamer. Repeat with the remaining won ton wrappers and filling.

5. Steam for 8 to 10 minutes. Serve the dumplings immediately with Soy Sesame Sauce.

—Eileen Yin-Fei Lo

• • •

BEGGAR'S PURSES

I think these shrimp-filled dumplings are too elegant for a name like Beggar's Purses. I'd call them Princess's Purses.

They can be frozen after they are cooked. To prepare for freezing, omit the scallion ties and steam for only 7 minutes instead of 10. Then wrap twice in plastic wrap and finally in foil. To serve, defrost and let return to room temperature; tie on scallion ribbons and steam for 3 to 4 minutes to heat through.

Makes About 5 Dozen

¼ cup dried Chinese black mushrooms
1 large bunch of scallions
¼ teaspoon baking soda
½ pound shrimp—shelled, deveined and finely diced
½ teaspoon salt
1½ teaspoons sugar
1 extra-large egg white, beaten
1½ teaspoons grated fresh ginger
1 tablespoon dry white wine
2 tablespoons cornstarch
2 teaspoons oyster sauce
1 teaspoon soy sauce
1½ teaspoons Oriental sesame oil
1½ tablespoons peanut oil
¼ cup finely diced jicama
¼ cup finely diced carrot
Pinch of freshly ground white pepper
65 round water dumpling skins (3¾ inches in diameter)
Lettuce leaves, for lining the steamer
3 tablespoons dry mustard
1½ teaspoons hot pepper sauce

1. Put the mushrooms in a small bowl, cover with hot water and let soak until softened, about 30 minutes. Drain the mushrooms. Discard the stems and mince the mushroom caps.

2. Meanwhile, trim off all of the scallion greens and reserve. Chop enough white part of the scallions to yield ¼ cup; set aside.

3. In a small saucepan, bring 2 cups of water to a boil over high heat. Add the baking soda. Add the scallion greens and blanch for 30 seconds. Drain immediately and rinse under cold running water; drain well. Cut each scallion green lengthwise into thin strands, or ribbons.

4. Place the shrimp in the bowl of an electric mixer. Beating on medium speed, add the salt, sugar, egg white, ginger, wine, cornstarch, oyster sauce, soy sauce, sesame oil and peanut oil, mixing thoroughly after each addition. Alternatively, combine all the above ingredients in a large bowl and mix and knead with your hand, slapping the mixture against the side of the bowl until it is well blended and stiffened.

5. Add the mushrooms, jicama, carrot, chopped scallions and white pepper; mix well. Transfer the filling to a shallow dish. Refrigerate for 4 hours, uncovered, or overnight, covered with plastic wrap.

6. To form each beggar's purse, hold a dumpling skin in your hand and spread about 1½ teaspoons filling in the middle. Holding the filling in place with the tip of a small blunt knife, slowly twist the dumpling skin to form a little satchel. Squeeze the neck between your fingers to seal. Open the dumpling skin near the top to stimulate the top of a sack. Tie a scallion ribbon around the neck of the purse. Repeat with the remaining dumpling skins and filling.

7. Line a large bamboo steamer with lettuce leaves. In batches without crowding, arrange a single layer of the beggar's purses on the lettuce and steam for 10 minutes.

8. Meanwhile, in a small bowl, mix the mustard with 3 tablespoons of water until blended. Stir in the hot sauce. Serve the dumplings hot with the mustard sauce.

—Eileen Yin-Fei Lo

• • •

PORK EMPANADITAS WITH YELLOW PEPPER SAUCE

The homemade corn pasta used to make these wonderful deep-fried empanaditas gives the hors d'oeuvres an extra measure of southwestern flavor.

Makes About 3½ Dozen

½ pound lean pork butt or shoulder, cut into 2-inch cubes
1 medium onion, coarsely chopped
4 garlic cloves, sliced
1 large jalapeño pepper, seeded and minced
1 bay leaf
1 cup chicken stock or canned unsalted broth
2 dried apricots
¼ teaspoon salt
¼ teaspoon freshly ground black pepper
1½ tablespoons chopped fresh coriander
1 tablespoon chopped fresh rosemary
2 teaspoons chopped fresh sage
Corn Flour Pasta (recipe follows)
1 egg, lightly beaten
¼ cup masa harina*
1 quart vegetable oil, for deep-frying
Yellow Pepper Sauce (p. 256)
****Available at Latin American markets***

1. In a small saucepan, combine the pork, onion, garlic, jalapeño, bay leaf and chicken stock. Bring to a boil over high heat. Reduce the heat to low and simmer, uncovered, until the meat is very tender, about 30 minutes.

2. Strain the pork mixture; reserve the meat and the liquid separately. Return the liquid to the pan and boil until reduced to about 2 tablespoons. Remove from the heat and add the apricots. Cover and set aside for 5 minutes.

3. Remove the bay leaf from the pork mixture. Add the meat, apricots, liquid, salt and pepper to a food processor. Turn the machine quickly on and off until the pork is coarsely chopped. Stir in the fresh coriander, rosemary and sage.

4. Divide the Corn Flour Pasta into 4 sections. One by one, roll each piece through a pasta machine up to the second to the last setting. Using a round cookie cutter, cut out 3-inch circles from the sheets of dough.

5. Lightly moisten the outer rim of a dough circle with the beaten egg. Scoop 1 heaping teaspoon of filling onto the center of each circle. Fold the dough over and press the edges together to seal in a semicircle. Toss the empanaditas with the masa harina to prevent them from sticking together. Set the empanaditas in a single layer on 2 baking sheets. *(The empanaditas can be prepared ahead to this point. Wrap and refrigerate for up to 1 day or freeze for up to 1 month.)*

6. In a large saucepan or deep-dryer, heat the vegetable oil over moderate heat to 375°. Fry the empanaditas in batches without crowding, turning once, until golden brown, about 2 minutes. Serve with Yellow Pepper Sauce for dipping.

—Brendan Walsh, Arizona 206, New York City

• • •

CORN FLOUR PASTA

Makes About 1 Pound

2 cups all-purpose flour
1 cup masa harina*
¾ teaspoon salt
2 whole eggs
1 egg yolk
****Available at Latin American markets***

1. In a food processor, combine the flour, masa harina, salt, whole eggs and egg yolk. With the machine on, pour in ¼ cup of water and process until the mixture resembles wet sand, about 20 seconds. Add a little more water if necessary.

2. Turn out onto a work surface and knead the dough until it forms a smooth ball, about 1 minute. Flatten into a disk and cover with plastic wrap. Let the dough rest at room temperature for at least 30 minutes, or in the refrigerator overnight, before rolling out.

—Brendan Walsh, Arizona 206, New York City

• • •

SALT COD FRITTERS

These fritters, called *accras de morue* in the French West Indies, are based on the ones Lucienne Salcède serves at Le Karacoli in Guadeloupe. They are frequently accompanied with fiery Scotch Bonnet (habañero) peppers, which you slice and rub over the fritters for heat; any other hot pepper can be used instead.

Makes About 3 Dozen

1 cup all-purpose flour
½ cup cornstarch
¼ teaspoon salt
½ pound skinless, boneless salt cod
2 tablespoons minced chives
2 tablespoons minced parsley
¾ teaspoon chopped fresh thyme or ¼ teaspoon dried
2 large garlic cloves, minced
1 jalapeño pepper, seeded and minced
1 teaspoon baking soda
About 3 cups vegetable oil, for deep-frying
Scotch Bonnet or other fresh hot peppers, cut in half

1. In a medium bowl, combine the flour, cornstarch and salt. Add 1½ cups of cold water and stir well to form a smooth batter. Cover with plastic wrap and refrigerate for at least 1 hour.

2. Meanwhile, in a medium saucepan, cover the salt cod with 2 inches of cold water. Bring to a boil over moderately high heat and cook until the cod is tender, about 20 minutes. Drain well.

3. Put the cod in a food processor and add the chives, parsley, thyme, garlic and jalapeño. Turn the machine quickly on and off until the fish is shredded and the seasonings are finely chopped.

4. Stir the baking soda into the batter. Add to the fish mixture and blend well.

5. In a large skillet or deep-fryer, heat about 3 inches of vegetable oil over moderately high heat to 375°. For each fritter, spoon 1 teaspoon of the batter into the hot oil. Fry in batches without crowding, turning once, until golden brown, about 3 minutes. Drain well on paper towels. Keep warm in the oven while frying the remaining batter. Serve hot, with the peppers on the side.

—Lucienne Salcède,
Le Karacoli, Guadeloupe

• • •

FRIED POLENTA WITH GORGONZOLA

Polenta is the perfect foil for the sharp, distinctive flavor of Gorgonzola cheese in this tempting hors d'oeuvre. When served with a green salad, these mini-sandwiches also make a good light lunch.

Makes About 4 Dozen

1½ teaspoons salt
1 cup instant polenta
½ pound Gorgonzola cheese, at room temperature
2 eggs
2 cups fine dry bread crumbs
Vegetable oil, for deep-frying

1. In a medium saucepan, bring 3 cups of water to a boil over high heat. Add the salt. Gradually stir in the polenta and cook, stirring constantly, for 10 minutes. Pour the polenta onto a lightly greased baking sheet and shape it into a square about 1 inch high, smoothing the surface with a wet spatula. Cover with a dampened kitchen towel and let cool to room temperature, about 30 minutes.

2. Cut the cooled polenta into even slices, about ¼ inch wide. Cut these slices into 2-inch lengths.

3. Take half of the polenta slices and spread each with 1 teaspoon of Gorgonzola. Cover with the remaining polenta slices to make small sandwiches.

4. Beat the eggs with a splash of water. Dip each sandwich into the egg wash and coat evenly with the bread crumbs; set aside. *(The recipe can be prepared to this point up to 12 hours ahead. Cover loosely and refrigerate.)*

5. Heat the vegetable oil in a deep-fryer to 375° to 400°. One at a time, drop the sandwiches into the hot oil in small batches so they are not touching and fry until golden brown, about 1 minute. Drain on paper towels. Repeat with the remaining sandwiches and serve hot.

—John Robert Massie

• • •

FIRST COURSES

BRAISED WILD MUSHROOMS

At Joseph Phelps Vineyards, this dish is made with the same wine as the one to be served with the meal.

8 First-Course Servings

1 long, narrow loaf of French bread, cut on the diagonal into ¼-inch slices
1 stick (4 ounces) unsalted butter, softened to room temperature
3 large garlic cloves, minced
⅛ teaspoon crushed hot pepper
1 tablespoon chopped fresh thyme or ¾ teaspoon dried
1 tablespoon chopped fresh marjoram or ¾ teaspoon dried
1 pound shiitake mushrooms, stems removed
½ pound chanterelles, stems removed
½ pound white tree mushrooms, stems removed
¼ teaspoon salt
¼ teaspoon freshly ground black pepper
1 cup dry white wine, preferably Chardonnay or Gewürztraminer
8 paper-thin slices of red onion, for garnish

1. Preheat the oven to 350°. Butter the bread with a total of 2 tablespoons of the butter. Set the slices on a baking sheet and bake until lightly browned, 15 to 20 minutes.

2. Meanwhile, in a large heavy skillet, melt the remaining butter over moderately high heat. Add the garlic, hot pepper, thyme and marjoram. Sauté until the garlic is fragrant and softened, about 2 minutes.

3. Add all of the mushrooms and toss quickly to coat with the herbed butter. Increase the heat to high and sauté until the mushrooms begin to brown slightly, about 3 minutes. Season with the salt and black pepper and add the wine. Bring to a boil and cook until the liquid is reduced by half and the sauce is slightly thickened, about 6 minutes.

4. Divide the slices of toasted French bread among 8 plates and top with the mushrooms and sauce. Garnish with the red onion slices.

—Joseph Phelps Vineyards, St. Helena, California

• • •

SPIEDINI WITH SAGE LEAVES AND MUSTARD SAUCE

If your sage leaves taste especially strong, blanch them in boiling water for about 30 seconds. Drain and dry with paper towels before using.

6 First-Course Servings

1 loaf of Italian bread—crusts removed and the loaf sliced ½ inch thick and cut into thirty 2-inch squares
10 ounces Italian Fontina cheese, sliced and cut into twenty-four 2-by-½-inch strips
2½ ounces sugar-cured ham, thinly sliced and cut into twenty-four 2-by-½-inch strips
24 large fresh sage leaves
¾ cup extra-virgin olive oil
1 tablespoon plus 1 teaspoon minced garlic
⅔ cup dry white wine
1 tablespoon plus 1 teaspoon chopped capers
1 tablespoon plus 1 teaspoon anchovy paste
1 tablespoon plus 1 teaspoon Dijon-style mustard
½ teaspoon freshly ground pepper

1. Preheat the broiler. On each of 6 metal skewers, alternate slices of bread, cheese, ham and 4 sage leaves (in effect making miniature sandwiches), using 5 slices of bread, 4 of cheese, 4 of ham and 4 sage leaves per skewer. Begin and end with a slice of bread. Arrange the skewers on a baking sheet.

2. In a medium saucepan, combine ½ cup of the olive oil and the garlic. Simmer over low heat until the garlic is fragrant but not browned, about 4 minutes. Increase the heat to moderately high and add the wine and capers. Boil for 2 minutes. Reduce the heat to low and whisk in the anchovy paste and mustard. Season with the pepper; remove from the heat.

3. Brush the remaining ¼ cup olive oil over the *spiedini*, mostly coating the bread and sage leaves. Broil in the middle of the oven for about 1½ minutes, or until partially browned. Turn the tray and broil for 1 minute longer or until the bread and sage are uniformly toasted and the cheese is just melted.

4. Rewarm the sauce over low heat and spoon an equal amount onto 6 warmed plates. Pull out the skewers and arrange the bread, cheese, ham and sage leaves on top of the sauce.

—Marcia Kiesel

• • •

MONTRACHET GOAT CHEESE SOUFFLE

For this first course, goat cheese is incorporated into the soufflé mixture and each soufflé is filled with additional crumbled goat cheese. The cooking time given below is for soufflés with a creamy center.
🍷 The affinity of goat cheese and Sauvignon (or Fumé) Blanc is based on their

similar, tart, acidic character. A crisp 1986 Chateau St. Jean Fumé Blanc or the vibrant 1986 Iron Horse Fumé Blanc would be top choices.

4 First-Course Servings

8 teaspoons freshly grated Parmesan cheese
1 large garlic clove, crushed through a press
1 teaspoon olive oil
4 tablespoons unsalted butter
3 tablespoons all-purpose flour
1 cup hot milk
3 ounces Montrachet or other mild goat cheese, crumbled
Pinch of salt
1/8 teaspoon freshly ground pepper
3 eggs, separated
1 1/2 teaspoons chopped parsley
1 1/2 teaspoons chopped chives
1/2 teaspoon chopped fresh thyme or 1/4 teaspoon dried

1. Preheat the oven to 400°. Butter four 6-ounce ramekins and coat each with 1 teaspoon of the Parmesan cheese.

2. In a small bowl, mash together the garlic and olive oil.

3. In a medium saucepan, melt the butter over moderate heat. Add the flour and cook, whisking, for 1 minute. Gradually whisk in the hot milk. Bring to a boil and cook until the sauce falls from the whisk in thin streams, about 2 minutes. Remove from the heat and stir in two-thirds of the goat cheese, the mashed garlic and oil and the salt and pepper. Whisk in the egg yolks and cover the pan.

4. In a large bowl, beat the egg whites until stiff but not dry. Fold one-fourth of the egg whites and the parsley, chives and thyme into the goat cheese mixture, then fold the lightened mixture back into the remaining egg whites.

5. Fill the ramekins with half the soufflé mixture. Divide the remaining goat cheese evenly among the ramekins and cover with the rest of the soufflé mixture. Using a spatula, smooth the tops of the soufflés and sprinkle each with 1 teaspoon Parmesan cheese. Set the ramekins on a baking sheet and bake until the soufflés are puffed and golden brown, about 10 minutes.

—Montrachet, New York City

• • •

PISSALADIERE

Nearly every bakery in Provence sells this substantial pizzalike bread. It's sold by the slice to eat on the spot or to take home and warm up in the oven.

🍷 Chilled white wine, such as 1986 Santa Margherita Pinot Grigio or 1986 Corvo White

6 to 8 First-Course Servings

2 tablespoons extra-virgin olive oil
4 medium onions, thinly sliced
2 large garlic cloves, thinly sliced
1 large sprig of fresh thyme or 1/2 teaspoon dried
2 large tomatoes—peeled, seeded and chopped
1/2 pound bread dough
8 flat anchovy fillets, rinsed and drained
12 oil-cured black olives, preferably from Nyons, pitted and halved

1. In a large skillet, heat the oil over moderately low heat. Add the onions, garlic and thyme and toss to coat with the oil. Cover and cook, stirring occasionally, until the onions turn a light golden color, about 20 minutes.

2. Stir in the tomatoes and cook until their liquid has evaporated and the mixture is thick, about 5 minutes. Discard the thyme sprig.

3. On a lightly floured surface, roll out the dough into an 11-by-14-inch rectangle. Transfer the dough to a baking sheet, cover and let rest for 15 minutes.

4. Preheat the oven to 450°. Spread the onion-tomato sauce evenly over the dough. Arrange the anchovies in a spokelike pattern on top and sprinkle with the olives. Let stand for 15 minutes.

5. Bake the *pissaladière* until the crust is crisp, 15 to 20 minutes. Slice and serve warm or at room temperature.

—Patricia Wells

• • •

EGGPLANT AND RED PEPPER PIZZA WITH ROSEMARY

Serve these pizzas with a big green salad for lunch or cut them into small pieces and serve as an hors d'oeuvre.

🍷 The far-from-subtle peppery, cheesy notes of this dish are most easily matched with a gutsy, direct-flavored red wine, such as 1981 Louis M. Martini Barbera from California or 1983 Jaboulet Gigondas from the Rhône.

Makes Eight 9-Inch Pizzas

1 envelope (1/4 ounce) active dry yeast
1/2 cup plus 2 tablespoons olive oil
5 cups all-purpose flour
2 3/4 teaspoons salt
2 large eggplants, thinly sliced lengthwise
4 large red bell peppers
2 large baking potatoes, thinly sliced
1 tablespoon plus 1 teaspoon cornmeal
1 tablespoon plus 1 teaspoon finely chopped rosemary
3/4 pound Bucheron goat cheese, crumbled
2 teaspoons freshly ground black pepper

1. Pour 1 1/2 cups of warm water into a large bowl. Sprinkle the yeast over the water and let stand until it dissolves, about 3 minutes. Stir in 2 tablespoons of the olive oil and 2 cups of the flour. Add 1 teaspoon of the salt and the remaining 3 cups flour. Turn the dough out onto a lightly floured work surface and knead until the dough is firm and pliable, about 5 minutes. Put the dough into a lightly oiled bowl and cover with plastic wrap. Set aside in a warm place until doubled in size, about 1½ hours. Punch the dough down and cut it into 8 equal pieces. Flatten each piece into a small disk and wrap individually in plastic wrap. Refrigerate until ready to use. *(The recipe can be prepared to this point and frozen for up to 1 month.)*

2. In a large nonreactive colander, layer one-third of the sliced eggplant and sprinkle with ¼ teaspoon of the salt. Repeat this procedure with two more layers of eggplant and ½ teaspoon of the salt. Place a plate over the eggplant and weigh it down with cans or a heavy pot; let drain for 1 hour.

3. Roast the red peppers directly over a gas flame or under the broiler as close to the heat as possible, turning, until charred all over. Place the peppers in a paper bag to steam for 5 minutes. Peel the peppers and remove the cores, seeds and membranes. Cut the peppers lengthwise into ¼-inch-wide strips. Place in a bowl; toss with 1 teaspoon of the oil.

4. Pat the eggplant dry with paper towels. In a large skillet, heat 1 tablespoon of the olive oil. Add one-quarter of the eggplant slices and cook over high heat, turning once, until browned, about 2 minutes on each side. Remove the cooked eggplant to a bowl. Repeat with the remaining 3 batches of eggplant and 3 tablespoons of olive oil.

5. Cook the potato slices in lightly salted boiling water until just tender, about 5 minutes; drain well.

6. Preheat the oven to 500°. Sprinkle a baking sheet with 1 teaspoon of the cornmeal.

7. On a lightly floured surface, roll out 1 piece of the pizza dough to form a 9-inch round ⅛ inch thick. Place the dough on the prepared baking sheet and brush lightly with some of the remaining olive oil.

8. Place a layer of potato in the center of the pizza, leaving about a ½-inch border. Sprinkle with ¼ teaspoon of the rosemary and 3 tablespoons of the goat cheese. Place 3 or 4 slices of eggplant over the cheese and brush the top with some of the remaining olive oil. Scatter one-eighth of the pepper strips over the pizza and season with an additional ¼ teaspoon rosemary, ⅛ teaspoon salt and ¼ teaspoon black pepper. Repeat with the remaining cornmeal, dough and toppings.

9. Bake 2 pizzas at a time on the lowest rack of the oven until crisp and golden, about 8 minutes. Cut into wedges and serve hot or at room temperature.

—Marcia Kiesel

• • •

OYSTERS WITH CAVIAR ON A BED OF SAVOY CABBAGE

Quickly cooked savoy cabbage makes a crisp, flavorful bed for chef David Waltuck's elegant poached oysters.

🍷 The extravagance of this dish—and its salty, briny flavors—would best be matched by a Blanc de Blancs Champagne, such as 1979 Taittinger "Comtes de Champagne," or 1983 Chateau St. Jean Blanc de Blancs from California.

—4 First-Course Servings—

24 Wellfleet or Blue Point oysters, shucked, liquor and concave shells reserved
1 cup heavy cream
3 tablespoons fresh lemon juice
2 tablespoons unsalted butter
⅛ teaspoon freshly ground pepper
1¼ cups finely shredded savoy cabbage
2 tablespoons minced chives
1½ ounces osetra caviar

1. Preheat the oven to 250°. Arrange the reserved oyster shells on a baking sheet and place in the oven to warm.

2. In a medium nonreactive saucepan, bring the oyster liquor to a boil over moderately high heat. Add the oysters and poach just until their edges begin to curl, 35 to 40 seconds. Using a slotted spoon, transfer the oysters to a small bowl and cover to keep warm.

3. Add the cream, lemon juice, butter and pepper to the saucepan and boil until reduced to ⅔ cup, about 10 minutes. Stir in the cabbage and chives and cook just until wilted, about 45 seconds.

4. Using a slotted spoon, make a small bed of the cabbage in each warm oyster shell. Place an oyster in each shell, spoon on about a teaspoon of the sauce and top each oyster with about ½ teaspoon of the caviar.

—David Waltuck, Chanterelle, New York City

• • •

CORN BREAD FRIED OYSTERS

Dean Fearing also uses these oysters as a garnish for his Red Snapper with Tomatillo-Serrano Chile Vinaigrette (p. 54).

—6 First-Course Servings—

1½ cups yellow cornmeal
½ cup all-purpose flour
2 eggs, lightly beaten
2 cups milk

1/4 cup melted bacon fat or butter
1 tablespoon baking powder
1/2 teaspoon salt
3 cups peanut oil, for deep-frying
36 freshly shucked oysters
Lemon wedges, as accompaniment

1. In a medium bowl, combine the cornmeal, flour, eggs, milk, bacon fat, baking powder and salt. Stir until the batter is smooth.

2. In a large saucepan or deep-fryer, heat the oil to 375°. Dredge each oyster in the cornmeal batter and fry in batches until golden brown, about 1 minute. Remove the oysters with a slotted spoon and drain on paper towels. Serve with lemon wedges.

—Dean Fearing, The Mansion on Turtle Creek, Dallas

• • •

EGGPLANT CREPES

Serve these crêpes as a first course or as an entrée. In preparing the eggplant, if you only have table salt, use half as much.

6 First-Course Servings

2 medium eggplants (about 2 pounds), peeled and sliced lengthwise 1/8 inch thick
1 teaspoon coarse (kosher) salt
1/4 cup all-purpose flour
1 1/2 cups peanut oil
1 tablespoon olive oil
1 medium onion, thinly sliced
8 garlic cloves, minced
1/2 cup dry white wine
1 can (35 ounces) crushed Italian peeled tomatoes, with their juice
1/4 teaspoon sugar
3/4 teaspoon salt
1/4 teaspoon freshly ground pepper
1/3 cup chopped fresh basil
1 teaspoon chopped fresh thyme or 1/2 teaspoon dried
1 teaspoon chopped fresh oregano or 1/2 teaspoon dried
2 pounds fresh spinach, stemmed
1 cup ricotta cheese (1/2 pound)
1/2 cup freshly grated Parmesan cheese
1 1/3 cups (about 4 ounces) shredded Gruyère cheese

1. Arrange the eggplant slices in a single layer on a large nonreactive jelly roll pan. Sprinkle with the coarse salt. Set a large cutting board or baking sheet on top of the eggplant and weight down with canned goods. Cover with plastic wrap and set aside at room temperature for 3 hours or refrigerate overnight.

2. Drain the liquid from the eggplant and pat the slices dry. Dredge in the flour; shake off any excess. In a large, heavy nonreactive skillet, heat the peanut oil over moderately high heat. Add the eggplant in batches and fry until golden brown, about 2 minutes per side; drain on paper towels. Pour off the oil and wipe out the skillet.

3. Add the olive oil to the skillet and warm over moderate heat. Add the onion and cook until softened, about 6 minutes. Add half the garlic and cook until fragrant, about 2 minutes. Add the wine and boil until it reduces to 1/4 cup, 3 to 5 minutes. Stir in the tomatoes and their juice, the sugar, 1/2 teaspoon of the salt and 1/8 teaspoon of the pepper. Simmer over moderate heat until slightly thickened, about 15 minutes. Stir in the basil, thyme and oregano and simmer for 5 minutes longer to blend the flavors.

4. Meanwhile, in a large pot, bring 2 quarts of water to a boil. Add the spinach and cook until just wilted, about 1 minute. Drain, rinse under cold water and squeeze dry.

5. In a food processor, combine the spinach, ricotta, Parmesan and remaining minced garlic, 1/4 teaspoon salt and 1/8 teaspoon pepper. Process until the spinach is finely chopped, about 1 minute.

6. Preheat the oven to 400°. Butter a large, shallow nonreactive baking dish. Spread an eggplant slice with about 2 tablespoons of the spinach mixture and roll up. Place the roll, seam-side down, in the baking dish. Repeat with the remaining eggplant slices and filling. Spoon the tomato sauce over the eggplant rolls and sprinkle the Gruyère cheese over the top. Bake until heated through and golden brown on top, 25 to 30 minutes.

—Adam Esman, La Colombe d'Or, New York City

• • •

SCALLOP PIES IN CREPE BONNETS

These little pot pies would be an ideal first course or brunch dish. The tangy scallops are neatly tucked into a ramekin and covered with a thin crêpe.

🍷 The garlic, tomatoes and lemon zest used in this dish require a wine that will echo those flavors but not compete with them—a fruity, crisp, refreshing dry white, such as the 1986 Parducci Sauvignon Blanc or the 1986 Maître d'Estournel Bordeaux Blanc Sec.

6 First-Course Servings

CREPE BONNETS:
1 egg
6 tablespoons milk
3 tablespoons cornstarch
1 1/2 teaspoons vegetable oil

½ teaspoon baking powder
Pinch of salt
6 long scallion greens

SCALLOP FILLING:
1½ pounds bay scallops, trimmed
3 tablespoons all-purpose flour
5 tablespoons unsalted butter
1½ tablespoons vegetable oil
⅓ cup dry white wine
1 small onion, minced
2 large garlic cloves, minced
1 large tomato—peeled, seeded and chopped
5 scallions, chopped
⅛ teaspoon thyme
½ teaspoon grated lemon zest
½ teaspoon salt
¼ teaspoon freshly ground pepper

1. *Make the crêpes:* In a blender, combine the egg, milk, cornstarch, oil, baking powder and salt. Blend until smooth, scraping down the sides once.

2. Lightly oil a 6-inch crêpe pan or nonstick skillet and heat over moderately high heat. Pour 2 tablespoons of the crêpe batter into the center of the pan and swirl to coat the bottom evenly. Cook until the underside is lightly browned and the edges are dry, about 20 seconds. Turn and cook the other side for 5 seconds. Transfer to a paper towel and repeat with the remaining batter, stacking the crêpes between paper towels.

3. Using a sharp knife, slit the scallion greens lengthwise, leaving 1 inch attached at the top. In a small saucepan, blanch in boiling water until just wilted, 5 to 10 seconds. Drain and pat dry.

4. *Make the filling:* Rinse the scallops under cold water. Drain and pat dry with paper towels. Sprinkle with the flour.

5. In a large nonreactive skillet, melt 3 tablespoons of the butter in the oil over moderately high heat. Add half of the scallops and sauté, tossing, until lightly browned, 1 to 1½ minutes. Using a slotted spoon, transfer to a bowl and repeat with the remaining scallops.

6. Increase the heat to high and stir in the wine. Add the onion and cook until softened slightly, about 1 minute. Stir in the garlic and cook for 2 minutes longer. Add the tomato, chopped scallions, thyme and any accumulated scallop juices. Cook over moderate heat until the sauce thickens, about 5 minutes. Add the scallops, lemon zest and salt and pepper.

7. Preheat the oven to 350°. Spoon the scallop mixture into six 4-ounce ramekins. Place a crêpe over the top of each ramekin and tie around the edges with a butterflied scallion green. Trim the crêpes neatly with scissors.

8. Melt the remaining 2 tablespoons butter. Set the ramekins on a baking sheet and brush the tops with the melted butter. Bake in the preheated oven for 15 minutes, until piping hot.

—Phillip Stephen Schulz

• • •

SEA SCALLOP FANTASY IN BLACK TIE

This stunning dish from chef Daniel Boulud calls for a little dexterity, but the fussing is well worth it. For an even more dramatic presentation, slice the cooked scallops in half so that the distinct layers of white scallops and black truffles can be seen.

—4 First-Course Servings—

16 very large sea scallops (1 ounce each)
2 ounces jarred black truffles, juice reserved
¼ cup dry white vermouth
1 tablespoon heavy cream
1 stick plus 3 tablespoons cold unsalted butter, cut into small pieces
¼ teaspoon salt
¼ teaspoon freshly ground pepper
1 pound fresh spinach, stemmed
1 tablespoon chopped chervil or parsley

1. Slice each scallop horizontally into 4 even slices. Cut the truffles into 48 very thin slices. Rinse and chop any remaining bits of truffle. Reassemble the scallops, layering every 4 scallop slices with 3 truffle slices, beginning and ending with scallop slices.

2. In a small nonreactive saucepan, boil the vermouth over high heat until reduced to ½ tablespoon, about 3 minutes. Reduce the heat to low and add the heavy cream and the reserved truffle juice and chopped truffles. Whisk in 1 stick plus 1 tablespoon of the butter, a few pieces at a time, until smooth and thick. Remove from the heat and season with the salt and pepper. Set aside.

3. In a large skillet, melt 1 tablespoon of the butter over high heat. Add the spinach and cook, tossing, until wilted, about 1 minute. Drain off any excess water, cover with foil and set aside.

4. In a large skillet, preferably nonstick, melt the remaining 1 tablespoon butter over moderate heat. Add the scallops and cook for 3 minutes. Using a spatula, carefully flip the scallops and cook on the other side for 3 minutes.

5. Rewarm the butter sauce over low heat, whisking constantly. Divide the spinach evenly among 4 warmed plates. Place 4 scallops on each bed of spinach, spoon over the sauce and garnish with the chopped chervil or parsley.

—Daniel Boulud, Le Cirque, New York City

• • •

GRILLED SEA SCALLOPS IN PUMPKIN SEED SAUCE

🍷 Because the slight sweetness of the scallops is accentuated by the spicy pumpkin seed sauce, a sharply acidic but fruity-sweet wine, such as a 1985 Schloss Vollrads Kabinett or 1986 Callaway White Riesling, would work best with this dish.

4 First-Course Servings

8 large garlic cloves, unpeeled
1 cup hulled raw pumpkin seeds (pepitas)*
1 large poblano pepper
1 small red bell pepper
3 large shallots, chopped
¼ cup chopped fresh coriander
¼ cup chopped fresh epazote* or Italian flat-leaf parsley
2½ tablespoons fresh lime juice
1½ tablespoons chopped seeded jalapeño pepper
½ cup tomatillos (fresh or canned), quartered
1 teaspoon salt
1⅛ teaspoons freshly ground black pepper
¾ cup olive oil
¼ cup hot pepper vinegar (see Note)
¾ pound sea scallops
1 cup tomato salsa, preferably homemade
Sprigs of fresh coriander, for garnish
****Available in health food stores and Latin American markets***

1. Preheat the oven to 400°. Wrap the garlic cloves in foil and roast in the oven until soft, about 45 minutes. Squeeze the garlic from the skin into a small bowl and mash to a paste. Set aside. *(The garlic can be roasted up to 1 day ahead.)*

2. Spread the pumpkin seeds on a baking sheet and bake in the oven until lightly toasted and fragrant but still green, about 4 minutes.

3. Roast the poblano and red pepper directly over a gas flame or under the broiler as close to the heat as possible, turning, until charred all over. Seal in a paper bag for 10 minutes, then rub off the blackened skin. Remove the stems, seeds and ribs. Cut both peppers into small dice and set aside separately.

4. Put the shallots, coriander and epazote in a food processor and finely chop by turning the machine quickly on and off. Add ¾ cup of the toasted pumpkin seeds, the lime juice, jalapeño, reserved garlic puree, tomatillos and 3 tablespoons each of the diced poblano and red peppers. Puree until smooth. Season with ½ teaspoon of the salt and ¾ teaspoon of the black pepper. With the machine on, slowly pour in 3 tablespoons of the olive oil. Thin with ½ cup of water. Set the pumpkin seed sauce aside.

5. In a small bowl, whisk together the hot pepper vinegar and ¼ teaspoon each of the salt and black pepper. Gradually whisk in ½ cup of the olive oil until blended. Stir in 2 tablespoons each of the diced poblano and red pepper. Set the pepper vinaigrette aside.

6. Divide the scallops among 4 wooden skewers. Brush them with the remaining 1 tablespoon olive oil and season with the remaining ¼ teaspoon salt and ⅛ teaspoon black pepper. Broil about 5 inches from the heat without turning until lightly browned, about 4 minutes.

7. Spoon ⅓ cup of the pumpkin seed sauce onto the center of each of 4 plates. Spread to cover evenly. Arrange the scallops in a circle around the plate. Spoon 1 teaspoon of the roast pepper vinaigrette over each scallop. Spoon ¼ cup of tomato salsa in the center of the plate and sprinkle each serving with 1 tablespoon of the toasted pumpkin seeds. Garnish with a sprig of fresh coriander.

NOTE: To make homemade hot pepper vinegar, soak fresh serrano chiles in rice wine vinegar for 3 days to 2 weeks; the longer, the hotter.

—Brendan Walsh, Arizona 206, New York City

• • •

SALMON SCALLOPINI WITH ENDIVE SAUCE

The sweet-tart-bitter accents in this endive sauce are perfectly complementary to the subtle richness of salmon.

4 First-Course Servings

½ pound salmon fillet, cut crosswise on the diagonal into 8 thin slices
½ teaspoon salt
⅛ teaspoon freshly ground pepper
2 tablespoons extra-virgin olive oil
3½ tablespoons unsalted butter
1 tablespoon chopped shallot
3 small Belgian endives, sliced crosswise ⅜ inch thick
¼ cup fresh orange juice
2 tablespoons fresh lemon juice
1 cup unsalted chicken stock
1 cup heavy cream

1. Place the salmon slices on a plate and sprinkle with the salt and pepper. Brush with the olive oil and cover with plastic wrap.

2. In a large heavy skillet, melt 2 tablespoons of the butter over moderately low heat. Add the shallot, cover and cook until softened but not browned, 2 to 3 minutes. Increase the heat to moderately high and add the sliced endives. Sauté until just tender, about 2 minutes. Spread the endives on a large plate and let cool.

3. Add the orange juice, lemon juice and stock to the skillet and boil over moderately high heat until reduced to ¼ cup, about 10 minutes. Stir in the cream and boil until reduced to ¾ cup, about 5 minutes.

4. In a large skillet, preferably nonstick, melt the remaining 1½ tablespoons butter over moderately high heat. Add the salmon and sauté in batches until just opaque throughout, about 30 seconds on each side. Transfer the fish to 4 warmed serving plates.

5. Stir the endives into the cream sauce and cook until warmed through, about 2 minutes. Spoon the sauce around the salmon and serve immediately.

—François Dionot

• • •

QUAIL WITH HAZELNUT AND GARLIC SAUCE

The quantity of garlic here may be intimidating, but roasting it gives it a sweet and more subtle flavor.

6 First-Course Servings

4 large heads of garlic
1½ tablespoons hazelnut oil
½ pound hazelnuts (filberts)
1 stick (4 ounces) unsalted butter, softened to room temperature
¾ teaspoon salt
¾ teaspoon freshly ground pepper
6 quail
¼ cup plus 2 tablespoons flavorless vegetable oil
⅓ cup dry white wine
¼ cup Brown Chicken Stock (p. 247) or canned beef stock

1. Preheat the oven to 375°. Place the garlic in a small baking dish and drizzle with the hazelnut oil. Bake until the garlic is soft, about 40 minutes. Let stand until cool enough to handle. Then squeeze the softened garlic from the skins into a bowl. Using a fork, mash the garlic to a puree.

2. Spread out the hazelnuts on a large baking sheet and bake until the skins crack and the nuts are lightly toasted, about 12 minutes. Rub the nuts together in a kitchen towel to remove most of the brown skins. Place the nuts in a food processor and process until finely ground. Add the softened butter and ¼ teaspoon each of the salt and pepper. Process until smooth.

3. Season the quail inside and out with ¼ teaspoon each of the salt and pepper. Loosen the skin around the neck opening of each bird. Place 2 teaspoons of the hazelnut butter in each cavity and place 1 teaspoon under the neck skin. Tie the legs together. *(The quail can be prepared to this point up to 6 hours ahead. Cover and refrigerate.)*

4. In a large skillet, heat the vegetable oil over moderately high heat. Add the quail and cook, turning, until browned all over and the breast meat is medium-rare, about 10 minutes. Remove from the pan and cover with foil to keep warm.

5. Drain the oil from the skillet. Add the wine and chicken stock and boil over high heat, scraping up any browned bits from the bottom of the pan, until the liquid is reduced to ¼ cup, about 2 minutes. Stir in the garlic puree and remove from the heat. Swirl in the remaining hazelnut butter and season with the remaining ¼ teaspoon each salt and pepper. Remove the strings from the quail. Spoon a small amount of the sauce onto each of 6 serving plates and place a quail on top.

—Mary Taylor & Bruce Healy

• • •

SOUPS

SHRIMP AND RED PEPPER BISQUE

This rich seafood soup can be prepared up to four days in advance, but the shrimp and cream should be added just before serving.

🍷 1985 California Chardonnay, such as Sonoma-Cutrer Russian River Ranches

8 to 10 Servings

4 large red bell peppers
2½ pounds medium shrimp—shelled, deveined and cut crosswise in half, shells reserved
3 tablespoons vegetable oil
1 large onion, finely chopped
1 large carrot, finely chopped
1 large celery rib, finely chopped
¼ cup all-purpose flour
¼ cup tomato paste
⅓ cup brandy
4 sprigs of fresh thyme plus ½ teaspoon fresh thyme leaves or 1¼ teaspoons dried
1 imported bay leaf
1½ cups heavy cream, at room temperature
1 teaspoon salt
¾ teaspoon freshly ground pepper

1. Roast the peppers directly over a gas flame or under a broiler as close to the heat as possible, turning occasionally, until they are charred all over, 15 to 20 minutes. Seal the peppers in a paper bag and let stand for 10 minutes. Remove the blackened skin, stems, seeds and ribs and puree the peppers in a food processor until smooth. Place the pepper puree in a small bowl and set aside.

2. Rinse the bowl of the food processor and add the shrimp shells. Chop into small pieces. In a large heavy saucepan or flameproof casserole, heat the oil over high heat. Add the chopped shrimp shells and sauté, stirring occasionally, until lightly browned, about 3 minutes. Add the onion, carrot and celery. Reduce the heat to low and cook, stirring occasionally, until the vegetables are softened and golden brown, about 10 minutes.

3. Stir in the flour. Add the tomato paste and cook 1 minute. Increase the heat to moderately high and whisk in the brandy, scraping up any browned bits from the bottom of the pan. Cook for 3 minutes, then whisk in 7 cups of water. Add the thyme sprigs or 1 teaspoon of the dried thyme and bay leaf and return to a boil, whisking frequently. Simmer the soup over low heat for 45 minutes.

4. Meanwhile, in a large saucepan, heat the cream over moderately high heat. Add the shrimp and cook, stirring occasionally, until they are pink and loosely curled, about 8 minutes. Pour the shrimp and cream into a large bowl and set aside.

5. Strain the soup through a fine-mesh sieve into a large bowl, pressing to extract all the liquid. Return the soup to the pan and stir in the red pepper puree.

6. Just before serving, stir in the shrimp and cream and season with the salt, pepper and remaining thyme.

—Marcia Kiesel

• • •

AVOCADO SOUP WITH PAPAYA PEPPER RELISH

This refreshing variation of chilled avocado soup is from Robert Del Grande.

8 to 10 Servings

2 teaspoons unsalted butter
1 small onion, minced
1 carrot, minced
2 small celery ribs, minced
1 garlic clove, minced
4 cups chicken stock or canned broth
1 cup heavy cream, chilled
1 small red bell pepper
1 poblano pepper
2 large ripe avocados (preferably Hass), cut into ¼-inch dice
2 tablespoons fresh lime juice
5 tablespoons minced fresh coriander
¼ teaspoon salt
¼ teaspoon freshly ground black pepper
1 small ripe papaya—peeled, seeded and cut into ¼-inch dice
1 teaspoon walnut oil
3 jalapeño peppers, seeded and minced

1. In a large saucepan or flameproof casserole, melt the butter over moderate heat. Add the onion, carrot, celery and garlic and cook, stirring, until softened but not browned, about 6 minutes. Add the chicken stock and bring to a boil. Remove from the heat and let cool to room temperature. Stir in the cream and refrigerate until well chilled, about 2 hours or overnight.

2. Roast the red bell pepper and poblano over a gas flame or under the broiler, turning, until charred all over. Put the peppers in a paper bag and let steam for 10 minutes. Peel and seed the peppers and discard the cores. Cut the peppers into ¼-inch dice.

3. Whisk the diced avocados into the chilled soup until they begin to break up and thicken it slightly. Stir in 1 tablespoon of the lime juice, 2½ tablespoons of the coriander, ⅛ teaspoon of the salt and ⅛ teaspoon of the black pepper. Refrigerate until the flavors are well blended.

4. In a small bowl, combine the papaya and the roasted red pepper and poblano with the remaining 1 tablespoon lime juice and 2½ tablespoons coriander. Stir in the walnut oil and the remaining ¼ teaspoon each of salt and black pepper. Serve the soup chilled, with a dollop of the papaya relish and a sprinkling of the minced jalapeños.

—Robert Del Grande, Cafe Annie, Houston

• • •

A fanciful tureen of Butternut Squash and Leek Soup (p. 39).

Proscuitto-Wrapped Hearts of Palm (p. 14).

Beggar's Purses (p. 20).

COOL ASPARAGUS SOUP

This creamy chilled soup makes a wonderful starter for a lazy Sunday lunch.

6 Servings

1½ pounds asparagus, trimmed
4 tablespoons unsalted butter
1 small onion, chopped
2 medium leeks, chopped
1 medium celery rib, chopped
1 large baking potato, peeled and cut into ½-inch dice
3½ cups chicken stock or canned broth
1 teaspoon fresh lemon juice
Salt
¾ teaspoon freshly ground white pepper
½ cup half-and-half
¼ cup plus 2 tablespoons crème fraîche or sour cream
Paprika, for garnish

1. Cut off the asparagus tips and set aside. Coarsely chop the stems.

2. In a large skillet, melt the butter over moderate heat. Add the asparagus tips, onion, leeks, celery and potato. Cover, reduce the heat to low and cook until soft, about 25 minutes.

3. Meanwhile, in a medium saucepan, bring the stock to a boil over high heat. Add the asparagus stems, cover and cook over low heat until soft, about 25 minutes. Strain into a large bowl pressing on the stalks to extract as much liquid as possible. Discard the stems.

4. Put the sautéed vegetables in a food processor and puree until smooth, about 30 seconds. Whisk the vegetable puree into the strained stock. Season with the lemon juice, salt and pepper. Cover with plastic wrap and refrigerate until chilled, about 1 hour.

5. When ready to serve, stir in the half-and-half; mix well. Top each soup bowl with 1 tablespoon of the crème fraîche and garnish each with a dash of paprika.

—*Lee Bailey*

Pork Empanaditas with Yellow Pepper Sauce (p. 21).

• • •

ROSEMARY-SCENTED SWEET RED PEPPER BISQUE

Serve this soup hot or cold at the start of an elegant meal or for a light supper.

🍷 Crisp white, such as 1986 Dry Creek Fumé Blanc.

6 Servings

4 medium sprigs of rosemary plus 6 tiny sprigs for garnish
2 medium sprigs of sweet marjoram
3 tablespoons fruity olive oil
6 large red bell peppers, cut into ½-inch strips
6 medium leeks (white part only), thinly sliced
2 large garlic cloves, crushed through a press
¼ teaspoon freshly ground black pepper
2½ cups beef stock or canned broth
¾ cup plus 6 tablespoons crème fraîche or sour cream, at room temperature
Salt

1. Tie the medium sprigs of rosemary and the marjoram in a double thickness of cheesecloth. Wring lightly to release the volatile oils.

2. In a large heavy saucepan, heat the oil over high heat until almost smoking, about 1 minute. Add the peppers and cook, tossing, until slightly softened, about 2 minutes. Add the leeks and garlic and cook, tossing, for 2 minutes longer.

3. Add the cheesecloth bag of herbs and the black pepper. Reduce the heat to very low, cover tightly and cook until considerable juices have accumulated and the peppers are very soft, about 1 hour.

4. Remove and discard the cheesecloth bag. Scrape the vegetables into a food processor or blender and puree until smooth.

5. Strain the puree into a medium saucepan and add the stock. Cook over moderate heat until just hot, 2 to 3 minutes. Stir in ¾ cup of the crème fraîche and season to taste with salt.

6. Ladle the soup into heated soup plates and garnish each serving with 1 tablespoon of the crème fraîche and a tiny rosemary sprig.

—*Jean Anderson*

• • •

DOUBLE CORIANDER-GINGER CREAM SOUP

This French-style light cream soup is flavored with fresh coriander and ginger.

4 to 6 Servings

4 tablespoons unsalted butter
2 teaspoons peanut oil
1 teaspoon Oriental sesame oil
½ cup finely chopped scallions
2 tablespoons finely chopped fresh ginger
½ cup minced shallots
2 teaspoons ground coriander
1 tablespoon sugar
4 cups chicken stock or canned broth
¼ teaspoon salt
⅛ teaspoon freshly ground white pepper
½ cup heavy cream
½ cup finely chopped fresh coriander
¼ cup minced chives
Fresh coriander leaves, for garnish

1. In a large saucepan or flameproof casserole, melt 2 tablespoons of the butter in the peanut oil and sesame oil over moderate heat. Add the scallions, ginger and shallots and cook until the shallots are softened but not browned, 2 to 3 minutes.

2. Stir in the ground coriander, sugar, chicken stock, salt and pepper. Bring to a boil, reduce the heat and simmer for 5 minutes. Remove from the heat and stir in the cream, fresh coriander and chives.

3. In a blender or food processor, puree the soup in batches until smooth. Return the soup to the saucepan and cook over moderately low heat until heated through, about 3 minutes. Stir in the remaining 2 tablespoons butter. Ladle the soup into a soup tureen or individual bowls and garnish with coriander leaves.

—Ken Hom

• • •

WATERCRESS SOUP

This low-calorie variation of the classic *potage au cresson* uses zucchini in place of potato. When pureed, the zucchini gives body to the soup, just as potatoes do. The zucchini is peeled, so the color of the soup resembles that of the original version and is not too dark.

Already low in calories, the soup can be lightened even further by omitting the cream. Either way, this soup is very quick and easy to make, and it can be served hot or cold as an elegant beginning to almost any meal.

6 Servings

1 tablespoon unsalted butter
3 leeks (white part only), chopped
1½ pounds zucchini, peeled and diced
4 cups chicken stock or canned broth
1 bunch of watercress, tough stems removed
⅓ cup heavy cream (optional)
Salt and freshly ground pepper

1. In a large heavy saucepan or flameproof casserole, melt the butter over moderately low heat. Add the leeks and cook until softened but not browned, 5 to 7 minutes.

2. Add the zucchini, increase the heat to moderately high and sauté for 2 minutes without browning. Add the stock and bring to a boil. Reduce the heat to moderate and simmer until the zucchini is just tender, about 5 minutes. Add the watercress and simmer for 1 minute longer.

3. Using a food processor or blender, puree the soup, in batches if necessary, until smooth. Add the cream, if desired, and season with salt and pepper to taste.

—Richard Grausman

• • •

CAULIFLOWER CRESS SOUP

In early summer, there are a number of varieties of cress that you might like to experiment with. A favorite of mine is referred to locally as "upland cress" and is cultivated in an ordinary garden instead of in running water. If you can, in this recipe, substitute a local type for the ubiquitous watercress.

4 to 6 Servings

1½ cups cauliflower florets
1½ cups low-fat milk
6 tablespoons unsalted butter
¾ cup chopped scallions
1½ cups baking potatoes, peeled and finely diced
2½ cups chicken stock or canned broth
10 cups (lightly packed) watercress sprigs (about 3 bunches)
Salt and freshly ground white pepper
¼ cup crème fraîche

1. In a medium saucepan, combine the cauliflower florets and milk. Bring to a boil over moderate heat. Reduce the heat to moderately low and simmer until the cauliflower is tender, about 5 minutes. Drain the cauliflower mixture over a bowl, reserving the cauliflower and the milk separately.

2. In a large saucepan, melt the butter. Add the scallions and sauté over moderately low heat until softened but not browned, 3 to 4 minutes. Add the potatoes and chicken stock. Increase the heat to moderately high and bring to a boil. Reduce the heat to moderately low, cover and simmer until the potatoes are tender, about 10 minutes.

3. Reserve 12 to 16 sprigs of watercress for garnish. Stir the remaining watercress into the stock and cook until the cress is tender, 5 minutes. Add the cauliflower to the soup and cook until heated through, about 3 minutes.

4. Working in batches, if necessary, puree the soup in a blender or food processor. Return to the saucepan and add the reserved milk. Reheat over moderately low heat, about 5 minutes. Season with salt and white pepper to taste. (If the soup is too thick, thin with a little more milk or water.) Serve warm and garnish each bowl with 1 tablespoon of crème fraîche and a few sprigs of watercress.

—Lee Bailey

• • •

INFORMAL SUMMER SOUP LUNCH

Soup is the perfect entrée in this casual lunch from Lee Bailey. There is a choice of soups, but either should be served family style, in a tureen. Serves 4 to 6.

Sweet Potato Vichyssoise (p. 39) or Cauliflower Cress Soup (p. 38)

Corn Wafers (p. 140)

Crisp White Wine

Tossed Green Salad with a Light Vinaigrette

Assorted Cheeses

Lemon Macadamia Cookies (p. 190)

Iced Coffee

SWEET POTATO VICHYSSOISE

I think you will like this takeoff on a traditional favorite. Although I think this soup is best served chilled, some of my friends also like it warm.

4 to 6 Servings

1¼ pounds sweet potatoes
1 cup (lightly packed) sliced scallions (white and 2 inches of the green)
2½ cups chicken stock or canned broth
Salt and freshly ground white pepper
¼ cup heavy cream
1 tablespoon chopped chives

1. Preheat the oven to 400°. Prick the sweet potatoes several times with a fork and bake for about 1 hour, until soft. Let cool; then scoop out the potato pulp from the skins.

2. Meanwhile, in a medium saucepan, combine the scallions with 1 cup of the chicken stock. Simmer over moderate heat, stirring occasionally, until the scallions are tender, about 10 minutes.

3. Pour the scallion-stock mixture into a food processor. Add the potato pulp and ½ cup more of the chicken stock. Puree until smooth, about 30 seconds.

4. Return to the saucepan and stir in the remaining 1 cup stock. Bring to a boil over moderate heat, reduce the heat to low and simmer for 5 minutes, to allow the flavors to blend. Season with salt and white pepper to taste. Let the soup cool to room temperature, then cover with plastic wrap. Refrigerate until chilled, about 4 hours.

5. Before serving, beat the cream in a medium bowl with a whisk until slightly thickened. Pour the soup into chilled bowls and swirl into each a tablespoon of the thickened cream. Garnish with the chives.

—Lee Bailey

• • •

BUTTERNUT SQUASH AND LEEK SOUP

This light, vibrant orange soup could also be made with another orange squash, such as hubbard or pumpkin.

8 Servings

4½ pounds butternut squash, halved lengthwise
5 tablespoons unsalted butter
4 large leeks (white and tender green), chopped
7 sprigs of fresh thyme or 1 teaspoon dried
5 cups chicken stock or unsalted canned broth
1¼ teaspoons salt
½ teaspoon freshly ground pepper
½ cup sour cream
3 tablespoons chopped chives
8 slices of bacon, fried crisp and crumbled

1. Preheat the oven to 350°. Place the squash, cut-side down, on a baking sheet and bake until tender, about 40 minutes. Let cool slightly. Using a spoon, scoop out and discard the seeds. Scrape the squash from the skin.

2. Meanwhile, in a large/heavy saucepan or flameproof casserole, melt the butter over low heat. Add the leeks and thyme and cook, stirring occasionally, until softened and lightly browned, about 40 minutes. Discard the thyme sprigs.

3. Stir in the stock and the squash. Simmer the soup over moderate heat for 20 minutes.

4. In a blender or food processor, puree the soup in batches until smooth. Pour the soup back into the pan and season with the salt and pepper. *(The recipe can be prepared to this point up to 2 days ahead. Reheat before proceeding.)*

5. To serve, ladle the soup into bowls and garnish each serving with 1 tablespoon sour cream, 1 teaspoon chopped chives and a sprinkling of the crumbled bacon.

—Tina Ujlaki

• • •

CREAM OF CARROT SOUP WITH BRANDY AND CHERVIL

For this simple recipe, chicken wings and carrots are cooked together to form a stock base for this delicious soup.

4 First-Course Servings

1 pound chicken wings, sectioned
1 tablespoon all-purpose flour
2 tablespoons unsalted butter
3 large shallots, chopped
1 pound carrots, peeled and chopped
½ cup brandy
½ cup dry white wine
1 cup plus 2 tablespoons chopped fresh chervil
½ cup heavy cream
1 teaspoon salt
½ teaspoon freshly ground pepper

1. Toss the chicken wings with the flour. In a large saucepan or flameproof casserole, melt the butter over high heat. Add the chicken wings and cook, stirring occasionally, until the chicken is browned, about 6 minutes.

2. Add the shallots and cook until softened and fragrant, about 2 minutes. Add the carrots, brandy and wine and cook over high heat for 1 minute. Add 2½ cups of water, return to a boil and reduce the heat to low. Cover and simmer until the carrots are very tender, about 45 minutes. Remove from the heat.

3. With a slotted spoon, remove and discard the chicken pieces. Stir in 1 cup of the chervil. Puree the soup in batches in a blender or food processor until very smooth. Return to the pan, stir in the cream and season with the salt and pepper. Divide the soup among 4 bowls, garnish each with the remaining chopped chervil and serve at once.

—Marcia Kiesel

• • •

BROCCOLI, ONION AND CHEESE SOUP

Serve this soup with homemade croutons or lots of crusty bread.

🍷 The sweetly aromatic onion and cheese flavors of this soup match with the fruity-pungent taste of Pinot Noir, such as 1985 Joseph Drouhin Laforet Bourgogne Rouge, served slightly cool.

8 to 10 Servings

5 tablespoons unsalted butter
2 large Bermuda onions, thinly sliced
1/4 teaspoon freshly ground black pepper
3 sprigs of fresh thyme or 1/2 teaspoon dried
1 tablespoon sugar
3/4 cup Riesling or other sweet white wine
3 cups Quick Chicken Stock (p. 246) or canned low-salt chicken broth
3 tablespoons all-purpose flour
1 1/2 cups milk
1/2 cup heavy cream
1/4 teaspoon dry mustard
1/8 teaspoon freshly grated nutmeg
Dash of cayenne pepper
1/2 pound Jarlsberg cheese, grated
1/2 cup grated Gruyère cheese
1 bunch of broccoli, separated into 1 1/2-inch florets (about 4 cups)
1 red bell pepper, cut into 1/4-inch dice

1. In a large flameproof casserole, melt 2 tablespoons of the butter over moderately high heat. Add the onions, black pepper, thyme and sugar. Reduce the heat to moderately low, place a circle of waxed paper directly over the top of the onions and cover tightly with a lid. Simmer, stirring occasionally, until the onions are very soft and golden, about 1 hour and 15 minutes.

2. Remove the cover and the waxed paper and increase the heat to moderate. Cook until the onions are golden brown, about 25 minutes.

3. Add the wine and boil until reduced by half, about 5 minutes. Add the chicken stock and 2 cups of water. Bring to a boil and simmer for 15 minutes.

4. In a large saucepan, melt the remaining 3 tablespoons butter over moderate heat. Whisk in the flour and cook, stirring, for 2 minutes without browning. Whisk in the milk, cream, dry mustard, nutmeg and cayenne and bring to a boil. Boil, stirring, for 2 minutes. Remove from the heat and stir in the Jarlsberg and Gruyère until smooth.

5. Scrape the cheese mixture into the hot soup, add the broccoli and cook until crisp-tender, about 8 minutes. Stir in the red pepper and cook until heated through, about 2 minutes.

—Mimi Ruth Brodeur

• • •

SPINACH SOUP

This soup is similar to one made by Mary Allen of Roxbury, Connecticut—and it's delicious.

6 to 8 Servings

4 tablespoons unsalted butter
1 large onion, minced
3 pounds fresh spinach, stemmed
2 cups chicken stock or canned broth
2 cups low-fat milk
1 teaspoon salt
1/2 teaspoon freshly ground pepper
Thin slices of lemon and minced chives, for garnish

1. In a large saucepan, melt the butter over moderate heat. Add the onion and reduce the heat to low. Cook until softened but not browned, about 10 minutes.

2. Increase the heat to moderate and add the spinach leaves by the handful, stirring to wilt them before adding the next handful. When all the spinach has been added, cook for about 1 minute to completely soften the spinach.

3. In a food processor, puree the soup in batches until smooth. Return the soup to the pan and stir in the stock and milk. Simmer over moderate heat until heated through. Season with the salt and pepper. Serve in soup bowls, garnished with a slice of lemon and a sprinkling of chives.

—Lee Bailey

• • •

LAMB BORSCHT

This hearty borscht can be made up to two days in advance.

🍷 Although there are fruity overtones in this soup, the dominant flavor is the meaty broth, which calls for a hearty but light red, such as the 1985 Paul Jaboulet Ainé Côtes du Rhône Parallèle 45.

8 Servings

1 tablespoon olive oil
1 large onion, chopped
8 garlic cloves, minced
3 large jalapeño peppers, minced with some seeds
2 1/2 pounds boneless lamb shoulder, trimmed of excess fat and cut into 1/2-inch cubes
2 sprigs of fresh rosemary, minced, or 1/2 teaspoon dried
2 cups (loosely packed) mint leaves, minced
1/2 teaspoon freshly ground pepper
7 cups Quick Chicken Stock (p. 246) or canned low-salt chicken broth
4 large beets, peeled and cut into 1/2-inch cubes, greens reserved, large stems removed
2 cans (19 ounces) cannellini or white navy beans, with their liquid

2 tablespoons grated orange zest
2 teaspoons grated lemon zest
1 cup sour cream, as accompaniment

1. In a large flameproof casserole, heat the oil over moderate heat. Add the onion, garlic and jalapeño peppers and cook until softened, about 10 minutes.

2. Increase the heat to moderately high and stir in the lamb, rosemary, 1 cup of the mint and the pepper. Cook, stirring occasionally, until the meat is browned, about 5 minutes. Add the chicken stock and 3½ cups of water; bring to a boil. Reduce the heat to moderate and simmer, skimming occasionally, until the meat is tender, about 1½ hours.

3. Add the beets, reserving the greens, and simmer until the beets are cooked through, about 25 minutes.

4. Meanwhile, in a food processor or blender, puree the bean liquid and 2 cups of the beans and stir them into the soup. Add the remaining whole beans, the orange zest, lemon zest, reserved beet greens and remaining 1 cup mint. Cook until the greens are just tender, about 5 minutes. Pass the sour cream separately.

—Mimi Ruth Brodeur

• • •

MONKFISH BOURRIDE WITH GARLIC CREAM

Monkfish—known as *lotte* in France—is a popular and plentiful Mediterranean fish, one that stands up well in flavorful soups such as this bourride. With the addition of the garlic-rich mayonnaise known as aioli, the soup is a meal all on its own. You can prepare the aioli earlier in the day, or even the day before, so that there is very little last-minute work.

🍷 With the soup, serve either a chilled white from Provence, such as a Cassis, or a Tavel or Bandol Rosé.

6 Servings

1 pound baking potatoes, peeled and thinly sliced
1 leek (white part only), sliced
1 fennel bulb, trimmed and thinly sliced
1 medium carrot, sliced
1 garlic clove, minced
1 teaspoon grated orange zest
3 imported bay leaves
1 cup dry white wine
Fish Stock (recipe follows)
2 pounds monkfish, membrane removed, cut crosswise into ½-inch slices
Aioli (p. 254)
2 egg yolks
¼ cup crème fraîche or heavy cream
½ teaspoon salt
¼ teaspoon freshly ground pepper
Toasted slices of peasant or French bread, as accompaniment

1. In a large nonreactive saucepan or flameproof casserole, combine the potatoes, leek, fennel, carrot, garlic, orange zest, bay leaves, wine and Fish Stock. Bring to a boil over high heat. Reduce the heat to moderately low and simmer until the vegetables are just tender, 12 to 15 minutes.

2. Add the monkfish and cook, skimming frequently, until the fish is opaque throughout, about 5 minutes. Discard the bay leaves.

3. With a slotted spoon, transfer the fish and vegetables to a warmed soup tureen. Cover to keep warm. Boil the soup over high heat until reduced to 3 cups, 5 to 10 minutes.

4. Meanwhile, in a medium bowl, combine ¾ cup of the Aioli with the egg yolks and crème fraîche; whisk to blend. Gradually stir ½ cup of the hot soup into the aioli mixture.

5. With the soup over low heat, whisk the warmed aioli mixture, or garlic cream, back into the remaining soup until blended. Cook, stirring, for 1 to 2 minutes to thicken slightly; do not let boil. Season with the salt and pepper and pour the soup over the fish and vegetables.

6. To serve, ladle the soup into warmed bowls, making sure everyone gets some fish and an assortment of vegetables. Pass the remaining Aioli and toasted bread separately.

—Hôtel Jules-César,
Arles, France

• • •

FISH STOCK FOR MONKFISH BOURRIDE

Makes 4 Cups

4 pounds non-oily fish bones, heads and trimmings—gills removed, well rinsed and cut up
1 medium onion, chopped
1 tomato, coarsely chopped
Bouquet garni: 12 parsley stems, 8 peppercorns, ¼ teaspoon thyme, ¼ teaspoon fennel seeds and 1 imported bay leaf tied in a double thickness of cheesecloth
Pinch of saffron threads
1 cup dry white wine

1. In a large nonreactive saucepan, combine the fish bones, heads and trimmings, the onion, tomato, bouquet garni, saffron and white wine. Add 6 cups of water.

2. Bring to a simmer over moderately low heat, skimming frequently. Simmer uncovered, skimming frequently, for 20 minutes.

3. Strain the stock through a sieve lined with a double layer of dampened cheesecloth. Measure the fish stock and, if necessary, boil until it is reduced to 4 cups.

—Lou Marquès restaurant,
Hôtel Jules-César, Arles, France

• • •

DUCK SOUP WITH ROASTED VEGETABLES

If desired, the duck skin can be crisped in the oven and added to the soup just before serving.

8 to 10 Servings

1 duck (5 pounds), neck and gizzard reserved
2 cups dry white wine
3 heads of garlic, cut horizontally in half
2 medium carrots, cut into 1-inch dice
1 large onion, cut into 1-inch dice
1 large baking potato, unpeeled and cut into 1-inch dice
1 pound Belgian endive, chopped
1/4 cup chopped parsley
3/4 teaspoon salt
1/2 teaspoon freshly ground pepper

1. Preheat the oven to 400°. In a large roasting pan, place the neck, gizzard and duck, breast-side up. Roast until the skin is golden brown and the breast meat is just slightly pink in the center, about 1 hour and 15 minutes. Remove the duck from the pan and set aside on a plate to cool. Pour off the fat from the pan, reserving and setting aside 2 tablespoons plus 2½ teaspoons.

2. Set the roasting pan on two burners over high heat. Add the wine and boil, scraping up any browned bits from the bottom of the pan, for 3 minutes. Pour the wine mixture into a large heavy stockpot or flameproof casserole along with the roasted neck and gizzard.

3. When the duck is cool enough to handle, remove the skin from the breasts, legs and thighs and cut all the meat into 1-inch pieces; set aside.

4. Cut up the remaining carcass as much as possible. Place the bones in the stockpot. Add 10 cups of cold water and bring to a boil. Reduce the heat to low and simmer, skimming occasionally, for 2 hours. *(The stock can be made to this point up to 3 days in advance. Let cool; cover and refrigerate.)*

5. Meanwhile, preheat the oven to 400°. Spread ½ teaspoon of the reserved duck fat on the bottom of each garlic half. Cover with the garlic tops and sit the garlic in a corner of the roasting pan. Add the carrots, onion and potato and toss with 1 tablespoon plus 1 teaspoon of the fat. Scatter the vegetables in an even layer over the bottom of the pan. Cover with aluminum foil and roast at 400° until the vegetables are cooked through and browned on the bottom, about 45 minutes. Leave the oven on.

6. Remove the garlic and set aside to cool. Scrape the remaining vegetables from the pan and place them in a separate bowl. Place the endive in the roasting pan and toss with the remaining 1 tablespoon duck fat. Roast the endive uncovered, until browned, about 20 minutes.

7. Place the pan with the endive on two burners over moderate heat and add 2 cups of water. Bring to a boil, scraping up any browned bits from the bottom of the pan. Reduce the heat and simmer, stirring occasionally, for 5 minutes. Add this mixture to the roasted vegetables.

8. When the garlic is cool enough to handle, squeeze to slip off the skins. In a small bowl, mash the garlic into a paste.

9. Strain the stock through a colander into a large bowl. Skim off the fat. Return the stock to the pot. Add the roasted vegetables and reserved meat and simmer over moderate heat for 10 minutes. Whisk in the garlic puree and season the soup with the parsley, salt and pepper.

—*Marcia Kiesel*

• • •

ESCAROLE SOUP WITH SAUSAGE

To serve this soup as a main course, accompany it with lots of warm crusty Italian or garlic bread and start the meal with a small salad of arugula, cherry tomatoes and mozzarella.

8 to 10 Servings

1 pound sweet Italian sausage
1/4 pound pancetta or lean bacon, finely diced
1 tablespoon olive oil
1 large onion, chopped
2 garlic cloves, minced
2 tablespoons tomato paste
Quick Chicken Stock (p. 246)
1 large head of escarole (about 1 pound), coarsely chopped
1/2 cup basmati rice
1 cup hot water
1/2 teaspoon salt
1/2 teaspoon freshly ground pepper
Grated Parmesan cheese

1. Put the sausage in a large saucepan. Add cold water to cover and bring to a boil over high heat. Reduce the heat to moderately low and simmer for 10 minutes. With a slotted spoon, remove the sausage to a plate. Bring the sausage water to a boil over high heat and add the pancetta. Boil for 30 seconds, stirring; drain and set aside. Slice the sausage ¼-inch thick and reserve.

2. In a large heavy saucepan or flameproof casserole, heat the olive oil over moderately low heat. Add the onion and garlic and cook, stirring occasionally, until the onion is soft, about 15 minutes.

3. Increase the heat to moderately high and add the pancetta. Cook, stirring, until the pancetta and onion begin to brown, about 3 minutes. Stir in the tomato paste and chicken stock. Bring to a boil and add the escarole. Boil for about 2 minutes; remove from the heat.

4. In a medium saucepan, cover the rice with the hot water. Bring to a boil over high heat, cover and reduce the heat to low. Cook without uncovering for 15 minutes. Turn off the heat and let the pan sit for 5 minutes. Uncover and fluff up the rice.

5. When ready to serve, stir the sausage and rice into the soup and season with the salt and pepper. Pass the grated Parmesan cheese on the side.

—Marcia Kiesel

• • •

STEAK SOUP

I've given instructions here for cooking a steak to use in the soup, but to my mind this recipe was tailor-made for leftover steak or roast beef.

4 to 6 Servings

1½ pounds boneless rib, strip, Delmonico or sirloin steak, cut about 2 inches thick
2 tablespoons unsalted butter
1 tablespoon olive oil
½ pound small leeks (white part only), finely diced
6 cups beef stock or canned broth
1½ pounds baking potatoes (about 3 medium), peeled and cut into 1-inch cubes
½ cup heavy cream
Salt and freshly ground pepper
2 tablespoons chopped fresh marjoram or parsley, for garnish

1. Preheat the broiler. Broil the steak about 4 inches from the heat, turning once, until rare, about 5 minutes per side. Remove the meat to a cutting board and let rest for 5 minutes. Cut the steak into ½-inch cubes.

2. In a large saucepan or flameproof casserole, melt the butter in the olive oil over moderately high heat. Add the leeks and toss to coat well. Reduce the heat to moderate and cook the leeks until softened, but not browned, about 5 minutes.

3. Add the steak, stock and potatoes. Bring to a boil over high heat. Reduce the heat to moderately low and simmer, uncovered, until the potatoes are very tender, about 30 minutes. With a wooden spoon, mash some of the potatoes to thicken the soup slightly. (*The recipe can be prepared ahead to this point. Refrigerate in a covered container for up to 3 days, or freeze for up to 3 months. Reheat before proceeding.*)

4. Stir in the cream and simmer for 3 minutes to heat through. Season the soup with salt and pepper to taste. Serve in large soup bowls, garnished with the chopped marjoram.

—Gayle Henderson Wilson

• • •

MUSHROOM, BEEF AND BARLEY SOUP

In this recipe, beef short ribs, wild mushrooms and barley are combined to create a satisfying cold-weather dish.

8 to 10 Servings

3 tablespoons vegetable oil
4½ pounds meaty beef short ribs, cut crosswise into 2-inch pieces (ask your butcher to do this)
1 tablespoon salt
¼ teaspoon freshly ground pepper
1 cup minced shallots (about 10)
1 pound fresh white mushrooms, minced
½ pound fresh shiitake mushrooms, stemmed, caps thinly sliced
1 cup dry red wine
¾ cup barley, rinsed and drained
2 teaspoons ground cumin
1½ teaspoons chili powder
4 sprigs of fresh thyme or ¾ teaspoon dried
1 imported bay leaf
1 can (35 ounces) Italian peeled tomatoes with their juice
3 tablespoons chopped Italian flat-leaf parsley, for garnish

1. In a large flameproof casserole, heat 2 tablespoons of the oil over moderately high heat. Add half of the meat and sauté, tossing, until browned, about 4 minutes. Remove the meat to a bowl and season with 1½ teaspoons of the salt and ⅛ teaspoon of the pepper. Repeat with the remaining meat, salt and pepper.

2. Drain off the fat from the casserole. Add the remaining 1 tablespoon oil and heat over moderately high heat. Add the shallots and mushrooms and cook until softened and lightly browned, about 8 minutes.

3. Add the wine and boil until reduced by half, about 5 minutes. Stir in 8 cups of water, the barley, cumin, chili powder, thyme and bay leaf; bring to a boil. Reduce the heat to moderately low and simmer, partially covered, until the meat is tender, about 1½ hours.

4. Remove the short ribs to a cutting board. Discard the bones and cut the meat into ½-inch pieces.

5. Skim the fat from the soup and return the meat to the casserole. Return to a boil and add the tomatoes and their juice. Simmer, uncovered, for 10 minutes. Sprinkle with parsley and serve.

—Mimi Ruth Brodeur

• • •

ROASTED SHALLOT SOUP WITH RABBIT

Here is an unusual way of presenting a soup: the solids are arranged attractively in shallow soup plates and presented to guests. The liquid soup is then ladled from a tureen at the table.

🍷 The subtle interplay of delicate rabbit, shallots, cream and wild mushrooms is tailor-made to showcase a fine oak-aged Chardonnay from California (such as 1985 Trefethen) or from Australia (such as 1986 Wolf Blass).

8 Servings

Coarse (kosher) salt
1 pound shallots, unpeeled
¼ pound sliced prosciutto
¼ cup plus 1 tablespoon peanut oil
½ pound fresh wild mushrooms (chanterelles, morels, shiitake)—stems removed and reserved, caps cut into small dice
6 cups strong chicken stock, preferably homemade
2 cups heavy cream
1½ teaspoons freshly ground pepper
2 saddles of rabbit on the bone, 1½ pounds (see Note)
½ teaspoon salt
1 teaspoon fresh thyme or ½ teaspoon dried

1. Preheat the oven to 375°. In a shallow medium baking dish, spread out a bed of coarse salt. Set half the shallots on top and roast until tender, about 20 minutes. Set aside briefly to cool, then carefully peel off the outer layers of the shallots, leaving a small central bulb. Reserve the bulbs and the peeled outer layers separately.

2. Peel the remaining uncooked shallots. Finely chop one and set aside; thinly slice the remaining shallots. Cut half of the prosciutto into fine dice and set aside. Coarsely chop the remaining prosciutto.

3. In a large heavy saucepan, heat 2 tablespoons of the peanut oil over high heat. Add the coarsely chopped prosciutto, the reserved mushroom stems and the sliced shallots. Cook, stirring constantly, until the shallots are softened and translucent. Add the stock and the reserved outer layers and peel of roasted shallots and bring to a boil. Reduce the heat to low and simmer for 20 minutes.

4. Puree the soup in a food processor or blender and strain into a clean saucepan. Bring to a simmer over moderate heat, add the cream and simmer, uncovered, for 15 minutes. Season the soup with ½ teaspoon of the pepper and strain again through a fine sieve. *(The soup can be prepared to this point up to 2 days in advance. Cover and refrigerate.)*

5. About 30 minutes before serving, preheat the oven to 450°. Season the saddles of rabbit on all sides with the salt and ½ teaspoon of the pepper. Brush with 1 tablespoon of the peanut oil and sprinkle with the thyme. In an ovenproof skillet, cook the saddles over high heat, turning, until browned all over. Place the skillet in the oven and roast the saddles until just cooked through, about 10 minutes. Remove from the skillet and let rest for 10 minutes.

6. Meanwhile, in a medium skillet, heat the remaining 2 tablespoons peanut oil. Add the diced mushroom caps and cook over moderately high heat, tossing, until nearly tender, about 2 minutes. Add the reserved diced prosciutto and the chopped shallot and continue to cook, tossing, until the mushrooms are tender, about 2 minutes longer. Season with the remaining ½ teaspoon pepper and set aside.

7. To assemble the soup, remove the loins from each saddle. Carve each loin into 8 slices and arrange 4 slices around the edges of each of 8 shallow soup plates. In between the slices, place the reserved roasted shallot centers and the sautéed mushroom mixture.

8. Return the soup to a simmer over moderate heat. Pour the hot soup into a tureen and ladle into the soup plates at the table.

NOTE: The original version of this recipe is made with hare; we've substituted rabbit because it is available fresh rather than frozen.

—Jean-Louis Palladin,
Jean-Louis, Washington, D.C.

• • •

FISH & SHELLFISH

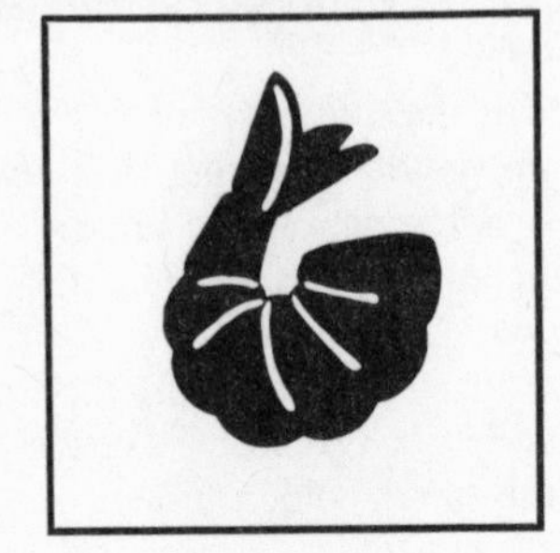

SALT COD GRATIN

This gratin is a delicious main course in any season, accompanied with bread and a green salad. The salt cod needs to soak for one to two days, so plan accordingly.

🍷 Serve with a chilled Tavel rosé, such as Domaine de la Genestière.

6 Servings

1 pound boneless, skinless salt cod
2 cups milk
2 teaspoons chopped fresh thyme
3 imported bay leaves
1 pound baking potatoes, peeled and thinly sliced
2 egg yolks
½ cup crème fraîche or heavy cream
½ teaspoon salt
½ teaspoon freshly ground pepper
1 garlic clove, cut in half
3 tablespoons unsalted butter

1. One to two days before preparing the gratin, depending on the saltiness of the fish, soak the salt cod in plenty of cold water. Change the water 3 or 4 times during the soaking period to remove excess salt. Drain and rinse the fish.

2. Put the cod in a large saucepan. Add cold water to cover and bring to a simmer over moderate heat. Immediately remove the pan from the heat, cover and let stand for 15 minutes. Drain well. Scrape off any fatty skin and remove any bones. Tear the fish into bite-size pieces.

3. In a large saucepan, combine the milk, thyme and bay leaves. Bring to a simmer over moderate heat. Remove from the heat, cover and let stand for 15 minutes.

4. Preheat the oven to 350°. Add the potatoes to the seasoned milk and simmer over moderate heat, covered, until the potatoes are tender, about 20 minutes.

5. In a small bowl, whisk together the egg yolks and crème fraîche. Remove the potatoes from the heat and stir in the egg and cream mixture. Season with the salt and pepper.

6. Rub the cut sides of the garlic over a medium gratin or baking dish. Grease with 1 tablespoon of the butter. Spoon half the potato mixture into the dish, cover with the cod and top with the remaining potatoes. Dot with the remaining 2 tablespoons butter. Bake the gratin until the top is golden brown, about 45 minutes. Serve hot.

—Patricia Wells

• • •

LUXURIOUS SUMMER LUNCH

Although the fish for this menu can be prepared any time of the year using the broiler, it is even more appealing when cooked on an outdoor grill. Serves 4.

Cream of Carrot Soup with Brandy and Chervil (p. 39)

Grilled Grouper with Yellow Pepper Sauce (p. 46)

Braised Black Beans (p. 47)

Corn Bread and Sweet Butter

🍷 *1985 Hermitage Blanc or 1985 Oregon Pinot Gris*

Belgian Endive Salad with Lemon Vinaigrette

Tangy Lime Tart (p. 201)

Café Filtre

GRILLED GROUPER WITH YELLOW PEPPER SAUCE AND BRAISED BLACK BEANS

Braised black beans pair beautifully with the grilled grouper served at the Hyatt Regency Tampa.

🍷 Although the fish is plain, the sauce is piquant, a combination that calls for an assertive white wine of equal bite—a 1985 Hermitage Blanc or 1985 Oregon Pinot Gris.

4 Servings

2 tablespoons balsamic vinegar
¼ cup plus 1 tablespoon minced shallots
1½ tablespoons minced garlic
1 teaspoon yellow mustard seeds, crushed
2½ teaspoons fresh thyme or ¾ teaspoon dried
2 teaspoons chopped fresh chervil or parsley
4 grouper fillets, 1 inch thick (about 6 ounces each)
2 large yellow bell peppers, chopped
¼ teaspoon crushed hot pepper
½ cup dry white wine
½ cup fish stock or bottled clam juice
Braised Black Beans (recipe follows)

1. In a medium bowl, combine the balsamic vinegar, 1 tablespoon of the minced shallots, 2 teaspoons of the minced garlic, the mustard seeds, thyme and chervil. Add the grouper fillets and toss gently to coat. Let marinate while you prepare the sauce.

2. In a medium nonreactive saucepan, combine the yellow peppers with the remaining shallots and garlic. Add the hot pepper, wine and fish stock and bring to a boil over high heat. Reduce the heat to moderate and simmer until the peppers are soft, 8 to 10 minutes. Transfer to a food processor or blender and puree until smooth. Strain the sauce through a sieve; cover to keep warm.

3. Preheat the broiler or a grill. Remove the grouper fillets from the marinade; pat dry with paper towels. Broil or grill about 4 inches from the heat until just cooked through, 3 to 4 minutes on each side. Serve with the warm yellow pepper sauce and Braised Black Beans.

—Roger Michel, Hyatt Regency Sarasota, Sarasota, Florida

• • •

BRAISED BLACK BEANS

4 Servings

2 cups dried black beans, rinsed and picked over
1 small onion stuck with 4 whole cloves, plus 1 cup diced onion
2 bay leaves
½ teaspoon crushed hot pepper
6 garlic cloves, crushed
1 medium tomato—peeled, seeded and diced

1. Put the beans in a large flameproof casserole and cover with at least 2 inches of cold water. Let soak overnight. Drain into a colander and rinse under cold running water. Return to the casserole. Add the whole and diced onions, bay leaves, hot pepper, garlic and enough water to cover by 1½ inches.

2. Bring to a boil over high heat. Reduce the heat to low, cover and cook until the beans are tender, about 1½ hours.

3. Drain the beans and remove the clove-studded onion and the bay leaves. Toss the beans with the tomato.

—Roger Michel, Hyatt Regency Sarasota, Sarasota, Florida

• • •

POACHED HALIBUT WITH WARM VINAIGRETTE

This light, herby halibut from chef Gilbert Le Coze can be prepared in less than half an hour.

🍷 1985 California Fumé Blanc, such as Robert Mondavi Reserve

4 Servings

1 teaspoon Dijon-style mustard
2 tablespoons sherry wine vinegar
2 tablespoons red wine vinegar
¼ cup extra-virgin olive oil
¼ cup vegetable oil
2 cups dry white wine
1 carrot, chopped
1 celery rib, chopped
1 small onion, chopped
Bouquet garni: 4 sprigs of parsley, 2 sprigs of thyme and 1 bay leaf tied in cheesecloth
8 whole black peppercorns
1 teaspoon salt
4 halibut steaks, 1 inch thick (about ½ pound each)
2 tablespoons minced shallots
1 tablespoon minced fresh chives
1 tablespoon minced fresh chervil
1 tablespoon minced fresh tarragon

1. In a small nonreactive saucepan, whisk together the mustard, sherry wine vinegar and red wine vinegar. Gradually beat in the olive oil and vegetable oil in a thin stream. Set the vinaigrette aside.

2. In a nonreactive skillet or casserole just large enough to hold the fish steaks in a single layer, combine the white wine, carrot, celery, onion, bouquet garni, peppercorns and salt with 4 cups of water. Bring to a boil over high heat and boil for 5 minutes. Reduce the heat to a simmer, add the halibut steaks and poach until almost opaque throughout, 5 to 7 minutes: do not overcook. Remove the fish with a slotted spatula and transfer to 4 warmed plates.

3. Meanwhile, warm the vinaigrette over moderate heat. Stir in the shallots, chives, chervil and tarragon, and spoon over the fish steaks.

—Gilbert Le Coze, Le Bernardin, New York City

• • •

MAHIMAHI FLORINADA

Fresh oranges and lemons add tropical flavor to this unusual dish from Down Under in Fort Lauderdale, Florida.

🍷 A subtle, elegant white wine, such as a 1985 Silverado Sauvignon Blanc from California, would point up the flavors without overpowering the dish.

4 Servings

2 medium seedless lemons
2 large seedless oranges
6 tablespoons unsalted butter
4 mahimahi or swordfish fillets, ¾ inch thick (6 to 7 ounces each)
1 cup milk
1 cup all-purpose flour
2 teaspoons finely chopped fresh mint
Salt and freshly ground pepper

1. Using a sharp knife, peel the lemons and oranges; pare away all the bitter white pith. Cut the fruit into small dice.

2. In a large, heavy nonreactive casserole or skillet, melt 2 tablespoons of the butter over moderately high heat.

3. Dip each mahimahi fillet in the milk and then dredge in the flour, shaking off any excess. Add the fish to the pan and sauté until browned, 2 to 3 minutes on each side. Remove to a platter and cover to keep warm.

4. In the same skillet, melt the remaining 4 tablespoons butter. Add the diced lemons and oranges and cook until heated through, 15 to 20 seconds. Stir in the chopped mint, season with salt and pepper to taste and spoon the sauce over the mahimahi; serve hot.

—*Down Under, Fort Lauderdale, Florida*

• • •

SIZZLING MONKFISH

This dish has a wonderful, nutty flavor. It's perfect for guests, especially if you aren't sure whether they're all fish fanciers, because everyone seems to really go for this.

6 Servings

1/3 cup peanut oil
2 monkfish fillets (1 1/2 pounds each), trimmed of all skin and membrane
1/3 cup soy sauce
2 bunches of scallions, coarsely chopped
Lemon wedges, for garnish

1. Preheat the oven to 450°. Line a large baking pan with foil. Lightly grease the foil with 1 tablespoon of the oil. Rub the fish with 1 tablespoon of the oil and 2 tablespoons of the soy sauce and place the fillets in the pan.

2. Bake the fish for 15 to 20 minutes, until just opaque throughout.

3. Cut the fish into 1/2-inch-thick slices and arrange on a heatproof platter. Sprinkle the fish with the remaining soy sauce and the scallions.

4. In a small saucepan, heat the remaining oil over moderate heat until it just begins to smoke. Immediately pour the oil over the fish and serve garnished with lemon wedges and extra soy sauce if desired.

—*Lee Bailey*

• • •

A SUPPER THAT SIZZLES

The centerpiece of this menu from Lee Bailey is a Chinese-inspired fish dish in which sizzling peanut oil is poured over baked monkfish just before serving, giving the dish its distinctive flavor. Serves 6.

Spinach Soup (p. 40)

Sizzling Monkfish (p. 48)

Rice with Toasted Pine Nuts (p. 136)

Braised Mustard Greens (p. 157)

🍷 *Dry White Wine*

Peppermint Pears (p. 226)

Coffee

BROILED OPAKAPAKA WITH BLACK OLIVES AND TOMATO HERB SAUCE

This delicious dish is from La Mer restaurant in Hawaii's Halekulani hotel.

🍷 Light, crisp Sauvignon Blanc from California, such as 1986 Rutherford Hill

6 Servings

6 opakapaka or red snapper fillets (about 8 ounces each)
12 black olives, pitted and cut lengthwise into quarters
1/4 cup olive oil
Tomato Herb Sauce (recipe follows)

1. Preheat the oven to 500°. With the tip of a knife, pierce 8 holes in each fish fillet. Stuff a piece of olive into each hole.

2. Brush a broiling pan with some of the olive oil, arrange the fillets on the pan and brush them with the remaining oil. Bake the fish until firm to the touch and just opaque throughout, about 5 minutes. Place one fillet on each of 6 plates and top with the tomato herb sauce.

—*Philippe Padovani, La Mer, Honolulu*

• • •

TOMATO HERB SAUCE

6 Servings

2 cups dry white wine
3 carrots, chopped
1 medium onion, chopped
2/3 cup chopped celery with leaves
1 cup (6 ounces) chopped shallots
2 garlic cloves, chopped
2 whole cloves
1/4 cup fresh lemon juice
1 bay leaf
1/8 teaspoon cayenne pepper
Salt
1/4 cup olive oil
2 pounds ripe tomatoes—peeled, seeded and diced
4 tablespoons unsalted butter
3 cups chopped mixed herbs (thyme, parsley, chives, tarragon and chervil)
Freshly ground white pepper

1. In a large nonreactive saucepan, bring the wine and 1 cup of water to a boil over high heat. Add the carrots, onion, celery, 2/3 cup of the shallots, the garlic, cloves, 2 tablespoons of the lemon juice, the bay leaf, cayenne and a pinch of salt. Reduce the heat to moderately low and simmer until the liquid is reduced to 1 cup, 25 to 30 minutes. Strain and reserve the broth.

2. In a large nonreactive skillet, heat the olive oil over moderate heat. Add the remaining ⅓ cup shallots and the tomatoes and cook until the shallots are translucent, 5 to 7 minutes. Add the reserved broth, remaining 2 tablespoons lemon juice, the butter and mixed chopped herbs. Whisk well and continue to simmer for 5 minutes longer. Season to taste with salt and white pepper.

—Philippe Padovani, La Mer, Honolulu

• • •

POACHED SALMON WITH HOLLANDAISE SAUCE

The classic presentation of *saumon poché sauce hollandaise* calls for a whole salmon to be poached in a court bouillon (a light vegetable stock) and served with the hollandaise sauce. Using salmon fillets or steaks makes cooking much faster and serving easier. If your fish is not extremely fresh, a little vinegar or white wine in the poaching water will help improve its flavor. Steamed potatoes are traditionally served with poached fish.

🍷 You will find that a dry white Sancerre, from the Loire Valley, such as 1985 Paul Cotat, is a perfect choice with the salmon.

6 Servings

3 pounds boned and skinned center-cut salmon fillet, about ¾ inch thick, cut into 6 servings, or 6 salmon steaks, ¾ inch thick
⅓ cup white wine vinegar or 1 cup dry white wine (optional)
Hollandaise Sauce with Chives (p. 253)

1. Fill a large flameproof casserole with about 10 cups of water, or enough to cover the salmon by at least 1 inch. If the salmon is not impeccably fresh, add the vinegar or wine. Bring to a boil over high heat.

2. Place the fish into the boiling water, reduce the heat so that the water barely simmers and poach the salmon until it is firm to the touch and just opaque throughout, 6 to 8 minutes. Drain the fish on paper towels. If steaks are used, remove the skin.

3. To serve, place the fish on warm plates or a platter and partially cover with hollandaise sauce, allowing 2 to 3 tablespoons per serving. Pass the remaining sauce on the side.

—Richard Grausman

• • •

GRILLED SALMON WITH TOMATILLO-PINEAPPLE SALSA

This zesty uncooked salsa manages to taste truly southwestern without being at all familiar. It is good with other flavorful oily fish, such as swordfish, shark, tuna or bluefish, as well as with chicken, pork or lamb; all should be mesquite-grilled since the smokiness of the wood pairs with the sweet heat of the salsa for a spectacular balance of flavors.

6 Servings

½ large, ripe pineapple—peeled, cored and cut into ½-inch dice (about 2¾ cups)
5 small fresh tomatillos—husked, rinsed in warm water and coarsely chopped
½ jalapeño pepper or 1 serrano chile, seeded and minced
2 to 3 tablespoons fresh lime juice
¼ teaspoon salt
¼ cup minced fresh coriander
6 salmon steaks, 1 inch thick (6 to 8 ounces each)
¼ cup olive oil

1. In a food processor, combine 1½ cups of the diced pineapple with the tomatillos, jalapeño, 2 tablespoons of the lime juice and the salt. Puree until smooth. Scrape the salsa into a bowl and stir in the remaining diced pineapple and the coriander. Taste for seasoning, adding more salt or lime juice if desired. Cover and let stand at room temperature for 1 hour.

2. If grilling the fish, soak a handful of mesquite chips in water. Prepare a charcoal fire and allow it to burn down until the coals are evenly white. Drain the mesquite chips and scatter them over the coals. Alternatively, preheat the broiler.

3. Position the grill rack or the broiling rack about 5 inches from the heat. Brush the salmon steaks with the oil and grill or broil, turning once, until lightly browned, 3 to 4 minutes per side. Serve at once, accompanied with the tomatillo-pineapple salsa.

—Michael McLaughlin

• • •

SALMON WITH LEMON-HERB SAUCE

The sauce can be prepared a day or two ahead; the salmon can be arranged on the platter, ready to cook and covered with plastic wrap, up to three hours before serving.

🍷 The tartness of this salmon dish calls for a crisp but rich white, such as the 1986 Antinori Cervaro della Sala or the 1986 Ruffino Libaio, both from Tuscany.

6 Servings

4 hard-cooked egg yolks
2 teaspoons anchovy paste
3 tablespoons chopped fresh parsley
2 tablespoons chopped fresh basil
2 tablespoons fresh lemon juice

½ cup extra-virgin olive oil
2 tablespoons capers, rinsed and drained
¾ teaspoon freshly ground pepper
½ teaspoon salt
2 pounds skinless salmon fillet, cut into 12 slices, ¼ inch thick

1. Preheat the oven to 400°. Press the egg yolks through a sieve into a small bowl. Beat in the anchovy paste, parsley, basil, lemon juice, olive oil, capers, ½ teaspoon of the pepper and ¼ teaspoon of the salt.

2. Lightly oil the bottom of a large ovenproof platter. Arrange the salmon slices on the platter, overlapping slightly. Brush lightly with olive oil, season with the remaining ¼ teaspoon each salt and pepper and bake for 4 minutes, or until just opaque throughout. Drizzle a little of the sauce over the salmon and pass the remainder separately.

—Nancy Verde Barr

• • •

SALMON WRAPPED IN GRAPE LEAVES

Serve this salmon with rice pilaf and a sautéed green vegetable, such as spinach or zucchini.

🍷 Dry rosé, such as 1986 Firestone Rosé of Cabernet Sauvignon.

6 Servings

¾ cup raisins
½ cup pine nuts
2¼ pounds salmon fillet, ½ to ¾ inch thick, cut into 6 equal pieces
18 large grape leaves, rinsed of brine, patted dry, stems removed
3 tablespoons fresh lemon juice
¼ teaspoon salt
¼ teaspoon freshly ground pepper
¾ cup extra-virgin olive oil
1 medium tomato—peeled, seeded and diced

1. Preheat the oven to 350°. Put the raisins in a small bowl and add hot water to cover. Let stand for 30 minutes.

2. Spread out the pine nuts on a baking sheet and bake, stirring them once, for 7 to 8 minutes, until lightly toasted.

3. Meanwhile, trim the salmon fillet of any fat and remove any remaining bones. Lay each piece of fillet on a grape leaf and use 1 or 2 more leaves to cover and wrap each piece. Set the packages on a lightly oiled broiling pan, cover lightly and set aside.

4. Preheat the broiler or light a charcoal grill. Drain the raisins and squeeze out any excess moisture. In a food processor, puree ¼ cup of the raisins with the lemon juice, salt and ⅛ teaspoon of the pepper. Scrape down the sides of the bowl. With the machine on, slowly add ½ cup plus 2 tablespoons of the olive oil. Transfer the sauce to a small bowl and stir in the whole raisins. (*The raisins can be prepared up to 3 hours in advance. Cover and set aside at room temperature.*)

5. Brush the grape leaf packets with the remaining 2 tablespoons olive oil and season with the remaining ⅛ teaspoon pepper. Broil or grill about 4 inches from the heat, turning once, for 3 to 4 minutes on each side, until the grape leaves are crisp and browned around the edges and the center of the fish is opaque but moist.

6. Transfer to individual warmed dinner plates. Spoon the sauce over each serving and sprinkle with the toasted pine nuts and diced tomato.

—Joyce Goldstein, Square One, San Francisco

• • •

GRILLED SALMON WITH PISTOU RAVIOLI

🍷 Salmon can take a deep-flavored wine, such as a 1985 Chalone Chardonnay or a 1985 Chapoutier Chante Alouette Hermitage Blanc.

6 Servings

5 cups (loosely packed) fresh basil leaves
⅓ cup plus 2 tablespoons olive oil
2 garlic cloves
¼ teaspoon salt
⅛ teaspoon freshly ground black pepper
24 won ton skins
12 small red potatoes
2 medium zucchini, halved lengthwise and sliced ¼ inch thick
2 yellow bell peppers, cut into 1-inch pieces
4 ears of baby corn (canned or frozen), sliced into ¼-inch rounds
3 tablespoons (loosely packed) fresh coriander leaves
12 cherry tomatoes
12 yellow pear tomatoes
6 skinless salmon fillets, ½ inch thick (about 6 ounces each)
Sprigs of fresh coriander, for garnish

1. In a blender or food processor, combine the basil with ⅓ cup of the olive oil and the garlic, salt and black pepper. Puree until smooth.

2. Lay 6 of the won ton skins on a work surface. Place about 2 teaspoons of the basil puree in the center of each, moisten the edges with water and lay another skin evenly over the top. Press the edges together to seal. Repeat with the remain-

ing 12 won ton skins and basil puree. Transfer the ravioli to a lightly oiled baking sheet.

3. Put the potatoes in a large saucepan, cover with water and bring to a boil over high heat. Boil until just tender, about 6 minutes. Drain and quarter the potatoes.

4. In a large heavy skillet, heat the remaining 2 tablespoons olive oil over moderately high heat. Add the potatoes and cook, tossing, until lightly browned, about 4 minutes. Add the zucchini, yellow peppers, corn and coriander leaves and sauté just until heated through, about 4 minutes. Add the cherry and pear tomatoes and toss until warmed slightly, about 1 minute.

5. Preheat the broiler. In a large pot of boiling salted water, cook the ravioli in 3 batches until tender but still firm, about 4 minutes per batch. With a slotted spoon, return the cooked ravioli to the baking sheet and cover loosely with foil.

6. Put the salmon fillets in an oiled baking dish in a single layer and broil about 3 inches from the heat, turning once, until opaque throughout, about 3 minutes per side.

7. To serve, place a salmon fillet in the center of each warmed dinner plate, arrange a ravioli on either side of the fish and the vegetables alongside. Garnish with sprigs of coriander.

—Roland Muller, Sonoma Mission Inn & Spa, Sonoma, California

• • •

GRILLED FISH DINNER

Serving grilled fish with a slice of colorful and peppery nasturtium butter on top adds an extra measure of elegance to an essentially simple menu. Serves 6.

Avocado Soup with Papaya Pepper Relish (p. 32)

Grilled Tilefish with Nasturtium Butter (p. 51)

Sautéed Cherry Tomatoes with Chives

Spanish Corn Bread (p. 140)

🍷 *Fruity Riesling*

Charlotte with Summer Fruit (p. 218)

Coffee

GRILLED TILEFISH WITH NASTURTIUM BUTTER

Tilefish meat is lean, moist and firm textured, not unlike white sea bass, which can be substituted.

🍷 The mildness of tilefish, here enlivened by grilling and the peppery nasturtium or watercress butter, suggests a relatively light wine such as 1986 Callaway, White Riesling or Clos du Bois Early Harvest Johannisberg Riesling.

6 Servings

2 pounds tilefish fillets, about 3/4 inch thick
2 tablespoons Hungarian or other sweet imported paprika
2 teaspoons dry mustard
1/4 teaspoon freshly ground pepper
2 tablespoons extra-virgin olive oil
2 garlic cloves, minced
Nasturtium Butter (recipe follows)

1. Place the fish fillets in a glass or ceramic dish. In a small bowl, combine the paprika, mustard and pepper and sprinkle over both sides of the fillets.

2. In a small bowl, combine the olive oil and garlic and brush over the fish. Cover and let stand at room temperature for 1 hour.

3. Meanwhile, light a charcoal grill or preheat the broiler. Brush the grill rack or broiler pan lightly with vegetable oil and cook the fish fillets either directly on the grill or in an oiled hinged basket, about 4 inches from the heat, turning once, until the fish is opaque throughout and flakes easily with a fork, 3 to 5 minutes on each side. Serve with the Nasturtium Butter.

—Phillip Stephen Schulz

• • •

NASTURTIUM BUTTER

Shredded watercress leaves may be substituted for the nasturtium.

Makes About 1/2 Cup

5 tablespoons unsalted butter, softened to room temperature
1 shallot, minced
1/8 teaspoon hot pepper sauce
1/2 cup nasturtium leaves and blossoms or watercress, shredded
1/4 teaspoon salt

In a bowl, cream the butter until light. Stir in the shallot, hot pepper sauce, nasturtium leaves and blossoms and salt. Cover and refrigerate for up to 4 days. Let stand at room temperature for at least 30 minutes before serving.

—Phillip Stephen Schulz

• • •

SEA BASS BAKED IN PARCHMENT WITH OLIVE OIL AND HERBS

Shredded basil leaves, a fine julienne of zucchini, lemon zest and a touch of truffles are all mingled with the delicate extra-virgin olive oil of Provence and the freshest of sea bass to create this light, elegant dish.

To slice the zucchini into julienne strips, use a Mouli julienne grater or the julienne blade of a food processor. As always, the truffles add a touch of luxury, although the dish will still be delicious without them.

🍷 To set off the direct but elegant flavors of this dish, try a luscious white Châteauneuf-du-Pape, such as that from Domaine du Vieux Télégraphe.

4 Servings

1/4 cup extra-virgin olive oil
2 medium zucchini, cut into thin julienne strips
1 1/2 teaspoons grated lemon zest
6 tablespoons fresh lemon juice
2 cups finely shredded fresh basil
1 or 2 truffles, cut into thin julienne strips (optional)
1 whole sea bass (about 2 pounds)
1/4 teaspoon salt
1/4 teaspoon freshly ground pepper

1. Preheat the oven to 450°. In a large bowl, toss together the olive oil, zucchini strips, lemon zest, lemon juice, basil and truffles.

2. Cut 2 pieces of parchment paper about 15 by 22 inches each. Set one of the pieces of parchment on a large baking sheet. Place the fish in the center of the paper and season with the salt and pepper. Spread the zucchini mixture over the fish. Place the second sheet of parchment on top and seal with a double-folded edge. Staple the edges at 2-inch intervals to secure.

3. Bake the fish in the center of the oven for 20 minutes. Carefully remove the package from the oven and cut it open with a scissors. Let the fish sit for about 3 minutes before removing the fillets and dividing them among 4 warmed dinner plates. Spoon some of the zucchini (and truffles if you added them) and sauce over each portion and serve at once.

—Jean-Paul Passédat,
Le Petit Nice, Marseilles

• • •

MAKO SHARK WITH ANCHOVY AND CAPER SAUCE

These marinated shark steaks served with a spicy sauce are a specialty at John Clancy's restaurant in Manhattan.

🍷 The zip of the sauce tunes this fish dish to red wine—preferably a low-tannin red, such as 1980 Gran Condal Rioja Reserva.

6 Servings

1/4 cup finely chopped onions
2 teaspoons coarsely chopped garlic
3 bay leaves
1/4 cup imported sweet paprika
1/4 cup fresh lemon juice
1 1/3 cups olive oil
1/4 teaspoon cayenne pepper
1/2 teaspoon salt
3/4 teaspoon freshly ground black pepper
6 mako shark or swordfish steaks (about 8 ounces each)
10 anchovy fillets, rinsed and finely chopped
1/4 cup dry white wine
2 tablespoons tarragon vinegar
2 whole cloves
1 can (35 ounces) Italian peeled tomatoes, drained and coarsely chopped
1 teaspoon sugar
1/4 teaspoon cinnamon
1 stick (4 ounces) unsalted butter
1/4 cup drained capers
1 small bunch Italian flat-leaf parsley, stemmed and finely chopped

1. In a large bowl, combine the onions, garlic, bay leaves, paprika, lemon juice, 1 cup of the olive oil, the cayenne, salt and 1/4 teaspoon of the black pepper. Add the shark steaks and set aside to marinate, turning every 20 minutes, for 1 hour.

2. Preheat the broiler. In a large nonreactive saucepan, sauté the anchovies in the remaining 1/3 cup olive oil over moderate heat until dissolved, about 2 minutes. Add the wine, vinegar and cloves. Reduce the heat to low; cook for 5 minutes. Strain; return the sauce to the pan.

3. Add the tomatoes, sugar and cinnamon and simmer the sauce over moderate heat until slightly thickened, 8 to 10 minutes.

4. Reduce the heat to low and add the butter, 1 tablespoon at a time, stirring until completely melted. Add the capers, parsley and remaining 1/2 teaspoon pepper; cover to keep the sauce warm.

5. Remove the shark steaks from the marinade and pat dry. Broil the steaks about 4 inches from the heat until just opaque throughout, about 5 minutes on each side. Pour the warm sauce over the fish and serve.

—John Clancy, John Clancy's
Restaurant, New York City

• • •

SHARK WITH PORCINI SAUCE

In this dish from New York's Manhattan Ocean Club, shark steaks are paired with a rich wild mushroom cream sauce and served over fettuccine.

🍷 This is intense enough to call for red wine, but the slight bitterness of Alsace Gewürztraminer, such as Hugel or Trimbach, would stand in for a red wine's tannic bite and still offer the crispness and coolness of a white.

4 Servings

2 cups (2 ounces) dried porcini mushrooms
½ cup brandy
2 cups heavy cream
1 tablespoon unsalted butter
½ cup chopped shallots
½ pound fresh mushrooms, sliced
2 large tomatoes—peeled, seeded and chopped
2 cups chicken or veal stock or canned chicken broth
Salt and freshly ground pepper
1 pound fettuccine, preferably fresh
4 shark or swordfish steaks, about ¾ inch thick (8 to 10 ounces each)
1 tablespoon chopped fresh parsley

1. Rinse the porcini mushrooms under cold running water. In a bowl, cover the mushrooms with the brandy; soak until the mushrooms are soft, about 1 hour.

2. Drain the porcini; strain and reserve the brandy. Cut the porcini into thin julienne strips.

3. In a medium saucepan, combine the porcini strips and the heavy cream. Bring to a boil over high heat, reduce the heat to moderately high and cook until the cream is reduced by half, about 10 minutes. Set aside.

4. In a large heavy saucepan, melt the butter over moderate heat. Add the shallots and cook until translucent, 2 to 3 minutes. Add the fresh mushrooms and cook, stirring, until they begin to brown, 8 to 10 minutes.

5. Add the reserved brandy and simmer for 2 minutes. Stir in three-fourths of the tomatoes and the stock and cook until the liquid is reduced to 2 cups, about 15 minutes.

6. Transfer the sauce to a food processor or blender and puree until smooth. Pour the sauce into a clean pan and stir in the reduced cream and porcini. Season with salt and pepper to taste. If the sauce is too thick, thin with additional stock or water.

7. Preheat the broiler or a grill. In a large pot of boiling salted water, cook the fettuccine until tender but still firm, about 10 minutes. Drain well.

8. Broil or grill the shark about 4 inches from the heat, until opaque throughout, 2 to 3 minutes on each side.

9. Combine the remaining chopped tomatoes and the parsley. Season with salt and pepper to taste. Place each steak on a bed of fettuccine and surround with porcini sauce. Garnish each serving with 1 tablespoon of the parslied tomatoes.

—Manhattan Ocean Club,
New York City

• • •

RED SNAPPER WITH VEGETABLE RAGOUT

🍷 The mildness of snapper is a classic match for very dry Champagne, but given the spicy vinaigrette sauce, a fruity-tart California sparkling wine, such as 1984 Iron Horse Brut or 1982 Piper-Sonoma Brut Reserve, would better complement this dish.

4 Servings

3 medium onions, sliced ½ inch thick
¾ cup plus 2 tablespoons olive oil
¼ cup chicken stock or canned broth
1 red bell pepper
1 yellow bell pepper
1 large poblano pepper
1 fennel bulb, trimmed and cut into ½-inch wedges
2 long, narrow Oriental eggplants, cut on the diagonal into ¼-inch slices
⅓ cup hot pepper vinegar (see Note)
1 pickled jalapeño pepper, seeded and minced
1 tablespoon coarsely chopped fresh oregano or thyme, or ¾ teaspoon dried
1 teaspoon salt
1 teaspoon freshly ground black pepper
4 red snapper fillets (6 to 7 ounces each), skinned

1. In a large skillet, cook the onions in ¼ cup of the olive oil over moderately low heat until softened and just beginning to color, about 10 minutes. Add the chicken stock and remove from the heat.

2. Roast the red and yellow bell peppers and the poblano directly over a gas flame or under a broiler as close to the heat as possible, turning, until charred all over. Seal in a paper bag for 10 minutes, then rub off the blackened skin. Trim off the stems, ribs and seeds. Cut the peppers into ½-inch strips.

3. In a medium bowl, toss the fennel and eggplant with 2 tablespoons of the olive oil. Broil or grill the vegetables until browned and just tender, about 3 mintues. Add to the onions.

4. In a small bowl, combine the vinegar, pickled jalapeño pepper, oregano, ⅓ cup of the olive oil and ½ teaspoon each of the salt and black pepper. Whisk to blend. Set the vinaigrette aside.

5. Brush the snapper fillets with the remaining olive oil and season with ¼ teaspoon each of the salt and pepper. Broil about 4 inches from the heat, or grill, without turning, until just opaque throughout, about 8 minutes.

6. Meanwhile, add ⅓ cup of the reserved vinaigrette to the vegetable ragout. Season with the remaining ¼ teaspoon each salt and pepper and cook over moderate heat until just hot.

7. With a slotted spoon, divide the vegetable mixture among 4 dinner plates. Place the fish on top of the vegetables and drizzle the remaining vinaigrette over the fish.

NOTE: Although you can buy hot pepper vinegar, you might want to make your own, as does Brendan Walsh. Soak whole fresh serrano chiles in rice wine vinegar for 3 days to 2 weeks; the longer it stands, the hotter it gets.

—Brendan Walsh, Arizona 206, New York City

• • •

RED SNAPPER WITH TOMATILLO-SERRANO CHILE VINAIGRETTE

Dean Fearing prefers to grill the snapper, but pan frying is a fine indoor alternative. He garnishes each plate with several Corn Bread Fried Oysters (p. 26).

🍷 The mildness of snapper is a classic match for very dry Champagne, but given the spicy vinaigrette sauce, a fruity-tart California sparkling wine, such as 1984 Iron Horse Brut or 1982 Piper-Sonoma Brut Reserve, would better balance the dish.

6 Servings

Peanut oil
6 red snapper fillets (about 6 ounces each), skinned
Salt and freshly ground pepper
Tomatillo-Serrano Chile Vinaigrette (p. 255)

1. Light a grill and set a lightly oiled rack over the fire. Lightly brush each snapper fillet with about 1 teaspoon oil and season to taste with salt and pepper. Grill the fish until just opaque throughout, about 2 minutes on each side. Alternatively, heat 2 tablespoons of oil in a large skillet. Add the fillets in batches and cook over moderate heat for 2 minutes. Turn and cook on the other side until the fish is just opaque throughout, about 3 minutes. Remove the fish to a large warm platter.

2. Spoon the Tomatillo-Serrano Chile Vinaigrette onto 6 warm dinner plates and arrange the snapper fillets in the center. Serve warm.

—Dean Fearing, The Mansion on Turtle Creek, Dallas

• • •

GRILLED RED SNAPPER WITH TOMATO AND ONION COMPOTE

Chef Michael Romano suggests serving this snapper with boiled potatoes or a mélange of baby vegetables.

🍷 Rosé Champagne, such as 1982 Lanson or Domaine Chandon Blanc de Noirs

4 Servings

6 large tomatoes
2 tablespoons plus 1 teaspoon unsalted butter
5 tablespoons olive oil
½ teaspoon salt
¼ teaspoon freshly ground black pepper
Pinch of cayenne pepper
1 medium onion, sliced paper-thin
½ teaspoon dried pink peppercorns
2 teaspoons sherry wine vinegar
1½ teaspoons chopped fresh tarragon or ½ teaspoon dried
4 red snapper fillets (about 5 ounces each), skin on

1. Coarsely chop 3 of the tomatoes. In a medium nonreactive saucepan, cook the tomatoes over moderate heat, stirring frequently, until they form a thick puree, about 15 minutes.

2. Strain the puree into a small nonreactive saucepan and cook over moderately low heat until slightly thickened, 1 to 2 minutes. Whisk in 1 tablespoon of the butter until thoroughly incorporated. Gradually whisk in 2 tablespoons of the olive oil. Season with ¼ teaspoon of the salt, ⅛ teaspoon of the black pepper and the cayenne; set the tomato sauce aside.

3. Preheat the oven to 400°. In a medium nonreactive skillet, melt 1 tablespoon of the butter in 1 tablespoon of the olive oil over moderately low heat. Add the onion and cook, stirring occasionally, until golden brown, 20 to 25 minutes.

4. Meanwhile, halve the remaining 3 tomatoes crosswise and place, cut-side down, on a rack set over a cookie sheet. Roast the tomatoes in the oven until soft and lightly browned, about 25 minutes; let cool slightly. Seed and skin the tomatoes, keeping the pulp in large pieces.

5. Preheat the broiler or a grill. Add the tomato pulp and the remaining 1 teaspoon butter to the onion and cook over moderate heat until warmed through. Stir in the pink peppercorns, vinegar, tarragon, and remaining ¼ teaspoon salt and ⅛ teaspoon pepper. Cook for 2 minutes longer; cover and keep warm. (*The recipe can be prepared to this point up to 8 hours ahead.*)

6. Reheat the tomato sauce. Brush the fish fillets with the remaining 2 tablespoons olive oil and season lightly with salt and black pepper to taste. If broiling, place the fillets on a broiling pan. Grill or broil the fillets, skin-side up, until opaque in the center, 4 to 5 minutes.

7. Spoon the tomato sauce onto 4 warmed dinner plates. Set the snapper fillets on the sauce and spoon the tomato and onion compote over the fish.

—Michael Romano, La Caravelle, New York City

• • •

BALLOTTINE OF SOLE

The *ballottine* is poached in fish stock and then leaves the roll in the cooking liquid overnight to chill and firm up. If you are short on time or if fish bones are unavailable, the *ballottine* can be poached in a court bouillon (instead of fish stock), made by combining four quarts of water and three cups of wine with sliced carrots, onions, a bouquet garni and whole peppercorns and simmering the mixture for 20 to 30 minutes.

🍷 Choose an elegant white that won't overshadow the delicacy and subtlety of this dish: an Alsace Riesling, such as the 1985 Trimbach "Cuvée Frédéric Emile," or the 1985 Chateau Ste. Michelle Johannisberg Riesling from Washington State.

8 to 10 Servings

2¼ pounds sole fillets
2 eggs, chilled
1¾ teaspoons salt
⅛ teaspoon freshly ground pepper
⅔ cup heavy cream, chilled
¼ pound skinless, boneless salmon fillet, cut into 4 rectangles, 2½ by ¾ inches
1 tablespoon vegetable oil
4 quarts Fish Stock (recipe follows)
Green Mayonnaise (p. 254)

1. Place the bowl and metal blade of a food processor in the freezer to chill. Cut the sole fillets in half lengthwise and remove the thin bony center strip.

2. Set aside 8 of the halved fillets for assembling the *ballottine.* Place the remaining fillets in the processor and puree until smooth. Add the eggs, ¾ teaspoon of the salt and the pepper and puree until smooth. With the machine on, gradually add the cream and process until well blended. Scrape the mousseline into a bowl.

3. Using a meat pounder or the flat side of a cleaver, lightly flatten the reserved 8 sole fillets to an even thickness. Sprinkle with the remaining 1 teaspoon salt.

4. Spread about 2½ tablespoons of the mousseline over each of the sole fillets. Place the salmon rectangles at the narrower end of 4 of the smaller fillets and roll up tightly. Wrap each of the salmon-filled rolls neatly in another sole fillet.

5. Spread about 1 tablespoon of the remaining mousseline over the ends of each double roll to seal.

6. Moisten a clean kitchen towel and spread it out on a work surface. Cover the towel with a sheet of parchment paper; brush the paper with the oil. Place the 4 rolls, end to end, along the bottom half of the parchment paper. Press the rolls together to form a neat log. Roll up the *ballottine* in the parchment paper. Then roll up snugly in the towel. Twist the ends of the towel to tighten the roll. Tie the ends with kitchen string, then tie at 2 intervals to secure.

7. Place the *ballottine* in a large pot or a fish poacher and add the Fish Stock. Bring to a boil over moderately high heat. Reduce the heat and simmer for 30 minutes. Remove from the heat and let cool, then refrigerate overnight in the stock.

8. The next day, remove the *ballottine* from the stock. Cut off the strings and unwrap. Pat dry with paper towels. To serve, trim off the very end of the *ballottine,* then slice crosswise ⅜ inch thick. Place 2 or 3 slices on each plate and serve with the Green Mayonnaise.

—André Soltner, Lutèce, New York City

• • •

FISH STOCK

Makes About 4 Quarts

4 pounds non-oily fish bones and trimmings
2 onions, minced
1 cup chopped mushroom stems
2 leeks, white and green, minced
2 carrots, minced
Bouquet garni: 2 sprigs of parsley, 2 sprigs of thyme and 1 bay leaf tied in cheesecloth
2 teaspoons salt
8 whole black peppercorns
1 bottle (750 ml) dry white wine

Place all the ingredients in a nonreactive stockpot and cover with 3½ quarts of water. Bring to a boil and skim the surface. Simmer the stock over moderate heat for 30 minutes, skimming occasionally. Strain through a fine sieve and let cool. (*The stock can be made up to 2 days ahead and refrigerated, covered.*)

—André Soltner, Lutèce, New York City

• • •

MARINATED AND GRILLED SWORDFISH MEDALLIONS WITH CREOJA SAUCE

Chef Hubert Keller serves this dish with steamed asparagus tips and croutons of toasted French bread spread with tuna-anchovy-olive tapenade at Fleur de Lys.
🍷 Rich, oaky Chardonnay, such as 1985 Jordan

4 Servings

1¼ pounds swordfish steaks, about ½ inch thick, cut into 4 equal pieces, skinned
3 tablespoons fresh lemon juice
¼ teaspoon salt
¼ teaspoon freshly ground pepper
½ cup extra-virgin olive oil
1 garlic clove, minced
1 tablespoon chopped fresh coriander
1 tablespoon chopped fresh thyme
1 bay leaf
1 small Belgian endive, cut into ½-inch slices
1 small head of Boston lettuce, torn into bite-size pieces
1 small head of radicchio, finely shredded
1 teaspoon Dijon-style mustard
1 cup Creoja Sauce (p. 256)

1. In a shallow glass baking dish, arrange the swordfish steaks in a single layer. In a small bowl, whisk together 2 tablespoons of the lemon juice with ⅛ teaspoon each of the salt and pepper and ⅓ cup of the olive oil. Stir in the garlic, coriander and thyme. Pour the marinade over the fish, add the bay leaf, cover and marinate at room temperature for 20 to 30 minutes, turning the fish once. Meanwhile, preheat the broiler or light the grill.

2. In a medium bowl, mix together the endive, Boston lettuce and radicchio. In a small bowl, whisk together the remaining 1 tablespoon lemon juice, ⅛ teaspoon each salt and pepper and the mustard. Slowly whisk in the remaining olive oil. Pour the vinaigrette over the salad and toss to coat.

3. Remove the swordfish steaks from the marinade and set them on a broiling pan or grill rack. Cook about 4 inches from the heat, turning once, for 3 minutes on each side, or until the fish is just opaque throughout; a skewer inserted in the center will feel hot to the touch.

4. Divide the mixed salad greens among 4 dinner plates. Place a swordfish steak on top of each bed of salad and spoon the Creoja Sauce over one half of each steak.

—Hubert Keller, Fleur de Lys, San Francisco

• • •

FISH FILLETS WITH TOMATILLOS AND CHILE PEPPERS

Felipe Rojas-Lombardi of The Ballroom Restaurant and Tapas Bar in New York City is known for his original, eclectic dishes. Here, the thick, tart tomatillo sauce is nipped by piquant chiles, sweetened with long-cooked onions and freshened with coriander.

4 Servings

2½ pounds fresh tomatillos, husked
¼ cup extra-virgin olive oil
2 jalapeño peppers, seeded and minced
3 large garlic cloves, minced
1 medium onion, chopped
½ teaspoon salt
½ teaspoon sugar
4 cod or halibut fillets, about 1½ inches thick (about ½ pound each), skin on
¼ cup minced fresh coriander

1. Rinse the tomatillos thoroughly in warm water. Set aside the 12 smallest ones; chop the remaining tomatillos.

2. In a large skillet, heat the oil. Add the 12 whole tomatillos and cook over moderate heat, stirring gently, until lightly colored and partially cooked, 3 to 4 minutes. Transfer the tomatillos to a dish.

3. Add the jalapeños and garlic to the skillet and cook over moderately low heat for 1 minute. Add the onion and cook, stirring, until softened, about 6 minutes. Stir in the chopped tomatillos, salt and sugar and cook over moderate heat until most of the liquid has evaporated, 20 to 25 minutes. Season to taste with additional salt and sugar.

4. Place the fish fillets in the skillet, skin-side down, on the sauce. Scatter the whole tomatillos between the fillets. Bring to a simmer and reduce the heat to low. Cover and cook until the fish is just opaque throughout, 15 to 20 minutes. Shake the pan every 5 minutes to prevent sticking. Sprinkle with the coriander and serve directly from the pan.

—Felipe Rojas-Lombardi, The Ballroom Restaurant and Tapas Bar, New York City

• • •

GRILLED TROUT WITH OLIVE BUTTER

Sablefish, butterfish, small coho salmon, even whole flounder are excellent options for this recipe. Trout fillets are so thin that a flat, hinged basket is useful to facilitate turning the fish on the grill. For this recipe the fish should be butterflied; that is, the bones are removed, but the fish remains attached by skin along the back. The fish heads may be left on.

🍷 Since the mildness of the trout is punctuated by a piquant olive butter, it calls for an herbaceous white to counterpoint the flavors, such as 1986 Groth Sauvignon Blanc or 1985 Lyeth White.

4 Servings

4 brook trout, heads removed, boned and butterflied
1 teaspoon salt
½ teaspoon plus ⅛ teaspoon freshly ground pepper
2 tablespoons Pernod
2 tablespoons extra-virgin olive oil
1 small shallot, coarsely chopped
¼ cup coarsely chopped black olives
4 tablespoons unsalted butter, softened to room temperature
1 teaspoon chopped chives
1 tablespoon chopped Italian flat-leaf parsley

1. Sprinkle the fish on both sides with the salt, ½ teaspoon of the pepper and the Pernod. Cover and let stand at room temperature for 30 minutes.

2, Brush each fish on both sides with the olive oil and let stand, covered, for 30 minutes longer.

3. In a food processor, place the shallot and olives and process until finely chopped, about 30 seconds. Add the butter, chives, parsley and remaining ⅛ teaspoon pepper and process until well blended, about 30 seconds. Transfer to a bowl, cover and refrigerate. (*The olive butter can be prepared to this point up to 2 days ahead. Remove from the refrigerator 30 minutes before serving.*)

4. Light a charcoal grill or preheat the broiler. Brush the grill rack or broiler pan lightly with vegetable oil and cook the fish, either directly on the grill or in an oiled hinged fish basket, about 4 inches from the heat, turning once, until opaque throughout, 2 to 3 minutes on each side. Serve with the olive butter.

—Phillip Stephen Schulz

• • •

PROVENCAL DINNER

If you have ever been to Provence, the flavors in this simple grilled fish dinner will take you right back. Serves 6.

Oil-Cured Olives

Pernod

Grilled Tuna with Herbed Tomato, Garlic and Lemon Sauce (p. 57)

Parslied Potatoes

French Green Beans with Butter and Chervil

🍷 *Côtes du Rhône*

Fennel Salad with Extra-Virgin Olive Oil and Lemon Juice

Crêpes Filled with Lemon Soufflé (p. 216)

GRILLED TUNA WITH HERBED TOMATO, GARLIC AND LEMON SAUCE

Throughout Provence, the fish markets abound with giant fresh red tuna (*thon rouge*), which is wonderful for slicing into steaks for grilling or broiling. The sauce—known as *sauce vierge*—is a Provençal accompaniment that sings with the flavors and aromas of the south.

🍷 Serve with a good red Côtes du Rhône, such as Château de Fonsalette.

6 Servings

3 tomatoes (about 1½ pounds)—peeled, seeded and chopped
½ cup extra-virgin olive oil
3 tablespoons fresh lemon juice
3 garlic cloves, minced
¾ teaspoon salt
½ cup finely chopped mixed fresh herbs, preferably a blend of chervil, chives, tarragon and parsley
2 tuna steaks, cut 1¼ inches thick (about 1 pound each)

1. In a medium bowl, stir together the tomatoes, olive oil, lemon juice, garlic and salt. Set aside for about 2 hours to allow the flavors to blend.

2. Light a grill or preheat the broiler. Stir the fresh herbs into the tomato sauce.

3. Grill or broil the tuna about 4 inches from the heat, turning once, until charred outside and still slightly pink in the center, 3 to 4 minutes on each side.

4. Transfer the tuna to a large platter and cut into thick strips. Top with half of the tomato sauce and pass the remainder.

—Patricia Wells

• • •

BLAFF

In a traditional Caribbean *blaff*, the fish is cooked in a large pot of simmering broth. For manageability's sake, we poach the fish in the oven. Any mild, firm-fleshed fish, such as halibut or tile, could be substituted for the cod.

4 Servings

1 tablespoon chopped fresh thyme
½ cup chopped Italian flat-leaf parsley
1 medium onion, minced
2 scallions, minced
2 small jalapeño peppers—1 minced, 1 thinly sliced
¼ cup fresh lemon juice
¼ cup lime juice
8 allspice berries, crushed
1½ teaspoons salt
1 teaspoon freshly grounded pepper
4 cod steaks (about 10 ounces each)
2 bay leaves

1. In a small bowl, combine 1½ teaspoons of the thyme, ¼ cup of the parsley, half of the onion and scallions, the minced jalapeño, 2 tablespoons each of lemon and lime juice, 4 crushed allspice berries, ¼ teaspoon of the salt and ½ teaspoon of the pepper.

2. Place the cod steaks in a large glass or ceramic baking dish. Rub the onion-spice mixture over both sides of the fish steaks and marinate at room temperature for 30 minutes.

3. Preheat the oven to 450°. In a medium saucepan, combine the remaining thyme, parsley, onion, scallion, sliced jalapeño, lemon and lime juice, crushed allspice berries, salt and pepper with the bay leaves and 3 cups of water. Bring to a boil over high heat. Reduce the heat to low and simmer the broth for about 10 minutes.

4. Pour the broth over the fish steaks and place the dish in the upper third of the oven. Bake for 8 minutes, turn the fish over and bake for 8 to 10 minutes longer, or until the fish is opaque throughout and the meat pulls away from the bone easily. Serve the fish in soup plates with a little of the broth.

—F&W

• • •

AMERICAN BOUILLABAISSE

The classic Marseilles recipe contains a list of up to 10 different fish, most of which cannot be found in this country. I use shellfish and whichever fish is freshest and most readily available. Although a purist would say that my recipe is not a true bouillabaisse, I have always enjoyed the results. The authentic recipes also contain a large amount of olive oil, as much as one cup, which I have reduced to a mere two tablespoons.

Two essential ingredients that may be hard to find are saffron and fresh fennel. There is no substitute for the saffron, but one teaspoon of fennel or anise seeds or one tablespoon of either Pernod or Ricard can replace the fennel.

If you make the fish soup or stock several days in advance, you will find the preparation easier. Although I do not use bivalves, such as oysters, clams and mussels, if you use them, make sure to steam them open before adding them with the other fish. The proportions below are merely a guide and can be changed according to availability and individual taste. If the fish is very fresh, leave the skin on; otherwise remove it.

Serve the bouillabaisse with toasted French bread, a bowl of *rouille* (spicy Provençal garlic mayonnaise) and grated Swiss cheese to sprinkle into the soup.

🍷 A chilled Rosé de Provence, such as 1985 Domaines Ott or Domaine Tempier, is sure to bring the Mediterranean right to your dining table.

8 Servings

2 tablespoons extra-virgin olive oil
1 medium onion, chopped
1 medium leek (white and tender green), chopped
½ fennel bulb, chopped, or 1 teaspoon fennel seeds
2 garlic cloves, minced
⅓ cup chopped parsley
1 large tomato—peeled, seeded and chopped
1 imported bay leaf
5 sprigs of fresh thyme or ½ teaspoon dried
Pinch of saffron threads
½ teaspoon salt
¼ teaspoon freshly ground pepper
2 pounds fresh lobster, split lengthwise and cut into 2-inch chunks in the shell, claws cracked
2 pounds thick fish fillets—sea bass, haddock or red snapper—cut into 3-inch chunks
Saffron Fish Stock (p. 248), at room temperature or cold
2 pounds medium shrimp, shelled and deveined
1 pound sea scallops
Rouille (p. 255), toasted French bread and grated Swiss cheese, as accompaniments

1. In a large stockpot, heat the oil over moderate heat. Add the onion, leek and fresh fennel and cook until softened but not browned, about 3 minutes. At this point, stir in the fennel seeds if used; add the garlic, parsley, tomato, bay leaf, thyme, saffron, salt and pepper and cook for 1 minute.

2. Add the lobster and the fish fillets and cover with the Saffron Fish Stock. Bring to a boil over moderately high heat. Reduce the heat to moderate and boil gently for 1 minute. Add the shrimp and scallops. When the soup returns to a boil, in 2 to 3 minutes, the seafood should be done. If not, simmer for an additional minute, but do not boil.

3. With a slotted spoon, transfer the seafood to a large serving platter. Return the soup to a boil, taste and adjust the seasonings if necessary. Strain, if desired, into a large soup tureen.

4. To serve, place a selection of the seafood in a large soup bowl and ladle some of the hot soup over it. Pass the Rouille, toasted bread and grated cheese separately.

—Richard Grausman

• • •

BISCUIT-CLOAKED SEAFOOD GUMBO PIE

This recipe was born in the heart of Cajun country in New Iberia, Louisiana. This gumbo, rich and dark, is an absolutely authentic bayou dish. The biscuit crust is pure Helen Johnson, whose eponymous restaurant was the culinary bright spot of the town when I was there, back in 1979. 🍷 Rich, satisfying and spicy, this gumbo would match nicely with the deep, mildly hoppy and slightly bitter flavors of a fine ale, such as Bass, Liberty or Palm.

6 Servings

GUMBO:

3 tablespoons plus 1 teaspoon vegetable oil
3 tablespoons all-purpose flour
3 tablespoons unsalted butter
3/4 pound smoked sausage, sliced
3/4 pound cooked boneless ham steak, cut into 2-by-1/4-inch strips
1 large onion, chopped
2 garlic cloves, minced
1/2 green bell pepper, chopped
1/2 red bell pepper, chopped
1 small celery rib, minced
3 tablespoons rice
2 cups chicken stock or canned broth
2 teaspoons fresh lemon juice
1/2 teaspoon cayenne pepper
3/4 pound shrimp, shelled and deveined
1/2 pound okra, sliced
Salt and freshly ground black pepper

BISCUIT TOPPING:

2 cups all-purpose flour
1 tablespoon baking powder
2 teaspoons sugar
1/2 teaspoon baking soda
1/2 teaspoon salt
6 1/2 tablespoons cold unsalted butter
3/4 cup buttermilk

1. *Make the gumbo:* In a heavy medium skillet, combine 3 tablespoons of the oil with the flour and cook over moderately low heat, stirring occasionally, until the roux is dark mahogany in color, about 1 hour. Do not let burn. Immediately remove from the heat. *(The roux can be prepared ahead and will keep indefinitely. Let cool, then cover and refrigerate.)*

2. In a medium flameproof casserole, melt 2 tablespoons of the butter with the remaining 1 teaspoon oil. Add the sliced sausage and cook over moderate heat until well browned, about 5 minutes. Transfer to a plate with a slotted spoon. Add the ham strips to the casserole and cook until lightly browned, about 7 minutes; add to the plate with the sausage slices.

3. Add the remaining 1 tablespoon butter and the onion to the casserole. Cook over moderate heat, stirring constantly, until softened and translucent, about 2 minutes. Reduce the heat to moderately low and add the garlic, green and red bell peppers, celery and rice. Cook, stirring, for 5 minutes longer.

4. Reheat the brown roux if necessary. Scrape it into the casserole with the vegetables and rice. Stir in the chicken stock and lemon juice. Bring to a boil over high heat. Add the sausages and ham, reduce the heat to moderately low and cook, covered, for 25 minutes.

5. Stir in the cayenne, shrimp and okra and season with salt and black pepper to taste. Cook, stirring once or twice, for 2 minutes. Remove from the heat. *(The recipe can be prepared to this point up to 2 days ahead. Let cool, then cover and refrigerate. Reheat before proceeding.)*

6. *Make the topping:* Preheat the oven to 450°. In a medium bowl, combine the flour, baking powder, sugar, baking soda and salt. Cut in 5½ tablespoons of the butter until the mixture resembles coarse crumbs. Stir in the buttermilk until a soft dough forms.

7. On a lightly floured surface, roll out the dough ½ inch thick. Using a 2½-inch round cutter, stamp out 12 biscuits.

8. Melt the remaining 1 tablespoon butter. Pour the hot gumbo into a shallow 9-inch round baking dish. Arrange the biscuits on top and brush with the melted butter. Bake until the biscuits are puffed and golden brown, about 20 minutes.

—Phillip Stephen Schulz

• • •

SEAFOOD POT PIE

This hearty seafood pie with its flaky crust and succulent filling makes a perfect winter entrée.

🍷 California dry Chenin Blanc, such as 1986 Chappellet

6 Servings

1/2 cup dry white wine
1 pound sea scallops, cut in half if very large
1 large baking potato, peeled and cut into 1/2-inch dice
3 tablespoons unsalted butter, softened to room temperature
1/2 cup peeled and minced tart apple
1 large carrot, minced
1 celery rib, minced
1 large onion, minced
1 garlic clove, minced
1 1/2 cups chicken stock or canned broth
1/4 cup heavy cream
2 tablespoons all-purpose flour
3/4 teaspoon salt
1/2 teaspoon freshly ground white pepper
Pinch of cayenne pepper
1 pound medium shrimp, shelled and deveined
1 cup corn kernels—fresh, frozen or canned
1 small jar (3 1/2 ounces) pimiento strips
2 tablespoons minced parsley
Flaky Pastry (recipe follows; see Note)

1. In a medium nonreactive saucepan, bring the wine to a boil over high heat. Add the scallops and cook until just opaque throughout, about 1 minute. Drain the scallops, reserving the liquid. In another medium saucepan of boiling salted water, cook the potato until just tender, 6 to 8 minutes; drain and set aside.

2. Preheat the oven to 425°. In a large saucepan, melt 2 tablespoons of the butter over moderately high heat. Add the apple, carrot, celery and onion and cook until the mixture softens and starts to brown, about 6 minutes. Add the garlic and cook for 1 minute longer. Pour in the chicken stock and increase the heat to high. Boil until most of the liquid has evaporated, about 5 minutes.

3. Transfer the apple-vegetable mixture to a food processor. Puree until smooth. Return to the saucepan and stir in the reserved scallop liquid and the heavy cream.

4. In a small bowl, blend the flour into the remaining 1 tablespoon of butter to form a paste. Bring the scallop cream to a simmer over moderate heat. Gradually whisk in the butter paste. Bring to a boil, whisking until thickened and smooth. Reduce the heat to low, season with the salt, white pepper and cayenne and simmer, whisking occasionally, until there is no raw flour taste, 2 to 3 minutes.

5. In a shallow 2-quart buttered baking dish, arrange the scallops in a single layer; top with the shrimp and then the corn, potato and pimiento. Sprinkle the parsley over the top. Pour on the sauce and gently shake the dish to distribute evenly. (*This dish can be prepared to this point up to 4 hours ahead. Cover and refrigerate. Bring back to room temperature before proceeding.*)

6. Roll out one portion of the dough (see Note) about 1/4 inch thick, a little larger than the dimensions of the baking dish. Place the dough over the top of the pan and press against the outside rim to seal the edges. Cut at least several steam vents into the top. Bake until the crust is golden brown, about 40 minutes. Serve hot.

NOTE: The pastry recipe makes enough dough for two pot pies; use only one ball of dough in Step 6.

—Lee Bailey

• • •

SAVORY SEAFOOD POT PIE SUPPER

Most of this meal from Lee Bailey can be readied in advance with only a minimum of finishing required to have it come off without a hitch. Serves 6.

Seafood Pot Pie (p. 60)

Baked Beet and Endive Salad (p. 127)

🍷 *Dry White Wine*

Pecan Brittle (p. 228) over Vanilla Ice Cream

Coffee

FLAKY PASTRY

Makes Enough for 2 Pot Pies

1 egg
About 1/4 cup ice water
2 1/2 cups all-purpose flour
1/2 teaspoon salt
1/2 cup vegetable shortening
4 tablespoons cold unsalted butter, cut into small pieces

1. In a measuring cup, lightly beat the egg. Add enough ice water to measure 1/2 cup.

2. In a food processor, combine the flour, salt, shortening and butter. Turn the machine quickly on and off about 10 times, until the mixture is the texture of coarse meal.

3. With the machine on, gradually pour in the egg and water. Process just until the dough begins to mass together; do not overmix.

4. On a sheet of waxed paper, knead the dough briefly into a smooth ball. Divide in half and pat each into a 6-inch disk. Wrap separately and refrigerate for at least 1 hour. (If the pastry is made a day ahead, let stand at room temperature for about 10 minutes, until malleable, before rolling out.)

—Lee Bailey

• • •

SHORT-CRUSTED NANTUCKET CLAM PIE

An old-time New England staple with a borrowing from the new Southwest, this pie is dependent on sweet, fresh clams and roasted red pepper. The crust may be short, but the flavor of the dish is long.

4 Servings

SHORT CRUST:

1½ cups all-purpose flour
1 teaspoon sugar
½ teaspoon salt
6 tablespoons vegetable shortening
1 egg yolk
1 teaspoon red wine vinegar
2 tablespoons cold water

CLAM FILLING:

¼ cup dry white wine
3 sprigs of parsley
1 small imported bay leaf
2 whole cloves
6 whole black peppercorns
24 large clams, scrubbed
2 strips of bacon
5 tablespoons unsalted butter
1 large onion, minced
1 small celery rib, minced
1¼ pounds baking potatoes, peeled and cut into ¼-inch dice
3 tablespoons all-purpose flour
¼ cup heavy cream
⅛ teaspoon hot pepper sauce
⅛ teaspoon freshly grated nutmeg
1 medium red bell pepper—roasted, peeled, seeded and chopped
¼ teaspoon freshly ground black pepper
1 egg white, lightly beaten

1. *Make the short crust:* In a medium bowl, combine the flour, sugar and salt. Cut in the vegetable shortening until the mixture resembles coarse crumbs. In a small bowl, lightly beat the egg yolk with the vinegar and water. Stir the liquid into the flour just until a soft dough forms, adding up to 1 tablespoon more water if necessary. Do not overwork. Flatten the dough into a 6-inch disk, cover with plastic wrap and refrigerate for 15 minutes.

2. *Prepare the clam filling:* In a large nonreactive pot, combine the wine, parsley, bay leaf, cloves and peppercorns and bring to a boil. Add the clams, reduce the heat to moderate, cover and cook for 5 minutes. Remove from the heat and let stand, uncovered, for 5 minutes. Discard any clams that do not open. Remove the clams from their shells over a bowl to catch the juices; discard the shells. Coarsely chop the clams. Add the clam cooking liquid to the juices in the bowl and strain through a sieve lined with cheesecloth. If you have more than 1 cup of liquid, boil to reduce to 1 cup.

3. In a medium skillet, fry the bacon over moderately high heat until browned and crisp, 3 to 5 minutes. Drain on paper towels, then crumble the bacon.

4. Pour off all the drippings from the skillet and add 3 tablespoons of the butter. Add the onion and cook over moderate heat, stirring, until golden, about 5 minutes. Stir in the celery and potatoes, cover and cook over moderately low heat until softened, about 5 minutes. Transfer to a medium heatproof bowl.

5. Preheat the oven to 400°. In the same skillet, melt the remaining 2 tablespoons butter over moderate heat. Whisk in the flour and cook, stirring constantly, for 2 minutes without allowing it to color. Whisk in the reduced clam liquid, bring to a boil and cook until thickened, about 2 minutes. Whisk in the cream, hot sauce and nutmeg. Simmer until the sauce is very thick, about 2 minutes longer. Pour the sauce over the vegetables in the bowl. Stir in the roasted red pepper, crumbled bacon, clams and black pepper.

6. Spoon the clam filling into a 10-inch glass or ceramic quiche dish. Roll out the short-crust dough on a lightly floured surface and lay it over the dish. Trim and flute the edges. Brush with the beaten egg white and cut a slash in the center of the pie. Bake for 25 minutes, or until the crust is golden brown.

—Phillip Stephen Schulz

• • •

STEAMED CRABS WITH BAY SEASONING

For a light, festive meal, serve the crabs with salad, bread and corn on the cob.

4 Servings

¼ cup Hungarian or other imported sweet paprika
¼ cup plus 1 teaspoon coarse (kosher) salt
1 teaspoon cayenne pepper
1 teaspoon freshly ground white pepper
2 teaspoons ground coriander
¼ teaspoon ground cloves
16 bay leaves, crumbled

8 garlic cloves, minced
2 bottles (12 ounces each) amber beer
2 lemons, cut in half
1 dozen large Blue Claw crabs

1. In a bowl, combine the paprika, salt, cayenne, white pepper, coriander, cloves, bay leaves and garlic, making sure the garlic is incorporated.

2. In a large stockpot with a lid, place a rack that will sit about 4 to 5 inches above the bottom. Pour in the beer. Squeeze the cut lemon halves into the pot and drop them in. Cover and bring to a boil over high heat.

3. Using tongs, arrange 6 crabs in an even layer on the rack. Sprinkle half the bay mixture over the back shells of the crabs. Place the remaining 6 crabs on top and sprinkle the remaining bay mixture over them. Cover and steam for 10 to 12 minutes, or until the meat in the crab claw is firm and juicy. Serve on newspapers with small mallets and nut picks.

—Marcia Kiesel

• • •

CRAB ENCHILADAS WITH CHERRY TOMATO SALSA

At The Mansion on Turtle Creek, Dean Fearing serves these with a lime-dressed salad of julienned jicama, red and yellow bell peppers, zucchini and carrot.

6 Servings

6 flour tortillas (7 inches in diameter)
3 tablespoons corn oil
10 ounces fresh lump crabmeat, picked over
1 cup grated Jalapeño Jack cheese (about 5 ounces)
1 cup shredded fresh spinach leaves
Cherry Tomato Salsa (p. 256)

1. Preheat the oven to 300°. Wrap the tortillas tightly in foil and bake for 10 to 15 minutes, until heated through.

2. In a medium skillet, heat the oil. Add the crabmeat and sauté over moderately high heat until heated through, 2 to 3 minutes.

3. Spoon the crabmeat onto the center of the warm tortillas and sprinkle with the cheese and the spinach. Roll the tortillas into cylinders and place on a warmed serving plate, seam-side down. Surround with the Cherry Tomato Salsa.

—Dean Fearing, The Mansion on Turtle Creek, Dallas

• • •

SCALLOPS PROVENÇAL ON TOAST

This scallop dish is an easy-to-assemble spring lunch or light supper. I like to accompany each serving with a green salad and a glass of white wine.

🍷 The Mediterranean seasonings in this dish would find their best match in the sharp, herbaceous flavors of a fresh California Sauvignon Blanc, such as 1986 Kenwood or 1986 Boeger.

6 Servings

3/4 pound lean thickly sliced bacon, cut into 1/8-inch matchsticks
2 tablespoons unsalted butter, softened to room temperature
1/4 cup olive oil
3 pieces of narrow French bread, cut 5 inches long and halved lengthwise
1/2 cup minced shallots
2 garlic cloves, minced
1/2 teaspoon fennel seeds, crushed
1/2 teaspoon thyme, crushed
1/2 teaspoon dill seeds, crushed
1 cup dry white wine
1/4 cup Pernod
1/2 cup canned Italian peeled tomatoes, chopped, 1/2 cup juice reserved
2 tablespoons minced parsley
2 pounds bay scallops
1 1/2 tablespoons fresh lemon juice
1/2 teaspoon salt
1 teaspoon freshly ground pepper
1/2 cup pitted black olives, sliced into rings

1. In a medium pot of boiling water, blanch the bacon for 10 minutes. Drain and set aside on paper towels.

2. Preheat the oven to 450°. In a small bowl, blend the butter with 1 tablespoon of the olive oil. Spread the mixture evenly over the cut sides of the bread.

SPRING LUNCH WITH A FRENCH TWIST

Here's a light and fresh-flavored lunch that is extremely easy to put together. To make matters even simpler, the dessert can be store-bought. Serves 6.

Salmon Rillettes (p. 13)

🍷 *Champagne*

Scallops Provençal on Toast (p. 62)

Quatorze's Chicory and Bacon Salad (p. 125)

🍷 *Sauvignon Blanc*

French Vanilla Ice Cream on Toasted Pound Cake with Raspberry Puree

Café Filtre

3. In a large nonreactive skillet, heat the remaining 3 tablespoons olive oil over low heat. Add the shallots and garlic and cook until softened, about 5 minutes. Add the reserved blanched bacon, fennel seeds, thyme and dill seeds and cook for 5 minutes longer.

4. Increase the heat to moderately high. Add the wine, Pernod, tomatoes with their juice and parsley and cook, stirring occasionally, until slightly thickened, about 10 minutes.

5. Add the scallops and cook, stirring well, until the scallops whiten, about 5 minutes. Remove from the heat at once and stir in the lemon juice, salt and pepper. Cover to keep warm.

6. Meanwhile, toast the bread directly on the oven rack until golden brown, about 5 minutes. Put 1 piece of toasted bread on each plate. Spoon the scallops and their sauce over the bread and sprinkle with the olives.

—W. Peter Prestcott

• • •

SEA SCALLOPS WITH ORANGE-BASIL BEURRE BLANC

This recipe from Jordan Vineyard is a stunner. The squares of aluminum foil called for are essential for transferring the scallops from the baking sheet to the plates.

4 Servings

20 large sea scallops (about 1½ pounds)
1 cup fresh orange juice
¼ cup plus 1 tablespoon minced shallots
¼ cup dry white wine
2 tablespoons Champagne vinegar or white wine vinegar
1 stick (4 ounces) plus 1 teaspoon unsalted butter
1 cup (packed) basil leaves, finely shredded
Dash of hot pepper sauce
½ teaspoon salt
¼ teaspoon freshly ground pepper
1 teaspoon vegetable oil
1 pound Italian plum tomatoes—peeled, seeded and chopped

1. From a double thickness of aluminum foil, cut out four 7-inch squares. Butter the top surface of each square and set them on a baking sheet.

2. Slice each scallop horizontally into ¼-inch rounds. Using a total of 5 whole scallops for each foil square, arrange the slices, slightly overlapping, to form a 6-inch ring. Leave a 2-inch circle empty in the center.

3. Preheat the oven to 450°. In a small nonreactive saucepan, bring the orange juice to a boil over moderately high heat. Boil until reduced to ¼ cup, 6 to 8 minutes.

4. In a nonreactive medium saucepan, combine ¼ cup of the shallots with the wine, vinegar and 2 tablespoons of the reduced orange juice. Bring to a boil over moderately high heat and boil until reduced to about 1½ tablespoons, about 3 minutes. Whisk in 1 stick of butter, 1 tablespoon at a time. Strain the sauce. Add more reduced orange juice, to taste. Stir in the basil, hot sauce, ¼ teaspoon of the salt and ⅛ teaspoon of the pepper. Cover and set over a pan of hot water to keep warm.

5. In a heavy medium skillet, melt the remaining 1 teaspoon butter in the oil over moderately high heat. Add the remaining 1 tablespoon shallots and cook until softened but not browned, about 1 minute. Add the tomatoes and the remaining ¼ teaspoon salt and ⅛ teaspoon pepper. Cook, tossing, until the excess liquid has evaporated, 2 to 3 minutes. Remove from the heat and cover to keep warm.

6. Bake the scallops until opaque throughout, 4 to 5 minutes. Carefully slide the rings of scallops off the foil squares onto heated plates. Spoon the cooked tomatoes into the center of each ring and spoon the sauce evenly over the scallops. Serve immediately.

—Franco Dunn & Jean Reynolds,
Jordan Vineyard & Winery,
Healdsburg, California

• • •

PRAWNS AND PEPPERS WITH SOPPRESSATA

Chef Rick O'Connell created this unusual blend of seafood and coarse Italian salami for RAF.

4 Servings

5 tablespoons extra-virgin olive oil
2 tablespoons minced carrot
2 tablespoons minced onion plus ½ cup thinly sliced onion
16 large shrimp, shelled and deveined, shells reserved and chopped
1 cup dry white wine
1 small garlic clove, minced
⅛ teaspoon crushed hot pepper
1 cup thinly sliced red bell pepper
½ cup thinly sliced yellow bell pepper
¾ cup thinly sliced fennel bulb
½ teaspoon salt
12 very thin slices of soppressata
1 tablespoon chopped Italian flat-leaf parsley, for garnish

1. In a medium saucepan, heat 2 tablespoons of the olive oil over moderately low heat. Add the carrot and minced onion and cook until the onion is softened but not browned, about 2 minutes. Stir in the shrimp shells. Add ½ cup of the white wine and 1½ cups of water. Bring to a boil, reduce the heat and simmer, uncovered, for 20 minutes.

2. Strain the stock, return it to the pan and boil over high heat until reduced to ½ cup, about 5 minutes. Strain and reserve the shrimp stock.

3. In a large skillet, heat the remaining 3 tablespoons olive oil over low heat. Add the garlic and hot pepper and cook for 1 minute. Stir in the sliced onion, red and yellow bell peppers and fennel. Season the vegetables with the salt and cook, covered, turning once, until soft, 8 to 10 minutes.

4. Add the remaining ½ cup white wine and the reserved shrimp stock. Bring to a boil, add the shrimp, reduce the heat and cook, covered, until the shrimp are pink and opaque throughout, about 3 minutes.

5. To serve, arrange 3 slices of soppressata on each of 4 plates. Using a slotted spoon, arrange 4 shrimp down the center of each plate and spoon the vegetables to each side of the shrimp. Boil the cooking liquid over high heat until reduced to ½ cup, about 3 minutes. Pour the sauce over the shrimp and garnish with the chopped parsley.

—Rick O'Connell, RAF, San Francisco

• • •

COCONUT SHRIMP

Passionately hot and slightly tropical, this sauté evokes Mexico's coastal abundance. The creamy tart sauce is the perfect foil for the crunchy sweet shrimp. Serve with white rice and cold beer.

4 Servings

1 small coconut
4 tablespoons unsalted butter
1 pound medium shrimp, shelled and deveined
½ teaspoon salt
3 jalapeño peppers, seeded and minced
3 garlic cloves, minced
½ cup thinly sliced scallions
1 large red bell pepper, cut into ¼-inch dice
1 cup heavy cream
¼ cup chicken stock or canned broth
1 tablespoon fresh lime juice
½ cup minced fresh coriander

1. Preheat the oven to 375°. Punch out the "eyes" of the coconut and drain out the liquid. Put the coconut in a baking pan and cook until the shell cracks, about 20 minutes. Cover with a towel and, using a hammer, crack the coconut open. Remove the coconut meat and, using a vegetable peeler, remove the tough brown skin. Coarsely grate enough coconut to yield ⅓ cup.

2. In a large skillet, melt 3 tablespoons of the butter over high heat. Add the shrimp, season with the salt and sauté until pink, curled and just tender, about 2 minutes. Using a slotted spoon, transfer the shrimp to a bowl; keep warm.

3. In the same skillet, melt the remaining 1 tablespoon butter over moderate heat. Add the jalapeño peppers, garlic, scallions and red pepper and cook, stirring occasionally, until softened, about 2 minutes. Add the cream and chicken stock to the skillet and bring to a boil. Reduce the heat and simmer until the sauce is slightly thickened, 2 to 3 minutes. Stir in the lime juice and minced coriander.

4. Spoon the sauce onto 4 serving plates. Arrange the shrimp on the sauce, sprinkle the grated coconut over the shrimp and serve.

—Michael McLaughlin

• • •

SHRIMP WITH GARLIC AND ROSEMARY

A robust extra-virgin olive oil should be used for these fragrant shrimp, which could be accompanied with crusty bread and a crisp salad of tossed greens.

4 to 6 Servings

1½ pounds large shrimp, shelled and deveined
2 medium garlic cloves, minced
3 tablespoons extra-virgin olive oil
¼ teaspoon freshly ground pepper
12 sprigs of fresh rosemary
1 tablespoon plus 1 teaspoon unsalted butter
½ cup dry vermouth

1. In a large shallow bowl, combine the shrimp, garlic, olive oil and pepper; toss well. Lightly crush 8 sprigs of the rosemary with your hands, add to the shrimp and toss again, using your hands. Cover with plastic wrap and let marinate in the refrigerator for 8 hours or overnight, tossing occasionally.

2. In a large heavy skillet, melt the butter over high heat. When the foam subsides, add the shrimp and marinade and sauté, tossing frequently until slightly pink, about 2 minutes. Reduce the heat to moderate, cover and cook until the shrimp are opaque throughout, about 3 minutes. With a slotted spoon, transfer the shrimp to a bowl. Discard the rosemary sprigs.

3. Pour the vermouth into the skillet and boil over high heat, stirring frequently, until it reduces to a moderately thick glaze, about 3 minutes. Reduce the heat to moderate. Return the shrimp to the pan along with any accumulated juices and toss in the glaze until evenly coated and heated through, about 1 minute.

4. Spoon the shrimp onto a warmed platter and garnish with the remaining 4 sprigs of rosemary.

—Jean Anderson

• • •

POULTRY

GRILLED CHILE CHICKEN

Fiery chile peppers inserted under the skin of the chicken to heighten the effect of the sauce are removed before serving.

6 Servings

4 ancho chiles, seeded
4 red bell peppers
2 tablespoons olive oil
1 small onion, chopped
6 garlic cloves—2 minced, 4 cut in half
2 tablespoons curry powder
1 teaspoon fennel seeds, crushed
1 teaspoon ground cumin
2 teaspoons sweet paprika
1/3 cup strongly brewed coffee
1 1/2 cups chicken stock or canned broth
1 stick (4 ounces) unsalted butter, cut into pieces
1/2 cup fresh orange juice
1/4 cup fresh lime juice
3 broiling chickens (2 1/2 pounds each), backbones removed
18 small dried red chile peppers, split and seeded
6 sprigs of fresh coriander
3 small unpeeled oranges, halved and thinly sliced

1. Place the ancho chiles in a small bowl and add enough boiling water to barely cover them. Let stand for 30 minutes. Drain and when cool enough to handle, remove the skins.

2. Roast the bell peppers directly over a gas flame or as close to the heat of a broiler as possible, turning frequently, until the skin is charred all over. Enclose the peppers in a paper bag and let stand for 10 minutes. Remove the stems, seeds and skins, wiping away any blackened particles with a damp cloth.

3. In a medium nonreactive saucepan, heat the olive oil. Add the onion and minced garlic and cook over low heat, stirring frequently, until softened but not browned, 3 to 5 minutes.

4. Add the curry powder, fennel seeds, cumin and paprika. Cook, stirring frequently, for 3 minutes.

5. Add the brewed coffee and the chicken stock. Bring to a boil. Add the peeled ancho chiles and the roasted bell peppers and simmer, stirring occasionally, for 30 minutes.

6. Pour the mixture into a blender or food processor. Add the butter and puree until smooth. Return to the saucepan. Blend in the orange juice, lime juice and additional stock to thin the sauce if necessary. Set the sauce aside, covered, to keep warm.

7. Preheat the broiler. Rub the chickens with the split garlic cloves and stuff the small, split dried chiles under the skin. Place the chickens, skin-side up, on a baking sheet and broil about 5 inches from the heat for 15 minutes, turning them with tongs every 3 to 4 minutes. Move the chickens to a lower rack about 7 inches from the heat and cook for 10 to 12 minutes, turning twice, until the skin is browned and the juices run clear.

8. To serve, split the chickens in half and remove the chiles from under the skin. Ladle the sauce over the chicken. Garnish the plates with a sprig of fresh coriander and thin slices of orange.

—Barbara Figueroa,
Sorrento Hotel, Seattle

• • •

GRILLED CHICKEN BREASTS WITH ANAHEIM CHILE BUTTER, CORN AND PEPPERS

All-American ingredients add freshness to this flavorful chicken from Taxi.

🍷 The piquancy of the chile butter on the chicken suggests a fruity, dry but simple white for contrast, such as the 1986 Chappellet Dry Chenin Blanc.

8 Servings

1/4 cup vegetable oil
2 large Anaheim chiles
1/2 jalapeño or 1 serrano pepper
1 small garlic clove
2 tablespoons fresh lemon juice
1 3/4 teaspoons salt
6 tablespoons unsalted butter
1 medium red bell pepper, cut into 1/4-inch dice
1 medium green bell pepper, cut into 1/4-inch dice
4 cups corn kernels, preferably fresh
3 sage leaves, preferably fresh, finely chopped
8 boneless chicken breast halves, skin on
Sprigs of fresh coriander, for garnish

1. In a medium skillet, heat the vegetable oil until very hot. Using long tongs, add the Anaheim chiles to the pan, being careful to avoid any splattering oil. Cook the chiles, turning, until the skins turn white, about 1 minute. Transfer the chiles to a plate lined with paper towels; reserve the oil.

2. When the chiles are cool enough to handle, remove and discard the skins, seeds and ribs. Place the chiles in a blender. Add the jalapeño pepper, garlic, lemon juice and 1/4 teaspoon of the salt. Puree until smooth. With the machine on, add 4 tablespoons of the butter, 1 tablespoon at a time, and blend until smooth. Transfer the butter to a sheet of plastic wrap and roll into a 4-inch-long cylinder. Place in the freezer. (*The chile butter can be prepared up to 2 months in advance and stored in the freezer.*)

3. In a medium saucepan, combine the red and green bell peppers, corn, sage, 1 1/2 cups of water and 1/2 teaspoon of the salt. Bring to a boil, reduce the heat to moderately low and simmer, uncovered, until the vegetables are tender, about 10 minutes. Drain and toss the vegetables with the remaining 2 tablespoons butter.

DOWN HOME CAJUN DINNER

Here's a hearty New Orleans-style chicken dish from Lee Bailey for those who like the authoritative flavors of Cajun cooking. Serves 6 to 8.

Chicken Sauce Piquant (p. 67)

Fluffy White Rice

Tossed Green Salad

Dry Red Wine

Chocolate Trifle (p. 217)

Coffee

4. In a large skillet, heat the reserved ¼ cup oil over moderate heat. In two batches, add the chicken breasts and sauté, turning, until golden brown, about 7 minutes on each side. Season with the remaining 1 teaspoon salt.

5. To serve, mound the vegetables in the center of 8 warmed dinner plates. Place a chicken breast on top of each. Cut the frozen chile butter into ½-inch rounds and set one on top of each piece of chicken. Garnish the plates with sprigs of coriander.

—*Taxi, San Francisco*

• • •

CHICKEN SAUCE PIQUANT

If you like your chicken with a very flavorful sauce, this is for you. Since the recipe creates a generous amount of sauce, it can be stretched to accommodate any last-minute guests. All you have to do is throw in a few more pieces of chicken.

Spicy California Zinfandel, such as 1983 Chateau Montelena

6 to 8 Servings

⅓ cup safflower or corn oil
4 large chicken breast halves
12 chicken thighs
2 medium onions, coarsely chopped
4 celery ribs, coarsely chopped
1 large green bell pepper, coarsely chopped
⅓ cup all-purpose flour
1 can (28 ounces) crushed Italian peeled tomatoes
¼ cup tomato paste
2 large imported bay leaves
2 large garlic cloves, minced
1 tablespoon lemon juice
1 teaspoon hot pepper sauce
1 teaspoon salt
½ teaspoon freshly ground black pepper
4 cups chicken stock or canned broth
2 tablespoons chopped scallion greens
2 tablespoons minced parsley
12 pimiento-stuffed olives, sliced

1. In a large flameproof casserole, heat the oil over moderately high heat. Add the chicken pieces in batches and sauté, turning, until browned, 4 to 5 minutes on each side. With a slotted spoon, transfer the chicken to a plate.

2. Add the onions, celery and green pepper to the casserole and cook over moderate heat, stirring, until softened but not browned, 5 to 10 minutes. With a slotted spoon, transfer the vegetables to another plate.

3. Whisk the flour into the remaining oil in the casserole and cook over moderate heat, stirring and scraping up the browned bits from the bottom of the pan, until the roux turns a rich brown, about 10 minutes.

4. Stir in the tomatoes with their juice, ½ cup of water, the tomato paste, bay leaves, garlic, lemon juice, hot sauce, salt, pepper and stock. Bring to a boil. Add the chicken and reserved sautéed vegetables to the casserole and simmer, uncovered, stirring and skimming the top occasionally, until the chicken is tender and the sauce thickened, about 1 hour. (*The recipe can be prepared to this point up to 1 day ahead. Let cool, then cover and refrigerate.*)

5. A few minutes before serving, stir in the scallions, parsley and olives.

—*Lee Bailey*

• • •

PROVENCAL CHICKEN WITH 40 CLOVES OF GARLIC

The garlic in this dish cooks so long that it mellows and is luscious spread on grilled or toasted French bread rounds.

1985 Alsace Pinot Blanc, such as Hugel or Trimbach

6 to 8 Servings

2 chickens (3 pounds each), cut into 8 pieces each
½ teaspoon salt
1 teaspoon freshly ground pepper
¾ cup extra-virgin olive oil
2½ teaspoons herbes de Provence (½ teaspoon each dried marjoram, oregano and summer savory and 1 teaspoon dried thyme), or use all thyme
40 whole garlic cloves, unpeeled
1 loaf of French or Italian bread, sliced and toasted

1. Preheat the oven to 375°. Season the chicken pieces with the salt and ½ teaspoon of the pepper. In a large flameproof casserole, heat 2 tablespoons of the olive oil over moderately high heat. Add the chicken in batches and brown evenly, about 3 minutes on each side.

2. Remove the casserole from the heat. Return all of the chicken to the casserole and add the herbes de Provence, garlic, remaining ½ cup plus 2 tablespoons olive oil and ½ teaspoon pepper. Toss to coat well. Place aluminum foil over the casserole and cover with the lid. Bake, without removing the lid, for 1 hour and 10 minutes.

3. Serve the chicken with the garlic cloves, to be spread onto the toasted French or Italian bread.

—Peter Kump

• • •

MISTRAL'S CHICKEN WITH GARLIC

This thoroughly Provençal dish—chicken smothered with garlic—is named after the region's favorite native son, the poet Frédéric Mistral. Chef Michel Gonod, of the Hostellerie Le Prieuré in Villeneuve-lès-Avignon, says this is one of the most popular dishes on his menu. With it, serve sautéed potatoes or rice.

🍷 A chilled rosé de Provence would be refreshing and have enough character to balance the volume of aromatic garlic in this dish.

4 Servings

1 chicken (3 to 4 pounds), cut into 8 serving pieces
1 teaspoon salt
¼ teaspoon freshly ground pepper
1 tablespoon unsalted butter
2 tablespoons extra-virgin olive oil
40 large garlic cloves, peeled
½ cup dry white wine
½ cup chicken stock or canned broth

1. Season the chicken with the salt and pepper. In a large heavy skillet, melt the butter in the oil over moderately high heat. Add the chicken in batches and sauté, turning, until browned, about 4 minutes on each side. Pour off the fat from the pan.

2. Reduce the heat to moderate and add the garlic cloves, tucking them under the chicken so that they settle in a layer at the bottom. Sauté, shaking the pan frequently, until the garlic is lightly browned, 8 to 10 minutes.

3. Pour in the wine and stock, stirring and scraping up any browned bits from the bottom of the pan. Cover and cook until the juices run clear when a thigh is pricked, 10 to 12 minutes. Serve the chicken with the garlic and pan juices.

—Michel Gonod, Hostellerie Le Prieuré, Villeneuve-lès-Avignon, France

• • •

CHICKEN SCALLOPS WITH SHALLOTS AND LEMON THYME

Although simple to prepare, the chicken must marinate overnight to absorb the herb flavor. I like to serve this dish with buttered noodles, steamed rice or boiled new potatoes.

🍷 This deliciously rich dish requires a white wine with assertive, direct flavors for contrast, such as the 1985 Jekel Arroyo Seco Pinot Blanc.

6 Servings

¼ cup plus 1 tablespoon fruity olive oil
3 large garlic cloves, slivered lengthwise
15 small sprigs of lemon thyme plus 1½ teaspoons minced fresh lemon thyme
1¼ pounds skinless, boneless chicken breast halves, pounded flat
3 shallots, minced
½ cup dry white wine or dry vermouth
¾ cup chicken stock or canned broth
1½ teaspoons Dijon-style mustard
¼ teaspoon freshly ground pepper
½ cup crème fraîche or heavy cream
Salt

1. Rub 1 tablespoon of the oil over the bottom of a 9-inch square baking dish. Scatter over one-third each of the garlic and the lemon thyme sprigs and top with half of the chicken. Repeat this layering 2 more times, using 2 more tablespoons of oil and ending with a sprinkling of the remaining garlic and thyme sprigs. Cover tightly with plastic wrap and let marinate in the refrigerator overnight.

2. In a large heavy skillet, heat the remaining 2 tablespoons oil over moderately high heat. Add the shallots and minced lemon thyme and stir-fry until golden, about 2 minutes. Using a slotted spoon, transfer the herbed shallots to a small plate.

3. Increase the heat to high, add the chicken in batches and sauté, turning, until browned, about 1 minute per side; transfer to a plate as they are cooked.

4. Add the wine to the skillet and bring to a boil, scraping up any browned bits from the bottom of the pan. Boil until the wine reduces to a rich amber glaze, 2 to 3 minutes.

5. Return the shallots to the skillet, add the chicken stock and blend in the mustard and pepper. Boil, stirring constantly, until the sauce has reduced by about two-thirds, 3 to 4 minutes. Stir in the crème fraîche and boil until reduced by half, about 2 minutes. Season the sauce with salt to taste.

6. Reduce the heat to low, return the chicken to the skillet and warm through, spooning the sauce over the top, about 2 minutes. Serve on heated plates.

—Jean Anderson

• • •

Roast Loin of Venison with Cranberries (p. 115).

Left, Guinea Hen with Black Olives (p. 86). Above, New Mexican Pork Pie with Cornmeal Crust (p. 103).

Above, Grilled Gingered Swordfish (p. 235). Right, Crusty Baked Ham (p. 104) with Gratin of Sweet Potatoes Flambéed with Bourbon (p. 161).

Left, Braised Pheasant with Polenta (p. 88). Above, Roast Pork Grand-Mère (p. 103).

CHICKEN BREASTS STUFFED WITH SAUSAGE AND LEMON ZEST

These aromatic chicken breasts would be delicious with buttered green beans and a rice pilaf for a spring supper.

🍷 Fruity white, such as 1985 Gaston Huet Vouvray, or 1985 Robert Mondavi Chenin Blanc

6 Servings

3 tablespoons olive oil
1 medium onion, finely chopped
1 garlic clove, minced
1/4 pound hot Italian sausage
1/4 pound sweet Italian sausage
2 teaspoons tarragon
2 tablespoons tomato paste
1/2 cup brandy
1 cup fresh bread crumbs
2 tablespoons minced parsley
1 tablespoon grated lemon zest
Pinch of salt
4 whole boneless chicken breasts, skin on, pounded lightly to flatten
3 tablespoons unsalted butter
1/2 cup dry white wine

1. Preheat the oven to 450°. In a large skillet, heat the oil over high heat. Add the onion and garlic; reduce the heat to low, cover and cook until the onion is very soft but not brown, about 20 minutes.

2. Meanwhile, put the hot and sweet sausages in a medium saucepan with water to cover. Bring to a boil, reduce the heat to moderate and simmer until the sausages are cooked through, about 15 minutes. Drain well and coarsely chop.

3. Add the sausages, tarragon, tomato paste and brandy to the skillet and cook, stirring occasionally, until most of the brandy has evaporated, about 5 minutes. Scrape the sausage mixture into a large bowl and stir in the bread crumbs, 1 tablespoon of the parsley, 2 teaspoons of the lemon zest and the salt.

4. Spoon one-fourth of the stuffing onto each chicken breast. Gather the sides around the stuffing to form a ball shape, and secure with wooden skewers.

5. In a large ovenproof skillet, melt 2 tablespoons of the butter over high heat. When the foam subsides, add the chicken breasts, rounded-side down, and cook until well browned, about 5 minutes; turn the breasts over and put the skillet in the oven. Bake for 25 minutes, or until the chicken breasts are white throughout but still juicy.

6. Transfer the chicken breasts to a large platter. Pour off the fat from the skillet and set it over high heat. Add the white wine and bring to a boil, scraping up any browned bits from the bottom of the pan. Boil until reduced to 3 tablespoons, about 3 minutes. Remove from the heat and stir in the remaining 1 tablespoon parsley and 1 teaspoon lemon zest.

7. Remove the skewers from the chicken and cut into slices about 3/8 inch thick. Pour any accumulated juices into the skillet and stir in the remaining 1 tablespoon butter. Drizzle the sauce over the chicken.

—W. Peter Prestcott

• • •

Shrimp with Garlic and Rosemary (p. 64).

NEW-FASHIONED CHICKEN POT PIE WITH PHYLLO CRUST

Chicken pot pie with a secret ingredient? Yes, jicama, that sweet, super-crisp tuber frequently found in Mexican cuisine. Jicama's crunch holds up remarkably well even after long cooking.

🍷 While a fruity white could be served with this dish, the slightly creamy, mild flavors would be nicely shown off by a light, bright-flavored red, such as a 1985 Ruffino or Frescobaldi Chianti.

4 to 6 Servings

1 chicken (about 3 1/2 pounds)
1 large onion, unpeeled
2 carrots—1 chopped, 1 cut into 1/4-inch dice
1 celery rib, chopped
1 turnip, peeled and chopped
1 parsnip, peeled and chopped
4 sprigs of parsley
4 cups chicken stock or canned broth
1 teaspoon cider vinegar
1 large leek (white and tender green), chopped
1 small jicama (1/2 pound), peeled and cut into 1/4-inch dice
5 tablespoons unsalted butter
1 1/2 tablespoons all-purpose flour
1 cup heavy cream
Pinch of ground allspice
Pinch of freshly grated nutmeg
1/2 teaspoon salt
1/4 teaspoon freshly ground pepper
8 sheets of phyllo dough
1 tablespoon fine bread crumbs

1. In a large saucepan, combine the chicken, onion, chopped carrot, celery, turnip, parsnip, parsley, chicken stock, and vinegar. Add enough water to cover the chicken and bring to a boil. Reduce the heat and simmer, partially covered, until the chicken is tender and white throughout, about 50 minutes. Remove from the heat and let cool for 30 minutes.

2. When the chicken is cool enough to handle, discard the skin and bones; cut the meat into bite-size pieces. Strain the cooking liquid and reserve.

3. In a medium saucepan, cover the leek with 1½ cups of the reserved cooking liquid and bring to a boil. Add the diced carrot and cook over moderately low heat until softened, about 10 minutes. Stir in the jicama and cook until softened slightly, about 5 minutes longer. Using a slotted spoon, remove the vegetables to a bowl and reserve. If necessary, add enough of the reserved cooking liquid to the pan to make 1 cup; set aside.

4. In a medium saucepan, melt 2 tablespoons of the butter over moderately low heat. Whisk in the flour and cook, stirring constantly, for about 2 minutes without coloring. Whisk in the reserved 1 cup of cooking liquid and bring to a boil. Boil, stirring frequently, for 3 minutes.

5. Whisk in the cream, allspice and nutmeg and return to a boil. Cook, stirring frequently, until thick, about 8 minutes. Remove from the heat and let cool, stirring occasionally. Stir in the chicken, cooked vegetables and the salt and pepper. Transfer the stew to a shallow 10-inch round baking dish.

6. Preheat the oven to 425°. Melt the remaining 3 tablespoons butter. On a work surface, lightly brush 2 sheets of the phyllo dough with melted butter and sprinkle with 1 teaspoon of the bread crumbs. Repeat twice more with the remaining phyllo, melted butter and bread crumbs, reserving a little of the butter. Place the last 2 sheets of phyllo on top and brush with butter. Invert the phyllo dough onto the baking dish and trim the sides to ½ inch beyond the edge. Brush the top and sides lightly with the remaining butter. Tuck under the sides.

7. Cut a hole in the center of the pie and bake for 30 minutes, or until the top is golden and crisp.

—Phillip Stephen Schulz

• • •

MEXICAN CASSOULET

A great party casserole, this dish needs nothing but a green salad to make a substantial meal. For added spice, you could serve an icy-cold fresh tomato salsa on the side.

8 to 10 Servings

1½ cups dried small red beans, rinsed and picked over
1½ cups dried pea beans (or other small white bean), rinsed and picked over
8 large dried ancho chiles
1 pound chorizo (Mexican sausage) or hot Italian sausage
1 chicken (3 to 4 pounds), cut into 8 pieces, or an equal amount of chicken parts
1 teaspoon salt
2 teaspoons freshly ground pepper
1 tablespoon chili powder
1 tablespoon ground cumin
3 cups chicken stock or canned broth
2 medium onions, cut into wedges
2 small fresh serrano or jalapeño chiles, minced, or 2 teaspoons minced pickled jalapeños
4 garlic cloves, crushed through a press
2 tablespoons chopped fresh oregano or 2 teaspoons dried
¼ teaspoon hot pepper sauce
2 medium chayote (about 1 pound), or 3 medium zucchini
1 can (28 ounces) Italian peeled tomatoes, cut in half and drained, liquid reserved
1½ cups fresh bread crumbs
3 tablespoons melted unsalted butter

1. In a large flameproof casserole, combine the beans with 8 cups of lightly salted water. Bring to a boil over moderately high heat and continue to boil for 40 minutes; remove from the heat. The beans will still be crunchy.

2. Meanwhile, rinse, stem and seed the ancho chiles. Soak in 2 cups of boiling water for 20 minutes. Puree the chiles and their soaking liquid in a blender or food processor. Set the chile puree aside.

3. Prick the sausages all over. In a large skillet, sauté the sausages over moderate heat, turning, until browned, 8 to 10 minutes. Transfer the sausages to a plate to cool slightly; reserve 2 tablespoons of fat in the skillet. Halve the sausages lengthwise, then slice crosswise ½ inch thick.

4. Preheat the oven to 350°. Rub the chicken pieces with the salt and pepper. Combine the chili powder and cumin. Sprinkle some over each piece of chicken. Reserve any that is not used.

5. Heat the 2 tablespoons reserved fat in the skillet. Add the chicken, skin-side down, in batches if necessary. Sauté over moderately high heat, turning once, until golden brown, 3 to 5 minutes on each side. Remove the browned chicken to a plate and pour off the fat in the skillet.

6. Mix 2 cups of the stock with the chile puree and add to the skillet. Bring to a boil over high heat, scraping up any browned bits from the bottom of the pan. Remove from the heat and set aside.

7. Cover the beans in the casserole with the onions, serrano chiles, garlic, oregano and hot sauce. Add the sausage and lay the chicken on top, wedging the pieces snugly together. Reserve 1 cup of the chile puree and pour the remainder into the casserole. Sprinkle any remaining chili powder and cumin over the top.

8. Cover the casserole and bake in the oven until the beans are just tender, about 2 hours; check the cassoulet after 1 hour and add the reserved 1 cup stock and chile puree if the beans look dry. (*The recipe can be prepared ahead to this point. Let cool, then cover and refrigerate for up to 2 days, or freeze for up to 1 month. Thaw the cassoulet, if frozen, and reheat before proceeding.*)

9. Meanwhile, peel and cut the chayote into 1-inch slices or slice the zucchini. Quarter each piece into pie-shaped wedges.

10. Remove the cassoulet from the oven and gently transfer the chicken to a plate. Add the chayote and tomatoes and enough of the reserved tomato juices to moisten the beans. Toss gently to mix. Return the chicken to the top of the casserole and bake for 20 to 30 minutes, until the chayote is tender and the beans are soft but not mushy.

11. Preheat the broiler. Mix the bread crumbs with the melted butter. Scatter the crumbs over the top of the cassoulet. Place the casserole under the broiler until the crumbs are browned, about 2 minutes, watching carefully.

—*Gayle Henderson Wilson*

• • •

CASSOULET RAPIDE

There are as many versions of cassoulet as there are cooks who prepare it. This one takes all the shortcuts except the one on taste.

🍷 Hearty red, such as C.U.N.E. Rioja Clarete or California Zinfandel, such as Kendall-Jackson

6 to 8 Servings

2 cups dried navy beans, rinsed and picked over
1 pound chicken gizzards
2 medium onions, coarsely chopped
1 bouquet garni: 8 parsley sprigs, 3 garlic cloves, 2 tablespoons thyme, 4 whole cloves and 2 bay leaves tied in cheesecloth
1 pound very lean bacon, cut into julienne strips
1 pound boneless smoked chicken or duck, cut into 2-inch chunks
1 pound smoked Polish sausage, sliced ¼ inch thick
1 tart apple, peeled and cut into ½-inch dice
½ cup dry red wine
½ cup Armagnac or brandy
3 tablespoons tomato paste
½ teaspoon freshly ground pepper
2 cups fresh bread crumbs
½ cup finely chopped parsley
4 tablespoons unsalted butter, melted

1. In a large heavy saucepan or flameproof casserole, bring 8 cups of water to a boil. Add the beans and cook for 1 minute. Remove from the heat and let stand, covered, for 1 hour.

2. Meanwhile, in a medium saucepan, cover the gizzards with 4 cups of water and bring to a simmer. Reduce the heat to low and cook for 1 hour. Strain the stock; discard the gizzards. Boil the stock over high heat until it is reduced to 1 cup. Set the reduced stock aside.

3. Add the onions and bouquet garni to the beans and bring to a boil over high heat. Reduce the heat to moderate and simmer for 1 hour. Drain the beans and discard the bouquet garni.

4. In a small saucepan, cover the bacon with cold water and bring to a boil. Cook for 3 minutes, then drain the bacon.

5. Preheat the oven to 400°. In a large bowl, combine the beans, reserved stock, smoked chicken, sausage, bacon, apple, wine, Armagnac, tomato paste and pepper. Toss to mix well. Turn into a large casserole.

6. In a medium bowl, toss the bread crumbs with the parsley and melted butter. Sprinkle evenly over the top of the casserole and bake, uncovered, for 20 minutes.

7. Reduce the oven temperature to 350° and bake for 1 hour longer.

—*W. Peter Prestcott*

• • •

CHICKEN IN RIESLING WINE SAUCE

The *poulet au Riesling* I ate in Colmar 20 years ago was made by simmering the chicken in a combination of wine and water. The resulting stock was used to make a roux-based velouté sauce, which was further thickened and enriched with egg yolks and cream. The mushrooms were poached separately, and their liquid was reduced and added to the sauce.

In the following recipe, the mushrooms are cooked along with the chicken. eliminating two steps, and only cream is used as an enrichment. Omitting the butter, flour and egg yolks from the sauce yields a smaller quantity, with greater intensity of flavor and, naturally, fewer calories.

🍷 Because Riesling is called for in the recipe, it's also the obvious wine to serve with this dish. The richness of the sauce points to a dry, savory, stylish example, such as the 1985 Hugel from Alsace or the 1985 Trefethen from California.

4 Servings

3 tablespoons unsalted butter
1 chicken (2½ to 3 pounds), quartered
¼ teaspoon salt
⅛ teaspoon freshly ground pepper
1 medium onion, cut in half
2 shallots, finely chopped
¼ pound mushrooms, sliced if medium size, halved if small
¾ cup plus 1 teaspoon Riesling wine
¾ cup heavy cream

1. In a large nonreactive skillet, melt the butter over moderate heat. Add the chicken and sauté, turning once, until lightly browned, about 3 minutes.

2. Pour off any fat from the pan. Season the chicken with the salt and pepper and add the onion, cut-side down. Cover and cook over low heat for 15 minutes.

3. Add the shallots, mushrooms and ¾ cup of the wine to the pan. Cover and simmer for 10 minutes.

4. With a slotted spoon, transfer the chicken and mushrooms to a serving platter and cover with foil to keep warm. Discard the onion and boil the liquid in the skillet over high heat until reduced to about ⅓ cup, 1 to 2 minutes.

5. Add the cream and boil, stirring, until thickened, 1 to 2 minutes. Add the remaining 1 teaspoon wine and season with additional salt and pepper to taste. Pour the sauce over the chicken and serve, surrounded by buttered noodles.

—Richard Grausman

• • •

SKILLET-ROASTED CORNISH GAME HENS ON A BED OF POLENTA

Cornish game hens are stuffed with sprigs of fresh sage and served over polenta.

4 Servings

2 Cornish game hens (about 1 pound each)
Salt and freshly ground pepper
4 sprigs of fresh sage or 6 dried leaves
2½ tablespoons unsalted butter
1½ tablespoons olive oil
3 cups chicken stock or 1½ cups canned broth diluted with 1½ cups water
1 cup instant polenta
¼ cup boiling water

1. Preheat the oven to 350°. Season the game hens inside and out with a pinch of salt and pepper. Stuff 1 sprig of sage (or 3 dried leaves) into each bird and truss with kitchen string.

2. In a large ovenproof skillet, melt 1½ tablespoons of the butter in the oil over high heat. Cook the birds, turning, until browned evenly all over, 8 to 10 minutes.

3. Turn the birds breast-side up, cover the skillet and place it in the oven. Cook until the birds are tender and the thigh juices run clear when pierced with a fork, 20 to 25 minutes. Transfer to a warm plate and cover loosely with foil.

4. In a medium saucepan, bring the stock to a boil over high heat. Add the remaining 1 tablespoon butter. Gradually stir in the polenta. Cook, stirring constantly, for 5 minutes. Add the boiling water and cook for 5 minutes longer.

5. Cut the game hens in half and reserve any cooking juices that escape. Stir the juices into the polenta. Spoon the polenta onto a large platter and arrange the hens on top. If you are using fresh sage, garnish the platter with the remaining sprigs.

—John Robert Massie

• • •

SMALL CHICKENS MARINATED IN TEQUILA AND LIME

This unusual marinade moves the margarita from the bar to the kitchen and results in moist and savory chickens every time. The birds can be cooked entirely in the oven, or they can be removed about 10 minutes early and finished on a grill over savory wood. They're good hot or at room temperature.

🍷 The tartness of the marinade and chiles in the accompanying salad calls for cold pitchers of a refreshing beer, such as Carta Blanca.

4 Servings

4 poussins (baby chickens) or Cornish games hens (about 1¼ pounds each), backbones removed
½ cup fresh lime juice

1/3 cup golden tequila
1/4 cup olive oil
2 tablespoons Cointreau
2 garlic cloves, minced
1/4 teaspoon salt
1/8 teaspoon freshly ground pepper

1. Flatten the chickens with the palm of your hand. In a large bowl, combine the lime juice, tequila, olive oil, Cointreau and garlic. Add the chickens and turn to coat with the marinade. Cover and marinate, turning once or twice, for up to 2 hours at room temperature or overnight in the refrigerator. Let return to room temperature before cooking.

2. Preheat the oven to 400°. Remove the chickens from the marinade and arrange them skin-side up in a shallow baking dish. Season with the salt and pepper. Bake on the upper rack of the oven, basting occasionally with the marinade, until the skin is golden and the juices from the thighs, pricked at their thickest, run pinkish-yellow, 25 to 30 minutes.

—Michael McLaughlin

• • •

DINNER SOUTH OF THE BORDER

This dinner requires a little research—to find baby chickens *(poussins)*—and some time spent in the kitchen, but your guests will thank you for it. Serves 4.

Grilled Sea Scallops in Pumpkin Seed Sauce (p. 29)

Dry Riesling or Beer

Small Chickens Marinated in Tequila and Lime (p. 80)

Black Bean, Corn and Poblano Pepper Salad with Toasted Cumin Vinaigrette (p. 129)

Dry Riesling or Beer

Honeydew in Jalapeño Syrup with Melon Sorbet (p. 227)

Coffee

GAME BIRD POT PIE

My father always made this recipe with wild birds, but for convenience, I usually use baby chickens or Cornish game hens. If you decide to make this with real game birds, substitute a dry red wine for the white wine called for below.

4 Servings

2 baby chickens (poussins) or Cornish game hens (1 to 1 1/4 pounds each)
1/3 cup all-purpose flour
1 1/4 teaspoons freshly ground pepper
2 tablespoons unsalted butter
2 tablespoons olive oil
1/2 pound carrots (3 or 4 medium), diced
3 medium leeks (white and tender green), chopped
1/2 cup dry white wine
2 1/2 cups chicken stock or canned broth
3/4 pound small red potatoes, unpeeled and cut into 1-inch cubes
1 cup peas, fresh or thawed frozen
1 garlic clove, minced
1 tablespoon minced fresh thyme or 1 teaspoon dried
Baking Powder Biscuits (p. 142)
Chopped fresh thyme or parsley, for garnish

1. Preheat the oven to 375°. Cut the birds lengthwise in half. Rinse and pat dry. In a shallow dish, combine the flour with the salt and pepper. Dust the birds with the seasoned flour, reserving the excess.

2. In a large skillet, melt the butter in the oil over moderately high heat. Add the chickens, skin-side down, in batches if necessary, and sauté, turning, until nicely browned, 3 to 5 minutes. Remove and set aside.

3. Add the carrots and leeks; cook for 2 minutes. Sprinkle the reserved seasoned flour over the vegetables and toss to coat. Cook, stirring, for 1 to 2 minutes without browning. Add the wine and stock and bring to a boil, scraping up any browned bits from the bottom of the pan. Add the potatoes, peas, garlic and thyme. Increase the heat to high and bring to a boil. Cook, stirring frequently, until the mixture is nicely thickened, 3 to 5 minutes.

4. Pour the vegetables and sauce into a large casserole. Arrange the chickens in a single layer on top of the sauce. Cover the casserole and bake for 20 minutes. (*The recipe can be prepared to this point up to 1 day ahead. Let cool, then cover and refrigerate. Reheat to lukewarm before proceeding.*)

5. Meanwhile, prepare the biscuits through Step 4.

6. After the casserole has baked for 20 minutes, increase the oven temperature to 425°. Arrange the biscuits over the birds. Return the casserole to the oven and bake, uncovered, until the biscuits are fluffy and golden brown, 12 to 15 minutes.

7. To serve, remove the biscuits; split if desired and divide among 4 warmed serving plates. Place a half chicken on each plate and cover generously with sauce and vegetables. Garnish with chopped thyme or parsley.

—Gayle Henderson Wilson

• • •

ROAST TURKEY WITH THREE-BREAD STUFFING

The stuffing for this turkey is based on one that Associate Editor Tina Ujlaki's mother, Lotte, prepares.

🍷 The medley of flavors on a Thanksgiving table requires an emphatic, fruity wine to complement both the turkey and the traditional sweeter side dishes as well. Try a sparkling wine, such as Domaine Chandon Blanc de Noirs, or a chilled light Nouveau red—either a Beaujolais Nouveau, such as Duboeuf, or a California example, such as Robert Pecota.

6 to 8 Servings

6½ tablespoons unsalted butter
14-pound fresh turkey, at room temperature, neck and giblets reserved
Three-Bread Stuffing (recipe follows)
½ teaspoon sweet Hungarian paprika
1 small onion, quartered
2 tablespoons all-purpose flour
½ teaspoon salt
¼ teaspoon freshly ground pepper

1. Preheat the oven to 450°. In a small saucepan, melt 4 tablespoons of the butter over low heat; remove from the heat. Dampen four 2-foot-long sheets of cheesecloth and soak them in the melted butter.

2. Shortly before you're ready to roast the turkey, loosely fill the large cavity with about 5 cups of the Three-Bread Stuffing; fill the neck cavity with another 2 cups. Wrap the remaining stuffing in buttered aluminum foil and refrigerate.

3. Skewer the neck cavity shut and truss the turkey with butcher's twine, tying the legs together to seal the large cavity. Set the turkey, breast-side up, on a rack in a large roasting pan. Cover the breast with the butter-soaked cheesecloth and place the turkey in the oven. Immediately reduce the heat to 325° and roast, basting occasionally with a bulb baster, until a meat thermometer inserted in the inner thigh reaches 155°, about 3½ hours.

4. Remove the cheesecloth and add the paprika to the pan. Place the remaining foil-wrapped stuffing in the oven to bake. Return the turkey to the oven and continue to roast, basting frequently, until the temperature in the inner thigh reaches 180°, about 1 hour longer.

5. While the turkey roasts, make the stock. In a medium saucepan, melt ½ tablespoon of the butter over moderately high heat. Add the onion and reserved neck and giblets and cook, turning, until well browned on all sides, about 10 minutes. Add 4 cups of water and bring to a boil. Reduce the heat to low and simmer, skimming occasionally, for 1½ hours. Strain the stock and set aside. You should have about 3 cups. (*The stock can be made up to 2 days ahead and kept in the refrigerator.*)

6. When the turkey is done, transfer it to a large platter and cover loosely with foil to keep warm. Remove the extra stuffing from the oven. Pour the pan juices into a wide cup or bowl and use a ladle to skim off the fat. Place the roasting pan over high heat and when it starts to sizzle and smoke, stir in the turkey stock, scraping up any browned bits from the bottom of the pan. Reduce the heat to moderate, stir in the pan juices and simmer for 5 minutes.

7. In a small bowl, mash the remaining 2 tablespoons butter with the flour until smooth. Whisk this paste into the gravy and bring to a boil, whisking until smooth. Reduce the heat to low and keep warm, stirring occasionally, while you carve the turkey. Season the gravy with the salt and pepper and stir in any accumulated juices from the turkey. Serve the turkey with the stuffing; pass the gravy separately.

—Tina Ujlaki

• • •

THREE-BREAD STUFFING

Makes About 11 Cups, Enough for a 14- to 16-Pound Turkey

½ pound rye bread, cut into 1-inch cubes
½ pound pumpernickel bread, cut into 1-inch cubes
½ pound sourdough bread, cut into 1-inch cubes
1 stick (4 ounces) unsalted butter
1 large onion, chopped
2 large celery ribs, chopped
1 teaspoon sweet Hungarian paprika
1 pound spicy sausage, such as Hungarian, hot Italian or chorizo
1 Granny Smith apple—peeled, cored and chopped
3 tablespoons chopped green olives
1 small jalapeño pepper, seeded and minced (optional)
¼ cup chopped parsley
1 tablespoon chopped fresh thyme or 1 teaspoon dried

½ teaspoon freshly ground black pepper
½ teaspoon salt
2 eggs, lightly beaten

1. Spread the bread cubes out in a large baking pan and let them dry overnight, uncovered.

2. In a large skillet, melt the butter over moderate heat. Add the onion and celery, reduce the heat to low and cook until softened but not browned, about 12 minutes. Sprinkle on the paprika and cook for 2 minutes longer.

3. In a medium saucepan, cover the sausage with 2 cups of water and poach over moderately high heat until cooked through, about 10 minutes. Drain, reserving 1 cup of the poaching liquid. Coarsely chop the sausage.

4. In a large bowl, combine the dried bread cubes with the cooked onion and celery, sausage, apple, olives, jalapeño, parsley, thyme, black pepper, salt, the reserved sausage poaching liquid and the eggs. Mix until well blended. Let cool completely before stuffing the turkey.

—Tina Ujlaki

• • •

ROAST WILD TURKEY WITH BLUE CORN BREAD AND CHORIZO STUFFING

This recipe from Stephan Pyles makes a particularly succulent roast turkey. Reserve the neck and giblets for the stock.

10 to 12 Servings

1 stick (4 ounces) plus 3 tablespoons unsalted butter
1 pound chorizo sausage, coarsely chopped
1 small onion, chopped
¼ cup diced celery
¼ cup diced carrot
4 serrano chiles or 2 jalapeños—seeded and minced
6 garlic cloves, minced
¼ cup diced peeled chayote (optional)
¼ cup bourbon
1 teaspoon minced fresh thyme or ½ teaspoon dried
1 teaspoon minced fresh sage or ¾ teaspoon dried
2 teaspoons chopped fresh coriander
Serrano Chile Blue Corn Bread (p. 139), crumbled
3¼ cups Turkey Stock (p. 247)
1¼ teaspoons salt
1 fresh turkey, preferably wild (about 10 pounds)
⅛ teaspoon freshly ground pepper
2 tablespoons all-purpose flour

1. In a large heavy skillet, melt 1 tablespoon of the butter over moderately high heat. Add the chorizo and cook, stirring occasionally, until lightly browned, 4 to 5 minutes. Remove and drain on paper towels. Wipe out the skillet.

2. In the same skillet, melt 4 tablespoons of the butter. Add the onion, celery, carrot, serrano chiles, garlic and chayote and cook over moderately high heat, stirring, until the vegetables soften slightly, about 3 minutes. Add the bourbon and cook until the liquid reduces by half, about 5 minutes.

3. Remove from the heat and stir in the thyme, sage, coriander, chorizo and crumbled Serrano Chile Blue Corn Bread. Moisten with ¼ cup of the stock and add 1 teaspoon of the salt; toss well.

4. Preheat the oven to 450°. Wash the turkey well and pat dry. Season the cavity with the remaining ¼ teaspoon salt and the pepper. Fill the cavity and the neck loosely with the corn bread stuffing. Wrap any extra stuffing in a buttered foil packet. Sew the openings of the turkey or skewer them shut, then truss the bird.

5. In a saucepan, melt 4 tablespoons of the butter. Soak a 2-foot-long double layer of cheesecloth in the butter. Set the turkey breast-side up on a greased rack in a roasting pan and cover the breast with the butter-soaked cheesecloth.

6. Put the turkey in the oven. Immediately, reduce the temperature to 325° and roast, basting with the pan juices every 30 minutes, until an instant-reading thermometer inserted into the thickest part of the thigh registers 155°, about 2 hours.

7. Remove the cheesecloth and continue to roast, basting every 20 minutes, until the internal temperature reaches 180°, about 1 hour longer. Bake the extra stuffing during the last 30 minutes.

8. Transfer the turkey to a carving board, cover loosely with foil and let rest for at least 15 and up to 30 minutes before carving.

9. Meanwhile, make the gravy. Mash the remaining 2 tablespoons butter and the flour together to form a paste. Skim the fat off the juices in the roasting pan. Pour in the remaining 3 cups stock and bring to a boil over moderately high heat, scraping up any browned bits from the bottom of the pan. Gradually whisk in the butter paste and boil, whisking constantly, until thickened. Reduce the heat and simmer for 5 minutes. Season the gravy with salt and pepper to taste.

10. Carve the turkey and serve with the stuffing. Strain the gravy into a sauceboat and pass separately.

—Stephan Pyles,
Routh Street Cafe, Dallas

• • •

CHILE-ROASTED TURKEY

To reduce the cooking time, I cut up the turkey before roasting it (see Step 3). This recipe was designed to be served cool, but it is also delicious hot. Just be sure to let the turkey rest for at least 15 minutes before slicing.

🍷 Despite the spiciness of the preparation, turkey is a mild meat best enhanced by a light, fruity red, which would also work well with the lively flavors of the side dishes. A 1987 Beaujolais-Villages from Louis Latour or Louis Jadot, or a 1985 Renato Ratti Dolcetto, would be delicious.

16 Servings

6 ancho chiles (about 3 ounces)
1 cup boiling water
3 garlic cloves, lightly crushed
1 medium onion, quartered
1 tablespoon fresh lime juice
1 tablespoon corn oil
½ teaspoon salt
12-pound turkey, preferably fresh

1. Preheat the oven to 350°. Arrange the ancho chiles on a baking sheet and heat in the oven until softened, about 2 minutes. Cut open the chiles and discard the stems, seeds and ribs. Rinse the chiles and place in a small bowl; cover with the boiling water and let soak for 30 minutes.

2. In a food processor, combine the chiles with ¼ cup of their soaking liquid, the garlic, onion, lime juice, corn oil and salt. Puree until smooth, about 2 minutes, scraping down the sides of the bowl once or twice. *(The chile puree can be made up to 3 days ahead and refrigerated in a covered container.)*

3. Cut up the turkey: Pull the turkey leg away from the body and, with a sharp knife, cut through the hip joint to remove the thigh and drumstick in one piece. Repeat with the other leg. Starting at the neck, cut the meat from one half of the breast, cutting and scraping against the bone and keeping the blade of the knife as close to the rib cage as possible. Cut through the wing joint and remove the wing and boneless breast half in one piece. Repeat with the other side. There will be 4 large pieces of turkey. Discard the neck, giblets and carcass or reserve them for stock.

4. Score the turkey skin at 1-inch intervals. Rub the chile puree all over the pieces of turkey. Let marinate at room temperature for 1 hour, or in a large plastic bag in the refrigerator for up to 24 hours. Let return to room temperature before cooking.

5. Preheat the oven to 450°. Arrange the turkey pieces, skin-side up, in a single layer in a large shallow baking pan and place in the middle of the oven. Reduce the oven temperature to 325° and bake for 1½ hours, or until the thickest part of the thigh registers 170° on an instant-reading thermometer and the juices run clear.

6. Remove the turkey from the oven and let cool. Separate the wings from the breast and carve each breast into thin slices. Cut the remaining meat off the thigh and leg bones. *(The turkey is, of course, best when freshly cooked, but it can be made up to 2 days ahead, wrapped well and refrigerated. Let return to room temperature before serving.)*

—Diana Sturgis

• • •

SUMMERTIME TURKEY BUFFET

Here's a no-fuss turkey dinner for the warm weather. The turkey is cut up before roasting, thus eliminating the stuffing and basting, as well as shortening the time the oven is on—an important consideration in the hot summer months. Serves 16.

Chile-Roasted Turkey (p. 84)

Composed Salad of Tomatoes, Peppers and Goat Cheese with Shallot Vinaigrette (p. 241)

Black Bean and Celery Salad (p. 129)

Corn on the Cob with Lime-Coriander Butter (p. 253)

Pepita and Bacon Corn Bread (p. 140)

🍷 *Mexican Beer, a Pitcher of Margaritas and Seltzer*

Strawberries and Blueberries with Whipped Cream

Iced Coffee

TURKEY GUMBO

This gumbo, developed by Associate Test Kitchen Director Marcia Kiesel, takes advantage of the turkey leftovers—carcass, meat and gravy.

6 to 8 Servings

1 turkey carcass, broken into pieces
2 large ancho chiles
1 cup boiling water
1 pound smoked hot andouille or chorizo sausage, sliced ¼ inch thick
Zest of 1 juice orange, cut into thin strips
2 large onions, chopped
2 large green bell peppers, chopped
2 large red bell peppers, chopped
4 medium celery ribs, chopped
8 garlic cloves, minced
3 tablespoons all-purpose flour
3 tablespoons tomato paste

⅓ cup fresh orange juice
Leftover turkey gravy (optional)
1 teaspoon thyme
1 teaspoon oregano
1 teaspoon basil
2 bay leaves
2 cups diced (1-inch) cooked turkey
½ pound okra, sliced
¾ teaspoon salt
2 tablespoons filé powder
6 cups cooked white rice, as accompaniment

1. Put the turkey carcass in a large, deep saucepan or flameproof casserole, cover with 2½ quarts cold water and bring to a boil over high heat. Reduce the heat to low and simmer, skimming occasionally, for 1½ hours.

2. Strain the stock and return it to the saucepan; there will be about 8 cups. Boil the stock over high heat until reduced to 6 cups, about 20 minutes. Set aside.

3. Meanwhile, in a small bowl, cover the ancho chiles with the boiling water. Cover with plastic wrap and let stand until the chiles are softened, about 30 minutes. Drain, reserving the liquid. Discard the stems and seeds from the chiles and puree in a food processor with ⅓ cup of the reserved soaking liquid until smooth.

4. In a large flameproof casserole or saucepan, brown the sausage slices over high heat. Remove with a slotted spoon and drain on paper towels.

5. Pour off all but 3 tablespoons of the fat and add the orange zest. Reduce the heat to moderately high and cook until the zest is lightly browned, about 3 minutes. Add the onions, green and red bell peppers, celery and garlic. Reduce the heat to low, cover and cook, stirring occasionally, until the vegetables are softened, about 25 minutes.

6. Uncover and increase the heat to high. Cook, stirring occasionally, until the excess liquid has evaporated and the vegetables start to brown, about 5 minutes. Add the flour and cook, stirring, for 1 minute. Stir in the tomato paste and cook for 1 minute longer. Whisk in the orange juice, reserved stock and leftover turkey gravy. Stir in the reserved ancho puree, the sausage slices and the thyme, oregano, basil, bay leaves and diced turkey. Reduce the heat to low and simmer, stirring occasionally, for 30 minutes.

7. Increase the heat to moderate, add the okra and cook until tender, about 8 minutes. Season the gumbo with the salt and stir in the filé powder. Simmer for 1 minute and remove from the heat. Serve with cooked rice on the side. (*The recipe can be prepared ahead to this point. Let cool completely, then cover and refrigerate for up to 3 days or freeze for up to 1 month. Let thaw, if necessary, and bring to a simmer before proceeding.*)

—*Marcia Kiesel*

• • •

DUCK BREASTS WITH HONEY AND CRANBERRIES

Chef Philippe Thème, of La Riboto de Taven in Les Baux-de-Provence, created this zesty dish, which includes a marvelous sauce flavored with lime zest, cranberries and honey.

🍷 The perfect wine with the rich duck and its tart sauce is a glass of sweet, honey-scented Muscat de Beaumes-de-Venise, from Domaine des Bernardins. If you prefer a red wine, try an intense, complex northern Rhône, such as 1983 Jasmin Côte-Rôti or 1983 Chapoutier Hermitage.

—4 Servings—

Grated zest of 2 limes
2 tablespoons extra-virgin olive oil
2 large carrots, finely diced
1 medium onion, finely diced
4 boneless duck breast halves, skin on (about 4 ounces each)
Salt and freshly ground pepper
¼ cup fresh lime juice
1 cup duck or chicken stock, or canned broth
1 tablespoon honey, preferably lavender honey
1 cup cranberries, fresh or frozen

1. Put the lime zest in a small saucepan and add 1 cup of cold water. Bring to a boil over high heat. Drain into a fine-mesh sieve, rinse the zest under cold running water and repeat the procedure once more. Drain the lime zest on paper towels and set aside.

2. In a large nonreactive skillet, heat 1 tablespoon of the oil over moderately high heat. Add the carrots and onion and sauté until the onion is golden brown, 6 to 8 minutes. Transfer to a warm bowl and cover to keep warm.

3. With a sharp knife, score the skin of the duck breasts. In the same large skillet, heat the remaining 1 tablespoon oil over moderately high heat. Add the duck, skin-side down, and sauté, turning once, until lightly browned outside and rare to medium-rare inside, 4 to 6 minutes on each side. Season lightly with salt and pepper. Remove from the pan and cover with foil to keep warm.

4. Pour off the fat from the skillet. Add the lime juice, stock and honey. Bring to a boil over moderately high heat, scraping up any browned bits from the bottom of the pan. Add the cranberries and cook until they begin to pop open, 1 to 2 minutes; remove from the heat. Using a slotted spoon, scoop out ¼ cup of the cranberries and reserve.

5. In a food processor, puree the remaining cranberries together with the cooking liquid. Pass the sauce through a sieve and return to the skillet. Set over low heat to keep warm.

6. Carve the duck breasts lengthwise into thin strips if desired. Divide the duck and the vegetables among 4 warmed dinner plates. Spoon the reserved cranberries and some of the sauce over the duck. Garnish with the grated lime zest. Pass any remaining sauce separately.

—Phillip Thème, La Riboto de Taven, Les Baux-de-Provence, France

• • •

DUCK WITH RASPBERRIES

Raspberry vinegar and fresh raspberries provide a tart counterpart to the rich, caramelized duck.

🍷 To stand up to the richness of the duck and the intensity of the raspberries, a fine young Bordeaux or California Cabernet Sauvignon would be excellent; even better, try a rich, youthful Pomerol such as the 1981 Château Trotanoy or the 1984 Duckhorn Napa Valley Merlot.

6 Servings

3 ducks (about 4½ pounds each), necks and gizzards reserved
2 carrots, thickly sliced
2 onions, thickly sliced
4½ cups dry white wine
1 stick (4 ounces) unsalted butter
1 tablespoon sugar
3 garlic cloves, lightly crushed
¾ cup raspberry vinegar
3 large tomatoes, coarsely chopped
1 tablespoon plus 2 teaspoons tomato paste
Bouquet garni: 6 sprigs of parsley, 1 bay leaf and 3 sprigs of thyme, tied together with string
Salt and freshly ground pepper
1½ cups fresh raspberries

1. Cut off the wing tips from the ducks and set aside. Cut off the leg/thigh pieces and the whole breasts. Using a heavy sharp knife, cut lengthwise through the bone to halve the breasts.

2. With the same knife or a cleaver, coarsely chop the remaining duck carcasses. Put the carcasses in a large nonreactive saucepan and add the reserved wing tips, necks and gizzards along with the carrots, onions, wine and 8 cups of water, or to cover. Bring to a boil, reduce the heat and simmer for 1½ hours.

3. Strain the stock into a large saucepan and boil over high heat until reduced to 2 cups. (*The recipe can be prepared to this point up to 2 days ahead. Cover and refrigerate the stock.*)

4. Meanwhile, melt 2 tablespoons of the butter in a large flameproof casserole. Add the duck pieces, in batches, and sauté over moderately high heat, turning, until nicely browned, about 3 minutes on each side.

5. Return all the duck to the casserole, sprinkle on the sugar and add the garlic. Cover and cook over moderately low heat for 20 minutes.

6. Drain the fat from the casserole and add the raspberry vinegar, scraping up any brown bits from the bottom of the casserole. Stir in the chopped tomatoes, tomato paste and bouquet garni. Cover and cook the sauce over moderate heat for 10 minutes.

7. Preheat the oven to 500°. Remove the duck to a baking dish or ovenproof platter. Add the duck stock to the casserole and boil over moderately high heat until the liquid is reduced by half, about 10 minutes. Remove from the heat. Cut the remaining 6 tablespoons butter into pieces and whisk into the sauce; season with salt and pepper to taste.

8. Strain the sauce over the duck, pressing hard on the solids to extract all the liquid. Sprinkle the raspberries over the duck and bake in the oven for about 5 minutes, or until just heated through.

—André Soltner, Lutèce, New York City

• • •

SOPHISTICATED SUPPER

This straightforward but extremely elegant meal comes from André Soltner, the Alsatian chef-owner of Lutèce restaurant in New York City. Serves 6.

Ballottine of Sole (p. 55)

Green Mayonnaise (p. 254)

🍷 *Alsace Riesling or Washington State Johannisberg Riesling*

Duck with Raspberries (p. 86)

Fresh Noodles

🍷 *Muscat de Beaumes-de-Venise or Côte-Rôti or Chapoutier Hermitage*

Orange Tart (p. 204)

GUINEA HEN WITH BLACK OLIVES

This recipe combines many of the finest ingredients of the Drôme, a sparsely populated area of northern Provence that includes Nyons, a lovely village surrounded by rolling fields of olive trees. The Drôme also has numerous farms that raise tender lamb, as well as the prized *pintade,* or guinea hen. If guinea hen is unavailable, this recipe could also be made with chicken.

🍷 Serve with a good red Côtes du Rhône, such as Cru de Coudelet.

4 Servings

3 ounces lean bacon, minced
4 shallots, minced
1 guinea hen (about 3 pounds), liver trimmed and reserved
3/4 cup (3 ounces) oil-cured black olives, preferably from Nyons, pitted and minced
1 tablespoon chopped fresh thyme or 1 1/2 teaspoons dried
1 tablespoon extra-virgin olive oil

1. Preheat the oven to 425°. In a large skillet, preferably nonstick, sauté the bacon and shallots over moderately high heat, stirring frequently, until the bacon is crisp and the shallots are browned, about 4 minutes. With a slotted spoon, transfer the bacon and shallots to a medium bowl.

2. In the bacon fat in the same pan, sauté the guinea hen liver over high heat until browned outside, about 1 minute on each side. Set aside to cool, then finely chop and add to the bacon and shallots. Stir in the olives and thyme.

3. Fill the cavity of the guinea hen with the olive stuffing and sew the opening closed. Brush the bird with the olive oil. Place on a rack and roast in the preheated oven, basting occasionally, until the juices run clear when you pierce a thigh with a skewer, about 1 hour.

4. Remove the bird from the oven and let rest for 10 minutes. Scoop the stuffing into a warmed serving bowl and carve the guinea hen.

—Patricia Wells

• • •

LE PERIGORD'S PHEASANT WITH CABBAGE

Chef Antoine Bouterin is especially partial to this light, flavorful dish in which crisp cabbage and tender pheasant breasts are perfumed with juniper.

4 Servings

2 pheasants (2 1/2 to 3 pounds each)
2 tablespoons plus 1 teaspoon olive oil
6 shallots, sliced
1 carrot, thinly sliced
1 teaspoon all-purpose flour
1 cup dry white wine
1 cup Brown Chicken Stock (p. 247)
1/2 teaspoon salt
1/2 teaspoon freshly ground pepper
1 teaspoon juniper berries
1 medium head of green cabbage, 4 large leaves reserved, the rest thinly sliced
1 1/2 tablespoons cold unsalted butter, cut into small pieces

1. Using a sharp knife, cut down the breastbone and along the rib cage to remove the breasts from the pheasants. Cut off the legs and thighs and reserve for another use. Chop the pheasant carcasses into small pieces.

2. In a large saucepan, heat 1 tablespoon of the olive oil over high heat. Add the pheasant bones, shallots and half the carrot slices, and reduce the heat to moderately high. Cook, stirring occasionally, until the bones and vegetables are browned, about 10 minutes.

3. Pour off the oil. Reduce the heat to moderate, add the flour and cook, stirring, for 1 minute. Add the wine, stock and a pinch of the salt and pepper. Crush 1 of the juniper berries, add to the stock and boil until the liquid is reduced to 1 cup, about 10 minutes. Strain the stock and set aside.

4. In a large steamer, place the shredded cabbage and remaining sliced carrot and juniper berries. Top with the cabbage leaves. Sprinkle with 1 teaspoon of the olive oil and steam until crisp-tender, about 8 minutes.

5. Preheat the broiler. Season the pheasant breasts with 1/4 teaspoon each of the salt and pepper. In a large skillet, heat the remaining 1 tablespoon olive oil over high heat. Add the breasts and sauté, turning once, until browned outside, about 1 1/2 minutes per side. Remove from the skillet and set aside. (They'll finish cooking later.)

6. Add the reserved pheasant stock to the pan and cook, scraping up any browned bits, until the liquid is reduced to 1/2 cup, about 2 minutes. Remove the pan from the heat and swirl in the cold butter. Season the sauce with the remaining 1/4 teaspoon salt and pepper.

7. Slice the pheasant breasts lengthwise about 1/4 inch thick and place on a baking sheet. Broil just until cooked through, about 1 minute. Place a large cabbage leaf on each plate and spoon the shredded cabbage mixture on the leaf. Arrange the pheasant slices on the cabbage and spoon the sauce over the meat.

—Antoine Bouterin, Le Périgord, New York City

• • •

BRAISED PHEASANT WITH POLENTA

This hearty pheasant dish is from Felidia Restaurant in New York City.

🍷 Fine, fruity Italian red, such as 1985 Gaja Vignarey Barbera d'Alba

4 Servings

2 teaspoons salt
7 tablespoons unsalted butter
3 imported bay leaves
1½ cups cornmeal, preferably Italian or coarse-grain
1 pheasant (3 to 3½ pounds), cut into 8 serving pieces
¼ cup extra-virgin olive oil
1 large onion, chopped
2 slices of bacon, chopped
1 teaspoon rosemary
4 whole cloves
2 teaspoons tomato paste
1 cup dry white wine
2½ cups chicken stock, preferably homemade
Freshly ground pepper
¼ cup freshly grated Parmesan cheese, or more as needed

1. Butter an 8-inch square pan or heatproof dish and set aside. In a large heavy saucepan, combine 4 cups of water with the salt, 1 tablespoon of the butter and 1 bay leaf. Bring to a simmer over moderate heat. Stirring constantly with a wooden spoon, very gradually sift in the cornmeal through the fingers of one hand. When all the cornmeal has been added, reduce the heat to moderately low. Cook, stirring frequently, until the polenta is thick and smooth and pulls away from the sides of the saucepan, about 15 minutes. Pour the polenta into the buttered pan and set aside to cool.

2. Rinse the pheasant pieces and pat dry with paper towels. In a large skillet or flameproof casserole, heat the olive oil. Add the onion, bacon, rosemary, cloves and 2 remaining bay leaves and cook over moderate heat, stirring occasionally, until the onion softens, about 5 minutes. Add the pheasant and cook, turning once, until golden, about 5 minutes per side.

3. Stir in the tomato paste until evenly distributed; then stir in the white wine, scraping up any browned bits from the bottom of the skillet. Add the chicken stock and bring to a boil. Reduce the heat to low and simmer, partially covered, until the pheasant is tender, about 20 minutes for the breast pieces and 40 minutes for the legs. With a slotted spoon, transfer the pheasant to a plate, cover and keep warm.

4. Increase the heat to high and boil the liquid in the skillet until it is reduced to 1 cup, about 10 minutes. Strain the sauce through a fine sieve into a clean pan; skim off any excess fat. Season with salt and pepper to taste and return the pheasant to the sauce. *(The polenta and pheasant can be prepared to this point up to 2 days ahead. Cover and refrigerate. Reheat the pheasant in the sauce before proceeding.)*

5. Turn the polenta out of the pan; cut into 2-inch squares. In a large heavy skillet, melt the remaining 6 tablespoons butter over moderate heat. Add the polenta squares. Cook, turning gently once or twice with a spatula, until the polenta is heated through and lightly glazed, about 5 minutes. (Keep warm on a baking sheet in a low oven if not serving immediately.)

6. Arrange 2 pieces of pheasant on each warm serving plate and flank with the polenta squares. Pour the sauce over and around the polenta and pheasant. Sprinkle the polenta with the grated Parmesan cheese and serve immediately.

—Lidia Bastianich,
Felidia Ristorante, New York City

• • •

A PHEASANT AFFAIR

If you've always wanted to serve a game bird for dinner but haven't known exactly where to begin, try this delicious Italian pheasant dish. Not only are domestic pheasant commercially available, but pheasant meat is remarkably un-gamey. Serves 4.

Prosciutto-Wrapped Hearts of Palm (p. 14)

Grissini

Campari and Soda

Braised Pheasant with Polenta (p. 88)

Buttered Carrots and Fennel

🍷 *Fruity Italian Red Wine*

Chicory and Red Pepper Salad

Gianduja Mousse Cake (p. 165)

Espresso

QUAIL WITH COFFEE AND SPICE RUB

At Arcadia restaurant in New York, Anne Rosenzweig has combined imaginative ideas with a sure sense of traditional American themes. The results are gracefully inspired, as typified by this recipe.

Because the dish is simple to prepare and most of the work is done the day before, it is excellent for entertaining. The quail are delicious with Coffee-Flavored Nutty Pulau (coffee-flavored rice), which appears on page 137.

🍷 The sweetness of a Late-Harvest California Riesling or Spätlese brings out the warm tones and enhances the smoky quality that the dark-roast coffee lends to the meat.

6 Servings

2 tablespoons sesame seeds
20 black peppercorns
25 coriander seeds
3 cloves
2 juniper berries
1/4-inch piece of cinnamon stick
1/4 bay leaf
3 tablespoons freshly ground espresso coffee
1 teaspoon sugar
1 teaspoon salt
12 quail, backbones removed
2 tablespoons soy or corn oil
6 sprigs of fresh coriander, for garnish

1. Preheat the oven to 300°. In separate piles in a medium ovenproof skillet or on a baking sheet, toast the sesame seeds, peppercorns, coriander seeds, cloves, juniper berries, cinnamon stick and bay leaf in the oven until the sesame seeds are golden brown, about 25 minutes. Finely grind the spices and 1 tablespoon of the sesame seeds with a mortar and pestle or in a coffee mill or spice grinder. Add the ground coffee, sugar and salt and grind until the coffee is pulverized.

2. Flatten the quail and rub the spice mixture evenly over the skin; cover and refrigerate overnight. (*The recipe can be prepared to this point up to 1 day in advance. Let the quail return to room temperature before proceeding.*)

3. In a large heavy skillet, heat the oil. Add the quail, skin-side down, and sauté over moderately high heat until lightly browned, about 1 minute. Turn and cook until medium-rare, 1 to 2 minutes. Sprinkle on the remaining 1 tablespoon sesame seeds and garnish with the coriander sprigs.

—Anne Rosenzweig, Arcadia, New York City

• • •

GRILLED QUAIL WITH SWEET POTATO PANCAKES AND JICAMA-ORANGE RELISH

In this dish, from Stephan Pyles of Dallas's Routh Street Cafe, the cooking of the quail couldn't be simpler; it's the combined flavors of the quail and its accompaniments that makes this dish so very special.

🍷 This delicate game bird, with its mild accompaniments, calls for a red wine, such as a 1985 California Pinot Noir from Robert Stemmler.

4 First-Course or 2 Main-Course Servings

1 large sweet potato (1 pound), peeled and grated
1 medium baking potato (1/2 pound), peeled and grated
1/2 medium onion, grated
1 egg, lightly beaten
2 tablespoons maple syrup
1 1/2 tablespoons all-purpose flour
1 tablespoon fresh bread crumbs
3/4 teaspoon salt
1/2 teaspoon freshly ground pepper
Pinch of freshly grated nutmeg
2 tablespoons vegetable oil
4 quail—split along back, breastbones and backbones removed
Jicama-Orange Relish (p. 260), as accompaniment

1. Put the grated sweet and white potatoes in a colander and press to drain off as much liquid as possible. In a medium bowl, combine the potatoes with the onion, egg, maple syrup, flour, bread crumbs, 1/2 teaspoon of the salt, 1/4 teaspoon of the pepper and the nutmeg.

2. Preheat the broiler. In a large skillet, heat 1 1/2 teaspoons of the oil over medium heat. Spoon 1/4 cup of the batter into the skillet for each pancake; flatten gently and cook 4 at a time. Reduce the heat to moderate and cook until browned on the bottom, 3 to 4 minutes. Turn and cook the second side until browned, 2 to 3 minutes longer. Remove to a plate and cover with foil to keep warm. Repeat with another 1 1/2 teaspoons of the oil and the remaining batter.

3. Brush the quail with the remaining 1 tablespoon oil and season with the remaining 1/4 teaspoon each salt and pepper. Place the quail skin-side up on a baking sheet and broil about 5 inches from the heat for 3 to 4 minutes, until crisp and browned outside but still pink in the center.

4. To serve, arrange the potato pancakes on warmed plates. Split the quail in half and place on top of the pancakes. Serve with Jicama-Orange Relish.

—Stephan Pyles, Routh Street Cafe, Dallas

• • •

GRILLED SQUAB WITH ANCHO CHILE SAUCE

At Cafe Annie, Robert Del Grande serves these sqaubs with the Corn and Avocado Torta (p. 155).

🍷 Consider serving a rich, assertive Chardonnay, such as a 1984 Simi or even a 1984 Llano Estacado Texas Chardonnay, to provide a flavor backdrop for the spicy but subtle nuances of the dish.

4 Servings

4 squabs (1 pound each)—gizzards, hearts and necks reserved
1 tablespoon vegetable oil
3 cups chicken stock or canned broth
2 ancho chiles, stemmed and seeded
1 small onion, quartered
1 garlic clove, sliced
1 tablespoon maple syrup
1/8 teaspoon freshly ground pepper
Salt

1. To bone each squab, use kitchen shears to cut down both sides of the backbone; reserve the bones. Using a sharp knife, remove the breastbones and ribs; keep the breast meat intact.

2. In a large skillet, heat the oil. Add the reserved squab bones, gizzards, hearts and necks and cook over moderate heat, stirring occasionally, until nicely browned, about 15 minutes. Add 2 cups of the stock and bring to a boil. Reduce the heat to moderately low and simmer uncovered for 30 minutes.

3. Meanwhile, in a small bowl, soak the ancho chiles in the remaining 1 cup chicken stock until plumped and softened, about 30 minutes.

4. In a food processor or blender, combine the onion, garlic, maple syrup and ancho chiles with their soaking liquid. Puree until smooth. Stir the puree into the squab stock and simmer over moderately low heat for 30 minutes.

5. Strain the sauce into a medium saucepan. If the sauce is very thin, simmer to reduce it to a coating consistency. Season with the pepper and salt to taste; cover and set aside.

6. Preheat the broiler or a grill. Broil or grill the squabs, skin toward the heat, about 5 inches from the heat for 10 minutes or until browned. Turn and broil or grill the other side for about 2 minutes, until the birds are medium-rate and the juices run pink. Serve with the ancho chile sauce.

—*Robert Del Grande, Cafe Annie, Houston*

• • •

FIVE-SPICE ROAST SQUAB WITH RICE WINE-BUTTER SAUCE

🍷 A deep and flavorful California Chardonnay with oak nuances, such as a 1985 Beaulieu Vineyard "Los Carneros Reserve," would provide a refreshing contrast to the mild spice of these birds.

4 Servings

4 squabs (12 to 14 ounces each) or Cornish game hens
1 tablespoon Oriental sesame oil
1 tablespoon five-spice powder*
2 teaspoons coarse (kosher) salt
1 teaspoon Szechuan peppercorns,* toasted and crushed
2 tablespoons grated orange zest
1/2 cup chicken stock or canned broth
1/2 cup Chinese rice wine or dry sherry
2 tablespoons cold unsalted butter, cut into small pieces
2 tablespoons minced scallions
****Available at Oriental markets***

EAST MEETS WEST MENU

The marriage of Oriental and Western ingredients in this menu is the hallmark of Ken Hom's simple and tasty food. Serves 4.

Rice Paper Shrimp Rolls (p. 18)

Double Coriander-Ginger Cream Soup (p. 37)

Five-Spice Roast Squab with Rice Wine-Butter Sauce (p. 90)

Curry Couscous with Fresh Chives (p. 136)

🍷 *California Chardonnay*

Chinese Apple Pear Compote with Candied Ginger (p. 227)

Vanilla Ice Cream

1. Cut along both sides of the squabs' backbones and remove them. Press down on each bird to break the breastbone and flatten the birds. Fold the wings tips under. With the tip of a knife, cut a hole through the skin on either side of the breast just above the thigh. Push the ends of the legs through the slits to secure them. Rub the birds all over with the sesame oil.

2. In a small bowl, combine the five-spice powder, salt, Szechuan peppercorns and orange zest. Spread 1½ tea-

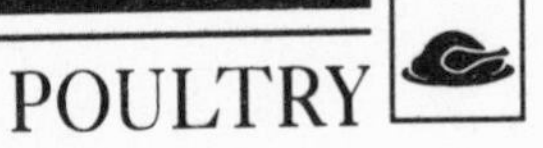

spoons of the seasoning under the breast skin of each squab and rub 1½ teaspoons over the skin. Place the birds, skin-side up, in a single layer in a small roasting pan or flameproof baking dish and let stand at room temperature for 1½ hours, or cover with plastic wrap and refrigerate overnight. (If refrigerated, let stand at room temperature for 1 hour before roasting.)

3. Preheat the oven to 475°. Roast the birds without turning until the skin is golden brown and the breast meat is just slightly pink near the bone, 15 to 20 minutes. Remove the squabs from the pan and skim off any fat from the juices.

4. Set the roasting pan over moderately high heat, add the chicken stock and rice wine and bring to a boil, scraping up any browned bits from the bottom of the pan. Boil, stirring, until the liquid is reduced to ½ cup. Remove from the heat and whisk in the butter and scallions.

5. Place a squab on each of 4 warmed dinner plates. Spoon a couple of tablespoons of the sauce over and around the squabs.

—Ken Hom

• • •

GRILLED SQUAB WITH DATE PUREE AND CUMIN-ORANGE SAUCE

Gifted chef Guenter Seeger of The Ritz-Carlton Buckhead in Atlanta was a *Michelin*-starred chef in his native Germany before he came to these shores a couple of years ago. Everything in this recipe can be prepared in advance; all you need to do at serving time is to grill the squab.

🍷 The slightly sweet puree and the intensity of the sauce that accompany this game bird require a powerful, tannic red wine, such as a 1981 Château de Pez or Château d'Angludet.

4 Servings

4 squab (10 to 12 ounces each)
2 tablespoons vegetable oil
1 small celery rib, chopped
1 small carrot, chopped
1 medium onion, chopped
1½ cups dry white wine
½ pound pitted dates
Zest of 2 large oranges, cut into thin julienne strips
1¼ cups fresh orange juice
¾ teaspoon cumin seeds
½ teaspoon salt
¾ teaspoon freshly ground pepper
1 tablespoon olive oil

1. With a sharp flexible knife, cut against the breastbones of the squab to remove each breast in a single piece. Cut off the leg/thigh pieces; set aside. Coarsely chop the remaining squab carcasses.

2. In a large saucepan, heat the vegetable oil. Add the carcasses and cook over moderately high heat, stirring frequently, until browned all over, about 4 minutes. Add the celery, carrot and onion, reduce the heat to moderate and cook, stirring, until the vegetables are browned, about 15 minutes.

3. Increase the heat to high and add the wine. Cook, stirring, until the wine is almost evaporated, about 10 minutes. Add 6 cups of cold water and bring to a boil. Reduce the heat to low and simmer, uncovered, for 1½ hours.

4. Strain the stock into a medium saucepan, pressing on the solids to extract as much liquid as possible. Boil the stock over high heat until reduced to 1½ cups, about 20 minutes.

5. Blanch the dates in a saucepan of boiling water for 30 seconds; drain well. While still hot, transfer the dates to a food processor. Add ½ cup of the reduced stock and puree until smooth. Strain the date puree through a sieve.

6. In a small saucepan of boiling water, blanch the strips of orange zest for 1 minute; drain well.

7. In a medium nonreactive saucepan, combine the orange zest, orange juice and cumin seeds. Boil over high heat until reduced by half, about 5 minutes. Add the remaining 1 cup squab stock and simmer until the sauce is slightly syrupy, about 8 minutes. Season with ¼ teaspoon each of the salt and pepper.

8. Preheat the broiler. Set the squab legs on one broiler rack and the breasts, skin-side up, on another. Season with the remaining ¼ teaspoon salt and ½ teaspoon pepper and brush with the olive oil. Broil the squab breasts about 5 inches from the heat until golden brown and medium-rare, about 4 minutes. Broil the legs until golden brown outside and medium inside, about 4½ minutes.

9. Reheat the orange sauce and the date puree. Spoon 1 tablespoon of the date puree onto two sides of 4 heated serving plates. Arrange the grilled squab in the center and spoon some of the orange sauce over the squab.

—Guenter Seeger,
The Ritz-Carlton Buckhead, Atlanta

• • •

AURORA'S PIGEON WITH SWEET GARLIC

Chef Gérard Pangaud serves this pigeon, or squab, with an assortment of green vegetables, such as fava beans, small peas, snow peas and thin green beans.

🍷 The richness of the bird and the use of garlic point to a rich, powerful red, such as the 1983 Jaboulet St. Joseph, or a California Pinot Noir, such as 1983 Soleterra.

4 Servings

2 tablespoons unsalted butter
4 squabs (about 3/4 pound each), trussed, livers reserved
24 garlic cloves, unpeeled
2 tablespoons dry white wine
1 cup Brown Chicken Stock (p. 247)
1/4 teaspoon salt
1/8 teaspoon freshly ground pepper
1 teaspoon minced parsley

1. Preheat the oven to 450°. In a large, heavy ovenproof skillet, heat the butter over moderately high heat. Add the squabs and sauté, turning, until lightly browned all over, about 2 minutes.

2. Scatter the garlic cloves around the birds. Place the skillet in the oven and roast until the squabs are medium-rare and their juices run pale pink when a skewer is inserted in a thigh, 12 to 15 minutes. Remove the birds from the skillet and cover with foil to keep warm.

3. Add the reserved livers to the skillet and sauté over moderately high heat until browned, about 2 minutes. Add the wine and scrape up any browned bits from the bottom of the skillet. Transfer the garlic, livers and liquid to a food mill and puree. Alternatively, puree in a food processor and strain through a fine sieve.

4. In a small saucepan, bring the stock to a boil. Reduce the heat to low and stir in the garlic and liver puree. Season with the salt and pepper and remove from the heat.

5. Place the squabs on a warmed serving platter. Spoon over some of the sauce and sprinkle with the parsley. Pass the remaining sauce separately.

—Gérard Pangaud, Aurora, New York City

• • •

MEAT

VEAL CHOP WITH TEXAS HAM, FRESH MOZZARELLA AND A RED PEPPER SAUCE

This recipe from Robert McGrath makes hearty portions for Texas-size appetites.
🍷 A lively, assertive red, such as a 1985 Saccardi or Podere Il Palazzino Chianti Classico, would underline the flavor of the sweet pepper sauce.

4 Servings

3/4 cup (about 6 ounces) wild rice
2 ounces wheat berries*
4 red bell peppers
1/4 cup chicken stock or canned broth
1 small garlic clove, minced
Pinch of salt
2 tablespoons heavy cream
1/8 teaspoon cayenne pepper
2 tablespoons unsalted butter
4 large veal chops (9 to 10 ounces each with the bone)
1/4 pound thinly sliced country ham, preferably from Texas, or Black Forest ham
1/4 pound fresh mozzarella cheese, thinly sliced
2 zucchini, cut into 2-by-1/2-inch strips
2 yellow squash, cut into 2-by-1/2-inch strips
****Available at health food stores***

1. In a heavy medium saucepan, combine the wild rice, wheat berries and 4 cups of salted water. Bring to a boil over moderately high heat. Reduce the heat to low, cover and simmer until the grains are tender, about 45 minutes. Keep warm.

2. Meanwhile, roast the red peppers over a gas flame or under the broiler, turning, until charred all over. Put the peppers in a paper bag and let steam for 10 minutes. Peel the peppers and discard the cores, seeds and ribs. Coarsely chop the peppers.

3. In a medium saucepan, combine the roasted peppers, chicken stock, garlic and salt. Bring to a boil over moderately high heat and add the cream. Reduce the heat and simmer for 1 minute.

4. Transfer the pepper mixture to a food processor or blender and puree until smooth. Stir in the cayenne and strain into a medium saucepan. Stir in 1 tablespoon of the butter.

5. Preheat the broiler. Using a small sharp knife, make a deep incision in the side of each veal chop to form a pocket. Fill the pockets with the ham and cheese slices and press to close. Set the chops on a lightly oiled rack and broil about 4 inches from the heat until browned, 4 to 5 minutes per side.

6. Meanwhile, in a large heavy skillet, melt the remaining 1 tablespoon butter over moderately high heat. Add the zucchini and yellow squash and sauté until crisp-tender, 5 to 6 minutes.

7. Spoon about 1/4 cup of the sauce onto 4 heated plates. Place a veal chop on one side of the plate. Arrange the zucchini, yellow squash, wild rice and wheat berries on the other side and serve.

—Robert McGrath,
Four Seasons Hotel, Dallas

• • •

A GRATIFYING MIDWINTER MEAL

The natural sweetness of carrots and onions adds a rich caramel flavor to this satisfying old-fashioned pot roast dinner from Lee Bailey. Serves 6.

Onion Pot Roast (p. 94)

Charred Carrot Puree (p. 153)

Shredded Cabbage with Sautéed Black Mustard Seeds (p. 154)

🍷 *Hearty Red Wine*

Tangerine Mousse (p. 211)

Coffee

ONION POT ROAST

This old-fashioned dish has a warm and satisfying taste. It cooks practically by itself in the oven and yields enough for about eight guests, or six with leftovers, which make marvelous sandwiches the next day.
🍷 Spicy red, such as 1985 Ravenswood Zinfandel

6 to 8 Servings

1 tablespoon safflower or corn oil
6 pounds first-cut brisket
6 large garlic cloves, crushed through a press
1 1/2 teaspoons fresh thyme or 1/2 teaspoon dried
1 teaspoon salt
1 teaspoon freshly ground pepper
4 large onions—2 coarsely chopped, 2 cut into 1/2-inch-thick rings
2 medium carrots, sliced 1/4 inch thick
1 cup beef stock or canned broth
2 tablespoons tomato paste
2 cups dry red wine

1. Preheat the oven to 300°. In a large nonreactive flameproof casserole, heat the oil over moderately high heat. Add the meat and sauté, turning, until browned, 3 to 5 minutes.

2. Rub the top of the meat with the garlic and thyme and season with 1/2 teaspoon each of the salt and pepper.

3. Turn the meat over and season the other side with the remaining 1/2 teaspoon each salt and pepper. Pack the coarsely chopped onions on top of the meat, transfer to the oven and bake the pot roast, uncovered, for 1 hour.

4. Turn the brisket over and sprinkle with the carrots and the onion rings. In a bowl, whisk together the stock and tomato paste until blended. Add to the brisket along with the wine. Cover and bake for another 3½ hours.

5. Transfer the meat to a carving board. Cut crosswise on the diagonal into ½-inch slices. Skim the fat off any remaining pan juices and spoon the vegetables and juices over the meat.

—Lee Bailey

• • •

BOILED BRISKET WITH LEMON HORSERADISH SAUCE

A lot of celery is called for in the brisket cooking liquid, which I find enriches its flavor noticeably.

6 Servings

4 pounds first-cut brisket
6 large celery ribs, chopped
3 medium onions—2 halved, 1 chopped
2 medium carrots, unpeeled and chopped
4 sprigs of parsley
2 bay leaves
¾ teaspoon thyme
1¾ teaspoons salt
4 tablespoons unsalted butter
2 tablespoons all-purpose flour
2 cups chicken stock or canned broth
⅓ cup drained prepared white horseradish
1 tablespoon fresh lemon juice
½ teaspoon grated lemon zest
¼ teaspoon freshly ground white pepper, or more to taste

1. In a large flameproof casserole or saucepan, combine the brisket, celery, halved onions, carrots, parsley, bay leaves, thyme and 1½ teaspoons of the salt with enough water to cover by 1 or 2 inches. Bring to a boil over high heat. Reduce the heat to low and simmer, partially covered, skimming occasionally, until the meat is fork-tender, about 4 hours. (*The brisket can be held in the warm liquid for up to 1 hour.*)

2. In a small saucepan, melt the butter over moderate heat. Add the chopped onion and cook until golden brown, about 15 minutes.

3. Sprinkle on the flour and cook, stirring, for 1 to 2 minutes without browning. Slowly whisk in the chicken stock. Bring to a boil, whisking, until thickened. Reduce the heat to low and simmer for about 10 minutes.

4. Stir in the horseradish, lemon juice, lemon zest, white pepper and remaining ¼ teaspoon salt. Simmer for 2 minutes. Serve warm, with the brisket.

—Lee Bailey

• • •

GRILLED FLANK STEAK WITH PECANS, BLACK BEANS AND FRESH CORIANDER

Stephan Pyles recommends serving this tasty steak with warm flour tortillas. Typical of the new southwestern style, the black beans are used here as a garnish rather than as a filler.

🍷 This hearty dish calls for a gutsy, straightforward red, such as 1983 Estrella River Syrah from California or a 1985 Vidal-Fleury Côtes du Rhône.

4 to 6 Servings

1 flank steak (1½ to 2 pounds)
1½ plus ⅓ cup dry red wine
¾ cup corn oil
2 tablespoons soy sauce
3 tablespoons chopped fresh coriander
2 jalapeño peppers with seeds, chopped
5 garlic cloves, 3 chopped, 2 left whole
1 tablespoon coarsely cracked black pepper
⅓ cup pecan halves
2 sticks (½ pound) plus 2½ tablespoons unsalted butter
4 serrano chiles (or 2 more jalapeños), seeded and diced
1 tablespoon minced chives
⅓ cup chicken stock or canned broth
⅓ cup red wine vinegar
1 large shallot, chopped
1 teaspoon fresh lime juice
¼ cup canned or cooked black beans, drained and rinsed
Salt and freshly ground pepper
Warm flour tortillas, as accompaniment

1. Put the flank steak in a shallow nonreactive pan. Add 1½ cups of the wine, the oil, soy sauce, 2 tablespoons of the coriander, the jalapeños, chopped garlic and coarsely cracked black pepper. Cover and marinate in the refrigerator for at least 2 hours or overnight.

2. Preheat the oven to 350°. In a small baking dish, toast the pecans until lightly browned, about 5 minutes. Remove from the oven and set aside.

3. Rub the remaining 2 whole garlic cloves with ½ tablespoon of the butter and roast in the oven until soft and light brown, about 20 minutes. Reduce the oven temperature to 250°.

4. In a mortar, combine the toasted pecans, roasted garlic and serrano chiles. Crush with a pestle. Blend in 2 tablespoons of the butter and the chives.

5. Preheat a grill or the broiler. In a medium nonreactive saucepan, combine the stock, remaining ⅓ cup red wine, the vinegar, shallot and 1 teaspoon of the corainder. Bring to a boil over moderate heat and boil until reduced to 2 tablespoons, 10 to 12 minutes.

6. Reduce the heat to low and whisk in the remaining 2 sticks of butter, 2 tablespoons at a time. Stir in the remaining 2 teaspoons coriander and the lime juice. Whisk in the pecan butter. Stir in the black beans and season the sauce with salt and pepper to taste. Keep the sauce warm over simmering water.

7. Lightly brush the flank steak with oil. Season with salt and pepper. Grill the steak over a moderately hot fire or broil until medium rare, 5 to 7 minutes.

8. Thinly slice the steak crosswise on the diagonal and arrange on warmed plates. Spoon the sauce over each serving and accompany with warm flour tortillas.

—*Stephan Pyles,*
Routh Street Cafe, Dallas

• • •

FILLET STEAKS ON FRIED TOAST

This tempting beef dish will alleviate any winter woes. (The steaks should be at room temperature before frying.)

🍷 Fruity red, such as 1984 Viña Cumbrero Rioja

6 Servings

6 slices of French bread slightly larger than the steaks, cut 1/2 inch thick
6 tablespoons unsalted butter, softened
6 fillet steaks, cut 1¾ inch thick (2¾ pounds total)
1 large garlic clove, cut in half
1/2 teaspoon salt
1/2 teaspoon freshly ground pepper
2 teaspoons safflower oil

1. Trim the crusts from the bread. Spread 4 tablespoons of the butter over both sides of the bread slices. In a large skillet, fry the bread over moderate heat until golden brown on the bottom, 3 to 4 minutes. Turn and fry the other side until golden, about 2 minutes. Drain on paper towels. (*The toast can be prepared several hours in advance. Let cool slightly; then cover loosely with waxed paper to keep crisp.*)

2. Preheat the oven to 400°. Rub both sides of each steak with a piece of cut garlic. Season the meat on both sides with the salt and pepper.

3. Heat a large, heavy ovenproof skillet, preferably cast iron, over high heat for 3 minutes. Add the oil and swirl to coat the bottom of the skillet with a thin film. Put the meat in the skillet and cook, turning once, until well browned, about 3 minutes per side. Drain the oil from the skillet and turn the steaks over.

4. Immediately transfer the skillet to the oven and bake for 5 minutes. Turn and bake for 5 minutes, until medium-rare. (If you like your meat rarer or better done, subtract or add 2 minutes.)

5. Immediately put each steak on a slice of fried toast and top each with 1 teaspoon of the remaining butter.

—*Lee Bailey*

• • •

FILLET STEAKS WITH MUSHROOMS AND BEARNAISE SAUCE

The combination of beef, mushrooms and béarnaise sauce is a treat for any steak lover.

All accompaniments should be ready in advance. Sautéed potatoes are excellent with the steaks and can be reheated at the same time as the mushroom duxelles. The sauce should be warm, and there should be sprigs of watercress for a bright green garnish.

🍷 Red Burgundy (or Pinot Noir) is the classic wine to serve with beef. The accompanying mushrooms and béarnaise sauce call for a robust example, either 1983 Beaune Clos des Mouches (Drouhin) or 1985 Saintsbury Carneros Pinot Noir.

6 Servings

2 tablespoons unsalted butter
4 large shallots, minced
¾ pound mushrooms, minced
1/4 teaspoon salt
1/8 teaspoon freshly ground pepper
1½ teaspoons tomato paste
1 tablespoon vegetable oil
6 center-cut fillet steaks (tournedos), 1 to 1¼ inches thick
Béarnaise Sauce (p. 253)
Sprigs of watercress, for garnish

1. In a large, heavy skillet, melt the butter over moderate heat. Add the shallots and cook until softened but not browned, about 2 minutes. Increase the heat to moderately high and stir in the mushrooms. Sauté until most of the moisture has evaporated, about 4 minutes. Season with the salt and pepper. Remove from the heat and stir in the tomato paste. (*The mushroom duxelles can be made up to 3 hours ahead. Set aside at room temperature.*)

2. In a large heavy skillet, heat the oil over moderately high heat. Add the steaks and sauté, turning, until rare or medium-rare, 3 to 4 minutes on each side. Season with additional salt and pepper to taste. Top each steak with a layer of the mushroom duxelles and partially coat with a couple of spoonfuls of the warm Béarnaise Sauce. Garnish with the sprigs of watercress. Pass the remaining sauce separately.

—*Richard Grausman*

• • •

BEEF DAUBE WITH WILD MUSHROOMS AND ORANGE

I am convinced that in Provence there are as many recipes for beef stew (daube) as there are households. This version, flavored with mushrooms and orange, comes from a favorite family restaurant—Auberge de la Madone—situated just north of Nice in the village of Peillon. Although chef Christian Millo uses wild cèpes, cultivated mushrooms are a worthy substitute when cèpes are not available. Plan to marinate the meat one day ahead. Steamed potatoes go well with this dish.

🍷 Serve with the same wine used in cooking, a solid red such as Nice's Bellet, Château de Crémat.

8 Servings

4½ pounds trimmed lean beef chuck, cut into 2-inch cubes
4 carrots, sliced
3 medium onions, coarsely chopped
2 garlic cloves
1 sprig of parsley
1 celery rib, thickly sliced
3 imported bay leaves
1 tablespoon fresh thyme or 1 teaspoon dried
¼ cup marc de Provence or Cognac
1 bottle sturdy red wine, such as Côtes de Provence
¼ cup plus 1 tablespoon extra-virgin olive oil
1 teaspoon peppercorns
3 whole cloves
3 tablespoons unsalted butter
1 pound fresh cèpes or cultivated mushrooms, trimmed and sliced
1 tablespoon tomato paste
1 teaspoon salt
¼ teaspoon freshly ground pepper
Grated zest and juice of 1 large orange

1. In a large bowl, combine the meat with the carrots, onions, garlic, parsley, celery, bay leaves, thyme, marc, red wine and 1 tablespoon of the olive oil. Tie the peppercorns and cloves in a piece of cheesecloth and add them to the bowl; toss well. Cover and refrigerate for 24 hours, stirring once or twice.

2. Let the meat and vegetables return to room temperature. With a slotted spoon, remove the meat from the marinade, drain well and pat dry on paper towels. With a slotted spoon, remove the vegetables and set them aside. Transfer the marinade and the cheesecloth bag to a large flameproof casserole and boil for 5 minutes over moderately high heat to reduce slightly. Remove from the heat.

3. In a large heavy skillet, melt the butter in the remaining ¼ cup oil over high heat. When the foam subsides, add half the meat and sauté, tossing, until browned all over, about 5 minutes. With a slotted spoon, transfer the meat to the liquid in the casserole. Repeat with the remaining meat.

4. In the same skillet, sauté the reserved vegetables until browned, about 7 minutes. Transfer the vegetables to the casserole. Add the mushrooms to the skillet and sauté until lightly browned, about 5 minutes; set aside.

5. Stir the tomato paste into the casserole and bring to a simmer over moderately low heat. Reduce the heat to very low and simmer, skimming occasionally, until the meat is very tender, 3½ to 4 hours.

6. Stir in the salt and pepper, the reserved mushrooms and the orange zest and juice. Remove the cheesecloth bag of cloves and peppercorns. *(The recipe can be prepared 2 to 3 days ahead and refrigerated. Reheat before serving.)*

—Patricia Wells

• • •

HEAVENLY BEEF PIE WITH RICH MASHED POTATO TOPPING

This dish is of mixed heritage. Not really a shepherd's pie, but a combination of two freely adapted Alice B. Toklas recipes that make an entirely new French connection.

🍷 1983 Spanish red, such as Torres Gran Coronas

6 Servings

BEEF FILLING:
2 pounds trimmed boneless sirloin steak (½ inch thick), cut into 1-inch pieces
½ cup Cognac or brandy
¼ pound salt pork, cut into ¼-inch dice
5 tablespoons unsalted butter
1 tablespoon vegetable oil
12 small white boiling onions, peeled
1 tablespoon all-purpose flour
2 cups dry red wine
Bouquet garni: 3 sprigs of Italian flat-leaf parsley, 1 sprig of thyme, 1 bay leaf, 5 peppercorns and 1 lightly crushed garlic clove tied in cheesecloth
1½ cups small mushroom caps

MASHED POTATO TOPPING:
2½ pounds baking potatoes
½ teaspoon salt
⅛ teaspoon freshly ground white pepper
⅛ teaspoon freshly grated nutmeg
4½ tablespoons unsalted butter, melted
2 egg yolks
3 tablespoons heavy cream

1. *Prepare the filling:* Put the steak in a shallow glass or ceramic dish and pour ⅓ cup of the Cognac over it. Cover and let stand at room temperature for 3 hours, or refrigerate for 6 hours.

2. In a small saucepan, cover the salt pork with water and bring to a boil; boil for 4 minutes. Drain well.

3. In a heavy nonreactive saucepan or flameproof casserole, melt 3 tablespoons of the butter in the oil over moderately high heat. Remove the steak from the dish and pat dry with paper towels. Add the meat to the pan in batches and cook, turning, until well browned, about 5 minutes. Transfer to a plate.

4. In the same pan, cook the salt pork over moderately high heat until golden brown, 3 to 5 minutes. Remove and add to the beef.

5. Cut a cross in the root end of each onion. Add to the pan and cook, tossing, until golden brown, 3 to 5 minutes. Using a slotted spoon, transfer to a bowl.

6. Drain off all but 1 tablespoon drippings from the pan. Whisk in the flour and cook over low heat, stirring constantly, for about 2 minutes without coloring. Whisk in the wine and ½ cup of water. Bring to a boil, scraping the sides and bottom of the pan with a wooden spoon.

7. Return the meat to the pan and add the bouquet garni. Pour the remaining Cognac into a small saucepan and carefully ignite. When the flames subside, pour over the meat. Cover and cook over moderately low heat for 1 hour.

8. Add the onions and cook, partially covered, until the meat and onions are just tender and the sauce is thickened, about 30 minutes.

9. Meanwhile, in a large skillet, melt the remaining 2 tablespoons butter over moderately high heat. Add the mushroom caps and sauté, turning, until browned on both sides, about 5 minutes. Remove and set aside. When the meat and onions are tender, stir in the mushrooms and remove from the heat.

10. *Make the topping:* Preheat the oven to 400°. Bake the potatoes until tender, about 1 hour; leave the oven on. When cool enough to handle, cut the potatoes in half and scoop out the insides; discard the skins. Rice the potatoes into a bowl and beat in the salt, white pepper, nutmeg and 4 tablespoons of the melted butter. Beat in the egg yolks and cream.

11. Spoon the beef stew into a 1½-quart shallow baking dish about 2 inches deep. Spread the mashed potatoes over the top. Drizzle on the remaining 1½ teaspoons melted butter and bake in the upper third of the oven for 15 minutes. If the top is not browned, run the pie under the broiler for 1 or 2 minutes.

—Phillip Stephen Schulz

• • •

CHILI FOR CHILI DOGS

You have two important decisions to make when you prepare chili dogs. The first is whether to degrease the chili or not. To degrease, refrigerate the chili overnight and spoon off and discard any fat that has congealed on the surface. The second is whether to peel your hot dogs if you're using those with the natural casings left on. If you don't peel, the hot dog stays crunchy; if you remove the skin, the chili sinks into the hot dog and the tastes become inseparably delicious.

Intensely flavored with cinnamon, this recipe is closer to Cincinnati chili than to real Texas chili. It's just as good on spaghetti as on a hot dog, so cook enough to freeze some.

Makes About 4 Cups

2 pounds skirt or flank steak
3 cups coarsely chopped canned tomatoes, drained, with ½ cup juice reserved
1½ tablespoons red wine vinegar or cider vinegar
1 tablespoon light corn syrup
2 teaspoons ground cumin
2 teaspoons minced fresh oregano or 1 teaspoon crumbled dried
1½ teaspoons ground cinnamon
1 teaspoon ground cloves
1 teaspoon cayenne pepper
½ teaspoon ground coriander
1 bay leaf
1 teaspoon salt
¼ teaspoon freshly ground black pepper
⅓ cup vegetable oil
2 large garlic cloves, minced
1 small red or green bell pepper, cut into ¼-inch strips
1 medium onion, coarsely chopped

1. Halve the steak following the grain, then slice the meat across the grain into ½-inch strips.

2. In a large bowl, mix together the tomatoes and the reserved juice, the vinegar, corn syrup, cumin, oregano, cinnamon, cloves, cayenne, coriander, bay leaf, salt and black pepper; set aside.

3. In a large nonreactive saucepan, heat the oil over moderately high heat. Add the meat and brown on all sides. Using a slotted spoon, transfer the meat to the tomato mixture.

4. Add the garlic, bell pepper and onion to the saucepan and reduce the heat to moderate. Cook, stirring, until the vegetables are just beginning to soften, about 5 minutes. Add the tomato and meat mixture and bring to a boil over high heat. Stir well, reduce the heat to low and simmer, uncovered, for 2 hours to reduce the liquid.

5. Cover the saucepan and simmer until the meat shreds easily, 1 to 1½ hours longer. Remove the meat from the saucepan, shred it and stir it back into the hot sauce.

—Linda Merinoff

• • •

TEN-CHILE CHILI

At Arizona 206, Brendan Walsh tops this very special chili with a garnish of julienned peppers—equal amounts of poblano peppers, Anaheim chiles, red and yellow bell peppers and jalapeños sautéed in a little olive oil—and serves it with a tart-flavored cilantro rice.

🍷 There's no fighting the pepperiness of this dish, but it can be effectively contrasted by a refreshing, slightly fruity sparkling wine, such as 1983 Van der Kamp Brut or 1984 Paul Masson Blanc de Noirs Centennial Cuvée, whose bubbles would cut across the spice.

12 to 18 Servings

1/3 cup cumin seeds
2 tablespoons coriander seeds
2 ancho chiles*
2 mulato chiles*
4 pasilla chiles*
6 pounds trimmed beef chuck, cut into 1 1/2-by-1/4-inch strips
1/2 pound thickly sliced lean bacon, cut crosswise into thin matchsticks
3/4 pound ham, finely diced
1 1/2 tablespoons corn oil
3 pounds large yellow Spanish onions, finely diced
3/4 cup diced celery
1 cup ground ancho chile powder*
1/2 teaspoon cayenne pepper
5 bay leaves
1 pequin chile* (optional)
3 jalapeño peppers, seeded and minced
3 serrano peppers, seeded and minced
1/2 can (3 1/2 ounces) chipotle chiles in adobo sauce,* coarsely chopped
1 smoked ham hock
2 cans (35 ounces each) Italian peeled tomatoes, drained
1/2 cup golden tequila
2 cups beef stock or canned broth
1/2 teaspoon rosemary
1 teaspoon crumbled sage leaves
1 teaspoon oregano
****Available at Latin American markets***

1. Preheat the oven to 500°. In a medium skillet, toast the cumin and coriander seeds over moderate heat until fragrant, 1 to 2 minutes. Immediately remove from the heat. Grind to a powder in a spice grinder or food processor.

2. Place the ancho, mulato and pasilla chiles on a baking sheet and toast them in the oven until fragrant and puffed up, about 2 minutes. Remove the stems and seeds and grind the chiles in a spice grinder or food processor until powdered.

3. In a stockpot or large flameproof casserole, combine the beef, bacon, ham and corn oil. Cook over moderate heat until the fat is rendered and the bacon is golden, about 20 minutes.

4. Add the onions and cook, stirring occasionally, until the onions are golden brown, about 20 minutes.

5. Add the celery, ground chiles and ancho chile powder. Cook, stirring frequently, until the celery is softened and the chile powder is fragrant, about 10 minutes.

6. Add the cayenne, bay leaves, pequin chile, jalapeño and serrano peppers, chipotle chiles, ham hock, tomatoes, tequila, stock, rosemary, sage and oregano. Simmer uncovered over low heat, stirring occasionally, for 4 hours.

—*Brendan Walsh, Arizona 206, New York City*

• • •

SAGE MEAT LOAF WITH CREAM SAUCE

If you have an herb garden or a well-stocked green grocer, try this delicious meat loaf made with fresh herbs.

🍷 Chianti Riserva, such as 1982 Montesodi

8 to 10 Servings

3 pounds ground lean beef chuck
1 1/2 cups coarse fresh bread crumbs
1 can (8 ounces) tomato sauce
2 eggs
1/3 cup freshly grated Parmesan cheese
2 tablespoons minced parsley
2 tablespoons minced capers
3/4 teaspoon salt
1/4 teaspoon freshly ground black pepper
2 tablespoons robust olive oil
1 medium onion, minced
2 medium garlic cloves, minced
1/4 cup minced green bell pepper
1/4 cup plus 1 1/2 teaspoons minced fresh sage
2 teaspoons minced fresh sweet marjoram
1/2 teaspoon minced fresh lemon thyme
3/4 cup heavy cream
Cherry tomato halves and sprigs of fresh sage, for garnish

1. Preheat the oven to 350°. In a large bowl, combine the ground beef, bread crumbs, tomato sauce, eggs, Parmesan, parsley, capers, salt and black pepper.

2. In a heavy medium skillet, warm the oil over moderately low heat. Add the onion, garlic and green pepper and cook until the onion is golden, about 5 minutes. Add 1/4 cup of the sage, the marjoram and lemon thyme and cook over low heat for 1 minute. Remove from the heat and let cool for 5 minutes, then add to the ingredients in the bowl.

3. Using your hands, thoroughly mix the meat loaf ingredients. Pack the meat firmly into a well-greased 9-by-5-by-3-inch loaf pan, mounding it slightly in the middle.

4. Bake the meat loaf for about 1½ hours, or until it has pulled away from the sides of the pan, is nicely browned and firm to the touch. Let cool in the pan on a rack for 15 minutes.

5. Strain all the meat loaf drippings from the pan into a small heavy saucepan. Skim off most of the fat. Boil the drippings over moderately high heat until reduced by two-thirds, about 10 minutes. Stir in the cream, reduce the heat to low and boil gently, stirring frequently, until reduced to 1 cup, about 7 minutes. Stir in the remaining 1½ teaspoons sage, reduce the heat to very low and keep warm.

6. Turn the meat loaf out of the pan and set it upright on a heated platter. Garnish with the cherry tomato halves and sprigs of fresh sage. Pass the sauce separately.

—Jean Anderson

• • •

FRESH HAM WITH PAN GRAVY

This is one of my favorite things. With a menu for six, you'll have plenty of leftovers, which won't last long.

🍷 1986 California Dry Chenin Blanc, such as Hacienda or Chappellet

8 to 12 Servings

8-pound butt end of fresh ham
¾ cup apple juice
¾ cup dry white wine
½ cup olive oil
¼ cup honey
¼ cup soy sauce
1 tablespoon dry mustard
⅛ teaspoon cayenne pepper
2 garlic cloves, crushed through a press
2 bay leaves
1 medium onion, coarsely chopped
2 cups chicken stock or canned broth
3 tablespoons all-purpose flour
2 tablespoons unsalted butter, softened to room temperature
½ teaspoon salt
½ teaspoon freshly ground pepper

1. Place the ham in a deep crockery or stainless steel bowl and pierce all over with a kitchen fork. In a medium bowl, whisk together the apple juice, wine, olive oil, honey, soy sauce, dry mustard and cayenne. Add the garlic, bay leaves and onion. Pour over the ham and cover tightly. Refrigerate for at least 24, and up to 48, hours, turning several times.

2. Preheat the oven to 450°. Remove the ham from the marinade and pat dry. Discard the marinade. Place on a rack in a shallow roasting pan. Put the meat in the oven and reduce the temperature to 325°. Roast for 1 hour. Baste with the pan drippings. (Do not be tempted to baste with the marinade, as the sugar in it will burn.) Continue to roast, basting occasionally with the pan drippings, until the internal temperature reads 185° on a meat thermometer, about 4 hours longer.

3. Remove the ham to a cutting board and cover loosely with foil. Let rest for at least 15 minutes before slicing.

4. Meanwhile, discard any burned bits and all the fat from the pan. Pour in the stock and bring to a boil on top of the stove, scraping up any browned bits from the bottom of the pan. Reduce the heat to a simmer. Mash the flour into the butter and stir into the stock. Simmer until the sauce is thickened and has lost its raw flour taste, about 5 minutes. Season with the salt and pepper.

—Lee Bailey

• • •

A HOMEY HAM SUPPER

Unless your guests have gargantuan appetites, there should be leftover fresh ham from this menu, which serves 6. Lee Bailey suggests using it to make a savory meat pie with potatoes (sweet or white), turnips, lima beans and carrots.

Fresh Ham with Pan Gravy (p. 100)

Sweet Potatoes with Grapefruit (p. 161)

Broccoli and Cauliflower in Mustard Butter (p. 153)

Thin Buttermilk Biscuits (p. 142) and Sweet Butter

🍷 *Dry Red Wine*

Store-Bought Dessert, such as Apple Crumb Cake and Vanilla Ice Cream

Coffee

BAKED FRESH HAM WITH COFFEE GLAZE AND TURNIPS

Surprising as it may be, this recipe from Chicago's Gordon restaurant calls for instant coffee. However, the instant is used here to fortify freshly brewed coffee, which allows the brew to stand up to the warm, hot notes of turnips and chiles without diluting the glaze with too much liquid. Gordon serves the ham and turnips on a bed of steamed turnip greens; kale or spinach works just as well.

🍷 Although ham normally calls for light-bodied red wines, the glaze in this case begs for added complexity. Try a California Zinfandel, such as Ridge or Phelps.

12 Servings

1 small bone-in shank end of fresh ham (about 7½ pounds)
8 cups strongly brewed coffee
4 cups pineapple juice
1 cup dry white wine
½ cup vegetable oil
2 Spanish onions, finely diced
1 head of garlic—separated into cloves, peeled and chopped

4 plum tomatoes, chopped
3 small dried red chile peppers, with seeds, chopped
1/4 cup white wine vinegar
2 teaspoons ground cumin
1/4 cup instant espresso powder or 3/4 cup instant coffee granules
1 cup chicken stock or canned broth
1 tablespoon coarse (kosher) salt
1 tablespoon freshly ground pepper
4 tablespoons unsalted butter
3 pounds turnips, peeled and thinly sliced

1. Trim the ham to remove the heavy skin and fat. Place in a large nonreactive pot and add the brewed coffee, pineapple juice and white wine. Cover and marinate in the refrigerator for 2 days, turning the ham 2 to 3 times daily. Remove the ham from the refrigerator about 2 hours before proceeding.

2. Preheat the oven to 300°. In a large heavy skillet, heat the oil. Add the onions and garlic and cook over moderate heat until softened but not browned, about 8 minutes. Stir in the tomatoes and hot peppers and sauté for 2 minutes longer. Add the vinegar, cumin, instant espresso powder and chicken stock. Boil until reduced by half, about 10 minutes.

3. Remove from the heat and stir in 1 cup of the ham marinade. Puree the mixture in a food processor or blender until smooth.

4. Remove the ham from the remaining marinade and discard the marinade. Season the ham with the salt and pepper and place meatier-side down on a rack in a large roasting pan. Brush the puree on the ham, lightly covering the top and the sides; reserve the remaining puree.

5. Bake the ham for 3½ hours, basting with the reserved puree every 30 minutes and turning every 1½ hours, ending with the meatier side up. Let stand for 15 minutes before thinly slicing.

6. Meanwhile, in a large heavy skillet, melt the butter over moderately high heat. Add the turnips and sauté, turning frequently, until golden and tender, 10 to 12 minutes. Arrange the carved ham and the turnip slices on a large platter and serve hot.

—Gordon, Chicago

• • •

HERB-CURED PORK LOIN

🍷 Among the wines that could pair successfully with this complexly seasoned dish is Gewürztraminer, such as the 1986 Rutherford Hill from California.

8 to 10 Servings

5 garlic cloves, minced
1 tablespoon coarse sea salt or kosher salt
1½ tablespoons minced fresh thyme or 1½ teaspoons dried
1½ tablespoons minced fresh basil, plus 1 tablespoon finely shredded basil (preferably a mixture of opal and Thai basil)
2 tablespoons chopped fresh chervil or parsley
1½ tablespoons sugar
Pinch of cayenne pepper
1 tablespoon Dijon-style mustard
1 tablespoon extra-virgin olive oil
1½ teaspoons rice vinegar
4 pounds center-cut boneless pork loin in one piece, trimmed and tied in a roll
2 large shiitake mushroom caps, cut into thin julienne strips
1 tablespoon minced fresh coriander
1 teaspoon minced fresh lemon grass or ½ teaspoon grated lemon zest
2 tablespoons chives that have been cut into 1-inch pieces
½ small red bell pepper, cut into thin julienne strips

1. In a small bowl, mash the garlic to a paste with the salt. Stir in the thyme, minced basil, chervil, sugar and cayenne. Add the mustard, oil and vinegar and mix until blended.

2. Place the pork in a nonreactive baking pan. Spread the herb marinade evenly over the meat. Cover with plastic wrap and refrigerate for at least 12 hours or up to 2 days. Let the pork return to room temperature before proceeding.

3. Preheat the oven to 325°. In a small bowl, combine the shiitake mushrooms, shredded basil, coriander, lemon grass, chives and red bell pepper. Cover and refrigerate until serving time.

4. Roast the pork until the internal temperature measures 150°, about 1¼ hours (or to an internal temperature of 160° if you prefer your pork with no trace of pink, about 1½ hours).

5. Transfer the pork to a cutting board. Cover loosely with foil and let rest in a warm spot for 15 minutes. Slice the meat and scatter some of the herb and mushroom garnish over each serving.

—Cindy Pawlcyn, Mustards Grill, Yountville, California

• • •

ROAST PORK LOIN WITH ROSEMARY-GARLIC GRAVY

I like to serve this roast with Tiny Potatoes Roasted on Rosemary Branches (p. 159). Just bake them in the oven with the roast.

🍷 A rich fruity red Rhône that's aromatic will complement the herbal rosemary and fragrant garlic, while the tannin will balance the unctuousness of the pork. Try Paul Jaboulet's 1985 Crozes-Hermitage Domaine de Thalabert.

4 Servings

2 teaspoons olive oil
3 pounds pork loin, boned and excess fat removed, bones reserved

1 medium onion, chopped
1 carrot, chopped
3 teaspoons whole rosemary leaves plus ½ teaspoon finely chopped rosemary
½ teaspoon salt
¾ teaspoon freshly ground pepper
1 head of garlic, separated into cloves and peeled
2 tablespoons all-purpose flour

1. In a large saucepan, heat 1 teaspoon of the olive oil. Add the reserved pork bones and cook over high heat, stirring occasionally, until the bones are browned all over, about 5 minutes. Add the onion and carrot and cook until they begin to brown, about 3 minutes. Add 4 cups of water and 1 teaspoon of the whole rosemary. Reduce the heat to low and simmer, skimming occasionally, for 1 hour. Strain the stock; skim off the fat.

2. Preheat the oven to 400°. Season the pork loin with ¼ teaspoon of the salt and ¼ teaspoon of the pepper. In a large cast-iron skillet, heat the remaining 1 teaspoon olive oil over high heat. Put the pork in the skillet, fat-side down, and cook until the fat is browned.

3. Turn the roast and place the skillet in the oven. After 10 minutes, add the remaining 2 teaspoons whole rosemary and the garlic cloves to the skillet. Cook the pork for 20 minutes longer, basting once or twice, until a meat thermometer reads 155°.

4. Transfer the pork to a warm serving platter. Pour the grease out of the skillet, leaving the rosemary and garlic in the pan. Place the skillet over moderately high heat. Add the flour and cook, stirring, for 30 seconds. Whisk in the reserved stock until smooth, scraping up any browned bits from the bottom of the pan. Bring to a boil, reduce the heat to low and simmer, whisking, for 4 minutes.

5. Strain the gravy, pressing the cooked garlic through the strainer, into a gravy boat. Season with the chopped rosemary, and the remaining ¼ teaspoon salt and ½ teaspoon pepper. Keep warm while you carve the roast. Add any accumulated juices from the carved roast and serve immediately.

—Marcia Kiesel

• • •

MARINATED PORK AND RED CABBAGE

This is a great one-platter dish for a warm June day. Since the meat is cooked the night before and easily assembled at serving time, the meal is simplicity itself. A lemony green salad, crusty bread and a chilled bottle of rosé or a frosty glass of lager beer would be excellent accompaniments.

8 to 10 Servings

3 pounds boneless loin of pork, trimmed
1 tablespoon crumbled sage leaves
1 tablespoon ground ginger
2 cups sweet Marsala
2 cups apple juice or sweet cider
⅔ cup safflower oil
⅓ cup olive oil
¼ cup rice wine vinegar
6 scallions (white and 1 inch of green), minced
2 garlic cloves, lightly crushed
2 tablespoons soy sauce
2 teaspoons sugar
3 tablespoons Dijon-style mustard
1 tablespoon fresh lemon juice
1 teaspoon salt
1 small head of red cabbage, very thinly sliced (6 to 7 cups)
1 large Granny Smith apple—peeled, cored and coarsely chopped
½ cup plain yogurt

1. Preheat the oven to 325°. Rub the pork all over with the sage, then the ginger. Roast the pork for 1 hour and 15 minutes, or until the internal temperature reaches 145°.

2. In a medium nonreactive saucepan, combine the Marsala, apple juice, safflower oil, olive oil, rice vinegar, scallions, garlic, soy sauce and sugar. Bring to a simmer over moderate heat.

SOUTHWESTERN SUPPER

The flavors of the southwest abound in this hearty home-style supper. If you're pressed for time, serve the guacamole with store-bought tortillas or (unsalted) tortilla chips. Serves 4 to 6.

Guacamole (p. 12)

Blue Corn Pizzelle (p. 141)

New Mexican Pork Pie with Cornmeal Crust (p. 103)

Sliced Beefsteak Tomatoes with Minced Fresh Coriander

Premium Mexican Beers

Chocolate Black Walnut Cake (p. 165)

Dark-Roast Coffee with Kahlúa

3. Pour the hot marinade over the meat and let cool to room temperature, turning once or twice. Cover with plastic wrap and refrigerate overnight.

4. Meanwhile, in a large bowl, stir together the mustard, lemon juice and salt. Add the cabbage, toss, cover with plastic wrap and refrigerate overnight.

5. About 1 hour before serving, remove the meat from the marinade and thinly slice on the diagonal. Reserve the marinade. Arrange the pork on a large platter. Pour the marinade into a measuring cup and use a ladle to skim off and discard the oil on top. Brush the pork with ¼ cup of the marinade.

6. Add the apple and yogurt to the cabbage and toss well. Add ½ cup of the marinade, toss again and arrange the cabbage alongside the meat.

—W. Peter Prestcott

• • •

ROAST PORK GRAND-MERE

🍷 The richness of this dish, particularly the use of prunes, calls for a spicy white such as a 1985 Landmann-Ostholt Gewürztraminer from Alsace or the 1985 Alexander Valley Vineyards Gewürztraminer from California.

8 Servings

20 pitted prunes
¼ cup Calvados
3½-pound boneless pork roast, trimmed of excess fat
2 garlic cloves, quartered lengthwise
1 teaspoon salt
½ teaspoon freshly ground pepper
2 tablespoons unsalted butter
½ teaspoon fresh thyme or ¼ teaspoon dried
3 medium carrots, sliced
2 small onions, sliced
8 shallots
3 cups Brown Chicken Stock (p. 247)

1. In a small bowl, soak the prunes in the Calvados.

2. Make 4 incisions on each side of the roast and insert the garlic. Season with the salt and pepper.

3. In a large flameproof casserole, melt the butter over moderately high heat. Add the pork and sauté, turning, until browned all over, about 5 minutes. Sprinkle with the thyme, reduce the heat to moderately low, cover and cook, turning once, for 25 minutes.

4. Add the carrots, onions and shallots and cook until the vegetables are tender, about 25 minutes. Add the prunes and Calvados and cook for 5 minutes longer.

5. Remove the roast to a carving board. Using a slotted spoon, transfer the vegetables and prunes to a bowl; cover and keep warm.

6. Add the stock to the casserole and boil over moderately high heat, scraping up the browned bits from the bottom, until the sauce thickens slightly, about 10 minutes.

7. Carve the roast and arrange on a serving platter with the vegetables and prunes. Pour some of the sauce over the meat and pass the remainder separately.

—Monique Hooker

• • •

NEW MEXICAN PORK PIE WITH CORNMEAL CRUST

This recipe hails from the Southwest, and although you may find versions topped with blue cornmeal in "uptown" dining spots, I'll take my cornmeal yellow, thank you.

🍷 This dish deserves the best Mexican beer you can find—icy cold and sluiced with fresh lime juice.

4 to 6 Servings

CORNMEAL CRUST:
1¼ cups all-purpose flour
½ cup yellow cornmeal
½ teaspoon salt
½ cup cold vegetable shortening
5 to 6 tablespoons ice water

PORK FILLING:
1¼ pounds boneless pork shoulder, trimmed of fat and cut into ½-inch cubes
3 tablespoons all-purpose flour
4 tablespoons unsalted butter
1 tablespoon vegetable oil
1 medium onion, finely chopped
2 garlic cloves, minced
1 medium tomato, seeded and chopped
1 can (13¾ ounces) beef broth
1 tablespoon chili powder
1½ teaspoons ground cumin
1 teaspoon chopped fresh oregano or ¼ teaspoon dried
1 green bell pepper, cut into ½-inch dice
1 red bell pepper, cut into ½-inch dice
1 cup corn kernels, preferably fresh
10 pimiento-stuffed green olives, sliced
½ teaspoon salt
¼ teaspoon freshly ground black pepper
1 egg white, lightly beaten
Hot pepper sauce

1. *Make the crust:* In a large bowl, combine the flour, cornmeal and salt. Cut in the shortening until the mixture resembles coarse crumbs. Add just enough of the water to form a fairly soft dough. Flatten the dough into a 6-inch disk, cover with plastic wrap and refrigerate for at least 15 minutes.

2. *Prepare the filling:* Pat the pork dry with paper towels. Sprinkle with the flour and toss to coat. In a large flameproof casserole, melt 2 tablespoons of the butter in the oil over moderately high heat. Add the pork in batches and cook until lightly browned on all sides, 3 to 5 minutes. Transfer to a bowl.

3. Add the onion to the casserole and cook over moderately low heat until softened slightly, about 1 minute. Add the garlic and cook until fragrant, about 2 minutes. Stir in the tomato and the beef broth, scraping up any browned bits from the bottom of the casserole with a wooden spoon.

4. Add the pork and season with the chili powder, cumin and oregano. Stir well, cover and cook, stirring occasionally, for 1 hour and 15 minutes. Uncover and cook, stirring occasionally, until the stew thickens, about 15 minutes longer.

5. Meanwhile, in a medium saucepan, melt the remaining 2 tablespoons butter. Add the bell peppers, cover and cook over moderately low heat until softened, about 10 minutes. Remove from the heat.

6. Preheat the oven to 400°. Add the peppers, corn kernels and olives to the meat and season with the salt and pepper. Spoon the stew into a shallow, buttered, 4- to 6-cup round or oval baking dish.

7. Roll out the dough between sheets of waxed paper. Peel off the top sheet of paper and invert the dough onto the baking dish. Trim and flute the edges. Brush with the beaten egg white. Using a sharp knife, make several slashes in the top to allow steam to escape. Bake the pie until golden, 15 to 20 minutes. Serve with hot pepper sauce on the side.

—Phillip Stephen Schulz

• • •

SMOKY SPARERIBS

Lapsang Souchong tea imparts its robust, smoky, hearty flavor to these roasted Chinese-style spareribs.

4 Servings

2 cups boiling water
2 tablespoons Lapsang Souchong tea leaves
⅓ cup soy sauce, preferably dark*
4 garlic cloves, lightly crushed
1 whole star anise pod*
2 tablespoons plus 1½ teaspoons sugar
3 pounds spareribs, cut between the ribs
4 tablespoons unsalted butter
2 large onions (about 2 pounds), halved and thinly sliced
****Available at Oriental markets***

1. In a heatproof glass bowl, pour the boiling water over the tea leaves. Let steep for 5 minutes. Strain the tea into a clean bowl and stir in the soy sauce, garlic, star anise and 2 tablespoons of the sugar; let cool completely.

2. Put the ribs in a large heavy-duty plastic bag and set the bag in a bowl. Pour the tea marinade into the bag and seal tightly. Tip the bag to thoroughly coat the ribs with the marinade. Refrigerate for 4 hours, turning often. Remove the ribs from the refrigerator at least 30 minutes before roasting.

3. Preheat the oven to 350°. Drain the ribs, reserving the marinade. Arrange the ribs, fat-side up, on 2 racks. Pour 1 inch of water into two 9-by-13-inch pans and set the racks on top. Brush the ribs with the marinade.

4. Roast the ribs, brushing once with the marinade, for 1 hour. Baste the ribs again, turn and roast, basting once more, for 30 minutes longer, or until the ribs are very tender.

5. Meanwhile, in a large heavy skillet, melt the butter over low heat. Add the onions and toss to coat evenly with the butter. Cover and cook until the onions are very soft and translucent, 20 to 30 minutes.

6. Sprinkle the remaining 1½ teaspoons sugar over the onions, increase the heat to moderately high and cook, stirring frequently, until the onions are caramelized to a rich brown, 15 to 20 minutes.

7. Reduce the heat to moderate, add ⅔ cup of the remaining marinade and simmer for 2 minutes. Transfer the onions and their liquid to a food processor or blender and puree until smooth.

8. When the ribs are tender, turn and brush with some of the pureed onion sauce. Roast for 5 minutes longer, or until the ribs are richly glazed. Serve the ribs with the onion sauce. Reheat the onion sauce if necessary.

—Ceri E. Hadda

• • •

CRUSTY BAKED HAM

This recipe details the favorite method of Managing Editor Warren Picower for dressing up a smoked ham.

🍷 Riesling has a natural affinity for ham and smoked meats. A 1986 Hogue Cellars Johannisberg Riesling from Washington State, with its crisp acidity, floral scent and fruity flavor, would be a fine choice.

6 to 8 Servings

5-pound boneless smoked ham
4 cups unsweetened apple cider
½ cup Calvados or applejack
¼ cup Dijon-style mustard
2 cups fresh bread crumbs
½ cup (packed) light brown sugar
2 teaspoons apple cider vinegar

MIDWINTER BUFFET

Hearty meals such as this are best served family style, or as a buffet, so that guests can pile their plates high, in keeping with the informal spirit of the menu. Serves 8.

Herbed Oyster Canapés (p. 15)

Muscadet

Crusty Baked Ham (p. 104)

Steamed Brussels Sprouts and Grapes (p. 152)

Braised Red Cabbage with Maple-Glazed Chestnuts (p. 152)

Mashed Potatoes with Onions and Garlic (p. 160)

Gratin of Sweet Potatoes Flambéed with Bourbon (p. 161)

Tossed Salad with Sherry Wine Vinaigrette (p. 126)

Beaujolais Moulin-à-Vent

Cranberry-Apple Pie with an Oatmeal-Almond Crust (p. 192)

Indian Pudding (p. 215)

Brandy Butter Sauce (p. 258)

Coffee

1. Place the ham in a deep nonreactive pot or casserole a bit wider than the ham. Pour in the cider and Calvados. Cover with plastic wrap and refrigerate for 8 hours or overnight, turning the ham occasionally. Remove the ham from the refrigerator early enough to allow it to come to room temperature before cooking, about 2 hours.

2. Preheat the oven to 350°. Remove the ham from the marinade and pat dry. Reserve the marinade. Spread the ham with 3 tablespoons of the mustard. On a long sheet of waxed paper, mix together the bread crumbs and brown sugar. Roll the mustard-coated ham in this mixture to coat evenly.

3. Put the ham in a roasting pan and bake until golden brown and heated through, about 1 hour. Let the ham rest for 15 minutes before slicing.

4. Meanwhile, in a small saucepan, boil the marinade over high heat until it is reduced to ½ cup, about 20 minutes.

5. Whisk in the remaining 1 tablespoon mustard and the vinegar. Serve a small amount of this sauce with each serving of ham.

—Warren Picower

• • •

COLOMBO OF LAMB

The complex seasonings that form the Colombo Paste lend a unique blend of flavors to this lamb stew. Chef Henri Charvet of Le Lafayette in Martinique makes this stew with goat.

6 to 8 Servings

2½ pounds boneless leg of lamb, trimmed of excess fat and cut into 1½-inch cubes
1½ teaspoons salt
¾ teaspoon freshly ground black pepper
Colombo Paste (recipe follows)
1 tablespoon unsalted butter
2 medium onions, finely chopped
2 tablespoons minced chives or scallion greens
2 garlic cloves, crushed through a press
6 sprigs of fresh thyme or ¾ teaspoon dried
4 bay leaves
2 cups dry white wine
1 tablespoon minced, seeded jalapeño pepper
2 carrots, cut into ½-inch dice
1 sweet potato, peeled and cut into ¼-inch dice
1 small boiling potato, peeled and cut into ¼-inch dice
1 chayote—peeled, seeded and cut into ¼-inch dice

1. In a bowl, season the meat with 1 teaspoon of the salt and ½ teaspoon of the black pepper. Add 2 tablespoons of the Colombo Paste and toss to coat.

2. In a large nonreactive flameproof casserole, melt the butter. Add half of the meat and cook over moderately high heat, stirring, until browned all over, 6 to 8 minutes. Remove to a plate. Repeat with the remaining pieces of meat.

3. Add the onions, chives, garlic, thyme, bay leaves and wine to the casserole. Return all the meat to the pan and cook, stirring, until the wine reduces by half, 15 to 20 minutes.

4. Add the jalapeño and enough water to just cover the meat. Reduce the heat to moderately low and simmer, stirring and skimming occasionally, until the meat is tender, about 1 hour.

5. Add the carrots, sweet potato, potato and chayote. Partially cover and cook until the vegetables are tender and the sauce thickens, 15 to 20 minutes.

6. Stir in the remaining Colombo Paste. Before serving, remove the bay leaves. Season the stew with the remaining ½ teaspoon salt and ¼ teaspoon black pepper.

—Henri Charvet, Le Lafayette, Fort-de-France, Martinique

• • •

COLOMBO PASTE

Makes About 1/4 Cup

2 tablespoons rice flour*
1/2 teaspoon ground coriander
1/2 teaspoon turmeric
1/4 teaspoon freshly ground black pepper
1 teaspoon ground cumin
2 garlic cloves, minced
1 large jalapeño pepper, halved and seeded
1/2 cup (loosely packed) Italian flat-leaf parsley sprigs
1/4 teaspoon salt
2 tablespoons vegetable oil
***Available at health food stores**

Combine all the ingredients in a food processor and puree until well blended.

—Henri Charvet, Le Lafayette, Fort-de-France, Martinique

• • •

RACK OF LAMB WITH ROSEMARY AND MUSTARD

The success of this recipe depends on the quality of the lamb, so order the best meat you can find. Have the butcher trim the rack, remove the chine bone and french the rib bones. Ask him to wrap up all the bones and trimmings—you will need them for the glaze.

🍷 The flavors of lamb and rosemary echo the often herbaceous scent and flavor of red wines based on Cabernet Sauvignon and Merlot, making them ideal for such pairings. A rich, soft 1983 Château Belair from St-Emilion or a 1983 Merlot from Clos du Val in Napa Valley would make a splendid choice.

A ROMANTIC DINNER FOR TWO

The oysters and pomegranate, with their reputation for smoothing the path to romance, add a whimsically hopeful touch to this meal from Bob Chambers. Serves 2.

Oysters on the Half Shell
Crusty Brown Bread
Sweet Butter
Lemon Wedges
🍷 *Pink Champagne*

Pomegranate Ice (p. 225)

Rack of Lamb with Rosemary and Mustard (p. 106) and Lamb Glaze (p. 249)
Eggplant and Spinach Timbales (p. 155)
🍷 *1983 Clos du Val Merlot and 1983 Chateau Belair*

Mixed Leaf Salad with Roasted Walnuts and Roquefort (p. 126)

Espresso Bavarian Cream (p. 213)
Chocolate Shortbread Hearts (p. 189)
Espresso
Cognac or Armagnac

2 Servings

2 teaspoons extra-virgin olive oil
1 trimmed rack of lamb (about 1 1/2 pounds)
1 cup fresh bread crumbs
2 tablespoons minced Italian flat-leaf parsley
2 teaspoons minced fresh rosemary
1/2 teaspoon freshly ground pepper
1 tablespoon grainy mustard
2 tablespoons Roasted Garlic Puree (p. 259)

1. In a heavy medium skillet, heat the olive oil. Add the lamb and cook over high heat, turning, until browned all over, about 1 1/2 minutes. Remove from the skillet and let cool completely.

2. In a small bowl, toss the bread crumbs with the parsley, 1 teaspoon of the rosemary and the pepper.

3. In another bowl, combine the remaining 1 teaspoon rosemary with the mustard and the Roasted Garlic Puree. Spread the mixture evenly over the lamb. Pat the seasoned bread crumbs onto the mustard coating. *(The lamb can be prepared to this point up to 8 hours ahead. Cover and refrigerate until 2 hours before roasting.)*

4. Preheat the oven to 500°. Place the lamb on a rack set in a shallow roasting pan. Put the lamb in the center of the oven and immediately reduce the temperature to 450°. Roast the lamb for 20 minutes, or until a meat thermometer inserted into the center registers 120° for medium-rare.

5. Remove from the oven, cover loosely with aluminum foil and let rest in a warm place for 10 minutes. Carve the lamb just before serving by slicing between the ribs.

—Bob Chambers

• • •

FILLET OF LAMB WITH MINT AND SAFFRON

At La Réserve, chef André Gaillard serves this lamb with baby vegetables and an asparagus flan.

6 Servings

1 saddle of lamb, boned and trimmed (about 2 pounds boneless loin and tenderloin)
3/4 teaspoon salt
1/4 teaspoon freshly ground pepper
1 tablespoon plus 1 teaspoon unsalted butter
1 shallot, minced
1/2 cup dry white wine
1/4 cup Pernod
1 cup heavy cream
1 tomato—peeled, seeded and finely diced
1 teaspoon minced fresh mint
Pinch of saffron threads

1. Season the lamb with ½ teaspoon of the salt and ⅛ teaspoon of the pepper. In a large, heavy nonreactive skillet, melt 1 tablespoon of the butter over moderately high heat. Add the lamb and sauté, turning, until browned on the outside and rare inside, 7 to 8 minutes for the loin and 6 for the tenderloin. Remove from the skillet and cover with foil to keep warm.

2. Pour off any fat from the skillet. Add the remaining 1 teaspoon butter and the shallot. Cook over moderate heat until soft, about 2 minutes. Add the wine and Pernod and cook until the liquid is reduced to ⅓ cup, about 5 minutes.

3. Stir in the cream, tomato, mint, saffron and remaining ¼ teaspoon salt and ⅛ teaspoon pepper. Cook until the sauce lightly coats a spoon, about 3 minutes.

4. Slice the lamb on the diagonal ¼ inch thick. Spoon some sauce onto 6 warmed plates. Arrange overlapping slices of lamb on the sauce and pass the remaining sauce separately.

—André Gaillard, La Réserve, New York City

• • •

MOUSSAKA

By combining some of the components rather than layering them individually, this simplified version of the classic Greek dish can be assembled in a flash. Although the recipe comfortably serves six to eight, it could easily be doubled to feed a large crowd.

🍷 Dry Provence Rosé, such as 1985 Domaines Ott

6 to 8 Servings

3 medium eggplants (1 pound each), sliced crosswise 1/4 inch thick
1 1/2 tablespoons salt
2 medium baking potatoes, peeled and cut into 1-inch dice
1 cup plus 3 tablespoons olive oil
1 cup all-purpose flour, for dredging
2 medium onions, coarsely chopped
3 garlic cloves, minced
2 pounds lean ground lamb
3 tablespoons tomato paste
3 tablespoons brandy
2 1/4 teaspoons cinnamon
1 1/4 teaspoons thyme
1 1/4 teaspoons freshly ground pepper
1 can (35 ounces) Italian peeled tomatoes, drained well and chopped
1 pound feta cheese, crumbled
4 eggs
1 cup heavy cream

1. Place the eggplant slices on paper towels and sprinkle with the salt. Let stand for 30 minutes.

2. Meanwhile, in a medium saucepan, cook the potatoes in boiling water until tender, about 10 minutes. Drain and set aside.

3. Pat the eggplant dry with paper towels. In a large skillet, heat ¼ cup of the olive oil over high heat. Dredge the eggplant slices in the flour; shake off any excess. Add the eggplant to the skillet in batches and fry over high heat, using up to ¾ cup more oil as necessary, until browned, about 2 minutes per side. Drain on paper towels.

4. Wipe the skillet clean. Add the remaining 3 tablespoons oil to the skillet set over moderate heat. Add the onions and garlic and cook, stirring occasionally, until the onions are soft and golden brown, 5 to 10 minutes.

5. Add the lamb and cook, breaking up the meat with a spoon, until no trace of pink remains, about 10 minutes.

6. Transfer the lamb mixture to a colander to drain, then return to the skillet. Stir in the tomato paste, brandy, cinnamon, thyme and pepper. Cook over moderate heat for 1 minute, stirring, to blend the flavors. Transfer to a large bowl and add the tomatoes, reserved potatoes and the feta cheese; stir well to combine.

7. Preheat the oven to 350°. Reserving about 30 slices for the top, line the bottom and sides of a 5- to 6-quart shallow baking dish with the fried eggplant slices, overlapping them slightly.

8. In a small bowl, lightly beat the eggs with the heavy cream. Spoon half the meat into the baking dish and pour on half the custard mixture. Repeat with the remaining meat and custard. Cover with the reserved eggplant slices, overlapping them slightly in a decorative pattern. (*The moussaka can be prepared to this point up to 2 days ahead. Cover with plastic wrap and refrigerate. Let return to room temperature before baking.*)

9. Bake until the custard is set and the top is nicely browned, about 45 minutes. Let stand for 10 to 15 minutes before serving.

—*W. Peter Prestcott*

• • •

RABBIT SIMMERED IN WINE WITH BACON AND APPLES

Frank Stitt, of Highland Bar & Grill in Birmingham, Alabama, has been a pioneer in seeking out locally raised ingredients. He even returns to his hometown of Cullman, Alabama, to buy rabbits from Venz's Bunny Farm.

🍷 The chef suggests serving this tasty braised dish with a cool, fruity, light red wine, such as a Fleurie or Juliénas (Beaujolais), or a Chinon or Zinfandel.

4 Servings

1 rabbit (3¾ pounds), cut into serving pieces
2 large carrots, sliced
1 large onion, sliced
2 shallots, sliced
2 garlic cloves, sliced
5 peppercorns, crushed
4 juniper berries, crushed
1 sprig of fresh thyme or ¼ teaspoon dried
1 sprig of fresh basil or ¼ teaspoon dried
1 cup dry white wine
¼ cup olive oil
¼ pound slab bacon, finely diced
Flour, for dredging
2 tablespoons Calvados or brandy
1 cup veal or chicken stock, preferably homemade
3 tablespoons unsalted butter
2 Granny Smith apples—peeled, cored and cut into ½-inch wedges
½ cup heavy cream
¼ teaspoon salt
¼ teaspoon freshly ground pepper
Chopped fresh parsley or basil, for garnish

1. In a large bowl, toss the rabbit with the carrots, onion, shallots, garlic, peppercorns, juniper berries, thyme, basil, wine and 2 tablespoons of the olive oil. Cover and let marinate overnight in the refrigerator.

2. Remove the rabbit pieces from the marinade and pat dry. Strain the marinade; reserve the liquid and vegetables separately. Discard the thyme, basil, peppercorns and juniper berries.

3. In a large ovenproof skillet, cook the bacon over moderate heat until crisp, about 10 minutes. With a slotted spoon, transfer the bacon to paper towels to drain. Pour off the fat from the skillet.

4. Preheat the oven to 325°. Dredge the rabbit pieces in the flour, shaking off any excess. Add the remaining 2 tablespoons olive oil to the skillet and heat over moderately high heat. Add the rabbit pieces and cook, turning once, until nicely browned, about 4 minutes per side. Add the Calvados, heat for a moment and then carefully ignite. When the flames subside, transfer the rabbit to a plate.

5. Add the reserved marinade vegetables to the skillet and cook over moderate heat, stirring occasionally, until softened, about 10 minutes. Add the marinade liquid and the stock and bring to a simmer. Return the rabbit to the skillet, cover and bake in the oven for 40 minutes, or until the rabbit is tender. (Check occasionally to see that the liquid is simmering gently; reduce the temperature if necessary.)

6. In another large skillet, melt 2 tablespoons of the butter over moderate heat. Add the apple wedges and cook, tossing, until just softened, about 10 minutes. Remove from the heat and cover to keep warm.

7. Transfer the rabbit pieces to a warm serving platter and cover loosely with foil. Boil the liquid over high heat, skimming any fat from the surface until reduced by half, about 5 minutes. Add the cream and any juices from the rabbit; simmer until the sauce thickens slightly. Season with the salt and pepper. Remove from the heat and swirl in the remaining 1 tablespoon butter.

8. Spoon the sauce over the rabbit. Scatter the bacon around the rabbit, garnish with the apple wedges and sprinkle with chopped parsley.

—*Frank Stitt, Highland Bar & Grill, Birmingham, Alabama*

• • •

Scalloped Potatoes with Sweet Marjoram and Parmesan Cheese (p. 159).

Left, Grilled Vegetable and Mozzarella Salad with Chipotle Vinaigrette (p. 118). Above, Salad of Pears and Mixed Greens with Chèvre (p. 125).

SWEET AND SOUR LAMB

One of the nicest features of this unusual Italian stew is the fact that it tastes even better a day or two after it is made.

🍷 Match the sweet-sour flavors in this stew with a tart but fruity red, such as an Italian Dolcetto d'Alba—a 1986 Vietti or 1986 Marchesi di Gresy—or a fruity California Zinfandel, such as 1985 Caymus.

6 Servings

¼ cup plus 1½ tablespoons olive oil
2 medium onions, sliced
3½ pounds boneless lamb shoulder, trimmed and cut into 1-inch cubes
⅓ cup tomato paste
½ cup red wine vinegar
2 tablespoons sugar
⅓ cup pine nuts
⅓ cup raisins
½ teaspoon salt
½ teaspoon freshly ground pepper

1. In a large flameproof casserole, heat ¼ cup of the olive oil. Add the onions and cook over moderately low heat until softened but not browned, 10 to 15 minutes.

2. In a large skillet, heat the remaining 1½ tablespoons of the oil over high heat. Add one-third of the lamb cubes and sauté, tossing frequently, until browned, about 5 minutes. Transfer the browned meat to the casserole. Repeat with the remaining lamb.

3. Pour off any fat from the skillet and add ¾ cup of water. Bring to a boil, scraping up any browned bits from the bottom of the pan. Add the liquid to the casserole along with the tomato paste, vinegar, sugar and another ¾ cup water. Simmer the stew over low heat, stirring occasionally, for 1 hour.

4. Add the pine nuts and raisins and cook until the meat is very tender, about 30 minutes longer.

5. Increase the heat to moderate and boil until the liquid thickens enough to lightly coat the meat, about 20 minutes. Season the stew with the salt and pepper.

—Nancy Verde Barr

• • •

ITALIAN SPRING DINNER PARTY

Here is a menu, from Nancy Verde Barr, that celebrates the advent of spring Italian style. Serves 6.

Crostini with Pea Puree (p. 15)

Tagliatelle with Asparagus (p. 133)

Salmon with Lemon-Herb Sauce (p. 49)

Sweet and Sour Lamb (p. 113)

Baked Fennel with Parmesan Cheese (p. 156)

🍷 *Dolcetto d'Alba or California Zinfandel*

Molded Ricotta and Mascarpone with Strawberries (p. 211)

BRAISED LAMB SHANKS WITH ROSEMARY

These tasty lamb shanks in a red wine sauce redolent of herbs and garlic couldn't be simpler or more welcome on a cold winter night. I like to serve them on a bed of steamed rice or couscous, with buttered green beans or peas.

🍷 California Cabernet Sauvignon, such as 1984 Alexander Valley Vineyards

4 to 6 Servings

5½ to 6 pounds lamb shanks, cracked by the butcher (6 to 8 shanks)
1 teaspoon salt
2 teaspoons freshly ground pepper
⅓ cup all-purpose flour
4 medium carrots, quartered lengthwise and cut into 1½-inch pieces
2 medium onions, coarsely chopped
10 to 12 garlic cloves, to taste, peeled and cut lengthwise in half
1 tablespoon chopped fresh rosemary or tarragon or ¾ teaspoon dried, crushed
2½ cups dry red wine

1. Preheat the broiler. In a large shallow roasting pan, place the lamb shanks in a single layer without crowding. Season with the salt and pepper. Broil about 4 inches from the heat, turning occasionally, until well browned, about 15 minutes.

2. Remove the browned meat to a large flameproof casserole. Generously dust the flour all over the lamb. Add the carrots, onions, garlic, rosemary, wine and 1½ cups of water. Bring to a boil over moderately high heat. Reduce the heat to low, cover and simmer, turning the meat occasionally, until tender when pierced with a knife, about 1½ hours.

Lemon Shrimp Salad (p. 119).

3. Uncover the casserole and increase the heat to moderately high. Boil until the liquid is thickened and reduced to a saucey consistency, about 10 minutes. Season with additional salt and pepper to taste. *(The recipe can be made ahead; if anything, the flavor will improve. Let cool, then refrigerate, covered, for up to 2 days, or freeze for up to 2 months. Reheat, covered, in a 300° oven, adding additional red wine if the sauce seems too thick.)*

—Gayle Henderson Wilson

• • •

RABBIT IN ANCHO CHILE SAUCE WITH RAISINS AND GARLIC

The rich, almost chocolatey taste of ancho chiles complements the full-flavored rabbit, while the raisins and garlic cloves add a savory note. This is one of those dishes that taste even better the next day. Serve plenty of steamed white rice for capturing the lush sauce and follow with a watercress, avocado and grapefruit salad.

Rabbits always come with a few pieces that seem too scrappy to serve to company. I freeze them for use in chicken stock. If rabbit is not your meat of choice, this dish would be delicious with chicken instead.

🍷 This intensely rich, spicy dish can be matched by an equally powerful, fruity red, such as a young California Zinfandel; 1985 Ridge Geyserville or Haywood would be ideal, or pour more of the same amber beer you used in the dish.

—6 Servings—

6 medium ancho chiles (4 ounces)
3½ cups chicken stock or canned broth
½ cup raisins
1½ teaspoons cumin seeds
2 rabbits (2½ to 3 pounds each), cut into serving pieces
¼ cup plus 2 tablespoons extra-virgin olive oil
24 garlic cloves, peeled
2 large onions, chopped
2 teaspoons oregano, preferably Mexican
1 cup amber beer, such as Dos Equis or New Amsterdam
1 can (28 ounces) Italian peeled tomatoes, drained and crushed
1½ teaspoons salt
¼ teaspoon freshly ground pepper

1. Put the ancho chiles in a large heavy skillet in a single layer. Place over moderate heat and toast, turning occasionally, until fragrant and softened slightly, 5 to 6 minutes. Remove from heat. When cool enough to handle, remove the stems, seeds and ribs. Tear the chiles into 1-inch pieces and place in a medium heatproof bowl.

2. In a medium saucepan, bring the chicken stock to a boil. Pour 3 cups of the stock over the chiles. In a small heatproof bowl, combine the remaining ½ cup stock with the raisins. Let the chiles and raisins stand for 1 hour.

3. In a small dry skillet, toast the cumin seeds over moderately high heat, tossing, until fragrant and golden brown, about 1 minute. Grind in a spice mill or finely chop on a cutting board.

4. Pat the rabbit pieces dry. In a large flameproof casserole, heat ¼ cup of the olive oil over moderately high heat. Working in 2 batches, sauté, the rabbit, turning, until lightly browned, 3 to 5 minutes on each side. Transfer to a bowl.

5. Add the remaining 2 tablespoons oil and the garlic cloves to the casserole, reduce the heat to low and cook, stirring occasionally, until tender and golden brown, about 20 minutes. With a slotted spoon, transfer the garlic cloves to a small bowl.

6. Add the onions, oregano and toasted cumin to the casserole. Cover and cook, stirring occasionally, until the onions are tender, 15 to 20 minutes.

7. Stir in the beer, tomatoes and ancho chiles with their soaking liquid. Return the rabbit and any accumulated juices to the casserole, season with the salt and pepper and bring to a boil. Reduce the heat to moderately low and simmer uncovered, turning the rabbit in the liquid, until tender, 35 to 45 minutes. Transfer the rabbit pieces to a bowl.

8. Let the sauce cool slightly, then skim off the fat. In a food processor, puree the sauce in 2 batches until smooth. Return the sauce to the casserole and stir in the raisins and their soaking liquid and the garlic cloves. Bring to a boil, reduce the heat and simmer, stirring frequently, until the sauce thickens slightly, 5 to 7 minutes.

9. Return the rabbit to the casserole. Heat through or let cool, cover and refrigerate overnight. Reheat before serving.

—Michael McLaughlin

• • •

MONSIEUR HENNY'S RABBIT WITH MUSHROOMS AND THYME

My local butcher, Monsieur Henny, is a wonderful source for recipes. Here's one that I scratched on the back of an envelope one sunny day as he dictated from behind the counter. As with any recipe using mustard as an essential flavoring, I advise using a freshly opened jar because it will have more punch. And if at all possible, use fresh thyme. Serve this tasty dish over pasta or rice.

🍷 Serve the rabbit with the same white wine used in cooking, such as Cassis Clos Ste-Magdelaine.

4 Servings

1 fresh rabbit (2½ to 3 pounds), cut into 8 pieces, liver reserved
½ teaspoon salt
½ teaspoon freshly ground pepper
3 tablespoons extra-virgin olive oil
5 ounces salt pork, rind removed, cut into ¼-inch dice
2 medium onions, coarsely chopped
2½ cups dry white wine
3 tablespoons Dijon-style mustard
½ pound mushrooms, thinly sliced
4 imported bay leaves and 1 fresh thyme sprig, tied in cheesecloth
½ cup fresh bread crumbs
⅓ cup fresh thyme leaves

1. Season the rabbit with the salt and pepper. In a large skillet, heat the oil over moderately high heat. Add half the rabbit pieces and sauté until well browned all over, about 7 minutes; transfer to a platter. Repeat with the remaining rabbit.

2. Add the salt pork to the skillet and sauté until browned, 5 to 6 minutes. Stir in the onions and cook until softened, about 5 minutes. Gradually stir in the wine, then add the mustard, mushrooms and the cheesecloth bag of herbs. Return the rabbit to the skillet. Cover, reduce the heat to moderately low and cook until the juices run clear when the thigh is pierced, about 20 minutes.

3. Transfer the rabbit to a warmed platter, cover and keep warm. Remove the cheesecloth bag.

4. In a food processor, combine the reserved rabbit liver, bread crumbs and thyme leaves. Puree until smooth. Add to the sauce in the pan and cook over low heat, stirring until well blended, about 1 minute; do not boil. Pour the sauce over the rabbit and serve hot.

—Patricia Wells

• • •

ROAST LOIN OF VENISON WITH CRANBERRIES

The Austrian-born chef Walter Plendner researches early American sources to devise intriguing monthly menus using indigenous American ingredients for the American Harvest Restaurant in Manhattan's Vista International Hotel. This is a delicious (and very American) illustration of how venison's flavor works well with tart fruit. In order to develop maximum flavor, the cranberries should be prepared several days in advance.

🍷 Fruity California red, such as 1982 Clos de Val Cabernet Sauvignon or 1983 Silverado Merlot

8 Servings

2 thick slices of lemon
2 thick slices of orange
2 slices of peeled fresh ginger
1½ cups sugar
1 small bay leaf
2 cups fresh cranberries
4 pounds boneless loin of venison, at room temperature
2 tablespoons olive oil
1 teaspoon salt
1¼ teaspoons freshly ground pepper
¾ teaspoon finely chopped juniper berries
2 cups dry red wine
2 cups strong beef or venison stock or canned broth
2 tablespoons cold unsalted butter, cut into pieces
Fresh thyme sprigs, for garnish

1. In a medium nonreactive saucepan, combine the lemon, orange, ginger, sugar and bay leaf with 1 cup of cold water. Bring to a boil over high heat, stirring to dissolve the sugar. Reduce the heat to moderate and boil, uncovered, until syrupy, 10 to 15 minutes.

2. Stir in the cranberries, then remove from the heat and let cool. Transfer the mixture to a glass or ceramic container, cover and refrigerate for 1 to 2 days, or up to 1 week, stirring once or twice during that time.

3. Preheat the oven to 400°. Rub the venison with the olive oil, ¾ teaspoon of the salt, 1 teaspoon of the pepper and ½ teaspoon of the chopped juniper berries, pressing the seasonings into the meat. Set the loin on a rack in a roasting pan and roast, basting frequently with the pan juices, until medium-rare (about 135° on an instant-reading meat thermometer), 25 to 30 minutes. Cover the venison loosely with foil and set aside for 10 to 15 minutes before carving.

4. Meanwhile, remove and discard the bay leaf and the lemon, orange and ginger slices from the cranberries. In a food processor or blender, puree half the cranberries and half the liquid until smooth.

5. In a medium nonreactive saucepan, boil the wine over high heat until reduced to ½ cup, about 5 minutes. Add the stock and bring to a boil. Add the cranberry puree, reduce the heat to low and simmer, uncovered, until slightly thickened, about 10 minutes. Remove from the heat.

6. Strain the remaining whole cranberries and add them to the sauce with the remaining ¼ teaspoon each salt, pepper and chopped juniper berries. Swirl in the cold butter.

7. Slice the venison about ⅛ inch thick. Reheat the sauce, if necessary, and stir in any juices from the venison. Spoon some of the sauce onto heated serving plates. Arrange 3 or 4 slices of venison on the sauce and spoon some of the whole cranberries over the meat. Garnish each plate with a thyme sprig and pass the remaining sauce separately.

—Walter Plendner, American Harvest Restaurant, New York City

• • •

GAME CHILI

This is a favorite recipe from Ottomanelli's butcher shop in New York City.

🍷 A substantial, spicy red with a fruity flavor would best pair with this hearty hunter's stew. A California Zinfandel, such as 1985 Lytton Springs, would be a top choice.

6 to 8 Servings

5 hickory wood chips
½ cup bourbon
½ pound bacon, chopped or coarsely ground
2 large onions, chopped
4 garlic cloves, chopped
2 pounds coarsely ground venison stew meat
1 pound coarsely ground beef stew meat
⅓ cup chili powder
2 teaspoons ground cumin
1½ teaspoons salt
1 can (35 ounces) Italian peeled tomatoes, with their juice
1 can (6 ounces) tomato paste
1 bottle (12 ounces) amber beer
Freshly ground pepper

1. Wrap the hickory chips in cheesecloth. Pour the bourbon into a small bowl, add the chips and let soak overnight.

2. In a large flameproof casserole, combine the bacon, onions and garlic. Cover and cook over moderate heat, stirring occasionally, until the onion is softened and translucent, about 7 minutes. Scrape the mixture onto a plate and set aside.

3. Season the ground venison and beef with the chili powder, cumin and salt. Add the meat to the casserole and cook over high heat, stirring with a large spoon to break up any chunks, until browned, about 10 minutes.

4. Add the cheesecloth-wrapped hickory chips and bourbon and the reserved bacon-onion mixture, the tomatoes with their juice, the tomato paste and the beer and bring to a boil over moderately high heat. Reduce the heat to low, cover and simmer the chili for 2 hours, stirring occasionally.

5. Remove and discard the cheesecloth bag. Season to taste with additional salt and pepper. Skim any fat from the surface and serve hot. *(The chili can be prepared up to 3 days ahead and refrigerated, or frozen for up to 6 months.)*

—O. Ottomanelli & Sons, New York City

• • •

SALADS

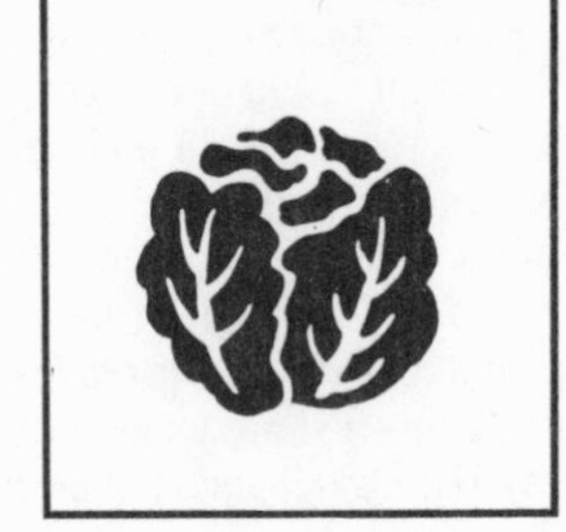

SINGAPORE NOODLE SALAD

One of my early-morning pleasures in Singapore and Thailand is to sample the spicy noodles available from almost every street vendor. This salad is excellent even when it is tossed up to a day in advance of serving and has been known to disappear during the silent hours of early morning.

—— *6 to 8 Main-Course Servings* ——

¼ cup sesame seeds
½ pound dried Chinese spaghetti-style noodles
2 tablespoons vegetable oil
1 bunch of broccoli, separated into 1-inch florets
1 pound asparagus, preferably pencil thin, tough ends snapped off, cut on the diagonal into 1-inch pieces
½ cup chicken stock or canned broth
½ cup peanut butter
¼ cup red wine vinegar
2 tablespoons soy sauce, preferably dark
1 tablespoon Oriental sesame oil
1 tablespoon dry sherry
2 teaspoons sugar
1½ teaspoons Chinese chili sauce
¼ cup minced scallions
2 tablespoons finely minced fresh ginger
1 large garlic clove, minced
1 cup bean sprouts
1 cup thinly sliced button or shiitake mushrooms or separated enoki
1 large red bell pepper, cut into thin julienne strips
2 tablespoons minced chives

1. In a small dry skillet, toast the sesame seeds over moderately high heat, tossing, until fragrant and golden brown, about 1 minute. Set aside.

2. In a large pot of boiling salted water, cook the noodles, separating them with a fork, until tender but still firm, about 2½ minutes. Drain and rinse under cold running water, drain well and toss with the vegetable oil.

3. Bring a large saucepan of salted water to a boil over high heat. Add the broccoli and cook until crisp-tender, 2 to 3 minutes. Using a slotted spoon, transfer to a bowl of ice water and chill until cold, about 5 minutes. Drain on paper towels. Repeat with the asparagus, cooking them for only 1 to 2 minutes.

4. In a small saucepan, bring the stock to a boil over moderately high heat; remove from the heat. Stir in the peanut butter, vinegar, soy sauce, sesame oil, sherry, sugar, chili sauce, scallions, ginger, garlic and toasted sesame seeds.

5. In a large bowl, toss together the noodles, broccoli, asparagus, bean sprouts, mushrooms and red pepper. Add the dressing and toss to coat. Sprinkle the chives over the top just before serving.

—Hugh Carpenter

• • •

GRILLED VEGETABLE AND MOZZARELLA SALAD WITH CHIPOTLE VINAIGRETTE

This is one of my favorite main-course salads. I love to grill the vegetables over a mesquite fire, but you could also use the broiler. Let the vegetables cool just to room temperature and serve the salad on large plates.

🍷 The smoky, complex flavors of this salad would overwhelm wine, but an elegant beer with a bite of hops—such as Anchor Steam, Samuel Adams or New Amsterdam—would be refreshing.

—— *6 Main-Course Servings* ——

1½ teaspoons Dijon-style mustard
1 egg yolk
2 chipotle peppers in adobo sauce,* stemmed and minced
2 tablespoons white wine vinegar
1¼ teaspoons salt
1 cup light olive oil
1 tablespoon adobo sauce from the can of chipotles
18 small red potatoes
½ teaspoon freshly ground black pepper
3 medium zucchini, quartered lengthwise
3 medium yellow squash, quartered lengthwise
18 large scallions
3 large red bell peppers, quartered
6 slices of peasant bread, cut 1 inch thick
1½ pounds fresh mozzarella cheese, at room temperature, cut into 6 wedges
****Available at Latin American markets***

1. In a medium bowl, whisk together the mustard, egg yolk, chipotle peppers, vinegar and ¼ teaspoon of the salt. Gradually whisk in ½ cup of the oil and the adobo sauce. Cover and set aside.

2. Preheat the oven to 500°. In a large saucepan, cover the potatoes with cold salted water. Bring to a boil over high heat, reduce the heat and simmer until just tender, 10 to 12 minutes. Drain the potatoes and cut into quarters.

3. Spread the potatoes on a baking sheet. Brush with 2 tablespoons of the olive oil and sprinkle with ½ teaspoon of the salt and ¼ teaspoon of the black pepper. Bake until crisp and golden brown, about 15 minutes. Remove from the oven the keep warm.

4. Prepare the grill, if using. Soak a handful of mesquite chips in water. Pre-

pare a charcoal fire and allow it to burn down until the coals are evenly white. Drain the mesquite chips and scatter them over the coals. Position the grill about 6 inches above the coals. Turn the oven to broil if you won't be grilling outdoors.

5. Brush the zucchini, yellow squash, scallions and bell peppers with 4 tablespoons of the oil and arrrange on the grill. Cook, turning once, until the vegetables are lightly browned, 3 to 4 minutes. Transfer the vegetables to a plate and season lightly with salt and black pepper.

Alternatively, spread the zucchini and yellow squash on a broiler rack, brush with 2 tablespoons of the oil, season with ¼ teaspoon of the salt and ⅛ teaspoon black pepper. Broil 6 inches from the heat until golden brown and softened, about 3 minutes on each side. Remove from the broiler, cover with aluminum foil and keep warm. Then spread the scallions and red peppers on the broiler rack, brush them with 2 tablespoons of the oil and season with the remaining salt and pepper. Broil until lightly browned, 2 to 3 minutes on each side. Remove, cover with foil and keep warm.

6. Brush the bread slices with the remaining 2 tablespoons oil and grill or broil until browned and crisp, 3 to 4 minutes on each side.

7. Arrange the mozzarella cheese and grilled vegetables on 6 dinner plates. Drizzle each serving with 1½ tablespoons of the chipotle vinaigrette and serve at room temperature. Pass the bread and the remaining vinaigrette separately.

—*Michael McLaughlin*

• • •

WARM SHRIMP SALAD WITH CHAMPAGNE VINEGAR SAUCE

At Lafayette, chef Jean-Georges Vongerichten tosses the mixed greens with edible wildflowers.

—6 First-Course Servings—

30 medium shrimp (about 1 pound), shelled
6 cups mixed salad greens such as watercress, radicchio, young chicory, arugula and mâche
6 large mushroom caps, peeled and cut into thin matchsticks
2 tomatoes—peeled, seeded and finely diced
3 shallots, minced
6 tablespoons Champagne vinegar or white wine vinegar
6 tablespoons heavy cream
1½ sticks (6 ounces) unsalted butter, at room temperature, cut into 12 pieces
¼ teaspoon salt
Pinch of cayenne pepper
Fresh chervil sprigs, for garnish

1. Split the shrimp along the back, leaving a small portion attached at the top and bottom. Remove the veins. Flatten each shrimp to form a circle. Steam the shrimp until just opaque throughout, about 1½ minutes.

2. Toss the salad greens and arrange on 6 salad plates. Scatter the mushrooms over the top. Place a small mound of diced tomatoes in the center of each salad and surround with 5 shrimp.

3. In a small saucepan, combine the shallots and vinegar. Bring to a boil over moderately high heat and cook until the liquid is reduced to 2 tablespoons, about 2 minutes. Stir in the cream and boil until reduced to 3 tablespoons, 2 to 3 minutes longer.

4. Remove from the heat and whisk in the butter, a few pieces at a time, until thoroughly blended. Stir in the salt and cayenne. Spoon the sauce over the salads and garnish with a sprig of chervil. Serve warm.

—*Jean-Georges Vongerichten, Restaurant Lafayette, New York City*

• • •

LEMON SHRIMP SALAD

Here's a twist on the usual pairing of chicken and lemon. I find shrimp particularly appealing on a hot summer night.

—4 Main-Course Servings—

1 pound medium shrimp, shelled and deveined
1 tablespoon minced lemon zest
¼ cup fresh lemon juice
2 tablespoons ginger syrup (from preserved stem ginger)*
1 tablespoon soy sauce
½ teaspoon Chinese chili sauce*
½ teaspoon salt
2 tablespoons finely minced fresh ginger
1 garlic clove, minced
3 cups safflower or other vegetable oil
8 won ton skins*, cut into ¼-inch-wide strips
2 ounces rice sticks*, separated into small bundles
8 large romaine lettuce leaves
1 cup shredded carrots
¼ cup thinly sliced scallions
****Available at Oriental markets***

1. In a large saucepan of boiling water, cook the shrimp until opaque throughout, 1½ to 2 minutes. Drain and transfer to a bowl of ice water. Split the cooled shrimp in half lengthwise, pat dry, cover and refrigerate.

2. In a small jar, combine the lemon zest, lemon juice, ginger syrup, soy sauce, chili sauce, salt, ginger, garlic and 2 tablespoons of the safflower oil. Cover tightly and shake vigorously.

3. In a large skillet, heat the remaining oil over moderate heat until it just begins to smoke. Cook the won ton strips in several batches until light golden brown, about 1 minute. Using tongs or a slotted spoon, transfer them to a tray lined with paper towels. Cook the rice stick bundles in the same oil until they puff, about 10 seconds; drain on paper towels. *(The recipe can be prepared to this point up to several hours in advance.)*

4. Stack the romaine leaves and roll up from a long side into a tight cylinder. Slice the roll at 1/8-inch intervals and transfer the shredded lettuce to a large mixing bowl. Add the carrots, scallions and cooked shrimp. Shake the dressing, pour it over the salad and toss. Gently fold in the fried won ton skins and rice sticks. Serve immediately.

—Hugh Carpenter

• • •

THAI PAPAYA SCALLOP SALAD

Cool papaya, fresh bay scallops, sweet red pepper and crisp cucumber mingle with buttery pine nuts in a Thai sweet and sour lime dressing.

—4 to 6 Main-Course Servings—

3/4 cup pine nuts
1 tablespoon unsalted butter
1 tablespoon peanut oil
1 small garlic clove, minced
4 teaspoons finely minced fresh ginger
1 pound bay scallops
3 tablespoons fresh lime juice
2 tablespoons (packed) light brown sugar
1 tablespoon light soy sauce or 2 tablespoons fish sauce (nuoc mam)*
1/2 teaspoon Chinese chili sauce
2 scallions, minced
1 tablespoon minced fresh coriander
1 1/2 ripe papayas (about 2 pounds total)—peeled, seeded and cut into 1/2- inch dice
1 medium red bell pepper, cut into 1/2-inch dice
1 small cucumber, seeded and cut into 1/2-inch dice
1 pound spinach—stemmed, washed and patted dry
****Available at Oriental markets***

1. Preheat the oven to 325°. On a small baking sheet, toast the pine nuts until golden, about 10 minutes.

2. In a large skillet, melt the butter in the oil with the garlic and 2 teaspoons of the ginger over moderately high heat. Add the scallops and cook, tossing, until firm when pressed with your finger and just opaque throughout, about 2 minutes. Transfer the scallops to a plate and let cool for 15 minutes. Cover and refrigerate until ready to use.

3. In a medium jar, combine the lime juice, brown sugar, soy sauce, chili sauce, scallions, coriander and the remaining 2 teaspoons ginger. Cover the jar tightly and shake vigorously to blend and dissolve the sugar.

4. In a large bowl, combine the papayas, red pepper and cucumber. Add the scallops, all but 2 tablespoons of the reserved pine nuts and the dressing. Toss well to coat.

5. Divide the raw spinach among chilled dinner plates. Spoon the salad on top. Sprinkle the remaining 2 tablespoons pine nuts over the salads and serve.

—Hugh Carpenter

• • •

JADE CRAB SALAD

The special ingredient in the dressing, red sweet ginger (preserved red ginger in syrup), is available at all Chinese markets (Koon Chun or Mee Chun are a couple of well-known brands).

—6 Main-Course Servings—

1/2 cup pine nuts
3 tablespoons red wine vinegar
2 tablespoons syrup from the jar of preserved red ginger (below)
2 tablespoons safflower oil
1 tablespoon minced fresh ginger
1 teaspoon grated orange zest
1/2 teaspoon Chinese chili sauce
1/2 teaspoon salt
3/4 pound fresh spinach, stems removed, leaves shredded
1/2 pound lump crabmeat
1 large red bell pepper, cut into thin julienne strips
1 bunch of enoki mushrooms, separated, stem ends trimmed

A STYLISH SUMMER LUNCH

Everything in this colorful summer menu from Lee Bailey can be served cold or at room temperature. Serves 6.

Lobster and Artichoke Salad (p. 121)

Tomato Bruschetta (p. 149)

Wine and Iced Tea

Apple Sorbet (p. 220)

Hazelnut Cookies (p. 190)

Coffee

2 scallions, thinly sliced on the diagonal
1/3 cup finely julienned preserved red ginger

1. Preheat the oven to 350°. Spread out the pine nuts on a baking sheet and toast in the oven until golden brown, about 10 minutes.

2. In a bowl, whisk together the vinegar, red ginger syrup, oil, minced fresh ginger, orange zest, chili sauce and salt.

3. In a large bowl, combine the spinach, crabmeat, red pepper, mushrooms, scallions, preserved red ginger and toasted pine nuts. Add the dressing; toss well.

—Hugh Carpenter

• • •

LOBSTER AND ARTICHOKE SALAD

This recipe is a flexible one. You can substitute shrimp, if you prefer, for half or all of the lobster. And if you're not partial to artichokes, you can use avocado slices instead. However, the avocados should not be marinated, but tossed in just before serving. Although I didn't include it in this recipe, you can also add steamed corn kernels to the salad for a sunny splash of color.

—6 Main-Course Servings—

1 egg yolk, at room temperature
1 1/2 tablespoons Dijon-style mustard
1/3 cup red wine vinegar
1/2 cup extra-virgin olive oil
1/2 cup peanut oil
1/2 teaspoon salt
1/4 teaspoon freshly ground pepper
3 tablespoons minced chives
3 tablespoons chopped parsley
1 medium shallot, minced
1 package (9 ounces) frozen artichoke hearts, thawed and halved, or 4 large cooked artichoke hearts, cut in eighths
6 live lobsters (1 1/4 pounds each) or 1 1/2 pounds cooked lobster meat
1 head of Boston lettuce, separated into leaves
4 hard-cooked eggs, cut into 4 wedges each
Black olives, for garnish

1. In a food processor, combine the egg yolk, mustard and vinegar. Process for 30 seconds. With the machine on, add the olive oil and peanut oil slowly through the feed tube. Process for another 30 seconds. Transfer the dressing to a medium bowl. Stir in the salt, pepper, chives, parsley and shallot. Add the artichoke hearts and toss to coat.

2. In a large stockpot of boiling water, cook the lobsters, covered, over high heat for 10 minutes. Turn off the heat and let the stockpot stand for 3 minutes longer. Take out the lobsters and let them stand until cool. Carefully remove all the lobster meat from the shells. Cut into 1-inch pieces and add to the bowl containing the artichoke hearts. Toss to mix well. Cover with plastic wrap and refrigerate for at least 1 hour.

3. Line a large serving platter with the lettuce leaves. Using a slotted spoon, spoon the lobster and artichoke salad onto the platter. Arrange the egg wedges around the edges of the platter and garnish with the black olives. Serve chilled or at room temperature.

—Lee Bailey

• • •

COUSCOUS SALAD

I have been making this salad, in one form or another, for years. It is what friends request when I ask if there's anything I can bring for supper, and it's what I make, doubling the recipe, when I have guests for the weekend. Sunny yellow, flavored with cumin, ginger, cinnamon and turmeric, this becomes a main-course salad with the addition of chicken.

—6 to 8 Main-Course Servings—

2 cups chicken stock or canned broth
3/4 teaspoon cinnamon
1/2 teaspoon ground ginger
1/2 teaspoon ground cumin
1/4 teaspoon turmeric
3 tablespoons extra-virgin olive oil
1/2 pound skinless, boneless chicken breast or leftover cooked chicken
1 cup couscous
1 medium carrot, cut into 1/4-inch dice
1 small red bell pepper, cut into 1/4-inch dice
1 small cucumber or zucchini, cut into 1/4-inch dice
1 small red onion, cut into 1/4-inch dice
1 small Granny Smith apple, cut into 1/4-inch dice
1/3 cup currants or raisins
1 cup canned chick-peas, rinsed and drained
1/4 cup fresh lemon juice
1/2 teaspoon salt
1/4 teaspoon freshly ground black pepper

1. In a heavy medium saucepan, whisk together the chicken stock, cinnamon, ginger, cumin, turmeric and 1 1/2 tablespoons of the olive oil. Bring to a boil, reduce to a bare simmer and add the chicken breast if you are using uncooked chicken. Poach until white throughout but still moist, about 15 minutes. Remove the chicken and set aside to cool.

2. Return the stock to a boil. Add the couscous in a slow steady stream, stirring constantly, and continue to boil, stirring, for 1 minute. Cover the pot tightly, remove from the heat and let stand for 15 minutes.

3. Fluff the couscous grains with a fork, transfer to a large mixing bowl and let cool. Then fluff again, rubbing with your fingers to break up any lumps.

4. Cut the chicken (poached or left-over) into ½-inch dice. Add the chicken to the couscous. Add the carrot, bell pepper, cucumber, onion, apple, currants and chick-peas and toss.

5. In a small jar with a lid, shake the remaining 1½ tablespoons olive oil with the lemon juice, salt and pepper until well mixed. Pour over the salad and toss well. Cover and refrigerate for several hours or up to 3 days. Season with additional salt, pepper and lemon juice to taste before serving.

—Dorie Greenspan

• • •

TRIPLE-MUSTARD CHICKEN SALAD

Toasted mustard seeds make this chicken salad extra special. This dish will feed large crowds during the holidays, but it is also great for warm-weather picnics.

🍷 Serve a clean, crisp, dry, but assertive white. Try 1986 Bordeaux Blanc Sec, such as Maître d'Estournel, which is refreshingly light.

16 Main-Course Servings

8 pounds skinless, boneless chicken breasts
2 cups mayonnaise
¼ cup Pommery mustard
½ cup extra-sharp Dijon mustard
½ cup fresh lemon juice
½ teaspoon salt
1 teaspoon freshly ground pepper
12 large stalks of celery, peeled and thinly sliced on the diagonal
¾ cup mustard seeds
¼ cup extra-virgin olive oil
4 large bunches of watercress, tough stems removed

1. Put the chicken in a large heavy pot and add enough cold salted water to cover by a least 1 inch. Bring to a simmer over moderate heat. Reduce the heat to low and simmer until the chicken is juicy but no longer pink in the center, about 20 minutes. Remove and cut the chicken into 1-inch dice. *(The recipe can be prepared to this point up to 1 day in advance. Cover and refrigerate.)*

2. In a medium bowl, combine the mayonnaise, Pommery and Dijon mustards, lemon juice and salt and pepper; whisk to blend well.

3. In a large bowl, combine the chicken, celery and mustard mayonnaise. Toss to coat well.

4. In a medium skillet, combine the mustard seeds and olive oil. Cook, covered, over moderate heat, shaking the pan, until the seeds begin to pop, 1 to 2 minutes. Immediately remove from the heat and continue shaking the pan until the seeds are toasted and fragrant and have stopped popping. Scrape the seeds and oil over the salad and fold to combine.

5. Transfer the salad to a large serving bowl or a platter and surround with the watercress. Serve slightly chilled or at room temperature.

—Susan Wyler

• • •

THAI CHICKEN SALAD

On our first night in Bangkok several years ago, we had dinner at a small, out-of-the-way restaurant. One of the dishes we ate that evening was a delicious chicken salad. Here is my version, reassembled from notes I scribbled on a napkin.

6 Main-Course Servings

3 cups vegetable oil, for frying
20 won ton skins, cut into ¼-inch strips*
8 cups shredded mixed salad greens
4 cups of bite-size pieces of barbecued or roast chicken (from a 3-pound bird)
1 cup bean sprouts
1 large yellow bell pepper, cut into thin julienne strips
½ European seedless cucumber (about 8 ounces), cut into thin julienne strips
6 tablespoons fresh lime juice
¼ cup fish sauce (nuoc mam)*
¼ cup (packed) light brown sugar
4 serrano chiles, seeded and minced
½ teaspoon freshly grated nutmeg
1 tablespoon finely minced fresh lemon grass* (optional)
1 tablespoon finely minced fresh ginger
¼ cup minced fresh mint
3 tablespoons minced fresh basil
¼ cup dry-roasted unsalted peanuts, coarsely chopped
****Available at Oriental markets***

1. In a large skillet, heat the oil over moderately high heat until a strip of won ton bounces across the surface. Add the won ton strips in batches and fry, turning, until crisp and golden, about 1 minute. Transfer to paper towels; drain well.

2. In a large bowl, combine the mixed greens, chicken, bean sprouts, yellow pepper and cucumber.

3. In a medium bowl, whisk together the lime juice, fish sauce, brown sugar, chiles, nutmeg, lemon grass, ginger, mint and basil. Add the dressing to the salad and toss well. Gently fold in the crisp won ton strips. Turn out onto a serving platter and sprinkle with the peanuts.

—Hugh Carpenter

• • •

SOUTH SEA BEEF SALAD

The special ingredient in this salad is fish sauce, which is available at all Oriental markets. Buy the brand having the lightest color and use the sauce sparingly, as it can overwhelm subtler flavors.

4 Main-Course Servings

1/2 pound beef tenderloin
1/2 pound snow peas
2 tablespoons fish sauce (nuoc mam)
2 tablespoons fresh lime juice
1 tablespoon sugar
1/2 teaspoon Chinese chili sauce
1 garlic clove, minced
1 medium red onion, thinly sliced
2 medium red bell peppers, thinly sliced
1/2 pound jicama, cut into thin strips
2 tablespoons chopped roasted peanuts
1 tablespoon grated lime zest
1/2 teaspoon freshly grated nutmeg
1/4 cup minced fresh coriander

1. Place the meat in the freezer until very firm, about 20 minutes. Then cut into paper-thin slices. Stack the beef slices and cut into matchstick-size pieces. Put the meat on a plate and press plastic wrap directly on it so the meat is covered airtight. Refrigerate until ready to use.

2. In a large saucepan of boiling water, cook the snow peas for 10 seconds. Drain and rinse immediately under cold running water until cool. Drain well and pat dry. Cut the snow peas lengthwise into thin strips.

3. In a small bowl, combine the fish sauce, lime juice, sugar, chili sauce, garlic and 2½ tablespoons of water. Stir to dissolve the sugar.

4. In a large bowl, combine the red onion, red peppers, jicama, snow peas and half of the beef strips. Toss with the dressing and turn out onto a serving platter. Decorate with the remaining beef. Sprinkle the peanuts, lime zest, nutmeg and coriander over the top.

—Hugh Carpenter

• • •

VIETNAMESE SALAD WITH CHILE-MINT DRESSING

This salad is composed in the Vietnamese style. It contains a small amount of meat, lots of vegetables and a generous sprinkling of peanuts. If you want to double the amount of meat, cook it in two pans and double the dressing. This dish makes a delicious light lunch.

🍷 The sharp-flavored, spicy yet slightly sweet components of this salad will not marry well with wine, but would be complemented by a fine beer, such as Ringnes Export Lager, or a slightly sweet ale, such as New Amsterdam.

4 Main-Course Servings

1/2 pound boneless pork shoulder, trimmed of excess fat and cut into 1/4-inch-thick strips
2 large garlic cloves, minced
2 tablespoons soy sauce, preferably mushroom soy*
1 tablespoon peanut oil
1 medium onion, thinly sliced
1 1/2 tablespoons cider vinegar
1 1/2 tablespoons fresh lime juice
2 teaspoons Oriental fish sauce (nuoc mam)*
1 1/2 tablespoons chopped mint plus 1 1/2 tablespoons shredded mint
1/8 teaspoon chopped hot chile pepper
1/4 teaspoon sugar
1/4 teaspoon salt
2 large white turnips, peeled
2 large carrots, peeled
3 cups thinly sliced romaine lettuce
3 cups thinly sliced cabbage
1/3 cup chopped unsalted peanuts
****Available at Oriental markets***

1. Preheat the oven to 350°. In a medium bowl, toss the pork strips with 1 clove of the minced garlic and 1 tablespoon of the soy sauce. Set aside to marinate at room temperature for about 1 hour.

2. In a medium ovenproof skillet, heat 2 teaspoons of the peanut oil. Add the onion slices and cook over moderately high heat, stirring occasionally, until the onions are evenly browned, about 5 minutes. Place the skillet in the oven and cook, stirring occasionally, until the onions are dry and deep brown, about 25 minutes. Remove from the skillet and set aside.

3. In a medium bowl, whisk the vinegar, lime juice, fish sauce, chopped mint, remaining minced garlic, hot pepper, sugar, salt and ⅓ cup of water to blend well.

4. Using a food processor fitted with the grating disk, shred the turnips. Place them in a small bowl and toss with 3 tablespoons of the dressing. Shred the carrots. Place them in another bowl and toss with 3 tablespoons of the dressing.

5. In a large skillet, heat the remaining 1 teaspoon peanut oil over high heat. Add the pork strips to the skillet in an even layer and cook, without stirring, until browned on the bottom, about 2 minutes. Turn and cook until browned on the second side, about 2 minutes longer. Add the remaining 1 tablespoon soy sauce and stir to coat the meat well. Remove the meat to a plate and set aside to cool.

6. In a large bowl, toss the lettuce, cabbage, shredded mint and pork with the remaining dressing and any accumulated dressing from the turnips and carrots. Arrange the turnip and carrot on opposite sides of each of 4 salad plates and place the pork and vegetable mixture in the center. Sprinkle the charred onions and chopped peanuts over all. Or place ingredients in separate bowl and allow guests to compose their own salads.

—Marcia Kiesel

• • •

WILD SOUTH SEA SALAD

This salad combines an ingredient never used in traditional Oriental food—wild rice—with shredded barbecued pork and a ginger-shallot rice vinegar dressing.

— 4 to 6 Main-Course Servings —

½ pound pork tenderloin
1½ tablespoons hoisin sauce*
1 tablespoon plum sauce*
1½ teaspoons oyster sauce*
1½ teaspoons honey
¼ teaspoon Chinese chili sauce
1½ tablespoons minced fresh ginger
1 large garlic clove, minced
¾ cup wild rice
1½ teaspoons salt
12 snow peas
2 ounces fresh shiitake mushrooms, stemmed, caps cut into thin julienne strips
1 small red bell pepper, cut into thin julienne strips
1 small yellow bell pepper, cut into thin julienne strips
1 bunch of arugula, shredded (optional)
½ cup fresh coriander sprigs, chopped
2 tablespoons rice wine vinegar
¼ cup safflower oil
1 shallot, minced
****Available at Oriental markets***

1. Put the pork tenderloin in a small baking dish. In a small bowl, combine the hoisin sauce, plum sauce, oyster sauce, honey, chili sauce, 1½ teaspoons of the ginger and the garlic. Spread this marinade all over the pork and let stand at room temperature for 1 to 2 hours.

2. Preheat the oven to 350°. Bake the pork tenderloin until the internal temperature measures 155°, 30 to 40 minutes. Let cool completely. Cut into thin julienne strips about 2 by ⅛ inch.

3. Put the wild rice in a strainer and rinse under cold running water; drain. In a medium saucepan, bring 3 cups of water to a boil over high heat. Stir in the wild rice and 1 teaspoon of the salt. Reduce the heat to low and simmer until the rice grains are puffed and tender, about 45 minutes. Drain and fluff with a fork or chopsticks. Let cool to room temperature and refrigerate until well chilled.

4. Bring a small saucepan of salted water to a boil over high heat. Add the snow peas and cook until brightly colored and crisp-tender, 6 to 8 seconds. Drain and rinse under cold running water until cool. Drain on paper towels and cut into thin julienne strips.

5. In a large serving bowl, combine the pork, wild rice, snow peas, mushrooms, red and yellow peppers, arugula and coriander. Toss to mix well.

6. In a small bowl, whisk together the vinegar, oil, shallot and remaining 1 tablespoon ginger and ½ teaspoon salt. Pour over the salad and toss to coat.

—Hugh Carpenter

• • •

BARLEY-HAM SALAD WITH HONEY MUSTARD DRESSING

I enjoy barley as much for its texture as for its taste. This salad highlights both. Make it at least several hours ahead, and you'll have a piquant blend of flavors from the honey mustard dressing and smokiness from the ham.

— 6 to 8 Main-Course Servings —

¼ cup plus 1 tablespoon peanut oil
1 cup pearl barley
2 cups chicken stock or canned broth
½ teaspoon salt
1½ tablespoons Dijon-style mustard
1½ tablespoons cider vinegar
1 tablespoon fresh lemon juice
2 tablespoons honey
¼ teaspoon freshly ground black pepper
Dash of hot pepper sauce (optional)
1 cup peas, fresh or frozen
3 carrots, shredded
½ cup finely diced red or yellow bell pepper
½ pound smoked ham, such as Black Forest, cut into ½-inch dice
Tomato wedges, for garnish

1. In a heavy medium saucepan, heat 1 tablespoon of the oil. Add the barley and sauté over moderate heat until the grains are coated with oil. Add the chicken stock, salt and 1 cup of water. Bring to a boil over high heat. Reduce the heat to moderately low, cover and simmer for 40 minutes, or until almost all of the liquid is absorbed. Remove from the heat and let stand, covered, for 10 minutes. Turn the barley into a bowl and let cool to room temperature.

2. In a blender or food processor, mix together the remaining ¼ cup oil, the

SOUP AND SALAD

Here's a lunch or light supper menu for any time of year. If you are preparing this in the summer, serve the soup cold instead of hot. Serves 6 to 8.

Watercress Soup (p. 38)

Barley-Ham Salad with Honey Mustard Dressing (p. 124)

Pumpernickel Rolls with Sweet Butter

Amber Beer

Coffee Ice Cream

Chocolate Chip Macadamia Nut Cookies (p. 189)

mustard, vinegar, lemon juice, honey, black pepper and hot sauce. Process for 2 minutes, or until the dressing is thickened and creamy.

3. If using fresh peas, blanch in boiling water until just tender, about 2 minutes; drain and pat dry. If using frozen peas, thaw and pat dry.

4. In a large salad bowl, toss the barley with the dressing. Add the carrots, bell pepper, ham and peas. Toss well and refrigerate for several hours or overnight. *(The salad can be made up to 3 days ahead.)* Garnish with tomato wedges before serving.

—Dorie Greenspan

• • •

MACHE, RADICCHIO AND BELGIAN ENDIVE SALAD

6 Servings

1/4 pound mâche lettuce (lamb's lettuce or field salad), about 2 cups
1 head of radicchio, leaves separated and torn into bite-size pieces
4 Belgian endives, sliced crosswise
2 tablespoons safflower oil or other flavorless vegetable oil
1 1/2 tablespoons extra-virgin olive oil
1 1/2 teaspoons Dijon-style mustard
1/4 teaspoon salt
1/4 teaspoon freshly ground pepper
1 tablespoon red wine vinegar

1. In a large salad bowl, combine the mâche, radicchio and endive.

2. In a small bowl, comine the safflower oil, olive oil, mustard, salt and pepper. Whisk in the vinegar and pour over the salad. Toss and serve.

—Lee Bailey

• • •

SALAD OF PEARS AND MIXED GREENS WITH CHEVRE

This refreshing salad from Laura Chenel would work as a first or a cheese course.

8 First-Course Servings

1/2 cup coarsely chopped walnuts
1 tablespoon red wine vinegar
1/2 cup walnut oil
1 garlic clove, lightly crushed
1/4 teaspoon salt
1/8 teaspoon freshly ground white pepper
2 heads of Bibb lettuce, torn into bite-size pieces
2 bunches of arugula, large stems removed, torn into bite-size pieces
3 ripe pears, cored and sliced
1/2 pound mild, creamy goat cheese, cut into 8 rounds

1. Preheat the oven to 350°. Spread the walnuts on a baking sheet and bake until lightly toasted, 10 to 12 minutes.

2. In a small bowl, whisk together the vinegar and oil. Add the garlic and set aside to steep at room temperature for at least 1 hour, or refrigerate overnight. Discard the garlic clove and season the dressing with the salt and pepper.

3. In a large bowl, toss the lettuce and arugula with two-thirds of the dressing. Divide the greens among 8 salad plates.

4. Toss the pears with the remaining dressing. Arrange the slices and a round of goat cheese alongside each salad and scatter the toasted walnuts over the top.

—Laura Chenel

• • •

QUATORZE'S CHICORY AND BACON SALAD

This recipe for a classic French salad called *frisée aux lardons* makes two very generous portions.

2 Servings

2 shallots, minced
2 tablespoons Dijon-style mustard
2 1/2 tablespoons red wine vinegar
1/8 teaspoon freshly ground pepper
1/2 cup extra-virgin olive oil
2/3 pound slab bacon, cut into 1/2-inch cubes
1/2 loaf French bread, crust removed, bread cut into 1/2-inch cubes
1 head of chicory (curly endive), torn into large pieces (about 6 cups)
Salt (optional)

1. In a small bowl, whisk together the shallots, mustard, vinegar and pepper. Gradually whisk in the olive oil in a thin stream.

2. In a medium skillet, cook the bacon over moderate heat until browned and crisp, about 10 minutes. Remove with a slotted spoon and set aside.

3. Pour off and discard all but 1/4 cup of the fat from the pan. Add the bread cubes to the hot bacon fat and sauté over moderately high heat, tossing until lightly browned, about 5 minutes. Remove and set aside.

4. Return the bacon to the skillet and toss until heated through. Remove from the heat and stir in the dressing.

5. Place the chicory in a large bowl. Add the dressing, bacon and bread cubes to the bowl and toss well. Salt lightly if desired. Serve immediately.

—Quatorze, New York City

• • •

MIXED LEAF SALAD WITH ROASTED WALNUTS AND ROQUEFORT

Slow roasting is the key to bringing out the true character of the walnuts in this salad. Any mix of greens can be used as the base, so don't feel confined by those listed below.

2 Servings

½ cup coarsely chopped walnuts
1 tablespoon red wine vinegar
1 tablespoon Dijon-style mustard
⅛ teaspoon salt
3 tablespoons extra-virgin olive oil
2 teaspoons minced parsley
Freshly ground pepper
4 cups mixed salad greens, such as arugula, radicchio, chicory and red leaf lettuce
⅓ cup crumbled Roquefort cheese

1. Preheat the oven to 275°. Spread the walnuts on a baking sheet and roast in the oven for 45 minutes, until fragrant and golden. Let cool.

2. In a small bowl, combine the vinegar, mustard and salt. Gradually whisk in the olive oil. Stir in the parsley and season with pepper to taste.

3. In a large bowl, toss the salad greens with the roasted walnuts, Roquefort and the vinaigrette. Divide the salad between 2 plates and serve immediately.

—Bob Chambers

• • •

SALAD OF PEARS AND STILTON WITH SAGE LEAVES

Sage blossoms are used here (although they are optional), so keep this recipe in mind the next time your sage plants bloom.

🍷 With its fresh fruit, raw greens and salty blue cheese, this dish provides a challenge that can be met by a deep-flavored wine, such as a Hunter Valley Semillon from Australia—1985 Tyrell's—or a white Hermitage from the Rhône—1985 Chapoutier Hermitage Chante-Alouette.

4 First-Course Servings

1 teaspoon Dijon-style mustard
1½ tablespoons Champagne vinegar or white wine vinegar
⅓ cup light olive oil
¼ teaspoon salt
¼ teaspoon freshly ground pepper
4 tablespoons unsalted butter
24 large fresh sage leaves plus 2 tablespoons chopped fresh sage
2 cups ½-inch French bread cubes
2 ripe pears, preferably Bosc—peeled, cored, halved and sliced into ¼-inch-thick wedges
½ head of Boston lettuce, torn into bite-size pieces
½ head of escarole, torn into bite-size pieces
½ head of romaine lettuce, torn into bite-size pieces
½ head of red leaf lettuce, torn into bite-size pieces
½ cup thinly sliced red onion
3 ounces Stilton cheese, crumbled
¼ cup sage blossoms (optional)

1. In a small bowl, whisk together the mustard, vinegar, olive oil, salt and pepper. Set the vinaigrette aside.

2. In a large skillet, melt 1 tablespoon of the butter over moderate heat. Add the whole sage leaves. Increase the heat to moderately high and fry until the leaves are golden brown and crisp on the bottom, about 1 minute. Turn the leaves and cook until crisp on the second side, about 1 minute longer. Remove to a plate.

3. Melt the remaining 3 tablespoons butter in the same skillet over moderate heat. Add the bread cubes and sprinkle the chopped sage over them. Toss to coat the bread evenly with the butter and sage. Cook, turning occasionally, until the cubes are golden brown and crunchy, about 4 minutes. Season the croutons with an additional pinch of salt.

4. In a medium bowl, toss the pears with 2 tablespoons of the vinaigrette until evenly coated. In a large bowl, combine the lettuces and red onion and toss with the remaining vinaigrette.

5. Place an equal amount of lettuce on each of 4 large plates and arrange the pear slices on top. Sprinkle each salad with Stilton cheese and top with the toasted sage leaves, croutons and sage blossoms.

—Marcia Kiesel

• • •

TOSSED SALAD WITH SHERRY WINE VINAIGRETTE

Here's a simple and tasty salad to serve to a crowd. As a side salad it will serve about 12 people, but in a buffet, along with other salads, it should serve as many as 50. To keep the salad from wilting when it's part of a large buffet, dress only one-fourth of the salad at a time and add more to the serving bowl as necessary.

50 Servings

1 large head of romaine lettuce, torn into bite-size pieces
1 large head of Boston lettuce, torn into bite-size pieces
4 heads of radicchio, torn into bite-size pieces

1 large head of chicory (curly endive), torn into bite-size pieces
3 tablespoons plus 1 teaspoon sherry wine vinegar
½ cup plus 2 tablespoons extra-virgin olive oil
1 teaspoon salt
1 teaspoon freshly ground pepper
2 medium red onions, thinly sliced
1 cup Niçoise olives

1. In a large bowl, combine the romaine, Boston lettuce, radicchio and chicory. *(The lettuce can be prepared up to 1 day in advance. Store in airtight bags in the refrigerator.)*

2. In a bowl, whisk the vinegar, olive oil, salt and pepper. Set aside.

3. When ready to serve the salad, toss one-fourth of the lettuce mixture, half of one sliced red onion and ¼ cup of the olives. Toss with one-fourth of the dressing. Refresh as necessary with more lettuce, onion, dressing and olives.

—Susan Wyler

• • •

CUCUMBER-TOMATO SALAD WITH RED ONIONS AND TOASTED CUMIN

Toasted cumin adds delicious flavor to this otherwise simple salad.

25 to 30 Servings

2 teaspoons cumin seeds
1 teaspoon dry mustard
1 teaspoon salt
½ teaspoon freshly ground pepper
½ cup red wine vinegar
1½ cups extra-virgin olive oil
3 cups thinly sliced red onions
6 pounds cucumbers
2 pints cherry tomatoes, halved

1. In a small skillet, toss the cumin seeds over moderate heat until fragrant and toasted, 2 to 3 minutes. Chop finely and set aside.

2. In a medium bowl, whisk the dry mustard, salt, pepper, vinegar, cumin seeds and olive oil. Add the onions and marinate in the refrigerator overnight.

3. Using a vegetable peeler, cut off the ends of the cucumbers. For a striped effect, peel alternate strips of the cucumber skin. Cut the cucumbers in half lengthwise and scoop out the seeds. Slice into ¼-inch-thick crescents.

4. Remove the onion from the vinaigrette; reserve the dressing. Toss the cucumbers with the onions and two-thirds of the dressing, and arrange on a large serving platter. Toss the cherry tomatoes with the remaining dressing and arrange them decoratively around the cucumbers and onions.

—Bob Chambers

• • •

JICAMA, MANGO AND PAPAYA SALAD WITH LIME-SESAME DRESSING

Clive du Val III serves this sweet-tart salad at his snazzy Latin restaurant, Tila's, in Houston, Texas, and sister establishment in Washington, D.C. For a fragrant variation on the dressing, he sometimes replaces the sesame seeds with the pulp of two passion fruits.

6 Servings

3 tablespoons hulled sesame seeds
2½ tablespoons fresh lime juice
2½ tablespoons fresh orange juice
1 tablespoon honey
½ teaspoon salt
1 large shallot, minced
⅛ teaspoon cayenne pepper
⅔ cup light olive oil
1 small head of romaine lettuce, torn into strips
1 small head of Bibb lettuce, torn into strips
1 medium jicama, peeled and cut into 3-inch matchsticks
1 large or 2 small papayas—peeled, halved, seeded and cut into long, thin slices
2 small mangoes, peeled and cut into long, thin slices

1. In a small nonstick skillet, toast the sesame seeds over low heat, stirring, until golden, 6 to 8 minutes. Let cool.

2. In a small jar, combine the lime juice, orange juice, honey, salt, shallot and cayenne; cover and shake to mix. Add the oil and the sesame seeds and shake until thoroughly blended.

3. In a large bowl, toss the romaine and Bibb lettuce with half the dressing. Arrange the salad on 6 plates and divide the jicama, papaya and mango over the greens. Spoon the remaining dressing evenly over the salads and serve.

—Clive du Val III, Tila's, Houston

• • •

BAKED BEET AND ENDIVE SALAD

6 Servings

2 bunches of beets, with ½ inch of tops
2 teaspoons green peppercorn mustard
¼ cup balsamic vinegar
2 teaspoons salt
1 teaspoon freshly ground pepper
¼ cup plus 2 tablespoons safflower oil
¼ cup light olive oil
4 Belgium endive, separated into individual leaves
2 tablespoons chopped chives

1. Preheat the oven to 425°. Line a large roasting pan with foil. Place the beets in the pan in a single layer. Cover the pan with foil and bake until the beets are tender, about 1 hour.

2. When the beets are cool enough to handles, remove the tops and slip off the skins. Cut the beets into ½-inch wedges.

3. In a small bowl, combine the mustard, vinegar, salt and pepper. Slowly whisk in the safflower and olive oils.

4. In a medium bowl, toss the beets with three-fourths of the vinaigrette. Arrange the endive leaves on a large plate, mound the beets on top, pour on the remaining dressing and sprinkle with the chopped chives.

—Lee Bailey

• • •

CRACKED WHEAT-SPINACH SALAD

Prepare the mushrooms and pear while the cracked wheat is cooking to prevent them from discoloring.

4 to 6 Servings

⅓ cup plus 2 teaspoons olive oil
2 large shallots, finely chopped
1 garlic clove, minced
½ cup cracked wheat
¼ teaspoon salt
¼ pound mushrooms
1 large pear
1 tablespoon Dijon-style mustard
2 tablespoons white wine vinegar
6 scallions, thinly sliced
4 plum tomatoes or 2 medium tomatoes, cut into ⅜-inch dice
3 tablespoons raisins
⅓ cup cashews or walnuts, broken or coarsely chopped
Freshly ground pepper
½ pound fresh spinach, stemmed and torn into large pieces

1. In a heavy medium saucepan, heat 2 teaspoons of the olive oil. Add the shallots and garlic and cook over moderate heat, stirring frequently, for 1 minute. Add the cracked wheat and continue to cook, stirring, until the kernels are covered with oil and the bottom of the pan is dry, about 1 minute. Add the salt and 1 cup of water, stir once and bring to a boil. Cover, reduce the heat to low and cook until the liquid is absorbed, 10 to 15 minutes. Remove from the heat, fluff with a fork and transfer to a bowl to cool to room temperature.

2. Trim and thinly slice the mushrooms. Cut the pear into small dice.

3. In a large bowl, whisk together the mustard and vinegar. Slowly beat in the remaining ⅓ cup olive oil, whisking until the dressing is blended and creamy. Add the mushrooms, pear, scallions, tomatoes, raisins and nuts; toss to coat with dressing.

4. Add the cooled cracked wheat and toss again. Season with additional salt and pepper to taste. Arrange the spinach around the edge of the bowl and fill the center with the tossed grain salad.

—Dorie Greenspan

• • •

SALAD BAR MENU

You may not want to serve as many salads as are listed here, but try to include a range of textures in those you choose. Serves 12 to 16.

Peasant Bread

Assorted Cheeses

Chiffonade of Belgian Endive, Scallion and Romaine with Light Vinaigrette

Warm Shrimp Salad with Champagne Vinegar Sauce (p. 119)

Jicama, Mango and Papaya Salad with Lime-Sesame Dressing (p. 127)

Chick-Pea Salad (p. 130)

🍷 White Wine Sangria

Pear Butterscotch Pecan Strips (p. 217)

Coffee

DILLED TABBOULEH

Fresh dill, smoked trout and bulgur make a luncheon salad that would be appealing packed into lettuce leaves, scooped up on endive leaves or stuffed into tomatoes.

6 Servings

1 smoked brook trout (about 8 ounces)
1 cup bulgur
¼ cup extra-virgin olive oil
⅓ cup fresh lemon juice
¼ cup minced fresh dill
¼ cup chopped red onion
2 tablespoons capers, rinsed and drained
½ teaspoon salt
¼ teaspoon freshly ground pepper
1 large tomato, cut into ½-inch dice

1. Remove the fillets from the smoked trout; peel off the skin. Break the fish into ½- to ¾-inch pieces.

2. In a large bowl, pour 2 cups of warm water over the bulgur, cover and let soak for about 1 hour, until the grains are puffed and softened.

3. Line a sieve with a double thickness of dampened cheesecloth and drain the bulgur into the sieve. Draw up the ends of the cheesecloth and gently squeeze the bundle until all the excess moisture is removed.

4. Place the bulgur in a large salad bowl and toss with the olive oil and lemon juice. Add the trout, dill, red onion, capers, salt and pepper; toss well. Cover and refrigerate for 2 to 3 hours, until chilled.

5. Before serving, add the tomato and toss into the salad.

—Dorie Greenspan

• • •

BLACK-EYED PEA SALAD WITH ORANGE-JALAPENO DRESSING

This salad with Southwest flavors is from Associate Test Kitchen Director Marcia Kiesel.

8 Servings

1 pound dried black-eyed peas, rinsed and picked over
1 bay leaf
1 large red onion, finely diced
2 teaspoons grated orange zest
1/4 cup fresh orange juice
5 garlic cloves, minced
2 tablespoons unsulphured molasses
1/3 cup red wine vinegar
1/4 teaspoon hot pepper sauce
1/2 teaspoon thyme
1 teaspoon salt
1/2 teaspoon freshly ground black pepper
3/4 cup light olive oil
1 large cucumber—peeled, seeded and cut into 1/2-inch dice
1 small jalapeño pepper with its seeds, minced

1. In a large saucepan, cover the peas with 4 inches of cold water. Add the bay leaf and bring to a boil over moderate heat. Reduce the heat to low and simmer, stirring occasionally, until the peas are tender, about 50 minutes; add water if the peas look dry.

2. Drain the peas in a colander and rinse well under cold water; discard the bay leaf. Transfer the peas to a large bowl and toss with the red onion.

3. In a medium bowl, combine the orange zest, orange juice, garlic, molasses, vinegar, hot sauce, thyme, salt and black pepper. Whisk in the olive oil. Add the dressing to the peas and toss well. Set aside at room temperature until serving time. *(The recipe can be prepared up to 1 day ahead. Cover and refrigerate.)*

4. Just before serving, fold in the cucumber and jalapeño.

—Marcia Kiesel

• • •

BLACK BEAN, CORN AND POBLANO PEPPER SALAD WITH TOASTED CUMIN VINAIGRETTE

This side salad could complement any southwestern meal, but seems especially appropriate alongside a grill entrée. It can be assembled one day ahead, and the quantities can be increased if a crowd is on the way. Cilantro (fresh coriander) fans will recognize this salad as a perfect vehicle for the herb. Chop the leaves and stir them into the salad just before serving.

4 to 6 Servings

1 1/2 cups dried black beans, rinsed and picked over to remove any grit
1 tablespoon plus 1 teaspoon salt
4 poblano peppers
1 tablespoon cumin seeds
1/4 cup sherry wine vinegar
1 tablespoon Dijon-style mustard
2 teaspoons freshly ground black pepper
1/2 cup olive oil
2 cups corn kernels—fresh, defrosted or drained canned
18 cherry tomatoes, cut in half
3 scallions, thinly sliced

1. In a large bowl, combine the beans with enough cold water to cover by at least 3 inches. Let stand for 24 hours at room temperature. Alternatively, cover the beans with water in a saucepan and bring to a boil. Remove from the heat and let stand, covered, for 1 hour.

2. Drain the beans and transfer to a large saucepan. Add enough fresh cold water to cover by at least 3 inches and bring to a boil over high heat. Reduce the heat and simmer, partially covered, for 30 minutes. Stir in 2 teaspoons of the salt and continue cooking until the beans are just tender, 35 to 45 minutes longer; drain.

3. Meanwhile, roast the poblanos directly over a gas flame or under a broiler as close to the heat as possible until the skins are lightly charred. Seal in a paper bag and let steam for 10 minutes. Rub away the charred skin. Stem and seed the peppers and cut into 3/4-inch squares.

4. In a small dry skillet, toast the cumin seeds over moderately high heat, tossing, until fragrant and golden brown, about 1 minute. Grind in a spice mill or finely chop on a cutting board.

5. In a small bowl, whisk together the vinegar, mustard, cumin seeds, black pepper and remaining 2 teaspoons salt. Slowly whisk in the oil.

6. In a large bowl, combine the black beans, poblano peppers and corn. Pour the dressing over the salad and toss well. *(The recipe can be prepared to this point up to 24 hours ahead. Cover and refrigerate. Let return to room temperature before proceeding.)*

7. Add the tomatoes and scallions to the salad, toss well and season with additional salt and pepper to taste. Serve at room temperature.

—Michael McLaughlin

• • •

BLACK BEAN AND CELERY SALAD

This flavorful salad, with its crunch of fresh vegetables, is tossed with a tangy lime dressing. You can make this a no-cook dish by substituting three 1-pound cans of black beans for the dried; if you do so, rinse and drain the beans and begin at Step 2.

16 Servings

1 pound dried black beans, rinsed and picked over to remove any grit
2 1/4 teaspoons salt

5 celery ribs, finely diced
1 large green bell pepper, finely chopped
3 red onions (about ¾ pound)—2 finely chopped, 1 thinly sliced
⅔ cup olive oil or other vegetable oil
⅓ cup fresh lime juice
¾ teaspoon freshly ground black pepper
Grated zest of 1 lime
Red onion rings, for garnish

1. Place the beans in a large saucepan or flameproof casserole and add enough cold water to cover by 2 inches. Let soak overnight. Alternatively, bring the water to a boil. Remove from the heat, cover and let soak for 1 hour.

2. Drain the beans, return them to the pot and add fresh cold water to cover by 2 inches. Bring to a boil, reduce the heat to low and simmer until the beans are almost tender, about 45 minutes. Add 1 teaspoon of the salt and cook until tender, 30 to 45 minutes longer. Drain the beans and set aside to cool. *(The beans can be cooked up to 3 days ahead. Refrigerate, covered.)*

3. In a large bowl, combine the black beans, celery, green pepper, chopped red onions and sliced red onion. Toss to mix.

4. In a small jar, combine the oil, lime juice, black pepper, lime zest and remaining 1¼ teaspoons salt. Cover with a tight lid and shake to blend.

5. Pour the dressing over the bean salad and toss well. *(The salad can be made up to 3 hours ahead and tossed again just before serving. Let stand at room temperature.)* Garnish with onion rings just before serving.

—Diana Sturgis

• • •

CHICK-PEA SALAD

I first sampled this dish at the Auberge d'Aillane, a casual family restaurant on the outskirts of Aix-en-Provence run by Madame Curto. In the summer months, I keep this salad on hand to serve as an appetizer or lunch dish or as a side dish with grilled fish or meats.

🍷 Drink a Côtes de Provence Rosé, such as Commanderie de Peyrassol.

8 to 10 Servings

1½ cups (8 ounces) dried chick-peas, rinsed and picked over to remove any grit
2 tablespoons red wine vinegar
5 garlic cloves, minced
½ teaspoon salt
⅛ teaspoon freshly ground pepper
2 tablespoons finely chopped mixed fresh herbs, such as rosemary, thyme, tarragon and parsley
½ cup extra-virgin olive oil
½ cup (2 ounces) oil-cured black olives, preferably from Nyons, pitted and halved
1 medium red onion, minced

1. Place the dried chick-peas in a medium saucepan and add enough cold water to cover by 2 inches. Set aside to soak overnight.

2. Drain the chick-peas, return them to the saucepan, cover again with cold water and bring to a boil over high heat. Reduce the heat, cover and simmer over low heat until tender, about 2 hours and 15 minutes.

3. In a medium bowl, whisk together the vinegar, garlic, salt, pepper and fresh herbs. Gradually whisk in the oil.

4. Drain the chick-peas. Add to the dressing along with the olives and onion. Toss to mix. Serve warm, at room temperature or chilled. *(The recipe can be made up to 3 days in advance and stored, covered, in the refrigerator.)*

—Patricia Wells

• • •

RED POTATO SALAD WITH GREEN BEANS AND RED PEPPER STRIPS

This vegetable salad can be composed to resemble a Christmas wreath.

32 Servings

½ cup minced shallots
⅓ cup Dijon-style mustard
½ cup tarragon wine vinegar or white wine vinegar
2 garlic cloves, crushed through a press
2 teaspoons tarragon
1 teaspoon salt
1½ teaspoons freshly ground pepper
3 cups olive oil
8 pounds small red potatoes
4 pounds green beans, trimmed and snapped in half
4 large red bell peppers, cut into 2-by-½-inch strips

1. In a medium bowl, whisk the shallots, mustard, vinegar, garlic, tarragon, salt and pepper. Whisk in the olive oil in a thin stream; set the dressing aside.

2. Put the potatoes in a large pot and add enough lightly salted cold water to cover. Bring the water to a boil. Simmer the potatoes until tender, 12 to 15 minutes; drain.

3. When just cool enough to handle, cut the potatoes in half. Toss the warm potatoes with half of the vinaigrette. Cover with plastic wrap and refrigerate overnight.

4. In a large pot of lightly salted boiling water, cook the beans until crisp-tender, 6 to 8 minutes. Drain and rinse under cold running water; drain well.

5. Toss the potatoes with ⅔ cup of the vinaigrette and place in the center of 2 large platters. Toss the beans and pepper strips with the remaining dressing and arrange around the potatoes.

—Bob Chambers

• • •

PASTA, RICE & BREADSTUFFS

PASTA KAHAWA

Hugo's in West Hollywood has long taken their coffee service seriously. Their best strong brew has often overflowed into the list of daily specials like this one.

🍷 The sweet aftertaste of the artichokes is balanced here by the acrid undertones of the coffee, which allows this rice sauce to be matched by an equally full-bodied white wine: a 1985 California Chardonnay, such as Beringer.

6 Servings

3 cups quartered trimmed baby artichokes or 2 packages (9 ounces each) frozen artichoke hearts
1 tablespoon lemon juice or vinegar (optional)
1 cup strongly brewed coffee
1½ cups heavy cream
2 tablespoons Dijon-style mustard
1 tablespoon chopped fresh rosemary
Salt and freshly ground white pepper
2 tablespoons olive oil
½ pound fresh shiitake mushrooms, stems removed
1½ pounds fresh egg fettuccine

1. Cook the fresh artichokes in a large pot of boiling salted water acidulated with the lemon juice or vinegar until the artichokes are just tender, 10 to 15 minutes. Scoop out the fuzzy choke from each piece. If using frozen artichoke hearts, simply defrost them.

2. In a large nonreactive saucepan or flameproof casserole, marinate the artichokes in the coffee for 10 minutes.

3. Stir in the cream and bring to a boil. Reduce the heat to moderately low and simmer until the liquid is reduced by one-fourth, about 10 minutes.

4. Blend in the mustard and rosemary. Season with salt and white pepper to taste. Remove from the heat and cover to keep warm.

5. Meanwhile, in a large skillet, heat the olive oil. Add the shiitake mushrooms and sauté over moderately high heat until lightly browned, 3 to 5 minutes. Set aside.

6. In a large pot, bring at least 4 quarts of salted water to a boil. Add the fettuccine and cook until just tender, 1 to 2 minutes; drain well.

7. Bring the cream and artichoke mixture to a simmer over moderately high heat. Add the pasta and toss in the cream sauce for 30 to 60 seconds. Divide the fettuccine with artichokes among 6 dinner plates and top with the sautéed shiitake mushrooms.

—Hugo's, West Hollywood, California

• • •

PASTA FOR SIX

Here is a delightful spring pasta from Lee Bailey that calls for such simple, but tasty, ingredients as flavored olive oil, scallops and green peas, bound together lightly with toasted bread crumbs. Serves 6.

Pasta with Bay Scallops, Pancetta and Peas (p. 132)

Mâche, Radicchio and Belgian Endive Salad (p. 125)

Crusty Parmesan Toast (p. 150)

🍷 *Hearty Red Wine*

Grape Tart with Red Currant Glaze (p. 202)

Coffee

PASTA WITH BAY SCALLOPS, PANCETTA AND PEAS

Here, the trick is to have all your ingredients ready so that this dish can be assembled quickly. Boil the water for the pasta while cooking the pancetta and peas. This dish can be served with freshly grated Parmesan cheese, but frankly I like it better without.

6 Servings

4 slices of French bread, cut 1 inch thick
½ pound pancetta or bacon, thinly sliced and finely diced
¾ cup extra-virgin olive oil
2 tablespoons minced garlic
¼ cup plus 2 tablespoons chopped shallots
1 package (10 ounces) frozen small peas, thawed
¼ cup chopped parsley
1¼ teaspoons salt
1 teaspoon freshly ground black pepper
¼ teaspoon crushed hot pepper
1¼ pounds linguine
1½ pounds bay scallops

1. Preheat the oven to 400°. Put the bread slices in a food processor and turn the machine quickly on and off until the bread forms very coarse crumbs, about 1 minute. Put the crumbs on a baking sheet and bake until golden brown, about 5 minutes. Transfer to a small bowl and set aside.

2. Put on a large pot of salted water to boil for the pasta. In a small saucepan of boiling water, cook the pancetta for 2 minutes. Drain well. In a large flameproof casserole, cook the pancetta over moderately high heat until crisp, about 3 minutes. Remove the pancetta with a slotted spoon and drain on paper towels.

3. Pour all of the fat out of the pan and add ½ cup of olive oil. Add the garlic and shallots and cook over moderately low heat, stirring frequently, until softened and translucent, 3 to 5 minutes. Stir in the peas, parsley, 1 teaspoon of the salt, the black pepper and the hot pepper. Cook until the peas are heated through, about 3 minutes. Remove from the heat and set aside.

4. Add the linguine to the pot of boiling water and cook, stirring occasionally, until tender but firm, about 12 minutes. Drain well.

5. Meanwhile, in another flameproof casserole, heat the remaining ¼ cup olive oil over high heat. When the oil starts to smoke, add the scallops and cook, stirring frequently, until just opaque throughout, about 3 minutes. Season with the remaining ¼ teaspoon salt. Add the scallops to the peas. Set over high heat and toss in the cooked linguine, pancetta and bread crumbs. Divide among 6 large bowls and serve at once.

—*Lee Bailey*

• • •

TAGLIATELLE WITH ASPARAGUS

The asparagus pieces can be blanched early in the day, but be sure not to overcook them so that they will maintain their bright green color. The noodles can be store-bought or your own freshly made.

🍷 Italian white, such as 1986 Antinori Cervaro della Sala or 1986 Ruffino Libaio

—6 Servings—

1 pound asparagus, peeled and cut into 1-inch pieces
1 stick (4 ounces) unsalted butter
¼ pound thinly sliced prosciutto, cut into thin strips
⅔ cup drained canned Italian peeled tomatoes, chopped
½ teaspoon salt
1 teaspoon freshly ground pepper
1 pound egg noodles
½ cup freshly grated Parmesan cheese

1. Cook the asparagus in a large pot of boiling salted water until just tender, about 3 minutes. Rinse under cold running water to cool; drain well.

2. In a large skillet, melt 6 tablespoons of the butter over low heat. Add the prosciutto and cook for 2 minutes. Add the tomatoes, salt and pepper and simmer until the sauce is slightly thickened, about 5 minutes; remove from the heat.

3. In a large pot of boiling salted water, cook the noodles until tender but still firm, about 8 minutes for dry and 2 minutes for fresh. Drain the noodles and return to the pot.

4. Add the asparagus to the tomato sauce and reheat. Pour the sauce over the noodles, add the remaining 2 tablespoons butter and the Parmesan cheese and toss well. Transfer to a platter and serve at once.

—*Nancy Verde Barr*

• • •

FRESH TOMATO SAUCE WITH MINT AND GARLIC ON SPAGHETTI

This flavorful minty tomato sauce can turn an ordinary plate of spaghetti into a delicious treat.

—4 to 6 First-Course Servings—

4 garlic cloves, minced
3 tablespoons extra-virgin olive oil
3 pounds tomatoes—peeled, seeded and chopped
½ teaspoon salt
½ teaspoon freshly ground pepper
1 tablespoon chopped fresh mint leaves, preferably spearmint, or more to taste
¾ pound spaghetti

1. In a large skillet, place the garlic and 2 tablespoons of the olive oil. Cook over low heat until the garlic is fragrant, about 2 minutes. Increase the heat to high and cook until the garlic is golden, about 10 seconds longer. Add the tomatoes and cook over high heat, stirring occasionally, until the sauce is thick but chunky and some tomato liquid still remains, about 10 minutes. Turn off the heat and season with the salt, pepper and mint.

2. In a large saucepan of boiling salted water, cook the spaghetti until tender but still firm, about 8 minutes. Drain and toss with the remaining 1 tablespoon olive oil. Reheat the sauce over moderate heat. Place the pasta in a large serving bowl and toss with a third of the sauce. Pour the remaining sauce over the spaghetti; toss lightly and serve.

—*Marcia Kiesel*

• • •

PASTA CUSTARD

Ideally this custard should be allowed to rest for just a few minutes before you remove it from the dish. However, if necessary, it can wait for up to 20 minutes before unmolding.

—6 Servings—

½ pound capellini or angel hair pasta
3 eggs
1½ cups low-fat ricotta cheese
1½ tablespoons minced parsley
1 teaspoon salt
¼ teaspoon freshly ground black pepper
⅛ teaspoon hot pepper sauce
½ cup heavy cream
1 cup chicken stock or canned broth
1 tablespoon unsalted butter
2 tablespoons freshly grated Parmesan cheese

1. Preheat the oven to 350°. Generously butter a 2-quart shallow ovenproof casserole or baking dish.

2. Break the pasta in half and drop into a large pot of boiling salted water. Separate the strands with a fork, if necessary, as the water returns to a boil. Cook for 1½ minutes, or until the pasta is half-cooked. Drain and rinse under cold water. Shake off excess moisture and place in the prepared casserole.

3. In a large bowl, beat together the eggs and ricotta cheese. Whisk in the parsley, salt, black pepper, hot sauce, cream and chicken stock. Pour over the pasta and dot with the butter. Sprinkle the Parmesan cheese over the top.

4. Bake for 45 minutes, or until the custard is set and the top is lightly browned. Let cool for a few minutes before running a knife around the edge and unmolding.

—Lee Bailey

• • •

RIGATONI WITH SAUSAGE, SHIITAKE AND SAGE

🍷 Spices, sausage, cheese and mushrooms call for a bright-flavored red as a suitable foil. Try a fresh young Zinfandel, such as 1985 Nalle, or a fruity 1985 Dolcetto d'Alba, such as Valentino.

8 to 10 First-Course Servings
or 6 Main-Course Servings

1 pound sweet Italian sausage
1 pound beet greens (from about 2 large bunches)
1 pound rigatoni
2 tablespoons extra-virgin olive oil
3 tablespoons unsalted butter
1 pound fresh shiitake mushrooms, stemmed, cups thinly sliced
6 garlic cloves, minced
3 tablespoons chopped fresh sage, or more to taste
1½ cups heavy cream
1 cup milk
2 cups ricotta cheese
1 teaspoon salt
1 teaspoon freshly ground pepper

1. Put the sausages in a large saucepan, cover with water and bring to a boil over high heat. Reduce the heat to moderate and simmer until the sausages are cooked through, about 12 minutes. Drain and remove the casings; coarsely crumble the meat. Set aside.

2. In a steamer basket set in a large saucepan, steam the beet greens until wilted, about 1 minute. Drain and rinse with cold water. Squeeze any excess water from the greens and set aside.

3. In a large pot of boiling salted water, cook the rigatoni until tender but still firm, about 10 minutes. Drain and toss with 1 tablespoon of the olive oil.

4. In a large flameproof casserole, melt the butter in the remaining 1 tablespoon olive oil over moderately high heat. Add the shiitake mushrooms and cook, stirring occasionally, until lightly browned and wilted, about 4 minutes.

5. Reduce the heat to low and add the garlic and sage. Cook, stirring, until the garlic is fragrant, about 2 minutes. Add the cream, milk and reserved sausage and beet greens. Increase the heat to moderate; add the rigatoni and simmer, stirring occasionally, until the mixture thickens slightly, about 2 minutes. Stir in the ricotta cheese and the salt and pepper.

—Marcia Kiesel

• • •

TWO-MUSHROOM RAVIOLI WITH MUSHROOM CREAM SAUCE

🍷 Enhance the earthiness of the mushrooms and creaminess of the sauce with a big-bodied, oaky Chardonnay, such as a 1985 Chateau St. Jean Robert Young Vineyards or a 1985 Trefethen. If you prefer red wine, try a light red, such as a 1984 Bouchaine Carneros Pinot Noir.

6 First-Course Servings

2½ tablespoons extra-virgin olive oil
2½ tablespoons minced shallots
¾ cup chicken stock or canned broth
⅓ cup heavy cream
½ cup diced (½-inch) fresh mushrooms
3 tablespoons freshly grated Parmesan cheese
1 tablespoon minced parsley
1 tablespoon minced scallion green
Pinch of freshly ground pepper
½ recipe Two-Mushroom Ravioli (recipe follows)

1. Heat 1½ tablespoons of the olive oil in a medium saucepan over moderately high heat. Add the shallots and cook, stirring, until softened but not browned, about 2 minutes.

2. Add the stock and bring to a boil. Stir in the cream and return to a boil. Add the mushrooms, again return to a boil and remove from the heat. *(The recipe can be prepared to this point up to 3 hours in advance. Cover and set aside at room temperature.)*

3. Shortly before serving, bring the sauce to a boil. Add the cheese and stir well. Stir in the parsley, scallion and pepper. Remove from the heat and cover to keep warm.

4. Bring a large pot of salted water to a boil. Add the remaining 1 tablespoon olive oil. Add the Two-Mushroom Ravioli and stir with a wooden spoon to prevent sticking. Let the water return to a boil and then cook the ravioli for 30 to 60 seconds, or until just tender. Remove from the heat and add 1 cup of cold water to the pot to stop the cooking.

5. Spread a thin layer of the mushroom cream sauce in a warmed deep platter. Using a slotted spoon, arrange about half the ravioli on top of the sauce. Cover with more sauce and then add the remaining ravioli. Top with the remaining sauce and serve at once.

—Eileen Yin-Fei Lo

• • •

TWO-MUSHROOM RAVIOLI

Egg roll wrappers make wonderful ravioli, and the contrasting tastes of the two mushrooms used here are quite special, indeed.

Since it's nice to have a batch of homemade ravioli in the freezer, I have deliberately made enough to serve 12 people. Freeze what you're not using as soon as they are made to prevent drying out. Of course, you can cut the recipe in half if you prefer. To freeze, lay the uncooked ravioli on a sheet of waxed paper in a single layer, cover with another sheet of waxed paper, then arrange another layer on top. Wrap all in plastic wrap and then in aluminum foil.

Makes About 60 Ravioli

1 ounce dried morels
2½ tablespoons olive oil
1 large onion, cut into ¼-inch dice
½ pound fresh mushrooms, cut into ¼-inch dice
1 teaspoon sugar
1 teaspoon salt
Pinch of freshly ground pepper
1 tablespoon brandy
2 tablespoons minced fresh basil
2 tablespoons minced parsley
¼ cup freshly grated Parmesan cheese
1 cup ricotta cheese, preferably fresh
1 egg, beaten
14 egg roll wrappers

1. Put the morels in a small bowl and cover with warm water. Let stand until softened, about 20 minutes. Drain the morels and rinse to remove any sand; drain well. Cut the morels into ¼-inch dice.

2. In a large skillet, heat the olive oil. Add the onion and sauté over moderately high heat, stirring frequently, until lightly browned, about 5 minutes.

3. Increase the heat to high, add the morels and cook, stirring, for 30 seconds, Add the fresh mushrooms and cook, stirring frequently, for 1 minute. Reduce the heat to moderate, add the sugar, salt and pepper and mix well. Cook, stirring frequently, until the mushrooms are tender, about 3 minutes.

4. Transfer the mushroom mixture to a medium bowl and let cool to room temperature. Add the brandy, basil, parsley, Parmesan cheese, ricotta cheese and egg; mix well.

5. To form the ravioli, place 1 egg roll wrapper over a ravioli mold (each wrapper will cover 6 pockets). One end of the wrapper should overhang by about ½ inch, leaving a wide strip on the other side. Make pockets in the wrapper with the ravioli plunger and brush water liberally around the edges of each pocket. Fill each pocket with 2 teaspoons of the mushroom filling. Cover with a second wrapper.

6. Using a rolling pin, begin rolling lightly from the center of the form to each of the ends, until the top surface is flattened. Then roll firmly in both directions to seal and cut the ravioli. Discard the narrow edges of the cut wrappers. Reserve the large strips.

7. Invert the ravioli mold onto a sheet of waxed paper to remove the ravioli. Place the large ravioli strips back on the form to make 3 additional ravioli using the same process. Repeat with the remaining wrappers and filling. *(The ravioli can be assembled up to 1 hour before cooking; set aside at room temperature, covered with plastic wrap and a kitchen towel. Freeze for longer storage.)*

—Eileen Yin-Fei Lo

• • •

THREE-MUSHROOM LASAGNA WITH GORGONZOLA SAUCE

Susan Wyler's rich mushroom lasagna can be made ahead and frozen, making it an ideal dish for entertaining.

🍷 A Côtes du Rhône, such as 1985 Domaine Rejardière

8 to 12 Servings

½ pound lasagna noodles, preferably fresh
1 ounce dried porcini or other dried imported mushroom
1 stick (4 ounces) unsalted butter
2 tablespoons olive oil
2 large shallots, minced
1 pound fresh mushrooms, minced
½ teaspoon salt
¼ teaspoon freshly ground black pepper
¼ teaspoon tarragon
Cayenne pepper
2 tablespoons fresh lemon juice
1 garlic clove, minced
6 ounces fresh shiitake mushrooms, stemmed, caps sliced ¼ inch thick
¼ cup all-purpose flour
1 cup milk
½ cup heavy cream
¼ pound Gorgonzola dolcelatte cheese
¼ cup plus 2 tablespoons freshly grated Parmesan cheese

1. In a large pot of boiling salted water, cook the lasagna noodles until just tender, about 1 minute for fresh noodles, 12 minutes for dried. Drain and rinse under cold running water. Transfer the noodles to a bowl of cold water, then place in a single layer on kitchen towels to dry. Cover with plastic wrap and set aside.

2. In a small bowl, cover the dried porcini with 1½ cups of boiling water. Set aside until softened, 20 to 30 minutes. Remove the mushrooms, chop them coarsely and set aside. Strain the soaking liquid through a double layer of cheesecloth; reserve 1 cup.

3. In a large heavy skillet, melt 2 tablespoons of the butter in 1 tablespoon of the olive oil over moderately high heat. Add 2 tablespoons of the minced shallots and all of the minced fresh mushrooms. Sauté, stirring frequently, until all the liquid has evaporated and the mushrooms are lightly browned, 5 to 7 minutes.

4. Season the mushroom duxelles with ¼ teaspoon of the salt, the black pepper and tarragon. Add a dash of cayenne and sprinkle with 1 tablespoon of the lemon juice. Scrape the mushroom duxelles into a bowl. Wipe the skillet with a paper towel and set aside.

5. In the same large skillet, melt 1 tablespoon of the butter in the remaining 1 tablespoon oil over moderately high heat. Add the remaining minced shallots and the garlic and sauté for 30 seconds. Add the shiitake and chopped porcini mushrooms and sauté, stirring frequently, for 1 minute. Reduce the heat to moderately low and cook, stirring frequently, for 3 minutes. Add ½ cup of the reserved porcini liquid and simmer, partially covered, until the mushrooms are tender but still slightly chewy, about 5 minutes. Uncover and cook, stirring frequently, until the remaining mushroom liquid evaporates, about 2 minutes. Season with the remaining lemon juice. Add this mixture to the mushroom duxelles; blend well.

6. In a medium heavy saucepan, melt 4 tablespoons of the butter over moderate heat. Add the flour and cook, stirring, for 2 minutes without letting the flour brown. Whisk in the remaining ½ cup mushroom liquid, the milk and the cream. Bring to a boil, whisking constantly, until the mixture is thickened and smooth. Reduce the heat and simmer, whisking frequently, for 5 minutes.

7. Remove from the heat; whisk in the Gorgonzola and ¼ cup of the Parmesan cheese until melted and smooth. Season with the remaining ¼ teaspoon salt and a dash of cayenne.

8. Preheat the oven to 375°. Generously butter a 13-by-8-by-2-inch baking dish. Arrange a layer of noodles in the bottom of the dish, trimming to fit if necessary and overlapping the edges slightly. Spread a thin layer of the mushroom mixture over the noodles and drizzle about 1 cup of the sauce over the mushrooms. Repeat with a second layer of noodles, mushrooms and sauce. Top with a final layer of noodles. Spread the remaining sauce over the noodles and sprinkle the remaining 2 tablespoons grated Parmesan cheese over the top. Dot with the remaining 1 tablespoon butter. *(The lasagna can be assembled to this point up to 1 day ahead; refrigerate, covered; or freeze for up to 2 weeks.)*

9. Bake the lasagna, uncovered, until heated through and golden on top, 15 to 20 minutes.

—Susan Wyler

• • •

CURRY COUSCOUS WITH FRESH CHIVES

Serve this couscous side dish with Five-Spice Roast Squab with Rice Wine-Butter Sauce (p. 90).

4 to 6 Servings

2 tablespoons olive oil
½ cup finely chopped onions
2 cups quick-cooking couscous
2 cups chicken stock or canned broth
1 tablespoon dark soy sauce
1 tablespoon unsalted butter
2 tablespoons Madras curry paste or powder
1 teaspoon sugar
⅓ cup chopped fresh chives
⅓ cup finely diced red apple
Salt and freshly ground white pepper

1. In a medium saucepan, heat the olive oil over moderately low heat. Add the onions and cook until softened but not browned, 3 to 5 minutes. Stir in the couscous and cook for 2 minutes longer. Remove from the heat.

2. In a small saucepan, bring the stock, soy sauce, butter, curry and sugar to a boil. Pour the hot liquid into the couscous and stir until well blended. Cover tightly and let stand for 10 to 15 minutes, until the liquid is completely absorbed. Stir in the chives and apple. Season with salt and pepper to taste.

—Ken Hom

• • •

RICE WITH TOASTED PINE NUTS

Every time I use nuts, I toast them. Pine nuts and pecans improve dramatically.

6 Servings

1½ cups rice
3 cups chicken stock or 1½ cups canned broth diluted with 1½ cups water
½ cup pine nuts
2 tablespoons unsalted butter
Freshly ground pepper

1. In a heavy medium saucepan, combine the rice and chicken stock. Bring to a boil over moderate heat, reduce the heat to a simmer and cook, uncovered, until tender, about 15 minutes.

2. Meanwhile, place the pine nuts in a dry medium skillet and cook, stirring over moderate heat, until lightly toasted, 3 to 5 minutes.

3. Place the rice in a colander and rinse under very hot water. Make sure to drain well.

4. Transfer the rice to a warmed bowl and toss with the butter and toasted pine nuts. Season with pepper to taste.

—Lee Bailey

• • •

COFFEE-FLAVORED NUTTY PULAU

Gaylord India, a New Delhi-based chain of Indian restaurants, makes this excellent pulau, a rice dish in which the rice, nuts, fruits and spices are all cooked together from the beginning. While coffee is not native to India, it is now grown and consumed there in abundance and accounts for an increasing amount of India's export earnings. Mysteriously, the good Indian coffees actually have overtones of cinnamon, cloves and cumin—three spices used regularly in Indian cooking.

6 Servings

¼ cup raisins
¼ cup walnuts
¼ cup pecans
3 tablespoons vegetable oil
3-inch cinnamon stick, halved
6 whole cloves
6 cardamom pods
¾ cup mixed dried fruit
1½ cups basmati rice* or converted long-grain white rice
1½ cups strongly brewed coffee
****Available at Indian markets and specialty food shops***

1. Mix together the raisins, walnuts and pecans. In a heavy medium saucepan, heat the oil over moderately high heat. Add the cinnamon, cloves, cardamom, ½ cup of the nuts and raisins and ½ cup of the dried fruits. Sauté until the nuts are lightly browned, about 15 seconds. Stir in the rice and add the coffee and 1½ cups of hot water.

2. Bring to a boil, reduce the heat to low, cover and simmer until the liquid is absorbed and the rice is tender, 25 to 30 minutes. Garnish with the remaining ¼ cup nut mixture and dried fruits.

—Gaylord India

• • •

JALAPENO RISOTTO WITH SONOMA DRY JACK CHEESE

This risotto, made with fresh hot chiles, Italian Arborio rice and California Dry Jack cheese, isn't from the menu of any trendy hot spot, but it might as well be. It is an amalgam of two cuisines that says everything there is to say about the assimilation of southwestern ingredients. If you cannot get the cheese called for, a mixture of equal parts of grated Monterey Jack and Parmesan can be substituted—not the same by any means, but savory nonetheless.

A properly made risotto should feature just-tender rice, bound in a generously creamy sauce that is really no more than the cooking liquid thickened by the starch of the grain. Actual cooking time and the amount of stock absorbed by the rice will vary, but I have found six to seven cups of liquid, absorbed slowly over 40 to 50 minutes, to be about right. Because the dish takes a bit of pot-watching anyway, you might as well taste as you go. If the stock runs out before the risotto is ready, continue with hot water.

6 First-Course Servings

6 to 7 cups unsalted chicken stock or 5 cups canned broth diluted with 2 cups water
1 stick (4 ounces) unsalted butter
1 cup minced onion
6 medium jalapeño peppers, seeded and minced
1 garlic clove, minced
1½ cups Arborio rice
1 cup grated Vella Sonoma Dry Jack cheese (about 4 ounces)

1. In a heavy medium saucepan, bring the stock to a boil over high heat. Remove from the heat and keep warm.

2. In a large heavy saucepan, melt the butter over moderately low heat. Add the onion, jalapeños and garlic and cook, stirring occasionally, until softened, 6 to 8 minutes. Add the rice and stir to coat well with butter. Stir in 1 cup of the hot stock and cook, stirring, until the liquid is absorbed, 10 to 12 minutes.

3. Continue to cook the risotto, adding the hot stock, ½ cup at a time, and stirring until it is absorbed and the grains are just tender but still firm to the bite, 30 to 40 minutes.

4. Stir ⅓ cup of the cheese into the risotto, cover and let stand for 3 minutes. Serve on plates and pass the remaining cheese and a pepper mill separately.

—Michael McLaughlin

• • •

MICROWAVE RISOTTO WITH WHITE TRUFFLES

For an extra measure of truffle flavor, store the truffle with the rice for the risotto for at least two days so that it takes on the truffle's earthy essence.

🍷 Try a smooth, rich Italian wine such as a red Rubesco di Torgiano Riserva of Lungarotti—a 1979 would be sensational—or a white Vernaccia di San Gimignano from Pietrafitta.

6 First-Course Servings

4 cups Microwave Veal Broth (recipe follows)
6 tablespoons unsalted butter
1 cup minced onion (about 1 large)
1½ cups truffled Arborio rice (see Note)
2 ounces freshly grated Parmesan cheese (about ¼ cup)
Salt and freshly ground pepper
4 ounces fresh white truffle, gently cleaned with a soft, dry brush

1. Pour the broth into an 8-cup glass measure and cover with microwave plastic wrap. Heat at 100 percent for 6 minutes. Cover to keep warm.

2. In an 14-by-11-by-2½-inch glass of ceramic dish, melt 4 tablespoons of the butter, uncovered, at 100 percent for 3 minutes.

3. Add in the onion and rice and stir to coat with butter. Cook at 100 percent for 6 minutes, or until the onion is softened and the rice is translucent.

4. Add the broth and cook, uncovered, at 100 percent for 12 minutes. Stir well and cook for 12 minutes longer. Remove from the oven.

5. Stir in the remaining 2 tablespoons butter, the cheese and salt and pepper to taste.

6. Bring the risotto to the table. With a flourish, thinly shave the truffle over the risotto with a truffle slicer or swivel-bladed vegetable peeler.

NOTE: Your truffles will come packed in rice. Measure the rice and add enough Arborio rice to make 1½ cups. In a glass jar with a tight-fitting lid, nestle the truffles in the rice. Cover and refrigerate for at least two days to allow the truffle essence to penetrate the rice.

—*Barbara Kafka*

• • •

MICROWAVE VEAL BROTH

Makes About 6 Cups

2½ pounds veal knuckle bones, cut into 4-inch pieces (ask your butcher to do this)
6 cups cold water

1. In a 3- to 3½-quart glass soufflé dish or heatproof bowl, cover the bones with the water. Seal with microwave plastic wrap. Cook at 100 percent for 25 minutes.

2. Strain the broth into another bowl and skim off the surface fat.

—*Barbara Kafka*

• • •

RISOTTO OF RADICCHIO

Lidia Bastianich and her husband, Felice, offer varied seasonal fare in their popular East Side restaurant, Felidia, in New York City. The chicken broth should be light-flavored in order not to overpower the flavor of the rice.

🍷 For this creamy Italian rice dish with its accents of anchovies and saffron, try a rich white such as 1985 Banfi Principessa Gavia or a light red, such as 1983 Prunotto Barbera d' Alba.

8 First-Course or 4 to 6 Main-Course Servings

6 tablespoons extra-virgin olive oil
3 tablespoons minced shallots
4 cups thinly sliced radicchio (10-ounce head)
1 medium onion, chopped
2 anchovy fillets, chopped
1 pound (2¼ cups) Arborio rice
¼ cup dry white wine
9 cups hot unsalted chicken stock or canned broth
¼ teaspoon (packed) saffron threads
2 tablespoons unsalted butter
1 cup freshly grated Parmesan cheese
Salt and freshly ground pepper

1. In a large saucepan, heat 3 tablespoons of the oil. Add the shallots and cook over moderate heat, stirring, until softened, about 2 minutes. Add the radicchio. Increase the heat to high and cook, stirring, until the leaves are wilted and almost all the liquid has evaporated, about 3 minutes. Transfer to a plate.

2. Add the remaining 3 tablespoons oil to the pan. Add the onion and anchovies and cook over moderate heat, stirring occasionally, until the onion is lightly colored, about 4 minutes. Add the rice and cook, stirring, until opaque, about 4 minutes. Stir in the wine, increase the heat to moderately high and cook, stirring, until evaporated.

3. Add 1 cup of the hot broth, the saffron and the radicchio to the rice. Reduce the heat so that the rice simmers in a lively fashion but does not boil and stick. Stir frequently until the liquid is absorbed.

4. Continue adding hot broth, ¾ cup at a time, stirring frequently, until the liquid is absorbed. After 30 to 35 minutes, taste the rice; each grain should be firm but no longer chalky in the center. (If you like your rice slightly more tender, add a little more broth and stir until absorbed.)

5. Remove from the heat and stir in the butter. With a spoon, vigorously beat in the Parmesan cheese. Season to taste with salt and pepper and serve immediately on warmed plates.

—*Lidia Bastianich, Felidia Ristorante, New York City*

• • •

ELEGANT COMFORT FOOD FOR DINNER

The creamy textures and earthy flavors in this menu are sure to warm the cockles of the heart as well as the stomach. Serves 6.

Braised Wild Mushrooms (p. 24)
Toasted French Bread

Risotto of Radicchio (p. 138)
Roasted Red Pepper Strips with Olive Oil and Balsamic Vinegar

Orange-Zested Nectarine Cobbler (p. 200)
Espresso

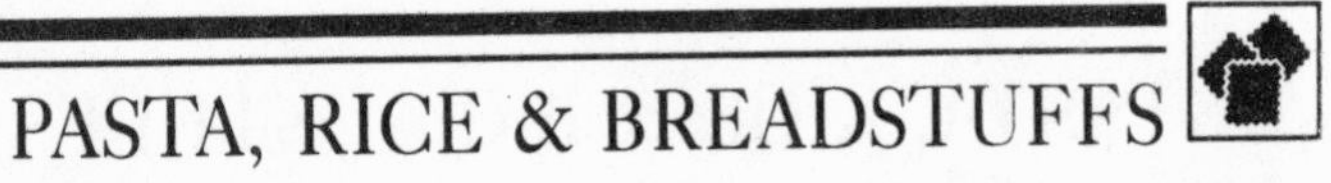

INSTANT POLENTA JOHNNYCAKES

Although these pancakes are American in origin and traditionally made from stone-ground cornmeal, we found that they work beautifully with instant polenta. For a sweet breakfast, serve the pancakes hot with butter and lots of maple syrup.

4 Servings

1¼ cups instant polenta
1 tablespoon sugar
1 teaspoon salt
1½ sticks (6 ounces) unsalted butter, melted
1½ cups boiling water
Maple syrup, as accompaniment

1. In a medium bowl, combine the polenta, sugar, salt and 1 stick of the melted butter. Add the boiling water and stir until thickened, about 2 minutes.

2. Place a large griddle or heavy skillet over moderately high heat and brush it lightly with some of the remaining butter. Stir 2 tablespoons of hot water into the batter.

3. Leaving enough room for the batter to spread, ladle about 3 tablespoons per pancake onto the hot griddle. (The griddle should be hot enough to make the batter bubble and produce lacy, crisp cakes.) Cook the johnnycakes until the tops are almost dry and the bottoms golden brown, about 8 minutes. Turn carefully with a spatula and cook until the second side is golden, about 4 minutes longer.

4. Transfer the cakes to a warmed plate and cover loosely with foil. Repeat with the remaining batter and melted butter. Serve with warm maple syrup.

—John Robert Massie

• • •

BREAKFAST POLENTA

In this warming dish, egg yolks are baked inside a ramekin of polenta. For a special occasion breakfast, add (in Step 3) a thin slice of foie gras atop each egg yolk before cooking.

8 Servings

2 cups chicken stock or 1 cup canned broth diluted with 1 cup water
1 teaspoon salt
1 cup instant polenta
1 tablespoon unsalted butter
½ cup freshly grated Parmesan cheese
¼ teaspoon freshly ground pepper
8 egg yolks
½ cup coarsely grated Gruyère cheese

1. Preheat the oven to 400°. In a large saucepan, combine the chicken stock and 2 cups of water. Bring to a boil over high heat and stir in the salt. Gradually stir in the polenta and cook over moderate heat, stirring constantly, until the polenta masses together and pulls away from the sides of the pan, about 10 minutes.

2. Stir in the butter, Parmesan cheese and pepper.

3. Spoon ½ cup of the hot, soft polenta into each of eight 1-cup ovenproof ramekins or custard cups. With a wet spoon, make an indentation in the polenta. Gently drop an egg yolk into the nest and cover with another ½ cup of polenta to completely enclose the yolk.

4. Sprinkle 1 tablespoon of the Gruyère cheese over each ramekin. Place the dishes on a baking sheet and bake until the cheese melts and begins to brown, about 10 minutes. Serve at once.

—John Robert Massie

• • •

SERRANO CHILE BLUE CORN BREAD

Serve this corn bread on its own or use it to stuff Roast Wild Turkey with Blue Corn Bread and Chorizo Stuffing (p. 83).

12 Servings

2 teaspoons vegetable oil
3 serrano chiles or 2 small jalapeños—seeded and minced
1 small red bell pepper, cut into ¼-inch dice
1 small green bell pepper, cut into ¼-inch dice
3 garlic cloves, minced
1 cup all-purpose flour
1¼ cups blue cornmeal
2 tablespoons sugar
1 tablespoon baking powder
1 teaspoon salt
2 eggs
6 tablespoons vegetable shortening, melted and cooled
6 tablespoons unsalted butter, melted and cooled
1 cup buttermilk, at room temperature
Pinch of baking soda
3 tablespoons chopped fresh coriander

1. Preheat the oven to 375°. Lightly butter an 8-by-12-inch baking pan.

2. In a small skillet, heat the oil. Add the serrano chiles, red and green peppers and garlic and sauté over moderately high heat until softened, about 2 minutes. Let cool.

3. In a large bowl, sift together the flour, cornmeal, sugar, baking powder and salt.

4. In a medium bowl, beat the eggs lightly and stir in the melted shortening and butter. In a small bowl, mix the buttermilk with the baking soda, then stir into the eggs. Pour this liquid into the dry ingredients and stir just until blended; do not overmix. Fold in the sautéed vegetables and the coriander.

5. Pour the batter into the prepared pan and bake for 50 minutes, or until the top is golden brown and a toothpick inserted in the center comes out clean.

6. Let cool on a rack. If using the corn bread for stuffing a bird, crumble it onto a cookie sheet and let it stand overnight or dry out in a 350° oven for 10 minutes.

—Stephan Pyles,
Routh Street Cafe, Dallas

• • •

SPANISH CORN BREAD

From Art Director Elizabeth Woodson's mother, Irene, this corn bread is loaded with chopped chiles and Cheddar cheese.

9 Servings

1 cup yellow cornmeal
1 cup all-purpose flour
1/4 cup sugar
1 tablespoon baking powder
1 teaspoon salt
1 egg, lightly beaten
1 cup milk
1 cup cottage cheese
1/3 cup corn oil
1 can (4 ounces) peeled whole mild green chiles—drained, patted dry and coarsely chopped
1 1/2 cups (about 6 ounces) grated sharp Cheddar cheese

1. Preheat the oven to 400°. Butter a 9-inch square baking pan.

2. In a large bowl, sift together the cornmeal, flour, sugar, baking powder and salt.

3. In a medium bowl, combine the egg, milk, cottage cheese and oil. Mix until blended. Add to the dry ingredients and stir gently until just mixed.

4. Spread half the batter into the prepared pan. Scatter the chiles evenly over the top and sprinkle with the cheese. Cover with the remaining batter.

5. Bake in the lower third of the oven for 35 minutes, or until the corn bread is golden brown. Cut into squares and serve slightly warm.

—Irene Woodson

• • •

PEPITA AND BACON CORN BREAD

The bacon and pumpkin seeds (pepitas) add an extra measure of richness to this moist and crumbly corn bread.

16 Servings

1/2 pound sliced bacon
1 cup pepitas (raw pumpkin seeds),* about 5 ounces
2 1/2 cups yellow cornmeal
1 1/2 cups all-purpose flour
1/4 cup sugar
2 tablespoons baking powder
1 1/4 teaspoons salt
1/4 teaspoon freshly ground pepper
4 eggs
2 cups sour cream
1/2 cup corn oil
1 can (4 ounces) chopped mild green chiles, drained
****Available at health food stores and Latin American markets***

1. Preheat the oven to 400°. Butter a 9-by-12-by-2-inch baking pan. Fry the bacon in a skillet or cook it in a microwave oven until crisp. Drain on paper towels; then crumble.

2. In a dry heavy medium skillet, toast the pepitas over moderate heat, stirring occasionally, until the seeds are lightly browned, about 5 minutes. Coarsely chop and set aside.

3. In a large bowl, combine the cornmeal, flour, sugar, baking powder, salt and pepper. Whisk to blend.

4. In a medium bowl, lightly beat the eggs. Whisk in the sour cream and oil until blended. Stir the egg mixture into the dry ingredients. Stir in the chiles, bacon and pepitas.

5. Scrape the batter into the prepared pan and spread evenly. Bake in the middle of the oven for 25 minutes, or until the top is golden brown and a toothpick inserted in the center comes out clean.

—Diana Sturgis

• • •

CORN WAFERS

These crisp cornmeal wafers have a dignified shape but the down-home taste of corn bread. Serve them with soup, such as Sweet Potato Vichyssoise (page 39) or Cauliflower Cress Soup (page 38).

Makes About 16 Wafers

3/4 cup white cornmeal
1/4 teaspoon salt
1 cup boiling water
2 tablespoons margarine or unsalted butter, cut into small pieces

1. Preheat the oven to 425°. Coat 2 cookie sheets with nonstick cooking spray. In a medium bowl, mix the cornmeal and salt. Stir in the boiling water. Add the margarine, or butter, and mix thoroughly, until smooth. Let stand for 5 minutes.

2. Restir the batter to blend well and then spoon 1 tablespoon onto the prepared cookie sheet. It should spread into a 3-inch circle. If it's too watery and thin to hold its shape, stir in 1 more tablespoon of the cornmeal. If it's too thick, add more water by teaspoons. Using a tablespoon, spoon the remaining batter for each wafer, onto the cookie sheets.

3. Bake the wafers for 20 minutes, or until they are crisp and golden brown around the edges. Serve with a crock of butter.

—Lee Bailey

• • •

BLUE CORN PIZZELLE

This peppery cracker is formed in a traditional flat pizzelle iron. It can be served as is or folded over, taco style, and filled with guacamole, salsa and cheese.

Makes 16 Pizzelle

2 tablespoons minced mild green chiles
3 eggs
3 tablespoons sugar
1 stick (4 ounces) unsalted butter, melted
1/2 cup masa harina*
2 teaspoons baking powder
3/4 teaspoon salt
1/4 teaspoon cayenne pepper
1/4 teaspoon freshly ground black pepper
1/4 teasooon freshly ground white pepper
1/4 teaspoon minced fresh thyme or 1/8 teaspoon crumbled dried
1/4 cup plus 3 tablespoons blue cornmeal (atole)*
****Available at Latin American markets***

1. Pat the chiles dry and, if using canned chiles, squeeze them between paper towels to remove any excess liquid.

2. Preheat the pizzelle iron on both sides. In a large bowl, beat the eggs with the sugar until thick and pale yellow in color, about 3 minutes. Beat in the melted butter.

3. In another bowl, mix together the *masa harina*, baking powder, salt, cayenne, and black and white peppers. Sift the mixture over the beaten eggs, add the chiles and the thyme and mix lightly. Fold in the blue cornmeal.

4. Grease the pizzelle iron only once, before making the first cracker. Place one tablespoon of the batter in the middle of the heated iron and gently press down the other half of the iron. Using a knife, scrape off any excess batter and place the iron over the burner for 1 minute. Flip the iron and cook on the second side until browned, about 30 seconds. Transfer the pizzelle to a rack to cool and repeat with the remaining batter. (*The pizzelle can be prepared a few hours ahead, but should be crisped in a 350° oven for 1 to 2 minutes before serving.*)

—Nancy Christy & Laure Cantor Kimpton

• • •

MEDITERRANEAN ANIMAL CRACKERS

These spicy crackers are studded with crunchy sesame seeds and flavored with garlic and thyme.

Makes 90 to 100 Crackers

1/4 cup hulled sesame seeds
1 1/2 teaspoons salt
1 1/2 cups all-purpose flour, sifted
1 1/4 cups whole wheat flour, sifted
1 teaspoon freshly cracked pepper
2 garlic cloves
3/4 teaspoon thyme
6 cups vegetable oil
1/2 cup olive oil

1. In a small skillet, toast the sesame seeds over moderate heat, stirring constantly, until lightly and evenly browned, about 2 minutes.

2. In a large bowl, combine the salt, sesame seeds, all-purpose and whole wheat flours and pepper.

3. Using a garlic press, crush the garlic into 1 cup of water and add the thyme.

4. Using a wooden spoon, stir the water mixture into the dry ingredients until thoroughly combined.

5. Turn the dough out onto a well-floured surface or pastry cloth. Sprinkle the dough with flour and divide it in half. Roll each piece into a 20-inch round about 1/16 inch thick. (Lift the dough occasionally and flour underneath to prevent it from sticking.)

6. Using 3- to 5-inch animal-shape cookie cutters, stamp out the crackers. Roll out any scraps of dough and cut out more crackers.

7. In a very large deep skillet or electric frying pan, heat the vegetable and olive oils to 425°.

8. Fry the crackers, a few at a time, turning once, until crisp, lightly browned and puffy, 1 to 2 minutes on each side. Using a slotted spoon, remove the crackers from the skillet and place on paper towels to drain. Dab off any excess oil. Sprinkle with salt and let cool.

—Nancy Christy & Laure Cantor Kimpton

• • •

PEPPERY PRETZELS

Everyone loves pretzels, and our version is flavored with garlic, black pepper, olive oil and thyme. Serve these tasty pretzels as an accompaniment to antipasto or with a wedge of gutsy Italian cheese.

Makes About 20 Pretzels

1 envelope (1/4 ounce) active dry yeast
Pinch of sugar
1 1/2 cups warm water (105° to 110°)
3/4 teaspoon finely minced garlic
1 1/2 tablespoons olive oil
4 cups unbleached all-purpose flour
1/2 teaspoon thyme
1/2 teaspoon freshly cracked pepper
2 tablespoons plus 1 teaspoon table salt
2 tablespoons coarse (kosher) salt
2 tablespoons hulled sesame seeds

1. In a medium bowl, combine the yeast, sugar and 6 tablespoons of the warm water. Set aside until the mixture foams, about 10 minutes. Add the remaining warm water, the garlic and olive oil and mix well.

2. In a large bowl, stir together the flour, thyme, pepper and 1 teaspoon of the table salt. Form a well in the flour mixture and pour in the yeast mixture. Gradually stir until the dough massses together.

3. Turn the dough out onto a floured work surface and knead until smooth, about 10 minutes. If the dough is still sticky, knead in a little additional flour. Place the dough in a clean bowl and cover with plastic wrap. Set aside in a warm place until doubled in size, about 30 minutes. *(The recipe can be prepared to this point up to 3 days ahead. Cover the dough and store in the refrigerator.)*

4. Turn the dough out onto a floured surface and knead for 15 minutes. Roll the dough into a 12-by-6-inch rectangle and cut it into about 20 strips. Roll each strip into a smooth 16-inch-long rope and form into a pretzel shape; secure the knots with a dab of water. Place the finished pretzels on baking sheets lined with parchment paper; set aside to rise for 10 minutes.

5. Preheat the oven to 425°. In a large saucepan, combine the remaining 2 tablespoons table salt and 3 quarts of water and bring to a boil.

6. Drop the pretzels, about 6 at a time, into the boiling water and cook until they rise to the surface. Using a slotted spoon, return the pretzels to the baking sheets. Sprinkle each pretzel with a pinch each of coarse salt and sesame seeds. Repeat with the remaining pretzels.

7. Spray the bottom and sides of the oven with water to create steam and bake the pretzels until evenly browned, about 30 minutes.

—*Nancy Christy & Laure Cantor Kimpton*

• • •

THIN BUTTERMILK BISCUITS

I think a lot of people have forgotten just how very simple it is to make biscuits, which are prepared from only a few ingredients and require practically no mixing. I don't even roll them out with a pin. Instead, I press and pat the dough with my hand to the proper thickness.

Makes About 2 Dozen

1¾ cups all-purpose flour
1 tablespoon baking powder
¼ teaspoon baking soda
1 teaspoon salt
6 tablespoons cold unsalted butter
¾ cup buttermilk

1. Preheat the oven to 450°. Into a medium bowl, sift together the flour, baking powder, baking soda and salt. Cut in the cold butter until it is the size of small peas. Add the buttermilk all at once and stir just until the dough forms a ball.

2. Turn out the dough onto a floured surface and dust with a little additional flour. Roll out the dough to a thickness of ¼ inch, or do as I do: flatten and smooth the dough with your hand.

3. Cut the dough into 3-inch biscuits and bake on an ungreased cookie sheet for 15 to 20 minutes, or until golden. Serve warm.

—*Lee Bailey*

• • •

BAKING POWDER BISCUITS

Serve these biscuits on their own, or use them to top Game Bird Pot Pie (p. 81).

Makes 8 to 10

4 tablespoons unsalted butter
2 cups all-purpose flour
1 tablespoon baking powder
1 teaspoon salt
¾ cup milk

1. Preheat the oven to 450°. In a food processor fitted with the metal blade or in a bowl using your fingertips, thoroughly blend the butter, flour, baking powder and salt until the mixture resembles coarse meal.

2. Add the milk and mix until the dough begins to mass together; do not overblend.

3. Turn the dough out onto a lightly floured surface and knead briefly, dusting lightly with additional flour if it sticks, until a soft, smooth dough forms, about 10 seconds.

4. Roll out the dough ½ inch thick on a clean lightly floured surface. Cut into 2-inch rounds.

5. Arrange the biscuits on a greased baking sheet and bake for 12 minutes, or until golden brown.

—*Gayle Henderson Wilson*

• • •

SAFFRON SCONES

These delicious, only slightly sweet tea biscuits have a gentle saffron taste that masks the flavor of the baking powder. They keep well in an airtight container for at least two weeks.

8 Servings

⅛ teaspoon (lightly packed) saffron threads
½ cup milk
1 egg
2 cups all-purpose flour
½ cup sugar
1 tablespoon baking powder
¼ teaspoon salt
1½ sticks (6 ounces) unsalted butter
⅓ cup currants

1. Preheat the oven to 425°. Crush the saffron into a fine powder and sprinkle into a small bowl. Add the milk and egg and beat until well blended.

2. In a large bowl, combine the flour, sugar, baking powder and salt. Cut 1 stick of the butter into small dice and sprinkle over the flour mixture. Cut in the butter until the mixture resembles coarse meal. Stir in the currants.

3. In a small saucepan, melt the remaining 4 tablespoons butter and set aside to cool.

4. Pour the saffron milk mixture over the flour, tossing to moisten the dough. Quickly stir into a mass and pat the dough into a ball; the dough will be very moist and sticky.

5. On a well-floured surface, roll out the dough to an 8-inch square about ½ inch thick. Using a floured knife, cut the square into 4-inch squares. Quarter each square diagonally.

6. Place the 16 triangles, about 1 inch apart, on a heavy baking sheet. Brush the scones lightly with the melted butter. Bake in the upper third of the oven for 13 minutes, or until lightly browned and firm to the touch. Serve warm or at room temperature. To store, let the scones cool completely and keep in an airtight container for up to 2 weeks or freeze.

—Julie Sahni

• • •

AFTERNOON TEA

Here is an institution that seems to be making a comeback in America, although this same menu with the addition of an egg dish or two would make a perfectly lovely brunch. Serves 10 to 12.

Cranberry Tea Bread (p. 143)

Saffron Scones (p. 142)

English Muffin Loaf (p. 149)

Assorted Jams and Jellies

Sweet Butter

Brown Butter Cardamom Shortbread Cookies (p. 180)

Tea and Coffee

CRANBERRY TEA BREAD

This moist, not-too-sweet quick bread flavored with orange zest is chock-full of juicy cranberries and chopped walnuts. It is best to let it sit for a day to allow the flavors to blend; then slice the loaf thin and eat plain or spread with a little sweet butter. (Chilling the loaf makes cutting neat slices easier.) We like it for breakfast or in the afternoon with a cup of tea.

Makes 1 Loaf

2 cups all-purpose flour
2 teaspoons baking powder
¼ teaspoon salt
4 tablespoons cold unsalted butter, cut into small pieces
¾ cup plus 1 tablespoon sugar
4 ounces chopped walnuts (1 scant cup)
1 tablespoon grated orange zest
1 egg
⅔ cup orange juice, preferably fresh
2 cups fresh cranberries
1 tablespoon milk

1. Preheat the oven to 350°. Butter a 9-by-5-inch loaf pan and line the bottom with waxed paper; butter the paper.

2. In a large bowl, mix together the flour, baking powder and salt. Cut in the butter until the mixture resembles fine bread crumbs. Add ¾ cup of the sugar, the walnuts and the orange zest and toss to blend.

3. In a small bowl, beat the egg with a fork until frothy. Beat in the orange juice. Pour this liquid over the dry ingredients and stir just until the dough begins to mass together. Before all the flour is thoroughly incorporated, add the cranberries and stir them into the dough until evenly distributed.

4. Scrape the batter into the prepared pan and spread evenly with a spatula. Brush the milk evenly over the surface of the batter and sprinkle the remaining 1 tablespoon sugar on top.

5. Bake the bread in the middle of the oven for 1 hour and 15 minutes or until the loaf is well risen, golden brown and crusty and a tester inserted in the center comes out clean. Transfer the loaf to a rack to cool for 20 minutes.

6. Run a thin knife around the inside of the pan and invert the loaf onto the rack. Peel off the waxed paper and turn the loaf right side up; let cool completely. Put the loaf in a tin with a tight-fitting lid and set aside overnight.

—Diana Sturgis

• • •

BASIC COUNTRY LOAF

A method of bread baking that we find appeals to people who bake bread on a regular basis is one we learned on a visit to Paris's well-known Poilane bakery. Instead of using all the kneaded and risen dough each time you bake, the trick here is to pull off a small portion of the dough and set it aside, covered with water. Next time you start to make bread, work this reserved dough, which the French call a *levain* (see Note), into your next mixture, and note how this addition of dough that has matured gives the new batch of bread better texture and added flavor. It's the kind of subtle touch that causes connoisseurs of bread to talk.

Makes 2 Round Loaves

SPONGE:
1 envelope (¼ ounce) active dry yeast
1½ cups warm water (105° to 110°)
2 cups unbleached all-purpose flour

DOUGH:
¾ cup coarsely ground whole wheat flour*
1 cup warm water (105° to 110°)
1 tablespoon coarse (kosher) or sea salt

About 5½ cups unbleached all-purpose flour
1 egg white, lightly beaten
Sesame seeds, poppy seeds, cracked wheat or flour, for topping (optional)
****Available at health food stores***

1. *Make the sponge about 12 hours ahead:* In a large bowl, dissolve the yeast in ¼ cup of the warm water. Let stand for 5 minutes. Stir in the remaining 1¼ cups water and the flour, beating by hand or in a mixer with a dough hook for 1 minute. Cover the bowl with plastic wrap and let the sponge stand at room temperature for 12 to 14 hours.

2. *Make the dough:* Stir the whole wheat flour, warm water, salt and about 4 cups of the all-purpose flour into the sponge until the dough becomes hard to work, then turn it out onto a well-floured surface. Let the dough rest while you clean the bowl. Now start kneading, slapping the dough around, scraping it up, gradually adding about 1½ cups more all-purpose flour and kneading until smooth and elastic, 8 to 10 minutes (this can also be done in a large electric mixer with a dough hook).

3. Return the dough to the bowl, cover with plastic wrap and let rise at room temperature until almost tripled in volume, about 2 hours.

4. Turn the dough out again onto a floured surface, punch it down, and tear off a small hunk (6 ounces) to reserve for the *levain* (see Note). Divide the remaining dough in half and shape each piece into a 1½-inch-thick disk. With the palms of your hands, coax the sides of each disk down and under all around, stretching the gluten cloak and plumping up each loaf into a round shape. Pinch together the seams on the bottom and place the rounds seam-side down on 2 lightly greased baking sheets. Cover loosely with a towel and let rise until doubled in volume, about 1 hour.

5. Preheat the oven to 450°. Paint the top and sides of the risen loaves with the beaten egg white to glaze. Sprinkle, if you wish, with one of the toppings and place on the middle rack of the oven. Immediately throw a few ice cubes on the oven floor to create steam. Add more ice after 3 minutes and again after 6 minutes. Bake for a total of 15 minutes. Then, reduce the oven temperature to 350° and bake for 20 minutes longer, or until the bread sounds hollow when the bottom is tapped. Turn the oven off and let the bread rest in the hot oven for 15 minutes. Remove to a rack and let cool.

NOTE: Put the hunk of reserved dough (about 6 ounces) in a covered jar with 1½ cups of warm water. This is the *levain*, which will go into the next loaf. Let stand at room temperature for 12 hours, then refrigerate. The *levain* will keep for up to 10 days; freeze for longer storage.

—Evan and Judith Jones

• • •

WHOLE WHEAT BREAD WITH MAPLE SYRUP, WALNUTS AND RAISINS

The subtly sweet flavor of this bread makes it ideal for breakfast or afternoon tea.

Makes 2 Round Loaves

1 envelope (¼ ounce) active dry yeast
¼ cup warm water (105° to 110°)
Levain (reserved from Step 4 of Basic Country Loaf, p. 143)
2 teaspoons coarse (kosher) or sea salt
½ cup maple syrup or molasses
2 tablespoons vegetable oil or softened butter
2 cups whole wheat flour
About 4¾ cups unbleached all-purpose flour
⅔ cup coarsely chopped walnuts
⅔ cup raisins
1 egg white, lightly beaten

1. In a large bowl, dissolve the yeast in the warm water. Add the *levain*, salt, maple syrup, oil, whole wheat flour and 4¾ cups all-purpose flour. Mix to blend well.

2. Turn the dough out onto a well-floured surface and knead until smooth and elastic, 8 to 10 minutes.

3. Return the dough to the bowl, cover with plastic wrap and let rise at room temperature until almost tripled in volume, about 2 hours.

4. Pat the dough down and separate into two 8-inch disks. Sprinkle the walnuts and raisins evenly over the dough and press gently to help them adhere.

5. Working with one disk at a time, roll up the edges of the dough over the filling, rotating the disk as you work. Continue to roll up, kneading lightly to enclose and evenly distribute the filling. Pinch the edges to seal.

6. Turn the rounds of dough over so that the smooth side is on top, set on two greased baking sheets and let rise until doubled in volume, about 1 hour.

7. Preheat the oven to 450°. Paint the top and sides of the risen loaves with the beaten egg white to glaze. Place on the middle rack of the oven and immediately throw a few ice cubes on the oven floor to create steam. Add more ice after 3 minutes and again after 6 minutes. Bake for a total of 15 minutes. Then, reduce the oven temperature to 350° and bake for 20 minutes, or until the bread sounds hollow when the bottom is tapped. Turn the oven off and let the bread rest in the hot oven for 15 minutes. Cool on a rack.

—Evan and Judith Jones

• • •

Pepita and Bacon Corn Bread (p. 140) and Composed Salad of Tomatoes, Peppers and Goat Cheese with Shallot Vinaigrette (p. 241).

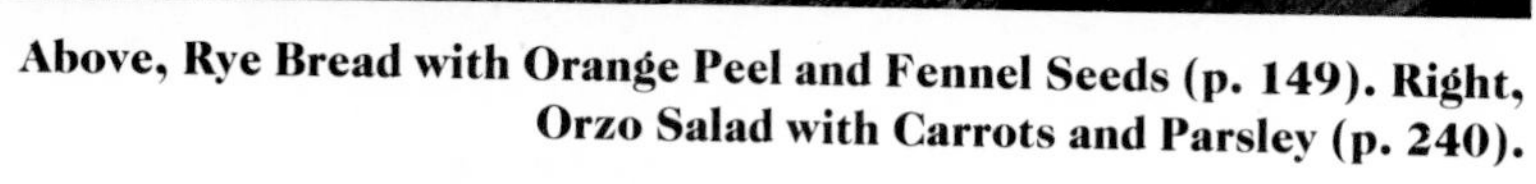

Above, Rye Bread with Orange Peel and Fennel Seeds (p. 149). Right, Orzo Salad with Carrots and Parsley (p. 240).

RYE BREAD WITH ORANGE PEEL AND FENNEL SEEDS

The touch of fennel and orange makes this bread a good accompaniment to a rich stew or soup.

Makes 2 Round Loaves

1 envelope (1/4 ounce) active dry yeast
1/4 cup warm water (105° to 110°)
Levain (reserved from Step 4 of Basic Country Loaf, p. 143)
2 teaspoons coarse (kosher) or sea salt
2 cups rye flour
About 3 1/2 cups unbleached all-purpose flour
2 teaspoons grated orange zest
1 1/2 tablespoons fennel seeds
1 egg white, lightly beaten

1. In a large bowl, dissolve the yeast in the warm water. Add the *levain,* salt, rye flour and 3½ cups all-purpose flour. Mix well.

2. Turn the dough out onto a well-floured surface and knead until smooth and elastic, 8 to 10 minutes. Return to the bowl, cover and let rise at room temperature until almost tripled in volume, about 2 hours.

3. Pat the dough down and separate into two 8-inch disks. Sprinkle the orange zest and fennel seeds evenly over the dough. Press gently to help them adhere.

4. Roll up the edges of the dough over the filling, rotating the disks as you work. Continue to roll up the dough, kneading lightly to enclose and evenly distribute the filling. Pinch the edges to seal.

5. Turn the rounds of dough over so that the smooth side is on top, set on 2 greased baking sheets and let rise until doubled in volume, about 1 hour.

6. Preheat the oven to 450°. Paint the risen loaves with the beaten egg white to glaze. Sprinkle, if you wish, with more fennel seeds and place in the middle of the oven. Immediately throw a few ice cubes on the oven floor to create steam. Add more ice after 3 minutes and again after 6 minutes. Bake for a total of 15 minutes. Then reduce the oven temperature to 350° and bake for 20 minutes, or until the bread sounds hollow when the bottom is tapped. Turn the oven off and let the bread rest in the hot oven for 15 minutes. Cool on a rack.

—Evan and Judith Jones

• • •

Tagliatelle with Asparagus (p. 133).

ENGLISH MUFFIN LOAF

George Bay of Bays English Muffins in Chicago came up with this delicious loaf based on their equally yummy muffins. This recipe makes two loaves, so bake both and freeze one for next Sunday. When ready to serve, thaw at room temperature for three to four hours and reheat at 350° for 10 minutes.

Makes Two 8-Inch Loaves

2 teaspoons cornmeal
1/4 cup instant mashed potatoes
2 cups hot milk
2 envelopes (1/4 ounce each) active dry yeast
2 tablespoons plus a pinch of sugar
1 tablespoon plus a pinch of salt
6 cups bread flour
1/4 cup plus 1 tablespoon unsalted butter, softened to room temperature

1. Lightly butter two 8-inch loaf pans. Sprinkle each with 1 teaspoon of the cornmeal to coat the insides. Tap out any excess.

2. Put the instant potatoes in a medium bowl. Whisk in the hot milk.

3. In a small bowl, combine the yeast, ½ cup of water and a pinch each of sugar and salt.

4. In a large mixing bowl, combine the flour and remaining 2 tablespoons sugar and 1 tablespoon salt. Pour in both the potato and the yeast mixtures and add the butter. Mix until well blended.

5. Transfer the dough to a lightly floured surface and knead until smooth and elastic, about 10 minutes. Put into a lightly buttered bowl. Cover with plastic wrap and let rise in a warm place until doubled in volume, about 1 hour.

6. Divide the dough in half. On a lightly floured surface, roll out each piece of dough into an 8-by-14-inch rectangle. Brush off any excess flour and then, starting at a short end, roll the dough up into a loaf shape. Pinch the bottom seam to seal. Put each piece of dough, seam-side down, into one of the prepared pans. Cover loosely with plastic wrap and let rise in a warm place until the dough extends about 2 inches above the pan, about 1 hour. Preheat the oven to 375°.

7. Bake for 35 to 40 minutes, until golden brown. Let cool on a wire rack before serving.

—Lee Bailey

• • •

TOMATO BRUSCHETTA

This is one of the innumerable variations on the classic Italian toasted bread. Although I like the tomatoes on my *bruschetta* broiled, others prefer it with uncooked tomatoes. Whichever way you prepare it, serve the *bruschetta* as an accompaniment to the main course or with some drinks before the meal.

6 Servings

1 loaf of Italian bread, halved lengthwise, cut crosswise on the diagonal into 1-inch slices
1 garlic clove, crushed through a press

2 tablespoons extra-virgin olive oil
2 large beefsteak tomatoes—peeled, seeded and chopped
¼ teaspoon salt
¼ teaspoon freshly ground pepper
½ cup julienned fresh basil

1. Preheat the broiler. Put the bread, cut-side up, on a baking sheet and broil 4 inches from the heat for about 30 seconds, until lightly browned.

2. In a small bowl, mix together the garlic and olive oil and brush over one side of the toasted bread.

3. Spread the tomatoes evenly over the bread. Season with the salt and pepper. Broil for about 30 seconds, just until the tomatoes are heated through. Sprinkle the basil over the *bruschetta* and serve at once.

—Lee Bailey

• • •

CRUSTY PARMESAN TOAST

I know the calorie conscious might balk when they read I use butter and olive oil to make this bread, but it's worth it! If you want to add garlic to the olive oil, you can.

6 Servings

6 slices of Italian bread, cut ½ inch thick crosswise on the diagonal
1 tablespoon unsalted butter, softened to room temperature
2 tablespoons extra-virgin olive oil
3 tablespoons freshly grated Parmesan cheese

1. Preheat the broiler. Broil one side of the bread slices, about 5 inches from the heat for 40 to 50 seconds, until lightly browned. Turn and butter the other side of each slice with ½ teaspoon butter. Broil for about 10 seconds, until the butter melts and bubbles.

2. Remove from the broiler and brush 1 teaspoon of olive oil over each buttered piece of toast. Sprinkle each with 1½ teaspoons Parmesan cheese. Broil for about 2 minutes, until the cheese melts and turns golden brown. Cut each slice in half before serving.

—Lee Bailey

• • •

CUCUMBER AND TOMATO TEA SANDWICHES

These tiny mouthfuls are a classic teatime savory. For best results use very thinly sliced bread at its freshest; flavorful red, vine-ripened tomatoes, and bright green fresh coriander leaves with no sign of wilting.

8 Servings

1 stick (4 ounces) plus 2 tablespoons unsalted butter, at room temperature
1 teaspoon prepared English mustard
½ teaspoon freshly ground pepper
½ teaspoon salt
¾ teaspoon fresh lemon juice
3 tablespoons minced fresh coriander
¼ cup alfalfa or radish sprouts (optional)
1 large tomato (about ½ pound)
1 cucumber, preferably seedless
8 very thin slices of white bread (see Note)
8 very thin slices of whole wheat bread (or substitute white bread)

1. In a small bowl, combine the butter, mustard, pepper, salt, lemon juice and coriander. Blend well. Stir in the sprouts.

2. Thinly slice the tomato and drain on paper towels. Peel the cucumber; cut ½ inch off the ends and discard. Cut the cucumber into 3-inch sections. Thinly slice each piece lengthwise.

3. Spread the flavored butter on one side of each bread slice. Arrange the tomato slices in a single layer on 4 slices and the cucumber in a single layer on 4 slices. (There may be extra tomato and cucumber slices.) Cover each sandwich with the remaining 8 buttered slices of bread and press gently together.

4. Using a sharp knife (preferably serrated), trim the sides to remove the crusts and reveal the filling. Quarter each sandwich diagonally to make into 4 little triangles. Serve immediately or stack the sandwiches carefully, wrap in plastic wrap to prevent drying out and store in the refrigerator for up to 2 hours. Remove from the refrigerator at least 15 minutes before serving.

NOTE: If you cannot find thinly sliced bread, flatten slices with a rolling pin.

—Julie Sahni

• • •

VEGETABLES

LAFAYETTE'S SPICY BAKED RED BEANS

For a taste of Martinique, serve these beans with steamed white rice.

6 Servings

1 pound small red beans
1 medium onion, peeled and stuck with 4 whole cloves
1 carrot, finely chopped
4 sprigs of fresh thyme or ½ teaspoon dried
2 bay leaves
¼ cup minced Italian flat-leaf parsley
2 tiny dried red chiles
¼ pound lean salt pork, cut into ¼-inch dice
4 to 6 tablespoons unsalted butter
2 shallots, finely chopped
½ cup finely chopped scallion greens
3 garlic cloves, crushed through a press

1. In a large flameproof casserole, cover the beans with at least 2 inches of water and bring to a boil over moderate heat. Remove from the heat, cover and set aside for 1 hour. Drain the beans and rinse under cold running water.

2. Return the beans to the casserole. Add the onion stuck with cloves, the carrot, thyme, bay leaves, 3 tablespoons of the parsley and the chiles. Add fresh cold water to cover by at least 2 inches. Bring to a boil, reduce the heat to moderate and simmer until the beans are just tender, about 1 hour.

3. Meanwhile, in a medium saucepan of boiling water, blanch the diced salt pork for 4 minutes. Drain and dry on paper towels. In a medium skillet, melt the butter over moderately high heat. Add the shallots, scallions and salt pork and cook until the salt pork browns, about 5 minutes.

4. Preheat the oven to 400°. Drain the beans, reserving 2 cups of the liquid. Add the salt pork mixture to the beans along with the garlic and remaining 1 tablespoon parsley; mix well. Pour in the reserved cooking liquid and bake, covered, for 40 minutes, or until the beans are tender. Remove the sprigs of thyme, bay leaves and chiles before serving.

—Henri Charvet, Le Lafayette, Fort-de-France, Martinique

• • •

STEAMED BRUSSELS SPROUTS AND RED GRAPES

Associate Test Kitchen Director Marcia Kiesel has found a succulent counterpoint to a traditional Thanksgiving vegetable.

6 to 8 Servings

2 pints brussels sprouts, trimmed and halved lengthwise
2 cups seedless red grapes
2½ tablespoons unsalted butter
1 tablespoon fresh lemon juice
½ teaspoon salt
¼ teaspoon freshly ground pepper

In a steamer basket, steam the brussels sprouts, covered, until tender, about 15 minutes. Add the grapes and steam 1 minute longer; drain well. Put the brussels sprouts and grapes in a serving bowl, add the butter, lemon juice, salt and pepper, and toss well.

—Marcia Kiesel

• • •

BRAISED RED CABBAGE WITH MAPLE-GLAZED CHESTNUTS

This cabbage dish combines sweet glazed whole chestnuts, tangy red cabbage and smoky Canadian bacon.

8 Servings

1 pound (about 2½ cups) fresh chestnuts or 10 ounces dried chestnuts (about 1¼ cups)*
1 head of red cabbage (2 pounds), cored and shredded
4 large garlic cloves, minced
4 large shallots, thinly sliced
½ pound Canadian bacon, cut into ½-inch dice
1 teaspoon caraway seeds
¼ teaspoon freshly grated nutmeg
½ teaspoon salt
¼ teaspoon freshly ground pepper
2 cups unsweetened apple cider
½ cup red wine vinegar
2 cups milk
1 teaspoon vanilla extract
3 tablespoons unsalted butter
⅓ cup maple syrup
****Available at Italian markets and some specialty food shops***

1. Preheat the oven to 350°. If using fresh chestnuts, cut a small cross into the flat side of each one, cutting through the woody outer shell; try not to cut into the meat. Arrange the chestnuts in a shallow pan in a single layer. Roast in the oven until the cross opens slightly, about 10 minutes. Peel the chestnuts. If using dried chestnuts, place them in a medium saucepan and cover with 4 cups of cold water. Bring to a boil over high heat, remove from the heat and let soak overnight; drain well. (*The chestnuts can be prepared to this point up to 3 days ahead and refrigerated in a covered container.*)

2. In a large nonreactive flameproof casserole, combine the red cabbage, garlic, shallots, bacon, caraway seeds, nutmeg, salt, pepper, apple cider and vinegar. Bring to a boil over moderately high heat. Reduce the heat to moderately low, cover and cook, stirring occasionally, until the cabbage is tender and the liquid is reduced to ½ cup, about 2 hours.

3. Meanwhile, in a medium saucepan, combine the chestnuts with the milk, vanilla and 2 cups of water. Bring to a boil over moderately high heat. Reduce the heat to moderately low, cover and simmer until the chestnuts are just tender, about 40 minutes. Drain well, rinse under warm water and drain again. (*The recipe can be prepared to this point up to 2 days ahead. Cover and refrigerate the cabbage and chestnuts separately.*)

4. In a large skillet, melt the butter. Add the chestnuts and maple syrup and cook over moderately high heat, tossing frequently, until the chestnuts are glazed and lightly caramelized, about 8 minutes.

5. Meanwhile, reheat the cabbage. Spoon the cabbage onto a serving platter and sprinkle the chestnuts over the top.

—*Mimi Ruth Brodeur*

• • •

HOMEMADE SAUERKRAUT

Food historians are still debating whether the Germans learned to make sauerkraut from the ancient Romans or whether it was brought to Europe by the Tatars 700 years ago. They are said to have learned it from the Chinese who lived on it while building the Great Wall.

It's impossible to think of hot dogs without thinking of sauerkraut, and if you don't have a European grocer near you who sells homemade kraut, you should consider making your own. It's very simple, and it tastes fresher and much less salty than the packaged variety.

Makes About 5 Cups

2 pounds shredded green cabbage
2 tablespoons coarse (kosher) salt
1 teaspoon sugar

1. In a large bowl, toss the cabbage with the salt and sugar. Set aside at room temperature until the cabbage has released about 1½ cups of liquid, about 1 hour. If there's not enough brine, the sauerkraut will go bad before it ferments.

2. Using your hands, squeeze the cabbage over the bowl to catch the liquid and place the cabbage in a tall 8-cup glass or glazed earthenware crock or canister. Using your fist, push down the cabbage to compact it. Pour in enough of the brine to cover the cabbage by at least 1 inch. Place a small plate in the crock to cover the cabbage and keep it submerged. Cover with a cloth and set aside at room temperature for 2 to 4 weeks, until it tastes like sauerkraut. Check the plate after a couple of days. If it's floating on the brine, place another small plate on top to weigh it down. Remove the plate(s) and store the sauerkraut, covered, in the refrigerator for up to 2 months.

—*Linda Merinoff*

• • •

BRAISED SAUERKRAUT

You may want to cook only as much sauerkraut as you're going to use on your hot dogs, in which case add fewer seeds. If you're using commercial sauerkraut, rinse it well before you cook it.

Makes About 5 Cups

5 cups sauerkraut, homemade or store-bought
3 tablespoons lard or meat drippings
1 teaspoon celery seeds
½ teaspoon caraway seeds
½ cup apple juice

Drain off the brine from the sauerkraut. In a large nonreactive saucepan, melt the lard over moderate heat. Add the sauerkraut, toss well and stir in the celery seeds and caraway seeds. Add the apple juice and bring to a boil over high heat. Reduce the heat to low, cover and simmer until the sauerkraut is heated through, about 15 minutes. Drain well and serve hot or cool.

—*Linda Merinoff*

• • •

CHARRED CARROT PUREE

A while ago, I read a recipe for charred carrot soup by Anne Disrude, former *Food & Wine* associate test kitchen director, and was intrigued. So here are my charred carrots, with thanks to Ms. Disrude for her inspiration.

6 Servings

6 tablespoons unsalted butter
1 tablespoon safflower or corn oil
3 pounds carrots, sliced ¼ inch thick
1 tablespoon lemon juice
½ teaspoon salt
¼ teaspoon freshly ground pepper
½ cup milk

1. In a large heavy skillet, melt 2 tablespoons of the butter in the oil over high heat.

2. Add the carrots and toss to coat evenly. Continue to cook, stirring them frequently, until they begin to char around the edges, 20 to 25 minutes.

3. Transfer the carrots to a food processor and add the remaining 4 tablespoons butter, the lemon juice, salt, pepper and milk. Puree until smooth. (*The puree can be made up to 1 day ahead; reheat over hot water in a double boiler.*)

—*Lee Bailey*

• • •

BROCCOLI AND CAULIFLOWER IN MUSTARD BUTTER

Simply steamed fall vegetables tossed with mustard butter make a wonderful side dish for baked ham.

6 Servings

4 tablespoons unsalted butter, softened to room temperature
1 tablespoon Dijon-style mustard
1 teaspoon fresh lemon juice

1 small bunch of broccoli, large stems removed, separated into florets
1 small head of cauliflower, separated into florets
1/4 teaspoon salt
1/4 teaspoon freshly ground white pepper

1. In a small bowl, blend together the butter and mustard. Mix in the lemon juice. Set the mustard butter aside.

2. Steam the broccoli and cauliflower, covered, until just tender, about 5 minutes. Drain and return the vegetables to the hot saucepan. Toss to evaporate any extra moisture. Season with the salt and white pepper. Add the mustard butter and toss to coat well.

—Lee Bailey

• • •

SHREDDED CABBAGE WITH SAUTEED BLACK MUSTARD SEEDS

This dish is easy to prepare at the last minute, but if you prepare it ahead, turn the heat on and toss the cabbage for a few seconds before serving.

6 Servings

1 tablespoon safflower or corn oil
1 tablespoon black mustard seeds
1 tablespoon unsalted butter
1 1/2 pounds shredded green cabbage
1 medium onion, chopped
1 teaspoon salt
1 teaspoon sugar
1 tablespoon tarragon vinegar
1/2 teaspoon freshly ground pepper

1. In a large flameproof casserole, heat the oil over moderately high heat. Add the mustard seeds, cover and shake the pan as the seeds pop. As soon as the popping subsides, add the butter, cabbage, onion, salt and sugar. Toss to mix and cover the casserole tightly.

2. Cook the cabbage over moderate heat, stirring once or twice to keep from sticking, until it is tender but still firm, about 5 minutes.

3. Add the vinegar and pepper and toss to mix well.

—Lee Bailey

• • •

CAULIFLOWER-ONION TART

🍷 Beaujolais—or a light Pinot Noir—would have the acidity and the emphatic fruitiness to contrast with the rich, pungent flavors of this dish. Try a 1985 Prosper Maufoux Saint Amour Beaujolais or a 1985 Saintsbury "Garnet" Pinot Noir served cool.

6 Servings

1 small head of cauliflower (1 1/2 pounds), separated into florets
1/2 teaspoon salt
1/8 teaspoon freshly ground pepper
2 tablespoons unsalted butter
1 large onion, thinly sliced
Partially Baked 9-Inch Tart Shell (recipe follows)
3 egg yolks
1 cup heavy cream
2 tablespoons chopped parsley

1. Preheat the oven to 350°. In a large saucepan, bring 2 quarts of water to a rolling boil. Add the cauliflower and cook, uncovered, until just tender, about 5 minutes. Remove and drain well on paper towels. Season with 1/4 teaspoon of the salt and the pepper.

2. In a medium skillet, melt the butter over moderately low heat. Add the onion and cook until softened but not browned, about 5 minutes. Let cool slightly. Spoon the onion over the bottom of the tart shell. Arrange the cauliflower in concentric circles over the onion.

3. In a medium bowl, whisk together the egg yolks, cream and remaining 1/4 teaspoon salt until blended. Pour the custard over the cauliflower and sprinkle with the parsley. Bake until the custard is set and a knife inserted in the tart's center comes out clean, 45 to 50 minutes.

—Myra Dorros

• • •

PARTIALLY BAKED TART SHELL

Makes One 9-inch Shell

1 cup all-purpose flour
1/8 teaspoon salt
1/4 cup vegetable shortening
2 tablespoons cold unsalted butter
2 tablespoons ice water

1. In a large bowl, combine the flour and salt. Cut in the shortening and butter until the mixture resembles coarse meal. Sprinkle the ice water over the mixture, 1 tablespoon at a time, tossing with a fork until the pastry can be gathered into a ball. (Use additional water if necessary.) Flatten the dough into a 6-inch disk, wrap in waxed paper and refrigerate for at least 30 minutes.

2. On a lightly floured surface, roll the pastry into a 12-inch circle, about 1/8 inch thick. Fold the circle into quarters or roll it loosely over a lightly floured rolling pin and transfer to a 9-inch tart pan with a removable bottom. Unfold and ease the pastry into the pan without stretching it. Trim off excess dough. Using a fork, prick the bottom of the tart. Cover with plastic wrap and freeze for 15 minutes before baking.

3. Preheat the oven to 450°. Line the tart shell with aluminum foil and fill with pie weights or dried beans. Bake until golden brown, about 15 minutes. Remove the foil and pie weights and let the shell cool.

—Myra Dorros

• • •

CELERY ROOT, GREEN BEAN AND POTATO PUREE

This soft, subtle dish pairs wonderfully with hearty roasts or steaks. Incidentally, if you have any of this puree left over, you can make patties out of it and fry them.

6 to 8 Servings

1/2 medium celery root (celeriac), peeled and cut into 1/2-inch dice
1 pound baking potatoes, peeled and cut into 1-inch cubes
1 pound green beans, cut into thirds
6 tablespoons cold unsalted butter
2 teaspoons salt

1. In a large saucepan, combine the celery root and potatoes. Cover with 2 inches of cold water and bring to a boil over high heat. Add the green beans and return to a boil. Reduce the heat to moderate and cook until the vegetables are tender, about 20 minutes; drain well.

2. Preheat the oven to 400°. Return the vegetables to the pan and cook over high heat, shaking the pan constantly to evaporate excess moisture, about 1 minute. Transfer the vegetables to a food processor or blender. Add 5 tablespoons of the butter and the salt. Puree, turning the machine quickly on and off, until smooth. (You may have to do this in two batches.)

3. Scrape the puree into a buttered 1½-quart casserole and smooth the top. Rub the remaining 1 tablespoon butter evenly over the top. (*The recipe can be prepared to this point up to 30 minutes ahead.*)

4. Bake the vegetable puree uncovered for 25 minutes.

—Lee Bailey

• • •

CORN AND AVOCADO TORTA

Robert Del Grande recommends serving this as an accompaniment to grilled squab, but it is also delicious on its own.

4 Servings

1 ear of corn or 3/4 cup corn kernels
2 tablespoons unsalted butter
1 red bell pepper, cut into 1/4-inch dice
1 jalapeño pepper, seeded and minced
3 scallions, chopped
1 ripe avocado (preferably Hass), cut into 1/4-inch dice
1/4 cup chopped fresh coriander
1 ounce goat cheese, crumbled
2 teaspoons walnut oil
1 teaspoon fresh lime juice
1/2 teaspoon salt
1/4 teaspoon freshly ground black pepper
2 flour tortillas (7 inches in diameter)
1/2 cup sour cream
Sprigs of coriander, as garnish

1. Cut the kernels from the corn cob. In a large skillet, melt 1 tablespoon of the butter over moderate heat. Add the corn and cook, stirring, until golden brown, about 10 minutes.

2. Stir in the red pepper, jalapeño and scallions and cook until softened, about 5 minutes. Remove from the heat and let cool slightly.

3. Stir in the avocado, coriander, goat cheese, walnut oil and lime juice. Lightly mash the avocado to bind the ingredients. Season with the salt and pepper.

4. Spread the avocado mixture over one of the tortillas. Cover with the second tortilla to make a sandwich, or torta.

5. In a large skillet, melt the remaining 1 tablespoon butter over moderate heat. Add the avocado torta and cook until golden brown on the bottom, about 2 minutes. Using a large spatula, carefully turn the torta and cook the other side until browned, about 2 minutes longer.

6. Using a sharp knife, cut the torta into quarters. Garnish each wedge with 2 tablespoons of the sour cream and a sprig of fresh coriander.

—Robert Del Grande,
Cafe Annie, Houston

• • •

EGGPLANT AND SPINACH TIMBALES

The Mediterranean flavor of these timbales makes them a perfect foil for lamb.

2 Servings

1 eggplant (about 1 pound)
1½ teaspoons salt
1/2 pound fresh spinach, stemmed
3½ tablespoons extra-virgin olive oil
1/3 cup finely chopped onion
1/3 cup finely chopped red bell pepper
1 egg, beaten
1 tablespoon minced basil
1 tablespoon minced parsley
2 teaspoons Roasted Garlic Puree (p. 259)
1/4 teaspoon freshly ground black pepper

1. Trim the eggplant and halve lengthwise. Using a sharp knife, score the flat surfaces with deep diagonal cuts. Sprinkle with 1 teaspoon of the salt and let drain on paper towels, cut-side down, for 1 hour.

2. Bring a large saucepan of water to a boil. Add the spinach leaves and blanch until wilted but still bright green, 5 to 10 seconds. Transfer to a colander and squeeze dry. Drain the leaves flat on paper towels.

3. Preheat the oven to 350°. Set the eggplant halves in a small roasting pan, cut-side up, and brush each half with 1 tablespoon of the olive oil. Bake until soft, about 1 hour. Let cool slightly, then use a spoon to scrape out the flesh; discard the skin. Finely chop the eggplant and place in a medium bowl.

4. In a small saucepan, heat 1 tablespoon of the oil. Add the onion and red pepper and cook over moderate heat, stirring frequently, until golden, about 5 minutes.

5. Add the onion to the chopped eggplant and blend in the egg, basil, parsley, Roasted Garlic Puree, black pepper and the remaining ½ teaspoon salt.

6. Brush two ⅔-cup ramekins with the remaining ½ tablespoon oil. Line the base and sides of the ramekins with the spinach leaves, overlapping them on the sides and letting them extend over the rims. Fill the ramekins with the eggplant mixture and fold the overhanging spinach leaves over the surface. Fold any remaining spinach neatly over the tops. *(The recipe can be prepared to this point up to 1 day ahead. Cover and refrigerate.)*

7. Set the ramekins in a steamer over boiling water and steam until a knife inserted in the center comes out clean and hot to the touch, 20 to 25 minutes. Remove from the steamer, cover with foil and let rest in a warm place for about 10 minutes.

8. To serve, run a knife around the inside of the ramekins, drain off any excess liquid and invert each timbale onto a warmed dinner plate.

—Bob Chambers

• • •

BAKED FENNEL WITH PARMESAN CHEESE

Try this classic Italian side dish with Sweet and Sour Lamb (p. 113).

6 Servings

5 small fennel bulbs (about 3 pounds), trimmed and cut into quarters
4 tablespoons unsalted butter
¼ teaspoon salt
½ teaspoon freshly ground pepper
⅓ cup chicken stock or canned broth
¼ cup freshly grated Parmesan cheese

1. Preheat the oven to 350°. Soak the fennel in cold water for 20 minutes; drain.

2. In a large pot of boiling salted water, cook the fennel for 5 minutes. Drain, rinse under cold water and dry well.

3. Grease a large shallow baking dish with 1 tablespoon of the butter. Cut the remaining 3 tablespoons butter into small pieces. Layer half of the fennel in the dish, scatter the butter over the fennel and season with ⅛ teaspoon of the salt and ¼ teaspoon of the pepper. Top with the remaining fennel, pack down and season with the remaining ⅛ teaspoon salt and ½ teaspoon pepper. (*The recipe can be prepared to this point up to 1 day ahead. Cover and refrigerate overnight.*)

4. Pour the stock over the fennel, cover with foil and bake for 45 minutes.

5. Increase the temperature to 400° and cook until the liquid has evaporated, about 20 minutes.

6. Sprinkle the Parmesan cheese over the fennel and bake uncovered until golden, about 10 minutes.

—Nancy Verde Barr

• • •

BAKED FENNEL AND BOSTON LETTUCE

From time to time I suppose it's usual for us to develop enthusiasms for particular foods. For me, recently, it has been fennel and cooked lettuce. I had always thought that fennel's flavor was too aggressive to suit me . . . until I got around to cooking it (I had always had it raw or not at all). Now I am putting it in everything. I expect my friends to start complaining any minute.

6 Servings

¼ pound pancetta or bacon, cut into 1-by-¼-inch strips
1 small carrot, coarsely chopped
1 small celery rib, coarsely chopped
1 small onion, coarsely chopped
2½ pounds fennel bulbs (about 3 large)
1 head of Boston lettuce (about ½ pound), leaves separated
¼ teaspoon freshly ground pepper
¾ cup chicken stock or canned broth
1 tablespoon fresh lemon juice
3 tablespoons unsalted butter
¼ teaspoon salt

1. Preheat the oven to 350°. In a small saucepan, blanch the pancetta in simmering water for 2 minutes; drain.

2. Sprinkle the pancetta and chopped carrot, celery and onion over the bottom of a large shallow gratin or baking dish.

3. Bring a large saucepan of water to a boil over high heat. Add the fennel bulbs and cook for 2 minutes. Remove with a slotted spoon and let cool slightly. Add the Boston lettuce leaves to the boiling water and cook for 2 minutes; drain.

4. Cut the fennel bulbs lengthwise into thick slices. Lay the fennel on top of the chopped vegetables. Sprinkle with the pepper. Lay the wilted lettuce leaves on top to cover the fennel completely.

5. In a small saucepan, heat the chicken stock, lemon juice, butter and salt over moderately high heat until the butter melts; pour over the fennel. Cover the dish with a sheet of buttered aluminum foil and bake for 45 minutes, or until the fennel is tender.

6. Carefully lift the lettuce off the fennel and place in a food processor. Arrange the fennel on a serving platter and cover with the foil to keep warm. Pour the pan juices along with the bacon, carrot, celery and onion into the processor with the lettuce. Puree to a sauce. Season with additional salt, pepper and lemon juice to taste.

7. Serve the fennel with a spoonful of the pureed vegetable sauce. Pass the remainder on the side.

—Lee Bailey

• • •

GLAZED ONIONS

These simple glazed onions can be prepared ahead of time and reheated in the oven before serving.

6 Servings

18 small white onions (about 1 inch in diameter)
4 tablespoons unsalted butter
2 tablespoons light brown sugar
¼ teaspoon salt
½ cup chicken stock or canned broth
½ cup dry red wine

1. Bring a large saucepan of water to a simmer. Add the unpeeled onions and simmer over moderate heat for 4 minutes; drain. Rinse the onions under cold running water to cool; pat dry with paper towels. Cut off the roots and tops of each onion. Peel off the outer skins.

2. In a large skillet, melt the butter over moderate heat. Add the onions and cook, tossing occasionally, until they begin to turn golden, about 10 minutes.

3. Sprinkle on the brown sugar and cook, tossing constantly, until the sugar melts and the onions are glazed to a deep brown, about 2 minutes longer. Season with the salt.

4. Increase the heat to high and add the chicken stock and wine. Cook, spooning the liquid over the onions, until the sauce is thick and the onions are tender, about 15 minutes. If the onions are still not tender, add a few more tablespoons of stock or water and continue to cook for a few more minutes.

—Lee Bailey

• • •

BRAISED MUSTARD GREENS

If you substitute fresh spinach for the mustard greens, the cooking time will be only 2 to 3 minutes, after the addition of the chicken stock.

6 Servings

2 tablespoons extra-virgin olive oil
1 medium onion, coarsely chopped
2 small shallots, minced
2 small garlic cloves, finely minced
2 tablespoons chicken stock or canned broth
2 pounds fresh mustard greens, rinsed, with large stems removed
2 teaspoons fresh lime juice
½ teaspoon salt
¼ teaspoon freshly ground pepper

1. In a large flameproof casserole, heat the oil over moderate heat. Add the onion, shallots and garlic and cook until golden, 8 to 10 minutes.

2. Add the chicken stock to the casserole. Arrange the mustard greens on top of the onion. Cover and cook, turning the greens several times, until tender, about 20 minutes. (The mustard greens will reduce in volume.) Season with the lime juice, salt and pepper. Toss and serve.

—Lee Bailey

• • •

GRILLED ONIONS AND PEPPERS

Although this vegetable mixture is traditionally served with Italian sausages, it's delicious on hot dogs, too. I developed this technique, which imitates barbecuing, after reading Paul Prudhomme's recipe for blackened redfish. You will need a cast-iron skillet to grill the vegetables, and it may smoke, so make sure all your doors and windows are open.

Makes About 1½ Cups

1 medium onion, thinly sliced
1 green bell pepper, thinly sliced
2 tablespoons minced fresh rosemary or 1 tablespoon crumbled dried

1. Keeping them separated, place the sliced onion and pepper on a lightly oiled rack in a steamer over boiling water. Steam until soft, about 15 minutes.

2. Place the rosemary in a cast-iron skillet. Set the skillet over high heat until the rosemary begins to smoke, 5 to 8 minutes. Add the onion and cook, turning once, until charred, about 2 minutes per side. Remove and set aside. Cook the pepper the same way, then remove and toss with the onion.

—Linda Merinoff

• • •

PEAS AND MUSHROOMS IN CROUSTADES WITH CHERVIL

These vegetable-filled croustades have a lovely chervil flavor. They make a good side dish or first course, but can also be served as an elegant light lunch.

4 Side-Dish Servings

5 tablespoons unsalted butter
8 thin slices of firm-textured white bread, crusts removed
¼ pound mushrooms, cut into dice
3 tablespoons minced fresh chervil
½ pound fresh shelled or frozen young peas
¾ cup heavy cream
¼ cup crème fraîche or sour cream
1 teaspoon fresh lemon juice
¼ teaspoon salt
¼ teaspoon freshly ground pepper

1. Preheat the oven to 400°. Melt 4 tablespoons of the butter. Brush over both sides of the bread slices. Gently press the bread into eight 2½-inch muffin tins. Bake until golden brown and crisp, about 20 minutes. Carefully lift the croustades from the tin and set aside. *(The croustades can be made up to 5 hours ahead. Store at room temperature in an airtight tin.)*

2. In a medium saucepan, melt the remaining 1 tablespoon butter over high heat. Add the mushrooms and sauté, without stirring, until brown, about 2 minutes. Reduce the heat to moderate and cook until tender, about 1 minute longer.

3. Remove the mushrooms to a small bowl and toss with 1 tablespoon of the chervil. Set aside for at least 10 minutes and up to 1 hour.

4. In a medium saucepan with a steamer basket, steam the peas until tender, 4 to 8 minutes depending on their size.

5. Remove the basket and discard the cooking water. Return the peas to the saucepan. Add the heavy cream and boil over high heat, stirring, until the cream is thick and reduced by half, about 3 minutes. Add the mushrooms and crème fraîche and stir to combine.

6. Remove from the heat, season with the lemon juice, salt, pepper and remaining 2 tablespoons chervil. Divide the warm mixture evenly among the croustades and serve at once.

—Marcia Kiesel

• • •

ITALIAN VEGETABLE DINNER

The steak-lovers in the crowd won't even miss the meat in this hearty and filling vegetable main dish. Serves 4.

Polenta with Peppers, Mushrooms and Onions (p. 158)

Chicory, Radicchio and Red Pepper Salad with Rosemary

Chocolate Pecan Pudding with Bourbon Sauce (p. 214)

POLENTA WITH PEPPERS, MUSHROOMS AND ONIONS

This delicious entrée can also be made completely vegetarian by substituting vegetable broth (or water and 1 teaspoon of salt) for the chicken stock.

4 to 6 Main-Course Servings

¼ cup olive oil
1 medium onion, sliced
1 garlic clove, minced
1 medium green bell pepper, sliced
1 medium red bell pepper, sliced
½ pound mushrooms, sliced
½ teaspoon salt
¼ teaspoon freshly ground black pepper
2 teaspoons chopped fresh oregano or ⅔ teaspoon dried
3 cups chicken stock or 1½ cups canned broth diluted with 1½ cups water
1 cup instant polenta
¼ cup boiling water

1. In a large skillet, heat the oil. Add the onion and garlic and cook over moderately high heat until the onion is softened and slightly browned, about 5 minutes.

2. Add the green and red peppers and the mushrooms. Season with the salt and black pepper. Reduce the heat to moderate and continue to cook, stirring occasionally, until the peppers are tender, about 15 minutes. Stir in the oregano, remove from the heat and cover to keep warm.

3. In a medium saucepan, bring the chicken stock to a boil over high heat. Gradually stir in the polenta and cook, stirring constantly, for 5 minutes. Add the boiling water and cook for 5 minutes

longer. Season with additional salt and black pepper to taste.

4. Spoon the polenta into a serving dish, smoothing it into an even layer with a wet spatula and mounding the edges slightly. Pour the sautéed vegetables into the center and serve.

—John Robert Massie

• • •

TINY POTATOES ROASTED ON ROSEMARY BRANCHES

You can also cook cubes of sweet potato, turnip and rutabaga on rosemary branches.

4 Servings

1½ pounds tiny new potatoes
4 long branches of rosemary, 6 to 8 inches each
1 tablespoon olive oil
⅛ teaspoon salt
¼ teaspoon freshly ground pepper

1. Preheat the oven to 400°. In a medium pot of boiling water, cook the potatoes over high heat until partially cooked, about 5 minutes. Drain and cool slightly.

2. Remove most of the leaves from the center of the rosemary branches, leaving a cluster of leaves at either end. Starting at the thicker end, skewer the potatoes onto the branches.

3. Place the potatoes on a baking sheet and drizzle with the olive oil; roll the branches to distribute the oil evenly. Season with the salt and pepper and bake until the potatoes are golden brown and crisp, about 25 minutes.

—Marcia Kiesel

• • •

SCALLOPED POTATOES WITH SWEET MARJORAM AND PARMESAN CHEESE

6 to 8 Servings

4 large baking potatoes, peeled and thinly sliced
1 teaspoon salt
¼ teaspoon freshly ground pepper
¼ teaspoon freshly grated nutmeg
2 medium garlic cloves, minced
¼ cup chopped fresh sweet marjoram
¼ cup freshly grated Parmesan cheese
2 cups heavy cream

1. Preheat the oven to 350°. Butter a 6-cup gratin dish or shallow casserole.

2. Layer one-fifth of the potato slices in the gratin dish and season with one-fourth each of the salt, pepper, nutmeg, garlic, marjoram and Parmesan. Repeat the layering 3 times. Top with a final layer of potato slices, overlapping them attractively.

3. Combine the cream with ½ cup of water and pour evenly over the potatoes. Cover the dish snugly with aluminum foil. Bake the potatoes for 1½ hours, then uncover and bake for 30 minutes longer, or until lightly browned. Remove from the oven and let stand for 10 minutes before serving.

—Jean Anderson

• • •

POTATO PIE FROM CHEZ LOUIS

This rustic potato dish from chef David Liederman can be assembled ahead and then baked shortly before serving. It is particularly good with a crisp, roasted chicken or other roasted meats.

4 Servings

2½ pounds large Idaho potatoes, peeled
5 garlic cloves—4 lightly crushed, 1 minced
3 tablespoons unsalted butter
3 tablespoons olive oil
½ teaspoon salt
⅛ teaspoon freshly ground pepper
1 tablespoon chopped parsley

1. Put the potatoes and 2 of the crushed garlic cloves in a large pot, with salted water to cover. Bring to a boil over high heat and cook until the potatoes are just tender, about 20 minutes; drain well. When the potatoes are cool enough to handle, slice them into ¼-inch rounds.

2. Preheat the oven to 450°. In a heavy 9-inch ovenproof skillet, melt the butter in the oil over moderately low heat. Add the remaining 2 crushed garlic cloves and cook until golden brown, about 4 minutes. Remove and discard the garlic.

3. In batches, add the potato slices to the garlic oil and sauté over moderately high heat, tossing, until lightly browned, about 6 minutes. Season the potatoes with the salt and pepper.

4. Return all the potato slices to the skillet and firmly press them down with the back of a spoon. Bake until the potatoes are golden brown and crisp, 20 to 25 minutes. Slide a spatula under the pie to loosen it, then invert onto a serving plate. Sprinkle with the parsley and minced garlic.

—David Liederman, Chez Louis, New York City

• • •

MASHED POTATOES WITH ONIONS AND GARLIC

These homey potatoes—the ultimate comfort food—are from Editorial Assistant Jim Brown.

6 to 8 Servings

1 stick plus 2 tablespoons unsalted butter
2 pounds onions, thinly sliced
8 garlic cloves, minced
5 pounds Idaho potatoes, peeled and cut into 2-inch chunks
1 cup milk
½ cup heavy cream
1½ teaspoons salt
1¼ teaspoons freshly ground pepper

1. In a large skillet, melt the butter. Add the onions, cover and cook over low heat, stirring occasionally, until softened, about 20 minutes.

2. Stir in the garlic, cover and cook until the onions are golden, about 10 minutes longer; set aside.

3. Meanwhile, in a large saucepan, cover the potatoes with hot water and cook over high heat until tender, about 15 minutes. Drain well and return the potatoes to the pan. Cook over high heat, tossing the potatoes until completely dry, about 1 minute. Turn off the heat and mash with a potato masher. Stir in the milk and heavy cream until thoroughly combined and fluffy. Stir in the onions, garlic, salt and pepper.

—James W. Brown, Jr.

• • •

PLANTAIN GRATIN

Clara Lesueur, chef/owner of Chez Clara in Guadeloupe, sometimes sprinkles the plantains with grated Gruyère cheese before baking.

6 Servings

½ small onion, sliced
2 garlic cloves, lightly crushed
1 jalapeño pepper, halved and seeded
3 whole black peppercorns
3 cups milk
1½ sticks (6 ounces) unsalted butter
3 large yellow plantains, thinly sliced
¼ cup plus 1½ teaspoons all-purpose flour
1 teaspoon salt
1 teaspoon freshly ground pepper
¼ cup fresh bread crumbs

1. In a medium saucepan, combine the onion, garlic, jalapeño pepper and black peppercorns. Add the milk and bring to a simmer over moderately high heat. Cover and set aside to infuse for 25 minutes.

2. Preheat the oven to 475°. In a large skillet, melt 3 tablespoons of the butter over moderately high heat. Add half of the plantain slices and sauté, turning once, until browned, about 2 minutes per side. Repeat the process using 3 more tablespoons of butter and the remaining plantains.

3. In another medium saucepan, melt the remaining 6 tablespoons butter over moderate heat. Set aside 1½ tablespoons of the melted butter. Add the flour to the melted butter in the saucepan and cook, stirring, for about 2 minutes without allowing the flour to color to make a roux.

4. Strain the seasoned milk into the saucepan, increase the heat to moderately high and bring to a boil, whisking constantly, until thickened. Reduce the heat to moderate and cook, whisking frequently, until the sauce is smooth and no longer floury tasting, about 2 minutes. Season with ¼ teaspoon each of the salt and pepper.

5. In a buttered medium gratin or baking dish, arrange the sautéed plantains in a single layer. Pour on one-third of the white sauce. Season with ¼ teaspoon each salt and pepper. Repeat the process twice more. Sprinkle the bread crumbs evenly over the top. Drizzle on the reserved 1½ tablespoons melted butter and bake for about 15 minutes, until bubbling and lightly browned on top.

—Clara Lesueur, Chez Clara, Ste. Rose, Guadeloupe

• • •

BUTTERNUT SQUASH GRATIN

This is an adaptation of the rich, creamy pumpkin gratin served at Le Lafayette in Fort-de-France, Martinique's capital.

6 to 8 Servings

1 butternut squash (about 3 pounds)
4 cups milk
1½ teaspoons salt
½ teaspoon freshly ground pepper
¼ teaspoon freshly grated nutmeg
1 garlic clove, crushed through a press
2 cups heavy cream

1. Preheat the oven to 375°. Halve the squash lengthwise. Scoop out the seeds and fibrous center and peel off the skin with a sharp knife. Cut into ¼-inch slices.

2. In a large saucepan, combine the squash with the milk and 2 cups of water. Add ½ teaspoon of the salt, ¼ teaspoon of the pepper, the nutmeg and the garlic. Bring to a simmer over moderately high heat. Reduce the heat to low and simmer until just tender, about 4 minutes; drain well.

3. Transfer the squash to a shallow 2-quart buttered gratin or baking dish and season with the remaining 1 teaspoon salt and ¼ teaspoon pepper. Pour the cream on top and bake for about 20 minutes, until browned. Serve hot, directly from the gratin dish.

—Henri Charvet, Le Lafayette, Fort-de-France, Martinique

• • •

GRATIN OF SWEET POTATOES FLAMBEED WITH BOURBON

This easy dish from Food Editor Susan Wyler is only slightly sweet and can make a grand entrance, if you choose to flambé it in front of your guests. For the best presentation, use a very large round or oval ovenproof dish.

6 to 8 Servings

3 pounds large sweet potatoes
4 tablespoons unsalted butter, at room temperature
¼ teaspoon salt
⅛ teaspoon freshly ground pepper
2 tablespoons sugar
¼ cup bourbon

1. Put the potatoes in a large pot of cold water. Bring to a boil over moderately high heat and cook until the potatoes are just tender around the edges but still firm in the center, 15 to 20 minutes. Drain and rinse under cold water. When the potatoes are cool enough to handle, peel them with a knife (the skins will come off easily).

2. Preheat the oven to 475°. Use 1 tablespoon of the butter to grease a large shallow baking dish, preferably a round or a large oval gratin dish. Cut the sweet potatoes into ¼-inch rounds. Arrange the slices, overlapping slightly in concentric circles. Spread the remaining butter all over the potatoes, covering them as well as you can. Season with the salt and pepper. Sprinkle the sugar evenly over the potatoes. *(The recipe can be prepared ahead to this point. Set aside at room temperature for up to 3 hours or cover and refrigerate overnight. Let return to room temperature before proceeding.)*

3. Bake the sweet potatoes for 20 minutes. Reduce the heat to 350° and bake for 20 minutes longer, or until the potatoes are tender and lightly glazed.

4. Pour the bourbon into a large metal ladle or small saucepan. Warm over low heat for about 20 seconds. Carefully ignite the bourbon and drizzle over the sweet potatoes.

—Susan Wyler

• • •

VEGETARIAN LUNCH

Although delicious any time of year, the ratatouille pie is best made toward the end of summer when all of the ingredients can be fresh from the garden. Serves 6.

Spinach-Stuffed Mushrooms with Cheddar and Chervil (p. 16)

Ratatouille Pie with Basil (p. 161)

Tossed Bitter Greens with Walnut Vinaigrette

Gorgonzola Dolcelatte

Poached Pears

Coffee

SWEET POTATOES WITH GRAPEFRUIT

Grapefruit gives this a very pleasant bittersweet taste, which I especially like with ham.

6 Servings

1¾ pounds sweet potatoes
1 large grapefruit
3 tablespoons unsalted butter
⅓ cup (firmly packed) light brown sugar
¼ teaspoon salt
2 eggs, well beaten

1. Preheat the oven to 375°. Put the potatoes, unpeeled, in a large saucepan and cover with water. With a swivel-bladed vegetable peeler, peel the yellow zest from the grapefruit and put it in with the potatoes. Bring to a boil, reduce the heat and simmer until the sweet potatoes are just fork-tender, about 20 minutes.

2. Meanwhile, with a long-pronged fork or tongs, dip the grapefruit into the boiling potato water and blanch, turning constantly, for 30 seconds. Rinse the grapefruit briefly under cold running water to cool and peel off the white pith. Section the grapefruit and peel off the membranes over a bowl to catch the juice. Reserve all the juice and pulp; discard any seeds.

3. When the sweet potatoes are done, drain and let cool; discard the grapefruit zest. Peel the potatoes and put them into a food processor along with the grapefruit pulp and juice, the butter, brown sugar and salt. Puree until smooth. Add the eggs and mix to blend.

4. Pour the sweet potato mixture into a well-buttered, 6-cup soufflé dish. Place in a pan of hot water and bake for 45 minutes, or until the center is set.

—Lee Bailey

• • •

RATATOUILLE PIE WITH BASIL CRUST

This is one for the vegetarian crowd to be sure, but it's not to be passed up even if you aren't a card-carrying member.

🍷 Highly seasoned and topped with tangy Parmesan cheese, this pot pie calls for the contrast of a clean, striking white, such as the 1986 Ruffino Libaio or 1986 Antinori Galestro.

—6 Main-Course Servings—

BASIL CRUST:

1½ cups plus 1 teaspoon all-purpose flour
1 teaspoon sugar
½ teaspoon salt
6 tablespoons vegetable shortening
1 egg yolk
1 teaspoon red wine vinegar
2 to 3 tablespoons cold water
2 tablespoons chopped fresh basil

RATATOUILLE:

1 large eggplant (about 1½ pounds)
¾ teaspoon salt
½ cup extra-virgin olive oil
2 small zucchini (about 1 pound), sliced
1 tablespoon unsalted butter
1 large onion, thinly sliced
2 large garlic cloves, minced
1 medium green bell pepper, thinly sliced
1 medium red bell pepper, thinly sliced
2 medium tomatoes, peeled and cut into ½-inch wedges
¼ teaspoon freshly ground black pepper
½ teaspoon hot Hungarian paprika
¼ cup chopped parsley
2 tablespoons chopped fresh basil
2 cups grated Italian Fontina cheese (about 6 ounces)
½ cup freshly grated Parmesan cheese
1 egg white, lightly beaten

1. *Make the crust:* In a medium bowl, combine 1½ cups of the flour with the sugar and salt. Cut in the vegetable shortening until the mixture resembles coarse crumbs. Lightly beat the egg yolk with the vinegar, water and basil. Mix the liquid into the flour mixture just until a soft dough forms. Sprinkle with the remaining 1 teaspoon flour, cover with plastic wrap and refrigerate for 1 hour.

2. *Prepare the ratatouille:* Halve the eggplant lengthwise and cut crosswise into ¼-inch-thick slices. Put the eggplant in a colander, sprinkle with ½ teaspoon of the salt and let stand for 30 minutes. Pat the eggplant dry with damp paper towels to remove the salt.

3. In a large heavy skillet, heat 2 tablespoons of the oil over moderately high heat. Add the eggplant slices in batches and sauté, tossing, until golden, about 2½ minutes per side. Repeat with the remaining eggplant, adding up to 5 tablespoons more oil as needed. Drain the eggplant on paper towels, then transfer to a bowl.

4. Add the remaining 1 tablespoon of oil to the same skillet, add the zucchini and cook over high heat, tossing constantly, until golden, 2 to 3 minutes. Reduce the heat to moderate and cook until soft, about 3 minutes longer. Drain and add to the eggplant in the bowl.

5. Wipe the skillet clean. Add the butter and melt over moderate heat. Add the onion and cook for 2 minutes. Stir in the garlic and green and red bell peppers, cover and cook until the peppers are soft, about 5 minutes. Stir in the tomatoes, remaining ¼ teaspoon salt, black pepper and paprika. Increase the heat to high and cook until all the liquid has evaporated, 2 to 3 minutes. Remove from the heat and add the eggplant, zucchini, parsley and basil; mix well.

6. Preheat the oven to 425°. Spoon one-third of the ratatouille into a buttered 10-inch glass or ceramic quiche dish. Sprinkle with one-third each of the Fontina and Parmesan cheeses. Continue layering until all the ingredients are used, ending with the Parmesan cheese.

7. Roll out the pastry on a lightly floured board and lay it over the dish. Trim and flute the edges. Cut a slash in the center of the pie. Brush with the beaten egg white and bake for 25 minutes, or until golden brown. Let stand for 5 minutes before serving.

—Phillip Stephen Schulz

• • •

CAKES & COOKIES

GINGERBREAD CHEESECAKE SWIRL

I love gingerbread and I love cheesecake, so this seemed to be a natural combination. The creamy texture of the cheesecake sets off the dense texture of the cake and vice versa. You can serve this at the most formal or most casual occasion. The cake can be refrigerated for up to 2 days or it can be frozen for up to 2 months.

8 to 10 Servings

1 pound cream cheese, at room temperature
1/2 teaspoon vanilla extract
4 eggs
1/2 cup plus 2 tablespoons granulated sugar
1/4 cup light unsulphured molasses
4 tablespoons unsalted butter, at room temperature
1 teaspoon ground ginger
1 teaspoon cinnamon
1/4 teaspoon freshly grated nutmeg
1/8 teaspoon ground cloves
1/4 teaspoon salt
1/2 cup (packed) light brown sugar
1 1/2 teaspoons baking soda
1 cup all-purpose flour

1. Preheat the oven to 350°. Butter a 9-inch springform pan. In a mixer bowl, beat the cream cheese on high speed until light and smooth, about 3 minutes. With the mixer on, beat in the vanilla. Add 2 of the eggs, 1 at a time, beating until thoroughly blended. Gradually add the granulated sugar and beat until the mixture is light and fluffy, about 3 minutes; set aside.

2. In a medium saucepan, heat the molasses over low heat until bubbles begin to form around the sides. Remove from the heat and stir in the butter, 1 tablespoon at a time, until completely blended.

3. Scrape the molasses into a medium bowl and stir in the ginger, cinnamon, nutmeg, cloves and salt. Add the brown sugar and beat with a wooden spoon until smooth. Let cool to room temperature.

4. Beat the remaining 2 eggs into the gingerbread batter, 1 at a time, until well blended. Stir in the baking soda, then beat in the flour in 3 batches until completely incorporated.

5. Using a tablespoon, drop half the gingerbread batter in dollops into the prepared pan. Use one-fourth of the reserved cream cheese mixture to fill in the empty spaces. Dollop the remaining gingerbread batter on top of the cream cheese mounds. Fill in with another one-fourth of the cream cheese mixture. Swirl with the flat edge of a knife to marbleize the batters. (Be careful not to overmix.) Smooth the remaining cream cheese mixture over the top.

6. Bake in the middle of the oven for 50 minutes, or until the top of the cake begins to crack in the center. (The cake may be lumpy since the gingerbread rises and the cheesecake sinks.) Let cool to room temperature. Remove the sides of the springform pan, cover and refrigerate. Serve chilled.

—Linda Merinoff

• • •

PISTACHIO CHEESECAKE

This elegant nut cheesecake from Georges Perrier of Le Bec-Fin in Philadelphia is even better the next day.

8 Servings

1 1/2 pounds cream cheese, preferably fresh, at room temperature
1 1/4 cups plus 1 tablespoon sugar
3 whole eggs, at room temperature
1/4 cup finely chopped unsalted pistachio nuts
1 egg white
1/2 cup finely ground almonds
3 tablespoons apricot preserves

1. Preheat the oven to 275°. Butter an 8-by-3-inch cheesecake pan or springform. Chill the pan for 5 minutes, then butter it again. If using a springform, wrap the outside with foil.

2. In a large bowl, beat the cream cheese with an electric mixer on medium speed until it is very soft. Gradually beat in 1 1/4 cups of the sugar until the mixture is light and smooth, about 5 minutes.

3. Beat in the whole eggs 1 at a time, beating well between each addition, until the mixture is smooth and thoroughly blended. Stir in the chopped pistachios.

4. Turn the batter into the prepared pan and place it in a larger pan. Add enough warm water to the larger pan to reach about two-thirds of the way up the cake pan. Bake the cheesecake in the middle of the oven for 1 1/2 hours, or until set. Remove from the water bath and let the cake cool in the pan on a rack. Refrigerate until chilled, at least 4 hours or overnight.

5. Preheat the oven to 500°. In a medium bowl, beat together the egg white, almonds and remaining 1 tablespoon sugar until well blended, about 1 minute. Unmold the cake onto a cookie sheet, wrapping a hot wet towel around the outside of the pan if necessary. Brush or spread the almond meringue over the top and sides of the cake and bake in the upper third of the oven until golden brown, about 3 minutes. Let cool.

6. In a small heavy saucepan, warm the apricot preserves until melted. Press through a sieve and brush all over the cake to glaze.

—Georges Perrier, Le Bec-Fin, Philadelphia

• • •

CHOCOLATE CAKE BONNE FEMME

This cake differs from a chocolate mousse cake because whole eggs are added instead of beaten egg whites. My friend Paule Basiaux, who gave me this recipe, bakes the cake in a 5- to 6-cup ring mold, a standard baking pan in the kitchens of French housewives. Here in New York, my students use either a bundt pan or a ring mold.

8 Servings

¾ cup Candied Orange Peel (p. 260)
8 ounces bittersweet chocolate, preferably Lindt, Tobler or Suchard, broken into small pieces
½ cup freshly brewed strong coffee or 2 teaspoons instant coffee dissolved in ½ cup boiling water
1 cup superfine sugar
2 sticks (8 ounces) unsalted butter, softened to room temperature
5 eggs
Custard Sauce (p. 257) or whipped cream, as accompaniment

1. Preheat the oven to 250°. Generously butter a 5- to 6-cup ring mold or bundt pan.

2. Chop ½ cup of the Candied Orange Peel; reserve the remaining strips for garnish.

3. In a double boiler, melt the chocolate with the coffee over moderate heat.

4. Meanwhile, in a medium mixer bowl, beat the sugar and butter until very smooth and creamy, about 5 minutes. Stir the butter mixture into the melted chocolate and continue to cook until the sugar is completely dissolved, about 5 minutes. Let cool slightly, about 10 minutes.

5. In a large bowl, whisk the eggs until well beaten, about 1 minute. Stir one-fourth of the egg mixture into the chocolate. Whisk the chocolate mixture into the remaining eggs. Stir in the chopped orange peel. Pour the batter into the ring mold.

6. Bake for about 2 hours, or until a cake tester inserted into the center of the cake comes out clean. Let cool for 10 minutes (the cake may sink in the center); then unmold onto a decorative platter. Garnish the top with the reserved ¼ cup Candied Orange Peel. Serve with Custard Sauce or whipped cream.

—Lydie Marshall

• • •

CHOCOLATE BLACK WALNUT CAKE

Black walnuts give this moussecake an unusually earthy flavor, but if you can't find any in your market, ordinary walnuts will work well.

8 to 10 Servings

1 pound semisweet chocolate, chopped
6 eggs, at room temperature
2 tablespoons sugar
1½ tablespoons dark rum
1 tablespoon vanilla extract
Pinch of salt
½ cup heavy cream
1 cup walnuts (about 4 ounces), preferably black, toasted and finely ground
Whipped cream, as accompaniment

1. Preheat the oven to 325°. Butter a 9-by-5-inch loaf pan. Line the bottom and sides of the pan with parchment or waxed paper.

2. Place the chocolate in a metal bowl over simmering water and stir just until melted. Remove from the heat and let cool slightly.

3. In a large metal bowl, whisk together the eggs, sugar, rum, vanilla and salt until blended. Set over a pan of simmering water and beat with an electric hand mixer until the egg mixture forms a slowly dissolving ribbon when the beaters are lifted, about 3 minutes. Remove from the heat and beat until cooled to room temperature.

4. In a medium bowl, beat the cream until soft peaks form. With a rubber spatula, fold the melted chocolate into the egg mixture until blended. Fold in the whipped cream and ground nuts until mixed. Pour into the prepared loaf pan.

5. Set the loaf pan in a larger pan in the oven and add enough hot water to reach halfway up the loaf. Reduce the oven temperature to 300° and bake for about 1¼ hours, or until set. Remove from the oven and let cool on a rack before unmolding. Slice the cake about ½ inch thick and pass a bowl of whipped cream on the side.

—Brendan Walsh, Arizona 206, New York City

• • •

GIANDUJA MOUSSE CAKE

Some girls go to Italy and fall in love with Gianfranco or Giuseppe. I fell in love with *gianduja*—that delicious, smooth chocolate hazelnut paste that is formed into bite-size candies and sold at many of Italy's confectionary shops. *Gianduja*-flavored ice cream is also a favorite at *gelaterie* in Florence and Rome. You can make good hazelnut paste in the food processor. Combine it with dark chocolate ganache and whipped cream, and the result is a chocolate hazelnut mousse that is delicious spread between layers of Tender Chocolate Cake.

Makes a 9-Inch Round Cake

2 cups shelled hazelnuts (filberts)
½ cup superfine sugar
2 cups heavy cream

9 ounces good-quality extra-bittersweet chocolate, coarsely chopped
Tender Chocolate Cake (recipe follows)

1. Preheat the oven to 350°. Spread the hazelnuts on a baking sheet. Bake until the nuts are toasted and the dark brown skins cracked, about 15 minutes. Rub the nuts in a kitchen towel to remove as much of the skins as possible. Coarsely chop 1 cup of the toasted nuts.

2. In a food processor, grind the remaining 1 cup hazelnuts with the sugar until the mixture forms a ball and holds its shape when pinched, about 3 minutes. (Do not overprocess or the mixture will become oily and runny.)

3. In a small saucepan, scald ⅓ cup of the cream. Remove from the heat and stir in 6 ounces of the chocolate until melted and smooth. Scrape the chocolate cream, or ganache, into a medium bowl. Refrigerate until cold but still pourable, about 5 minutes. Whisk the ganache until light and slightly stiff, about 1 minute. (If the mixture becomes too stiff, warm it slightly.) Stir in the hazelnut-sugar mixture.

4. Using a long serrated knife, trim the top of the Tender Chocolate Cake level; reserve the trimmings. Slice the cake horizontally into 3 even layers. Place the cake trimmings in a food processor and process until crumbly, about 5 seconds.

5. In a large chilled bowl, beat 1⅓ cups of the heavy cream until stiff peaks form, 1 to 2 minutes. Fold one-fourth of the whipped cream into the chocolate-nut mixture to form a mousse. Fold in the remaining whipped cream. Fold ¾ cup of the reserved chopped nuts into the mousse.

6. Line a 9-by-2-inch round cake pan with 2 perpendicular pieces of plastic wrap, letting them overhang at least 4 inches all around. Place the bottom layer of the cake, crust-side down, in the pan. Smooth half of the mousse evenly over the cake. Repeat with the remaining cake layers and mousse, ending with the third cake layer. Wrap in the plastic and refrigerate for at least 2 hours.

7. In a small heavy saucepan, scald the remaining ⅓ cup cream over high heat. Remove from the heat and stir in the remaining 3 ounces chocolate until melted and smooth. Let cool slightly.

8. Invert the chilled cake onto a rack or an upside-down cake pan. Pour the chocolate glaze over the cake, smoothing the top and sides. Refrigerate for 5 minutes. Pat the reserved cake crumbs onto the sides of the cake and around the top edge. Decorate the top of the cake with the reserved ¼ cup chopped nuts and any additional crumbs. Transfer to a platter and serve.

—Peggy Cullen

• • •

TENDER CHOCOLATE CAKE

The secret to the tenderness of this cake is in the use of cake flour, which has a lower protein content than all-purpose flour.

Makes a Single 9-Inch Round Layer

1½ cups plus 2 tablespoons cake flour
½ cup plus 1 tablespoon Dutch-process unsweetened cocoa powder
1 teaspoon baking powder
½ teaspoon baking soda
1 stick (4 ounces) plus 2 tablespoons unsalted butter, softened to room temperature
1⅓ cups superfine sugar
2 eggs
1 teaspoon vanilla extract

1. Preheat the oven to 325°. Butter and flour a 9-by-2-inch round cake pan. Sift together the flour, cocoa, baking powder and baking soda into a medium bowl.

2. In a large bowl, beat the butter on medium-high speed until light and fluffy, about 2 minutes. Gradually add the sugar and beat until dissolved, about 3 minutes.

3. Add the eggs, 1 at a time, beating well after each addition. Add the vanilla. Sift one-third of the flour mixture into the butter-sugar mixture; mix well. Stir in ⅓ cup of water. Repeat 2 more times with the remaining flour and ⅔ cup of water.

4. Scrape the batter into the prepared pan and bake for 40 to 50 minutes, or until a tester inserted into the center comes out clean. Let the cake cool in the pan on a rack for 10 minutes. Remove from the pan and cool completely, right-side up.

—Peggy Cullen

• • •

BASIC GINGERBREAD CAKE

This is how most of us remember the plain gingerbread cakes of our childhood: simple and even textured, with a pleasantly spicy taste. Serve it with whipped cream, ice cream or toasted and spread with butter for breakfast.

9 Servings

1½ teaspoons ground ginger
1½ teaspoons cinnamon
¼ teaspoon freshly grated nutmeg
¼ teaspoon ground cloves
1 teaspoon baking soda
½ teaspoon salt
½ cup dark unsulphured molasses
1 stick (4 ounces) unsalted butter, at room temperature
½ cup (packed) dark brown sugar
3 eggs
2 cups all-purpose flour

1. Preheat the oven to 350°. Butter an 8-inch square baking pan.

2. In a small bowl, combine the ginger, cinnamon, nutmeg, cloves, baking soda and salt.

3. In a small saucepan, heat the molasses over low heat until bubbles begin to form around the sides. Remove from the heat and stir in the butter, 1 tablespoon at a time, until melted and blended.

4. Scrape the molasses into a large mixer bowl. Gradually beat in the spice mixture, brown sugar and ¼ cup of water. Add the eggs, 1 at a time, beating until well blended, 3 to 5 minutes. Add the flour and beat on low speed for 1 minute, then increase the speed to moderate and beat until well combined.

5. Pour the batter into the prepared pan and bake for 45 to 50 minutes, or until a skewer inserted into the center of the cake comes out clean.

—Linda Merinoff

• • •

SPONGE CAKE

A French housewife would never attempt a genoise, as it belongs to the realm of professional *pâtissiers*, but she will bake this very simple sponge cake, soak it with a sugar syrup and rum or Cointreau and serve it with homemade preserves or a fruit compote. The plain cake can also be used as a substitute for ladyfingers.

—Makes an 8-Inch Square Cake—

5 eggs
½ cup sugar
⅛ teaspoon salt
1 cup all-purpose flour

1. Preheat the oven to 375°. Butter an 8-inch square baking pan and line the bottom with a piece of waxed paper. Butter the paper.

2. In a large bowl, beat the eggs, sugar and salt with an electric mixer on high speed until the mixture is pale and slowly dissolves in a ribbon when the beaters are lifted, about 12 minutes.

3. In 3 batches, sift the flour over the egg mixture and fold until well blended.

4. Pour the batter into the prepared pan and bake for 25 to 30 minutes, or until the cake is golden and a toothpick inserted in the center comes out clean. Unmold onto a rack and let cool completely.

—Lydie Marshall

• • •

LEMON-CARDAMOM POUND CAKE

This recipe is an adaptation of my grandmother Nana's wonderful lemon loaf, which she serves at her weekly bridge party. As an afterdinner dessert, I like to serve it with Wintry Fruit Salad (p. 226).

—Makes 2 Loaves—

½ cup currants
¼ cup sweet sherry
2 cups cake flour
1 tablespoon ground cardamom
2 teaspoons baking powder
¼ teaspoon salt
2 sticks (8 ounces) unsalted butter, softened to room temperature
1 cup plus 2 tablespoons superfine sugar
4 eggs
2 teaspoons grated lemon zest
1 tablespoon heavy cream

1. Preheat the oven to 350°. Butter and flour two 9-by-5-inch metal loaf pans.

2. In a small bowl, cover the currants with the sherry and let macerate for 15 minutes.

3. In a medium bowl, sift the cake flour, cardamom, baking powder and salt.

4. In a large mixer bowl, beat the butter until light and fluffy. Gradually beat in 1 cup of the sugar. Add the eggs, 1 at a time, beating well after each addition. Beat in the lemon zest. With the mixer on low speed, gradually beat in the flour mixture, 1 cup at a time; beat until well blended. Fold in the sherry with the currants.

5. Scrape the batter into the prepared pans and smooth the tops evenly. Drizzle the cream over the loaves and sprinkle with the remaining 2 tablespoons sugar. Bake for 50 minutes, or until the cakes are golden brown and a toothpick inserted in the center comes out clean.

—Mimi Ruth Brodeur

• • •

CANDIED ORANGE CAKE

It's really worth the time to candy your own orange peel because it beats the commercial product by a mile.

🍷 Serve this cake with a cup of espresso and an after-dinner liqueur.

—6 to 8 Servings—

1 large navel orange
1¼ cups sugar
1 cup all-purpose flour
2 tablespoons cornstarch
1 teaspoon baking powder
1½ sticks (6 ounces) unsalted butter, softened to room temperature
3 eggs, at room temperature
¼ cup heavy cream
3 ounces semisweet chocolate, chopped
3 ounces milk chocolate, chopped
2 tablespoons fresh orange juice
2 tablespoons orange liqueur

1. Remove the peel of the orange, including the white pith. Cut the peel into ¼-inch dice. Section the orange and reserve for garnish if desired.

2. In a small saucepan, bring 4 cups of water to a boil. Add the diced peel and

boil over moderate heat for 10 minutes. Drain, rinse well and drain again.

3. In a small heavy saucepan, combine 1 cup of water with ½ cup of the sugar and bring to a boil, stirring to dissolve the sugar. Add the orange peel and cook over moderate heat until 1 or 2 tablespoons of thick syrup remain, about 10 minutes. With a slotted spoon, spread the peel out on a baking sheet to dry, about 1 hour. (On a rainy day or if you're in a hurry, dry the peel in a 325° oven for 10 minutes.)

4. Preheat the oven to 350°. Butter and flour an 8-by-2-inch round cake pan and line the bottom with waxed paper; butter the paper. In a small bowl, toss together the flour, cornstarch and baking powder.

5. In a large mixer bowl, beat the butter until pale and creamy. Add the remaining ¾ cup sugar and beat until light and fluffy, about 5 minutes. Add the eggs, 1 at a time, beating well after each addition. Fold in all but 1 tablespoon of the flour mixture.

6. Set aside 1 tablespoon of the candied orange peel for garnish. Sprinkle the reserved 1 tablespoon of the flour mixture over the remaining candied peel and toss until evenly coated. Fold the floured peel into the cake batter, then spread the batter evenly in the prepared pan.

7. Bake on the middle rack of the oven for 30 minutes, or until the cake is golden and slightly shrunken from the sides of the pan. Let cool on a rack for 15 minutes, then invert the cake, peel off the paper and let cool, right-side up.

8. Meanwhile, in a small saucepan, bring the cream to a boil. Remove from the heat and add the semisweet and milk chocolates. Stir the ganache until completely smooth. Let cool to room temperature.

9. Combine the orange juice and orange liqueur and drizzle over the cake. Spread the chocolate ganache over the top and sides of the cake and refrigerate until set, about 15 minutes.

10. Toss the reserved 1 tablespoon candied peel with a pinch of sugar and place it in the middle of the cake. Decorate the cake or the platter with the drained orange sections if desired.

—Diana Sturgis

• • •

PINEAPPLE CRUMBCAKE

Many types of fruit can replace the pineapple in this moist cake. In early summer, try it with fresh apricots or sour cherries, then with peaches or nectarines and finally with prune plums in the fall.

10 to 12 Servings

2 sticks (8 ounces) unsalted butter, softened to room temperature
1¼ cups sugar
1 whole egg
3 egg yolks
1 teaspoon vanilla extract
2½ cups unbleached all-purpose flour
1 teaspoon baking powder
1 medium pineapple (2 to 2½ pounds)
¼ teaspoon cinnamon

1. Preheat the oven to 350°. Butter a 10-by-2-inch round cake pan and line the bottom with parchment or waxed paper.

2. In a large mixer bowl, beat 1 stick of the butter and ¾ cup of the sugar until light and fluffy. Add the whole egg and continue beating until well blended. Gradually add the egg yolks, 1 at a time, beating well after each addition. Beat in the vanilla.

3. Sift together 1¼ cups of the flour and the baking powder. Stir into the butter mixture. Turn the batter into the prepared pan and spread evenly.

4. Cut the skin and "eyes" from the pineapple. Quarter and core the pineapple. Cut the quarters crosswise into ½-inch-thick slices. Arrange the slices on top of the batter in concentric circles, overlapping slightly and leaving a margin of about 1 inch around the edge. (Don't be concerned if the pineapple mounds slightly in the center, the top will even out as the cake bakes.)

5. In a small saucepan over low heat or in a glass bowl in a microwave oven, melt the remaining 1 stick butter. Let cool slightly.

6. In a medium bowl, combine the remaining ½ cup sugar, 1¼ cups flour and the cinnamon. Pour the melted butter over the flour mixture and rub together with your fingertips to form coarse, pea-size crumbs. Scatter the crumbs evenly over the pineapple and batter.

7. Bake the cake for 55 to 60 minutes, until a knife inserted in the center comes out clean. Let cool in the pan for 15 minutes. Unmold onto a plate and remove the paper. Invert back onto a rack to cool. Serve warm or at room temperature.

—Nicholas Malgieri

• • •

PLUM CAKE

This simple yeast cake is the perfect dessert for a late-summer picnic or a buffet. The French housewife buys fresh yeast at the bakery, but active dry yeast also works well. If you wish, the dough can be prepared several days ahead and stored in the least cold section of your refrigerator. Be sure to let it return to room temperature before proceeding with the recipe.

Makes 2 Cakes

2¼ cups all-purpose flour
1 teaspoon salt
1 cup sugar
1 envelope (¼ ounce) active dry yeast
1 egg

3 sticks (12 ounces) unsalted butter, at room temperature
¾ cup warm milk (105° to 110°)
2 pounds Italian prune plums, pitted and halved (or quartered if large)
1 tablespoon kirsch
½ cup crème fraîche or sour cream, sweetened to taste, as accompaniment

1. Butter two 11-inch tart pans with removable bottoms. Wrap a piece of aluminum foil around the bottom of each pan to catch any drips.

2. In a medium bowl, stir together the flour, salt and 3 tablespoons of the sugar.

3. In a medium bowl, dissolve the yeast in ¼ cup of warm water. Let stand for 5 minutes. Stir in the egg, 1 stick of the butter and the milk until well blended. Gradually stir in the flour mixture. (The dough will be sticky.) Beat the dough with a wooden spoon until smooth and light, about 5 minutes. Cover the bowl with plastic wrap and set aside in a warm place to rise until doubled in volume, 30 to 45 minutes.

4. In a large bowl, toss the plums with ¼ cup of the sugar and the kirsch. Let macerate for 1 hour.

5. In a bowl, combine the remaining 2 sticks butter and ½ cup of the sugar.

6. Using a wooden spoon, deflate the yeast batter and divide in half. Pat one portion of the dough evenly into one of the prepared pans. Arrange half the plums, cut-side down, on the dough and spread half the butter/sugar mixture on top. Assemble the second galette in the same manner. Let rise in a warm place until doubled in size, about 25 minutes.

7. Preheat the oven to 400°.

8. Place the galettes on baking sheets and bake for 25 to 30 minutes, until puffed and golden. Sprinkle each galette with ½ tablespoon of the remaining sugar and serve warm with sweetened crème fraîche or sour cream.

—Lydie Marshall

• • •

PLYMOUTH BAY BERRY CAKE

One of my most pleasant summer memories is of an August spent on Cape Cod, where we hiked through the pines collecting buckets of wild blueberries. Once home, we ground hard yellow corn into a fine grain and made hearty blueberry corn muffins and pancakes. The rich, moist Plymouth Bay Berry Cake evokes those blue and yellow summer days by the sea.

12 Servings

Cornmeal Cake (recipe follows)
2½ cups heavy cream, chilled
¾ cup plus 3 tablespoons superfine sugar
1 pint blueberries (about 2 cups)
1 cup diced fresh fruit, such as nectarines, peaches, sliced bananas and strawberries or raspberries
5 egg whites, at room temperature
Pinch of salt

1. Preheat the oven to 500°. Using a long serrated knife, trim the top of the Cornmeal Cake to make an even surface. Slice the cake horizontally into 4 even layers. Place the bottom layer, crusty-side down, on a springform pan base.

2. In a large chilled bowl, beat the cream until it begins to thicken, about 1 minute. Gradually add 3 tablespoons of the sugar and beat until stiff, about 1 minute.

3. Using a spatula, spread ⅔ cup of the sweetened whipped cream over the bottom cake layer to within ¼ inch of the edge. Top with half of the blueberries. Cover with 1 cup of the whipped cream, spreading it evenly and keeping a ¼-inch border. Place the second cake layer on top and cover with a layer of whipped cream and ¾ cup of the diced fruit. Top with the third cake layer and the remaining blueberries and whipped cream. Top with the last cake layer, cover with plastic wrap and refrigerate.

4. Meanwhile, in a large mixer bowl, beat the egg whites on medium speed until frothy. Add the salt and beat until soft peaks form, about 2 minutes. Gradually beat in the remaining ¾ cup sugar, 1 tablespoon at a time, increasing the speed to high before adding the last 3 tablespoons. Beat until the meringue forms stiff peaks, about 1 minute.

5. Cover the top and sides of the cake with the meringue, swirling it on top into a decorative pattern. Place the cake (on its springform base) on a cookie sheet and bake for 4 to 5 minutes, or until the top and sides are golden brown. Transfer to a serving platter and decoratively garnish the top of the cake with the remaining ¼ cup diced fruit.

—Peggy Cullen

• • •

CORNMEAL CAKE

Makes a 9-Inch Round Cake

¾ cup yellow cornmeal
½ cup plus 3 tablespoons all-purpose flour
2 teaspoons baking powder
¼ teaspoon salt
2 sticks (8 ounces) unsalted butter, softened to room temperature
1¼ cups superfine sugar
4 whole eggs, at room temperature
5 egg yolks, at room temperature
1 teaspoon vanilla extract

1. Preheat the oven to 350°. Butter a 9-inch springform pan. Sprinkle 2 table-

spoons of the cornmeal into the pan and tilt and shake to coat the bottom and sides; tap out any excess.

2. In a medium bowl, sift together the flour, baking powder, salt and remaining ½ cup plus 2 tablespoons cornmeal.

3. In a large mixer bowl, beat the butter on medium-high speed until light and fluffy, about 1 minute. Gradually add the sugar and beat until the sugar is completely dissolved, about 3 minutes. Add the whole eggs and egg yolks, 1 at a time, beating well after each addition. Beat in the vanilla.

4. Gradually fold in the flour mixture until well blended. Scrape the batter into the prepared pan and bake for 40 to 45 minutes, or until the cake is golden brown and a toothpick inserted into the center comes out clean. Let cool on a rack for 10 minutes. Invert to unmold onto the rack and let the cake cool completely. *(The recipe can be prepared up to 1 day in advance, wrapped in plastic wrap and stored at room temperature or frozen for up to 2 months.)*

—*Peggy Cullen*

• • •

POPPY SEED TANTE CAKE

Made solely with egg whites, the starkness of this cake creates a striking contrast to the blue-black poppy seeds.

Makes a 9-Inch Round Cake

1 vanilla bean
⅔ cup milk
⅔ cup poppy seeds
1⅔ cups cake flour
2 teaspoons baking powder
½ teaspoon salt
1½ sticks (6 ounces) unsalted butter, softened to room temperature
1¼ cups superfine sugar
4 egg whites, at room temperature
Cream Cheese Icing (recipe follows)

1. Slit the vanilla bean lengthwise and cut off the tips. In a small saucepan, scald the milk with the vanilla bean.

2. In a small bowl, combine the scalded milk, vanilla bean and poppy seeds. Let cool to room temperature. Scrape the inside of the vanilla bean into the milk mixture and discard the pod.

3. Preheat the oven to 325°. Butter a 9-by-2-inch round cake pan. Sift together the flour, baking powder and salt into a medium bowl.

4. In a large mixer bowl, beat the butter on high speed until light and fluffy, about 2 minutes. Gradually add 1 cup of the sugar and continue to beat until very light and creamy, about 5 minutes.

5. Sift in one-third of the flour mixture; stir to combine. Beat in half of the milk-poppy seed mixture. Repeat 2 more times with the remaining dry ingredients and milk.

6. In a medium bowl, beat the egg whites on medium speed until frothy. Add a pinch of salt and continue beating until soft peaks form, about 2 minutes. Beat in the remaining ¼ cup sugar, 1 teaspoon at a time, increasing the speed to high before adding the last 2 teaspoons. Beat until the meringue is stiff and shiny, about 1 minute. Fold one-fourth of the meringue into the cake butter. Fold in the remaining meringue.

7. Scrape the batter into the prepared pan and bake for 50 to 55 minutes, or until a tester inserted into the center comes out clean. Let cool in the pan on a rack for 10 minutes. Remove the cake from the pan and let cool, right-side up, on the rack. *(The cake can be baked up to 1 day in advance, wrapped in plastic and stored at room temperature, or frozen for up to 1 month.)*

8. Using a long serrated knife, trim off the crusty top of the cake. Slice the cake horizontally into 3 even layers; set aside the middle layer to use as the top. Place the bottom layer on the inverted cake pan. Spread ¾ cup of the Cream Cheese Icing over the bottom cake layer. Repeat with the second cake layer. Top the cake with the middle layer. Frost the sides of the cake with a thin layer of icing. Refrigerate for 10 minutes, then refrost the sides with enough Cream Cheese Icing to cover completely.

9. If desired, use a pastry bag fitted with a #2 star tip to pipe a decorative border of icing around the top edge of the cake.

—*Peggy Cullen*

• • •

CREAM CHEESE ICING

Makes About 2½ Cups

11 ounces cream cheese, at room temperature
2 sticks (8 ounces) unsalted butter, at room temperature
1 vanilla bean, split lengthwise
¾ cup confectioners' sugar, sifted

1. In a medium mixer bowl, beat the cream cheese until light and fluffy. With the mixer on low speed, gradually beat in the butter until well blended, about 4 minutes.

2. Scrape the seeds from the inside of the vanilla bean into the mixture; discard the pod. Sift in the confectioners' sugar and continue to beat on low speed, scraping the bowl frequently, until well blended, about 2 minutes. Refrigerate until ready to use, but do not let harden.

—*Peggy Cullen*

• • •

BOARDWALK BUTTERCRUNCH CAKE

This candy-studded cake is especially for those who are most happy with something crunchy and sweet.

—Makes a 9-Inch Round Cake—

Butter Cake (recipe follows)
3/4 cup heavy cream
Caramel Pastry Cream (at right)
Pecan Buttercrunch (p. 173)
6 ounces extra-bittersweet chocolate, finely chopped

1. Trim the crusty top off the Butter Cake to even it. Slice the cake horizontally into 3 even layers. Reserve the bottom layer to use as the top.

2. In a medium bowl, beat 1/4 cup of the heavy cream until stiff peaks form. Gently whisk the Caramel Pastry Cream until smooth; fold in the whipped cream. Fold in 1 2/3 cups of the Pecan Buttercrunch (use the largest pieces of candy).

3. Place the first cake layer on an inverted cake pan and cover with 1 1/2 cups of the buttercrunch filling. Place the second cake layer on top and cover with the remaining filling. Top with the bottom cake layer, bottom-side up, to create a smooth, flat surface. Smooth any filling around the sides and refrigerate the cake on the pan until the filling is firm, about 30 minutes.

4. In a small heavy saucepan, scald the remaining 1/2 cup of the cream and remove from the heat. Add the chocolate and stir until melted and smooth; set aside to cool. (The glaze should be pourable but not too warm.)

5. Pour the cooled chocolate glaze over the cake, smoothing the top and sides with a spatula. Use any drippings to touch up bare spots. Press the remaining buttercrunch onto the sides of the cake and the rim of the top. Refrigerate the cake on the pan until the chocolate is set, about 30 minutes. Transfer the cake to a platter and serve.

—Peggy Cullen

• • •

BUTTER CAKE

Makes a Single —9-Inch Round Layer—

2 sticks (8 ounces) unsalted butter, softened to room temperature
1 cup superfine sugar
3 eggs, at room temperature
1 1/2 cups all-purpose flour
2 teaspoons baking powder
1/2 teaspoon salt
1/4 cup plus 2 tablespoons milk, at room temperature
1 teaspoon vanilla extract

1. Preheat the oven to 350°. Butter and flour a 9-by-2-inch round cake pan.

2. In a medium mixer bowl, beat the butter until soft. Gradually add the sugar and beat until light and fluffy. Add the eggs, 1 at a time, beating well after each addition.

3. In a medium bowl, combine the flour, baking powder and salt. Sift one-third of the dry ingredients into the butter mixture until blended. Beat in half of the milk and vanilla. Repeat with another third of the dry ingredients and the remaining milk and vanilla. Add the remaining dry ingredients and mix to blend well.

4. Scrape the batter into the prepared pan, spreading it slightly higher around the edges. Bake for 40 to 45 minutes, or until the cake is golden brown and a tester inserted into the center comes out clean. Immediately remove the cake from the pan and let it cool completely, right-side up, on a rack.

—Peggy Cullen

• • •

CARAMEL PASTRY CREAM

—Makes About 2 1/2 Cups—

3/4 cup sugar
1/4 teaspoon fresh lemon juice
1/4 cup heavy cream
1 3/4 cups milk
1 vanilla bean
6 egg yolks
1/3 cup cornstarch

1. Put 1/2 cup plus 2 tablespoons of the sugar into a medium nonreactive saucepan. Add the lemon juice and rub it into the sugar until evenly dispersed. Cook over moderate heat, stirring, until the sugar melts and turns deep amber, 6 to 8 minutes.

2. Remove from the heat and slowly stir in the cream and milk. Slit the vanilla bean lengthwise and scrape the seeds into the milk mixture. Add the pod, return to moderate heat and cook, stirring occasionally, until the mixture just reaches a boil. If the sugar is not completely dissolved, reduce the heat and continue to cook, stirring, until all of the sugar is melted. Remove the caramel milk from the heat; strain.

3. In a heavy medium saucepan, beat the egg yolks and the remaining 2 tablespoons sugar until light and slightly thickened. Sift in the cornstarch and whisk to combine.

4. Whisk the hot caramel milk into the egg yolks until smooth. Bring to a boil over moderately high heat, whisking constantly, until the pastry cream is thick, about 1 minute. Scrape into a bowl and press plastic wrap onto the surface. Refrigerate until cool, about 2 hours.

—*Peggy Cullen*

• • •

VERMONT MAPLE BRUNCH CAKE

This cake is the perfect accompaniment to a hot cup of coffee on a cold winter day. Its flavor improves when it is left to stand overnight at room temperature.

—Makes a 9-Inch Round Cake—

1 cup walnut pieces
1½ cups plus 2 tablespoons cake flour
2 teaspoons baking powder
½ teaspoon salt
2 sticks (8 ounces) unsalted butter, softened to room temperature
⅔ cup (packed) light brown sugar
¼ cup plus 1½ teaspoons maple syrup
1 teaspoon vanilla extract
2 cups old-fashioned rolled oats
⅓ cup milk, at room temperature
6 egg whites, at room temperature
⅓ cup superfine sugar
1 tablespoon vegetable oil
Maple Buttercream Frosting (recipe follows)
12 walnut halves, for garnish

1. Preheat the oven to 350°. Butter and flour a 9-by-2-inch round cake pan.

2. In a food processor, combine the walnuts and 2 tablespoons of the flour. Process until the nuts are finely ground, about 30 seconds.

3. In a medium bowl, sift together the remaining 1½ cups flour, the baking powder and salt.

4. In a large mixer bowl, beat the butter until light and fluffy, about 1 minute. Gradually add the brown sugar and beat until light and fluffy, about 3 minutes. Beat in ¼ cup of the maple syrup and the vanilla.

5. On low speed, beat in 1½ cups of the oats and the walnuts. Alternating with the milk, sift in the flour mixture in 3 additions.

6. In a medium mixer bowl, beat the egg whites on medium speed until frothy. Add a pinch of salt and continue beating on medium-high speed until soft peaks form, about 1 minute. Gradually beat in the superfine sugar, 1 tablespoon at a time, increasing the speed to high before adding the last 2 tablespoons. Beat until stiff and shiny, about 1 minute. Using a spatula, stir one-fourth of the meringue into the batter until blended. Fold in the remaining meringue.

7. Scrape the batter into the prepared pan and bake for 45 to 50 minutes, or until golden brown. (A tester inserted into the center will have one or two tiny crumbs clinging to it.) Let cool in the pan on a rack for 10 minutes; then invert the cake onto the rack to cool completely. Leave the oven on.

8. On a cookie sheet, toss the remaining ½ cup rolled oats with the oil and the remaining 1½ teaspoons maple syrup. Spread into an even layer and bake, stirring once or twice, until golden brown, about 15 minutes. *(The recipe can be made to this point up to 1 day ahead. Wrap the cake in plastic wrap and store at room temperature. Keep the toasted oats in a covered container.)*

9. Using a long serrated knife, trim the top of the cake level. Slice the cake horizontally into 3 even layers. Place the bottom layer on an inverted cake pan and cover evenly with a scant cup of the Maple Buttercream Frosting. Repeat with the second cake layer, reserving the most evenly sliced layer for the top. Frost the sides and top with the remaining buttercream. Gently pat the toasted oats onto the sides of the cake and garnish the top with the walnut halves. Transfer the cake to a plate and serve.

—*Peggy Cullen*

• • •

MAPLE BUTTERCREAM FROSTING

—Makes About 3½ Cups—

2 cups maple syrup
6 egg yolks
3 sticks (12 ounces) unsalted butter, at room temperature
1 teaspoon instant coffee
½ teaspoon rum or water

1. In a medium saucepan, bring the maple syrup to a boil over moderate heat, washing down the sides of the pan with a wet pastry brush. Continue to cook until the syrup reaches 240° on a candy thermometer or until a spoonful of syrup dropped into a glass of cold water forms a soft ball, about 20 minutes.

2. Meanwhile, in a medium mixer bowl, beat the egg yolks until they are pale, thick and fluffy, 15 to 20 minutes. Gradually beat in the maple syrup in a thin stream. Place the bowl in a larger bowl of ice water, increase the speed to high, and beat until the mixture is very stiff and completely cool, about 5 minutes. Gradually beat in the butter.

3. In a cup, mix together the coffee and rum until dissolved. Beat into the buttercream.

—*Peggy Cullen*

• • •

PECAN BUTTERCRUNCH

This buttercrunch also makes a great topping for ice cream.

Makes About 2¾ Cups

1¼ cups sugar
½ teaspoon fresh lemon juice
4 tablespoons unsalted butter
1½ cups pecan halves

1. Oil a large cookie sheet and a metal spatula. Place the sugar in a heavy medium saucepan. Add the lemon juice and rub it into the sugar until dispersed.

2. Add the butter and cook over moderately high heat, stirring until the sugar melts and becomes a deep amber color, about 10 minutes. Remove from the heat and stir in the pecans.

3. Immediately pour the mixture out onto the prepared cookie sheet. Using the oiled spatula, turn the sugar over onto itself until it stops spreading. Press the buttercrunch flat and set aside at room temperature to cool, about 15 minutes.

4. Chop the buttercrunch into 1-inch pieces. Place one-third of the buttercrunch in a food processor and chop coarsely into ½-inch pieces. Repeat with the remaining buttercrunch, adding it to the processor in 2 batches. (Any large pieces can be cut with a knife.)

—Peggy Cullen

• • •

CHOCOLATE BOURBON CREAM CAKE

Any number of liquors and liqueurs, such as brandy, Kahlúa and Grand Marnier, can be used in place of the bourbon called for here. To decorate the top with lines and squiggles, simply pipe melted semisweet chocolate through a paper cone.

16 Servings

6 ounces bittersweet chocolate, broken into pieces
¼ cup plus 2 tablespoons bourbon
2½ cups heavy cream
2 tablespoons granulated sugar
Buttermilk Chocolate Fudge Cake (recipe follows)
¼ cup confectioners' sugar
1 teaspoon vanilla extract
Sliced strawberries, unsweetened cocoa powder, crystallized violets, rose petals or fancy candies, for decoration

1. In a small heavy saucepan, combine the chocolate, 3 tablespoons of the bourbon and ½ cup of the cream. Cook over low heat, stirring, until smooth and just beginning to simmer, about 3 minutes. Remove the chocolate glaze from the heat and let cool.

2. Meanwhile, in a small saucepan, combine the granulated sugar with 2 tablespoons of water. Cook over moderately high heat until the sugar dissolves, about 2 minutes. Remove from the heat and stir in the remaining 3 tablespoons bourbon; let cool.

3. Using a long serrated knife, split the Buttermilk Chocolate Fudge Cake in half horizontally. Brush the cut side of each layer with the bourbon syrup. Let stand for 10 minutes before frosting.

4. Set the bottom layer of the cake, cut-side up, on a large round serving platter and slide wide strips of waxed paper under the base to keep the plate clean. Pour half of the chocolate glaze onto the center of the cake and spread just to the edge of the cake in a thick, even layer. Refrigerate for 10 minutes to set the glaze.

5. Meanwhile, in a large bowl, beat the remaining 2 cups heavy cream with the confectioners' sugar and vanilla just until stiff.

6. Using a metal spatula, spread half of the whipped cream over the chocolate glaze to within ½ inch of the edge. Top with the second cake layer, cut-side down. Pour the remaining chocolate glaze onto the center of the cake, letting it cascade over the sides. Run a long metal spatula lightly across the top so the glaze will not be too thick. Spread the glaze evenly and smoothly around the sides. Refrigerate the cake for 10 minutes to set the glaze.

7. Pull out the strips of waxed paper. Spread the remaining whipped cream over the top of the cake in an even layer. Decorate the cake as desired. Serve at room temperature.

—Mimi Ruth Brodeur

• • •

BUTTERMILK CHOCOLATE FUDGE CAKE

This is my favorite recipe for chocolate cake. It is simple to prepare and absolutely delicious. Frost it with whipped cream and top with fresh strawberries, or spread with your favorite icing. Because of its rich, dense texture, the cake is at its best when served at room temperature.

Makes a 10-Inch Round Cake

4 ounces unsweetened chocolate
2 sticks (8 ounces) unsalted butter, softened to room temperature

1¾ cups (packed) dark brown sugar
3 eggs
1 teaspoon vanilla extract
1½ cups all-purpose flour
½ teaspoon baking soda
½ teaspoon baking powder
⅛ teaspoon salt
1 cup buttermilk, at room temperature

1. Preheat the oven to 350°. Butter the bottom and sides of a 10-inch springform pan. Line the bottom with parchment or waxed paper. Butter the paper and dust the pan with flour.

2. Put the chocolate in the top of a double boiler over hot water; let stand, stirring occasionally, until melted and smooth. Set aside to cool.

3. In a large mixer bowl, beat the butter until light and fluffy. With the mixer on high speed, gradually beat in the brown sugar until well blended and light, about 8 minutes. Add the eggs, 1 at a time, beating well after each addition. Beat in the cooled chocolate and the vanilla.

4. In a large bowl, sift together the flour, baking soda, baking powder and salt. On low speed, beat one-third of the dry ingredients into the chocolate mixture until well blended. Beat in one-third of the buttermilk. Repeat 2 more times with the remaining dry ingredients and buttermilk.

5. Scrape the batter into the prepared pan and smooth the surface. Bake for 1 hour and 10 minutes, or until a cake tester inserted in the center comes out clean. Let cool on a rack for 10 minutes before unmolding. Let cool completely before frosting. *(The cake can be prepared 1 day ahead. Cover with plastic wrap and set aside at room temperature, or freeze for up to 1 month. Let return to room temperature before frosting.)*

—Mimi Ruth Brodeur

• • •

RASPBERRY AND PISTACHIO CHOCOLATE CAKE

A party cake for birthdays, dinners and teas, this fabulous creation proves that three great flavors are better than one.

10 Servings

1 cup shelled unsalted pistachio nuts (5 ounces)
3 cups fresh raspberries
2 tablespoons sugar
2¾ cups heavy cream
10 ounces semisweet chocolate, cut into 1-inch chunks
Chocolate Genoise (recipe follows)

1. Preheat the oven to 350°. Spread the pistachio nuts on a baking sheet and bake until lightly toasted, 8 to 10 minutes. Cool the nuts and coarsely chop.

2. Set aside 12 perfect raspberries. In a food processor, puree 1¾ cups of the remaining raspberries with the sugar until smooth, about 1 minute. Strain the puree into a small bowl.

3. In a small heavy saucepan, bring ¾ cup of the cream to a boil over moderate heat. Reduce to a simmer and add the chocolate. Remove from the heat and let stand for 5 minutes; stir until smooth.

4. Drop the reserved 12 raspberries into the chocolate and cream. Spoon them out, one at a time, letting the excess chocolate drip back into the pan. Place the chocolate-dipped raspberries on a plate lined with waxed paper. Let stand until set; refrigerate.

5. Trim the top of the Chocolate Genoise to level. Using a long serrated knife, cut the cake horizontally into 2 equal layers. Center the bottom layer on a plate. Using a spatula, spread half of the raspberry puree over it and gently work some of the puree into the cake. Spread a ¼-inch-thick layer of the cool chocolate and cream over the puree. Scatter 2 tablespoons of the chopped pistachio nuts and the remaining 1¼ cups raspberries over the chocolate cream.

6. In a mixer bowl, beat the remaining chocolate cream on medium speed. Slowly add the remaining 2 cups heavy cream. Increase the speed to high and continue beating until the mixture is slightly stiff and spreadable, about 1 minute.

7. Spread one-third of this mixture over the top of the pistachio nuts and raspberries. Top with the second genoise layer. Spread the remaining raspberry puree on top of the cake. Using a spatula, cover the top and sides of the cake with the remaining whipped chocolate cream frosting. Spread the frosting evenly over the cake.

8. Using your open palm, press the remaining chopped pistachio nuts onto the sides of the cake. Decorate the top with the chocolate-covered raspberries, spacing them evenly around the edge of the cake. Chill until ready to serve.

—Jim Dodge, Stanford Court, San Francisco

• • •

CHOCOLATE GENOISE

Makes a Single 9-Inch Layer

½ cup cake flour
3 tablespoons Dutch-process unsweetened cocoa powder
½ cup plus 3 tablespoons sugar
4 egg yolks
4 whole eggs
4 tablespoons unsalted butter, melted and cooled to lukewarm

1. Preheat the oven to 300°. Butter the bottom and sides of a 9-by-2-inch round cake pan. Line the bottom with a circle of parchment or waxed paper; dust the sides of the pan with flour.

2. Sift together the flour, cocoa and 2 tablespoons of the sugar twice.

3. In a large saucepan, bring about 2 inches of water to a boil. In a large stainless steel bowl, beat together the egg yolks, whole eggs and remaining sugar. Place the bowl over the boiling water and whisk constantly until the mixture is hot, about 3 minutes. Remove from the heat and beat with an electric mixer on high speed until doubled in volume, about 2 minutes. Reduce the speed to medium-high and beat until the mixture is cool and forms a thick ribbon when the beaters are lifted, about 6 minutes.

4. Sift the flour-cocoa mixture over the batter and fold in just until blended. Transfer one-fourth of the batter to a small bowl and stir in the tepid melted butter. Fold this mixture back into the remaining batter. Working quickly, pour the batter into the prepared cake pan.

5. Bake until a toothpick inserted in the center of the cake comes out clean, about 1 hour and 10 minutes. Let the cake cool in the pan for 10 minutes. Unmold onto a wire rack, peel off the paper and let cool completely.

—Jim Dodge, Stanford Court, San Francisco

• • •

PECAN CAKE WITH CHOCOLATE CREAM

This was referred to as "Plantation Cake" when I was growing up, probably because those grand long-gone houses almost all had groves of pecan trees nearby.

6 to 8 Servings

1½ cups sifted all-purpose flour
1 teaspoon baking powder
½ teaspoon salt
1½ cups finely chopped pecans (about 5 ounces)
1 stick (4 ounces) unsalted butter, softened to room temperature
1¾ cups plus 2 tablespoons sugar
¼ cup bourbon mixed with ½ cup water
4 egg whites
1 ounce unsweetened chocolate, coarsely chopped
2 cups heavy cream
2 teaspoons vanilla extract
1 teaspoon powdered espresso (optional)

1. Preheat the oven to 375°. Grease two 8-inch round cake pans; line the bottoms with waxed paper. Grease the paper and then lightly flour the pans; tap out any excess.

2. In a medium bowl, sift together the flour, baking powder and salt. Add the pecans and mix well.

3. In a large bowl, cream the butter and 1½ cups of the sugar with an electric mixer until light and fluffy. Add the pecan flour in four parts alternately with the diluted bourbon, beginning and ending with the flour and mixing well after each addition.

4. In a large bowl, beat the egg whites until stiff but not dry. Fold one-third of the egg whites into the cake batter to lighten it and then fold in the remaining egg whites. Pour into the prepared pans.

5. Bake the cakes for 25 minutes, or until a cake tester inserted in the center comes out clean. Let cool for about 10 minutes; then run a knife around the edges and unmold onto a rack. Let cool.

6. In a small heavy saucepan, combine the chocolate, ¼ cup of the sugar and 2 tablespoons of the cream. Cook over moderate heat, stirring, until the chocolate is melted and the mixture is smooth. Remove from the heat and whisk until cooled.

7. Beat the remaining cream until fairly stiff. Divide into 2 parts. Place half the cream in another bowl. Fold the cooled chocolate mixture and 1 teaspoon of the vanilla into one bowl of cream until blended. Whisk the remaining 2 tablespoons sugar and 1 teaspoon vanilla into the other. Cover both bowls and refrigerate until ready to use.

8. When the cakes are cooled, peel off the waxed paper. Pile the chocolate whipped cream onto one layer of cake and top with the second layer. Frost the top and sides with the vanilla cream. Sprinkle the powdered espresso over the top. Refrigerate, lightly covered with waxed paper, for up to a day before serving.

—Lee Bailey

• • •

SAVANNAH CREAM CAKE

This dessert from Elizabeth Terry of Elizabeth on 37th in Savannah, Georgia, is a real crowd pleaser that's so down-home it's almost shameful. Squares of light-as-air angel food cake folded into a sherry-flavored custard unmold into a spectacular ring, which is served with whipped cream and colorful fresh berries. Since the sherry is not cooked, its flavor remains true, so it's important to use a good brand.

10 to 12 Servings

1 envelope (¼ ounce) unflavored gelatin
5 extra-large egg yolks
1 cup sugar
½ cup dry sherry
2¾ cups heavy cream, chilled
1 tablespoon vanilla extract
Angel Food Cake (recipe follows), cut into 1-inch squares
1 cup fresh strawberries, sliced
1½ cups fresh raspberries
1½ tablespoons fresh lemon juice

1. In a small bowl, sprinkle the gelatin into ½ cup of cold water and let soften.

2. In a medium bowl, beat the egg yolks and ½ cup of the sugar until the mixture thickens and turns pale yellow, about 2 minutes. Stir in the sherry and ¼ cup of water.

3. Scrape the egg yolk mixture into a heavy medium saucepan and cook over moderate heat, stirring constantly, until the custard thickens enough to coat the back of a spoon lightly; do not let boil. Strain the custard into a large bowl and whisk in the softened gelatin; set aside.

4. In a large bowl, whip 2 cups of the cream until it begins to thicken. Gradually beat in ¼ cup of the sugar and the vanilla. Continue to beat until moderately stiff. Cover and refrigerate the whipped cream.

5. Set the bowl containing the custard and gelatin into a larger bowl of ice and water. Whisk gently until the custard is cold and beginning to set, 3 to 4 minutes. Remove from the ice and fold in the whipped cream.

6. Fold the Angel Food Cake squares into the custard cream until they are completely coated. Spoon this mixture into a buttered 10-inch tube pan. Cover and refrigerate until set, 1 to 2 hours.

7. Meanwhile, in a food processor, combine the strawberries, 1 cup of the raspberries, the remaining ¼ cup sugar and the lemon juice; puree until smooth. Strain if desired to remove the seeds. Cover and refrigerate the strawberry-raspberry sauce until chilled.

8. Beat the remaining ¾ cup cream until moderately stiff.

9. To unmold the cake, wrap the tube pan briefly in a hot wet towel; run a knife around the edge. Unmold the cake onto a platter and cover with the whipped cream. Garnish the cake with the remaining ½ cup raspberries and serve the strawberry-raspberry sauce on the side.

—*Elizabeth Terry, Elizabeth on 37th, Savannah, Georgia*

• • •

ANGEL FOOD CAKE

Makes a 10-Inch Tube Cake

1 cup plus 2 tablespoons cake flour
¼ teaspoon nutmeg, preferably freshly grated
1½ cups sugar
12 extra-large egg whites
1¼ teaspoons cream of tartar
½ teaspoon salt
1 teaspoon vanilla extract

1. Preheat the oven to 375°. Sift together the cake flour, nutmeg and ½ cup of the sugar.

2. In a large bowl, beat the egg whites until frothy. Add the cream of tartar and salt. Continue beating until soft peaks form. Gradually beat in the remaining 1 cup sugar, 1 tablespoon at a time, until very stiff shiny peaks form. Beat in the vanilla and fold in the flour mixture.

3. Turn the batter into an ungreased 10-inch tube pan and bake for 30 minutes, or until a cake tester inserted in the center comes out clean. Invert onto a rack to cool.

—*Elizabeth Terry, Elizabeth on 37th, Savannah, Georgia*

• • •

BUTTER-ALMOND FINANCIER

The name of this traditional French dessert probably comes from its richness. It is an unusual batter in which ground almonds, sugar, flour and a large quantity of melted butter are folded into egg whites that have been beaten with more sugar. Of course, the egg whites fall and liquefy as the butter is folded in, but the Financier rises impressively, nonetheless. For a change, try this recipe with a combination of almonds and hazelnuts or with all hazelnuts.

10 to 12 Servings

1 cup whole blanched almonds (about 5 ounces)
1½ cups sugar
1 cup unbleached all-purpose flour
1 stick plus 2 tablespoons unsalted butter
2 tablespoons dark rum
2 teaspoons vanilla extract
8 egg whites
Pinch of salt
¼ cup sliced blanched almonds
Confectioners' sugar, for garnish

1. Preheat the oven to 350°. Butter a 10-by-2-inch round cake pan. Line the bottom with a round of parchment or waxed paper. Butter the paper.

2. Combine the whole almonds and ¾ cup of the sugar in a food processor. Turn the machine quickly on and off until the nuts are finely ground. Pour into a bowl and stir in the flour.

3. In a small saucepan over moderately low heat or in a glass bowl in a microwave oven, melt the butter. Remove from the heat and add the rum and vanilla. Set aside to cool slightly.

4. In a large bowl, beat the egg whites with the salt until they form very soft peaks. Gradually beat in the remaining ¾ cup sugar in a very slow stream and continue beating until the egg whites form soft peaks.

5. In 3 batches, alternately fold the almond and the rum-butter mixtures into the egg whites, beginning with the almond and ending with the rum-butter. Pour the batter into the prepared pan.

Smooth the top and sprinkle with the sliced almonds.

6. Bake the Financier for 50 minutes, or until well risen and golden on top. The center of the cake should feel firm when pressed with the palm of the hand.

7. Let the Financier cool briefly on a rack before unmolding. If some of the almonds on the surface fall off, replace them. Garnish the top of the cake with a very light dusting of confectioners' sugar.

—Nicholas Malgieri

• • •

CHOCOLATE ROLL WITH MOCHA CREAM

The deep chocolate flavor of this popular dessert, enhanced by the addition of unsweetened cocoa to semisweet chocolate, is sure to make it one of your holiday favorites. This ethereal flourless roll should be eaten the day it is made.

—8 Servings—

8 ounces semisweet chocolate, broken up
2 tablespoons unsalted butter
6 eggs, separated
¾ cup granulated sugar
¼ cup plus 3 tablespoons unsweetened cocoa powder
4 teaspoons instant espresso
1 tablespoon boiling water
2 teaspoons vanilla extract
1⅓ cups heavy cream, chilled
⅓ cup plus 1 teaspoon confectioners' sugar

1. Preheat the oven to 350°. Lightly butter a 15½-by-10½-inch jelly-roll pan. Line the bottom and sides of the pan with waxed paper; butter the paper.

2. In a small heavy saucepan, melt the chocolate with the butter over low heat, stirring until smooth. Let cool slightly.

3. In a medium mixer bowl, beat the egg yolks with ½ cup of the granulated sugar on high speed until pale and thick, about 2 minutes. Beat in ¼ cup of the cocoa. Fold in the cooled melted chocolate until blended.

4. In a large bowl, beat the egg whites until soft peaks form. Beat in the remaining ¼ cup granulated sugar, 1 tablespoon at a time, until stiff.

5. Stir one-fourth of the beaten egg whites into the chocolate batter, then pour the chocolate mixture over the beaten whites and fold until just blended.

6. Pour the batter into the prepared pan; lightly spread it into the corners. Bake for 15 to 17 minutes, until the top of the cake feels dry when touched. Let cool on a wire rack for 15 minutes, then cover the cake with a kitchen towel to prevent it from drying out; cool completely.

7. Meanwhile, in a medium bowl, combine the espresso, boiling water and 4 teaspoons of the cocoa. Cool for 1 minute, then stir in the vanilla. Add the heavy cream and beat until soft peaks form. Sift ⅓ cup of the confectioners' sugar over the cream and continue beating until stiff.

8. Uncover the cake and run a knife around the sides of the pan to loosen. Place a 16-inch sheet of waxed paper on a work surface. Evenly sift the remaining cocoa over the paper; invert the cake onto the cocoa. Peel the waxed paper from the surface of the cake.

9. Spread the mocha cream evenly over the cake, leaving a ½-inch border on all sides. Using the waxed paper as a guide, roll up the cake from a long edge to form a log. Without removing the paper, slide the cake onto a cookie sheet and refrigerate until chilled.

10. Trim a thin slice from each end of the log. With 2 long spatulas, transfer the cake to a large platter. Sift the remaining 1 teaspoon confectioners' sugar over the roll and refrigerate until serving time.

—Diana Sturgis

• • •

BLACK CURRANT TEA BROWNIES

These brownies are brushed with a mixture of black currant tea and crème de cassis (black currant liqueur) and then with a thin layer of black currant preserves before being frosted with a tea-infused chocolate ganache. Other fruit-flavored teas, such as raspberry and apricot, along with their corresponding liqueurs and preserves, may be substituted for the black currant in this recipe.

—Makes 32 Bite-Size Brownies—

⅓ cup boiling water
1 tablespoon plus 1 teaspoon black currant-flavored tea leaves
2 squares (1 ounce each) unsweetened chocolate
1 stick (4 ounces) unsalted butter
2 eggs, at room temperature
¾ cup sugar
½ cup all-purpose flour
¼ teaspoon salt
1 tablespoon crème de cassis
¼ cup black currant preserves
½ cup heavy cream
3 ounces bittersweet chocolate, finely chopped

1. Preheat the oven to 350°. Butter an 8-inch square baking pan.

2. In a heatproof cup, pour the boiling water over 2 teaspoons of the tea; let steep for 5 minutes. Strain the tea into a small bowl.

3. In a heavy saucepan, melt the unsweetened chocolate with the butter over low heat. Let cool for 10 minutes.

4. In a medium mixer bowl, beat the eggs at high speed until well blended. Gradually beat in the sugar, beating until the mixture thickens slightly. Reduce the mixer speed to low and beat in the melted chocolate, then beat in 3 tablespoons of the strained tea. Fold in the flour and salt until just blended.

5. Pour the batter into the prepared pan and bake for 25 to 30 minutes, or until the top is shiny and firm and the batter begins to shrink from the sides of the pan. Let cool on a rack for 10 minutes.

6. In a small bowl, combine the remaining strained tea and the crème de cassis. Brush over the warm brownies and let cool completely on the rack.

7. In a small saucepan, melt the preserves over moderate heat, stirring frequently. Strain the preserves and brush them over the brownies.

8. In a small heavy saucepan, bring the cream to a boil over moderately high heat. Remove from the heat and stir in the remaining 2 teaspoons tea leaves; let steep for 5 minutes.

9. Strain the cream into a small clean saucepan and return to a boil. Remove from the heat and add the bittersweet chocolate. Stir until the chocolate is melted and the ganache mixture is smooth. Let cool for 5 minutes.

10. Using a flat spatula, spread the chocolate ganache over the brownies in an even layer. Refrigerate until the ganache is partially set, then cut the brownies into bite-size bars. Store in the refrigerator, lightly covered with plastic wrap. Serve the brownies at room temperature.

—Ceri E. Hadda

• • •

MYSTERY BITES

My mother made the original version of this recipe for many a Christmas when I was growing up. I used to eat off the top part first, then the bottom. Because of the honey in this recipe, the two layers are not as distinct as in the original. I recommend using freshly ground spices in this sweet bar cookie, but if you don't, you may want to use a bit more of each spice.

Makes 16 Small Squares

½ cup whole wheat flour
½ cup plus 2 tablespoons all-purpose flour
1 cup (packed) dark brown sugar
1 stick (4 ounces) cold unsalted butter, cut into ¼-inch dice
2 eggs
½ cup honey
1 cup (4 ounces) chopped almonds, walnuts or pecans
⅔ cup unsweetened shredded coconut*
2 teaspoons cinnamon
1 teaspoon vanilla extract
½ teaspoon baking powder
½ teaspoon ground cardamom
½ teaspoon freshly grated nutmeg
¼ teaspoon ground cloves
¼ teaspoon salt
****Available at health food stores***

1. Preheat the oven to 300°. In a medium bowl, mix the whole wheat flour, ½ cup of the all-purpose flour and ½ cup of the brown sugar. Add the butter and toss well. Using a pastry blender or 2 knives, cut in the butter to form a coarse meal; some pea-size pieces of butter will still be visible.

2. Gently press the crumbly dough into the bottom of an ungreased 8- or 8½-inch square glass baking pan. Bake for 45 minutes, until the crust is browned and slightly firm to the touch. Transfer the pan to a rack and let the crust cool to room temperature. *(The recipe can be prepared to this point up to 2 days ahead; cover and refrigerate.)*

3. Preheat the oven to 350°. In a medium bowl, beat the eggs until frothy. Whisk in the remaining ½ cup brown sugar and 2 tablespoons all-purpose flour. Stir in the honey, nuts, coconut, cinnamon, vanilla, baking powder, cardamom, nutmeg, cloves and salt. Spread the topping over the cooled crust and bake for 25 to 30 minutes, until dark brown and set. Let cool on a rack, then cut into 16 squares. *(Individually wrapped in foil and stored in an airtight container, these cookies will keep at room temperature for several weeks.)*

—Ed Brown

• • •

BASIC GINGERBREAD COOKIES

These cookies can be cut into any shape and decorated with icing, raisins, nuts or small candies.

Makes About 2 Dozen

3 cups unbleached all-purpose flour
2½ teaspoons ground ginger
1¼ teaspoons cinnamon
½ teaspoon ground cardamon
½ teaspoon freshly grated nutmeg
¼ teaspoon ground cloves
½ teaspoon baking soda
¼ teaspoon salt
¾ cup dark or light unsulphured molasses
1 stick (4 ounces) unsalted butter, at room temperature
½ cup sugar
1 egg

1. In a large bowl, stir together the flour, ginger, cinnamon, cardamom, nutmeg, cloves, baking soda and salt.

2. In a small saucepan, heat the molasses over low heat until bubbles begin to form around the sides. Remove from the heat and stir in the butter, 1 tablespoon at a time, until completely incorporated. Scrape the molasses into a large bowl. Beat in the sugar and 2 tablespoons of water until well blended. Beat in the egg.

3. Make a well in the center of the dry ingredients and pour in the molasses mixture. Gradually stir in the flour mixture until blended. Turn the dough out onto a floured surface and knead lightly until smooth. Pat the dough into a 6-inch disk, cover with plastic wrap and refrigerate overnight or for up to 3 days.

4. Preheat the oven to 350°. Roll out half the dough ⅛ inch thick. (Keep the remaining dough well wrapped until ready to use.) Cut out shapes using a cookie cutter. Place the cookies about ½ inch apart on greased cookie sheets and bake for 10 to 12 minutes, until firm and slightly puffed. Transfer the cookies to a rack to cool. Repeat with the remaining dough. Decorate the cookies or leave plain. *(The cookies can be stored in an airtight container for up to 2 weeks.)*

—Linda Merinoff

• • •

GINGERSNAP-CHOCOLATE SANDWICH COOKIES

You can eat these cookies plain, make them into sandwiches, or spread each cookie with chocolate. I like these best the day they're made; they become harder and less chewy over time, and it's the chewiness that I love.

Makes About 2½ Dozen

¼ cup dark unsulphured molasses
6 tablespoons unsalted butter, at room temperature
½ cup granulated sugar
¼ cup (packed) dark brown sugar
¼ teaspoon ground ginger
¼ teaspoon cinnamon
⅛ teaspoon ground cardamom
Pinch of ground cloves
Pinch of freshly grated nutmeg
1 whole egg
1 egg yolk
½ cup plus 2 tablespoons all-purpose flour
4 ounces bittersweet chocolate, cut into pieces

1. Preheat the oven to 350°. In a small saucepan, heat the molasses over low heat until bubbles begin to form around the sides. Remove from the heat and stir in the butter, 1 tablespoon at a time, until completely blended.

2. Scrape the molasses into a large bowl. Add the granulated sugar, brown sugar, ginger, cinnamon, cardamom, cloves and nutmeg. Beat until well blended. Beat in the whole egg and the egg yolk. Add the flour and mix well.

3. Drop level teaspoons of the dough onto buttered and floured cookie sheets, leaving about 2 inches between the cookies. Bake for 8 to 10 minutes, or until the edges are golden brown. Let the cookies cool on the sheets for 5 minutes, then transfer to a rack to cool completely.

4. Place a small saucepan over simmering water and add the chocolate. Remove the pan from the heat and let stand, stirring occasionally, until the chocolate is melted and smooth, about 5 minutes.

5. Spread the flat side of half the cookies with the chocolate. Top with the remaining cookies and press lightly to make them adhere. Refrigerate for 10 minutes to set the chocolate. The cookies can be stored in an airtight container for up to 3 days.

—Linda Merinoff

• • •

DEPRESSION COOKIES

These are thin, crisp cookies whose crunch increases measurably the longer they are baked. A tip if you don't have heavy cookie sheets: stack two together to reinforce the bottoms and create more even heating.

Makes About 6 Dozen

2 sticks (8 ounces) unsalted butter, softened to room temperature
1 cup sugar
1 egg
¼ cup dark unsulphured molasses
2 cups sifted all-purpose flour
2 teaspoons baking soda
2 teaspoons ground cloves
1 teaspoon ground ginger

1. Preheat the oven to 300°. In a medium mixer bowl, beat the butter with the sugar until light and creamy, about 5 minutes. Add the egg and the molasses and beat until well blended.

2. In a small bowl, combine the flour, baking soda, cloves and ginger. Gradually add the dry ingredients to the butter and beat until well blended. Cover and refrigerate for 20 minutes.

3. Remove from refrigerator. Drop rounded teaspoons of the dough onto greased cookie sheets, leaving 2 inches in between. Bake for 15 to 18 minutes, until the cookies are a deep golden brown. Let cool for 1 minute, then transfer to a rack to cool completely. *(These cookies will keep for up to 1 week at room temperature in a tightly covered tin.)*

—David Munn

• • •

CINNAMON SUGAR COOKIES

A tablespoon of cinnamon may sound excessive, but not to worry—the proof is in the cookie.

Makes About 2½ Dozen

2¼ cups sifted all-purpose flour
1 tablespoon cinnamon
2 sticks (8 ounces) unsalted butter, softened to room temperature
2 cups sugar
1 egg

1. In a medium bowl, combine the flour and cinnamon. In a large mixer bowl, beat the butter with 1 cup of the sugar until light and creamy, about 5 minutes. Beat in the egg. Gradually beat in the flour until well blended. Cover and refrigerate the dough until firm but not hard, 1 to 1½ hours.

2. Preheat the oven to 350°. Using your hands, shape the dough into 1½-inch balls and arrange on buttered baking sheets, about 2 inches apart.

3. Pour the remaining 1 cup sugar onto a small plate. Lightly butter the bottom of a glass. Dip the glass into the sugar and use it to flatten each ball of dough to a round, about 1/4 inch thick, sugaring the glass as necessary.

4. Bake 15 to 18 minutes, until the cookies are golden brown. Let cool slightly, then transfer to a wire rack. *(These cookies will keep for up to 2 weeks at room temperature in a tightly covered tin.)*

—Carol Field

• • •

AMARETTO BUTTER COOKIES

The festive combination of sliced almonds, orange rind and amaretto makes this a cookie with across-the-board holiday appeal. These are heavenly with a cup of coffee, either with or after dessert.

Makes 40 Squares

2 sticks (8 ounces) unsalted butter, softened to room temperature
1 cup sugar
1 egg, separated
1 1/2 tablespoons amaretto (almond liqueur)
2 teaspoons grated orange zest
1/4 teaspoon salt
2 cups all-purpose flour
3/4 cup sliced almonds

1. Preheat the oven to 300°. In a large mixer bowl, beat the butter with the sugar until light and creamy, about 5 minutes. Add the egg yolk, amaretto, orange zest and salt and beat until well blended. Stir in the flour and blend well. Spread and pat the dough evenly into a 10-by-15-inch jelly-roll pan.

2. In a small bowl, beat the egg white until foamy. Brush evenly over the dough. Sprinkle the almonds over the top. Bake for 40 minutes, or until light golden. Cut into 2-inch squares while still warm and transfer to a rack to cool. *(These cookies will keep for up to 2 weeks at room temperature in a tightly covered tin.)*

—Marion Cunningham

• • •

GINGER SHORTBREAD

These are very, very easy to make, and the results are delicious. It's a perfect recipe to make with kids because it's impossible to mess up, and there are no fussy techniques.

Makes 12 Wedges

3/4 cup sifted cornstarch
2/3 cup sifted all-purpose flour
1/2 cup sifted confectioners' sugar
1 stick (4 ounces) plus 2 2/3 tablespoons unsalted butter, softened to room temperature
1/3 cup very thinly sliced candied ginger, not longer than 3/4 inch

1. Preheat the oven to 325°. Butter a 9-inch round springform or cake pan. In a small bowl, stir the cornstarch, flour and confectioners' sugar.

2. In a medium mixer bowl, beat the butter until light and creamy, about 3 minutes. Gradually beat in the dry ingredients until well blended. Stir in the ginger.

3. Press the dough evenly into the prepared pan. Using a sharp knife, score the dough into 12 pie-shaped wedges. With the tines of a fork, pierce the dough along the score lines, then use the fork to crimp the outer edges as you would a pie.

4. Bake the shortbread for 40 to 45 minutes, turning the pan midway through to insure even baking, until light golden. While still warm, again pierce the score lines with the fork. Run a sharp knife around the edge. Set the pan on a rack and let cool completely.

5. Using a sharp knife, cut along the score lines and remove the wedges of shortbread from the pan. If using a springform pan, remove the sides first. *(These shortbread cookies will keep for up to 2 weeks at room temperature in an airtight container.)*

—Margaret Fox, Cafe Beaujolais, Mendocino, California

• • •

BROWN BUTTER CARDAMOM SHORTBREAD COOKIES

These buttery cookies with a hint of cardamom are not as heavy as traditional shortbread.

Makes About 3 1/2 Dozen

2 sticks (8 ounces) unsalted butter
3 cups all-purpose flour
6 cardamom pods, peeled, seeds crushed into a fine powder
1/2 cup superfine sugar
1/2 teaspoon salt
1/4 cup milk
1 teaspoon vanilla extract

1. In a small saucepan, simmer the butter over moderately low heat until the moisture from the fat evaporates and the milk solids brown and settle at the bottom of the pan, 25 to 30 minutes.

2. Strain the clear clarified butter into a shallow bowl or lipped plate and chill until firm; discard the browned solids at the bottom of the pan.

3. Preheat the oven to 325°. In a large bowl, stir the flour, cardamom, sugar and salt. Cut the clarified butter into small dice and add to the flour mixture. Rub with your fingertips until the mixture forms a coarse meal. Sprinkle on the milk and vanilla while tossing to blend. Gather the dough into a ball.

4. On a lightly floured surface, roll out the dough about 1/8 inch thick. Using a 2-inch round cookie cutter, cut into rounds. Gather up the scraps of dough and reroll to make more cookies. Repeat until all the dough is used.

5. Arrange the cookies on ungreased baking sheets and bake for 35 to 40 minutes, or until very lightly browned on the edges. Let cool. Store in an airtight container.

—Julie Sahni

• • •

Cranberry Crumb Tart (p. 200).

Left, Espresso Bavarian Cream (p. 213) with Chocolate Shortbread Hearts (p. 189). Above, Cannoli Siciliani (p. 216).

Above, Wintry Fruit Salad (p. 226) and Lemon-Cardamom Pound Cake (p. 167). Right, Chocolate Pecan Pudding with Bourbon Sauce (p. 214).

Left, Banana Walnut Tart (p. 204) and Apple and Prune Cobbler with Buttermilk Biscuit Crust (p. 199). Above, Honeydew in Jalapeño Syrup with Melon Sorbet (p. 227).

CHOCOLATE SHORTBREAD HEARTS

These shortbread cookies are laden with chocolate and sinfully rich.

Makes About 10 Cookies

4 tablespoons unsalted butter, softened to room temperature
2½ tablespoons sugar
½ teaspoon vanilla extract
½ cup all-purpose flour
2½ tablespoons unsweetened cocoa powder
⅛ teaspoon salt

1. Preheat the oven to 275°. In a small bowl, cream the butter until pale and fluffy. Add the sugar and vanilla and beat until well blended.

2. On a piece of waxed paper, sift together the flour, cocoa and salt. Stir the dry ingredients into the butter mixture until smooth. Wrap the dough in plastic and refrigerate for at least 15 minutes.

3. On a lightly sugared surface, roll out the dough to form a ⅜-inch-thick circle. Stamp out the cookies with a 2½-inch heart-shaped cookie cutter. Transfer the hearts to a lightly buttered cookie sheet and prick all over with the tines of a fork.

4. Bake the cookies in the middle of the oven for 40 to 45 minutes, or until firm to the touch. Let rest for 5 minutes on the sheet, then transfer the cookies to a rack to cool. *(The cookies can be stored in an airtight tin for up to 1 week.)*

—Bob Chambers

• • •

PECAN PRALINE SANDIES

This recipe is a bit involved, but it isn't difficult in the least if you take it in steps. The pecan praline is the magic formula that gives these a sublime personality. At the Bakeshop, the Londons roll these cookies in vanilla sugar, which is made by mixing the seeds scraped from 1 vanilla bean into 1 cup confectioners' sugar.

Makes About 4 Dozen

1 cup plus 3 tablespoons pecan halves (about 4 ounces)
⅔ cup granulated sugar
2¼ cups unbleached all-purpose flour
2 sticks (8 ounces) unsalted butter, softened to room temperature
½ cup plus 2 tablespoons confectioners' sugar
1½ teaspoons vanilla extract

1. Preheat the oven to 350°. Spread ½ cup of the pecan halves on an ungreased cookie sheet and bake for 10 minutes, until crisp. Let cool to room temperature and then transfer the nuts to a bowl. Grease the cookie sheet. Turn the oven off.

2. In a heavy medium saucepan, cook the granulated sugar over moderate heat, stirring, until it begins to melt. Stop stirring and continue cooking until the caramel is a deep brown, about 6 minutes.

3. Remove from the heat and stir in the toasted pecan halves until well coated. Quickly scrape the praline onto the greased cookie sheet and spread into a thin layer. Let cool to room temperature, about 15 minutes.

4. Break the praline into small chunks and grind to a powder in a food processor. Add the remaining pecans and process until finely ground. Transfer to a medium bowl and toss with the flour.

5. In a large bowl, beat the butter until light and creamy. Beat in ½ cup of the confectioners' sugar and the vanilla until well blended. Gradually add the flour and nut mixture and mix well. Cover and refrigerate until cold but not hard, about 1 hour.

6. Preheat the oven to 350°. Shape the dough into 1-inch balls and gently roll each one to elongate, tapering the ends slightly to form a cocoon shape. Arrange 1½ inches apart on greased cookie sheets. Bake for 18 minutes, or until the edges begin to brown slightly. Let cool for 2 minutes, then transfer to a wire rack to cool completely. Sift the remaining 2 tablespoons confectioners' sugar over the cookies. *(The cookies will keep for up to 2 weeks at room temperature in a tightly covered tin.)*

—Michael and Wendy London,
Mrs. London's Bakeshop,
Saratoga Springs, New York

• • •

CHOCOLATE CHIP MACADAMIA NUT COOKIES

This is the ultimate chocolate chip cookie. The rich, deep chocolate base is packed with chocolate chips and toasted macadamia nuts. You will be strongly tempted to eat all of these cookies within minutes but, instead, do what I do—tuck them into little holiday gift baskets.

Makes 3½ to 4 Dozen

2 cups (10 ounces) macadamia nuts
8 ounces semisweet chocolate
2 sticks (8 ounces) unsalted butter, softened to room temperature
¾ cup (packed) light brown sugar

Poppy Seed Tante Cake (p. 170).

3/4 cup granulated sugar
2 eggs
1 teaspoon vanilla extract
2 cups unbleached all-purpose flour
1 teaspoon baking soda
3/4 teaspoon salt
2 cups chocolate chips

1. Preheat the oven to 350°. Spread the macadamia nuts on a baking sheet and bake until lightly browned, about 8 minutes. Let cool, then coarsely chop the toasted nuts. Increase the oven temperature to 375°.

2. In a medium saucepan, melt the semisweet chocolate over a pan of simmering water, stirring until almost smooth. Remove from the heat and let stand, stirring occasionally, until the chocolate is completely melted and smooth; let cool.

3. Meanwhile, in a large mixer bowl, beat the butter until creamy. Gradually add the brown sugar and granulated sugar and beat until light, about 5 minutes. Add the eggs, 1 at a time, beating well after each addition. Beat in the cooled chocolate and the vanilla.

4. In a medium bowl, combine the flour, baking soda and salt. Stir the dry ingredients into the chocolate mixture until well blended. Fold in the macadamia nuts and the chocolate chips.

5. Drop mounded tablespoons of the dough onto greased cookie sheets, leaving about 2 inches between each cookie. Bake in the lower third of the oven for 15 to 18 minutes, until the tops feel firm when lightly pressed. Let cool for 5 minutes, then transfer the cookies to a rack to cool completely. *(These cookies will keep for up to 1 week at room temperature in a tightly covered tin.)*

—Sarabeth Levine, Sarabeth's Kitchen, New York City

• • •

HAZELNUT COOKIES

These nutty, buttery cookies serve as a perfect accompaniment to Apple Sorbet (p. 220). Store any leftover cookies in an airtight container.

Makes About 3 Dozen

3/4 cup hazelnuts (filberts)
1 stick (4 ounces) unsalted butter, softened to room temperature
3/4 cup (packed) light brown sugar
1 egg
1 teaspoon vanilla extract
1 1/4 cups all-purpose flour
1/2 teaspoon baking soda
1/2 teaspoon salt

1. Preheat the oven to 350°. Spread the nuts on a baking sheet and bake for about 10 minutes, or until the dark skins are cracked and the nuts are lightly browned. Put the nuts in a towel and rub off the skins. Let cool, then coarsely chop. Increase the oven temperature to 375°. Grease 2 large cookie sheets.

2. In a medium mixer bowl, beat the butter and brown sugar together on high speed until light and creamy, about 5 minutes. Add the egg, vanilla and 1 teaspoon of hot water. Beat until blended.

3. In a medium bowl, sift together the flour, baking soda and salt. Stir the dry ingredients into the butter mixture until well blended. Fold in the chopped toasted hazelnuts.

4. Drop mounded teaspoonfuls of the dough onto the cookie sheets, leaving about 2 inches between each cookie. Bake for 12 minutes, or until golden brown. Transfer to a rack to cool.

—Lee Bailey

• • •

LEMON MACADAMIA COOKIES

These are scrumptious served with a few figs macerated in a tangy lemon syrup. This recipe makes a lot, so keep any remaining cookies fresh in an airtight container. Or you can make the entire amount and freeze half the dough for later.

Makes About 5 Dozen

1 1/2 cups macadamia nuts (about 6 ounces), coarsely chopped
2 eggs
1 1/3 cups (packed) light brown sugar
1/2 cup plus 1 tablespoon all-purpose flour
1/4 teaspoon baking powder
2 teaspoons grated lemon zest
2 teaspoons fresh lemon juice
Pinch of salt

1. Preheat the oven to 375°. Spread the nuts on a baking sheet and bake until lightly browned, 8 to 10 minutes. Let cool.

2. In a medium mixer bowl, beat the eggs with an electric mixer on high speed until they are light and fluffy, about 3 minutes. Add the sugar and continue to beat until well blended, 1 to 2 minutes. Stir in the flour, baking powder, lemon zest, lemon juice, salt and the toasted nuts; mix well.

3. Coat 2 cookie sheets with nonstick cooking spray. Drop rounded teaspoons of the dough about 3 inches apart onto the cookie sheet. Bake for 7 to 9 minutes, until the cookies are golden with darker edges. Transfer to a rack, and let cool. Repeat with the remaining dough.

—Lee Bailey

• • •

PIES & TARTS

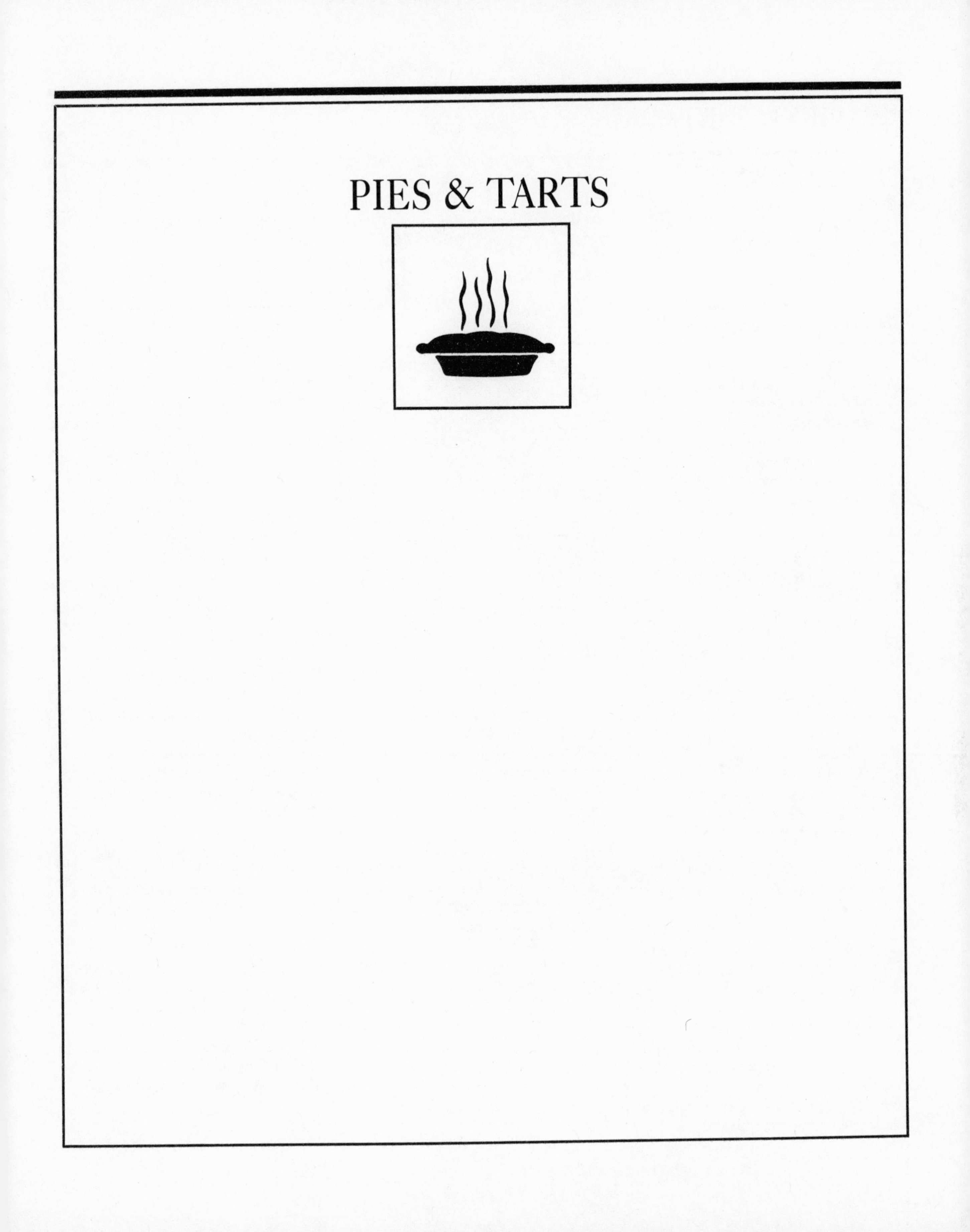

PEAR AND GINGER PIE

Very often fruit pies are obscured with too many spices. This one is flavored only with fresh ginger, which adds a subtle sparkle.

—8 to 10 Servings—

All-Butter Pie Dough (recipe follows)
2½ pounds firm-ripe pears
1-inch piece of fresh ginger, peeled and finely grated
⅓ cup sugar
3 tablespoons unbleached all-purpose flour
2 tablespoons unsalted butter
1 egg
Pinch of salt

1. Preheat the oven to 450°. Divide the dough in half. On a lightly floured work surface, roll out half the dough into an 11-inch disk, ⅛ to ¼ inch thick. Fit without stretching into a 9-inch glass pie pan. Trim the dough even with the edge of the pan.

2. Peel, quarter and core the pears and cut each quarter crosswise into 5 or 6 slices. Place the pears in a large bowl and toss with the grated ginger.

3. Combine the sugar and flour and sprinkle 2 tablespoons of the mixture over the pastry in the pan. Pour the remaining sugar and flour over the pears and toss gently to mix. Turn the filling into the prepared pastry shell and smooth the top as much as possible. Dot the filling with the butter.

4. On a lightly floured surface, roll out the remaining dough to an 11-inch disk. Place the dough over the filling and trim the edge of the dough so that there is an even ½-inch edge of overhang. Tuck the excess dough under the edge of the bottom crust. Flute the edge of the crust. Cut 3 or 4 vent holes in the center of the top crust with the point of a paring knife. Beat the egg and salt together and paint the top of the pie with the glaze.

5. Bake the pie on the bottom rack of the oven for 15 minutes. Reduce the oven temperature to 350° and bake for 35 minutes longer, or until the crust is deep golden and the juices are just beginning to bubble up. Let the pie cool on a rack. Serve warm or at room temperature.

—Nicholas Malgieri

• • •

ALL-BUTTER PIE DOUGH

The greatest problem in making all-butter crusts is getting them flaky and tender at the same time. The addition of the cake flour in this recipe cuts down the gluten development in the all-purpose flour and results in a more tender dough. The bit of baking powder helps the dough to expand very slightly, contributing both to tenderness and to a firm contact between the bottom crust and the pan; it also ensures that the crust bakes evenly throughout.

—Makes a Double 9-Inch Pie Crust—

2 cups unbleached all-purpose flour
¼ cup cake flour
¼ teaspoon baking powder
¼ teaspoon salt
2 sticks (8 ounces) unsalted butter
5 to 6 tablespoons ice water

1. Combine the all-purpose flour, cake flour, baking powder and salt in a mixing bowl. Stir well to blend.

2. Cut each stick of butter into 6 or 8 pieces and, using your fingertips, rub the butter into the dry ingredients until the mixture is mealy with no large pieces of butter visible.

3. Adding only enough to make the dough hold together, sprinkle the water over the flour and butter mixture and toss with a fork to moisten. Knead the dough into a ball and flatten into a 6- to 8-inch disk. Wrap in plastic and refrigerate for about 1 hour, or until firm.

—Nicholas Malgieri

• • •

CRANBERRY-APPLE PIE WITH AN OATMEAL-ALMOND CRUST

This pie has a red-jeweled interior that is surrounded by crunchy almonds and oats. The crust for this pie is an excellent choice for any berry pie.

—8 Servings—

1 package (12 ounces) fresh cranberries
1 large Granny Smith apple—peeled, cored and chopped
1¾ cups (packed) brown sugar
2 teaspoons grated orange zest
¼ teaspoon ground cloves
1½ tablespoons quick-cooking tapioca
½ cup finely ground almonds
⅓ cup old-fashioned rolled oats
2 tablespoons all-purpose flour
½ teaspoon salt
3 tablespoon cold unsalted butter, cut into ¼-inch dice
Oatmeal-Almond Dough (recipe follows)

1. In a large bowl, combine the cranberries, apple, 1¼ cups of the brown sugar, the orange zest, cloves and tapioca; stir well. Set aside at room temperature.

2. In a medium bowl, combine the remaining ½ cup brown sugar with the ground almonds, oats, flour and salt. Work in the butter until large crumbs form; cover and refrigerate.

3. Preheat the oven to 425°. Roll out the dough to form an 11-inch circle, ⅛ inch thick. Fit the dough into a 9-inch pie pan without tearing or stretching. Shape the rim into an even ridge and flute; refrigerate for 10 minutes.

4. Spread the reserved cranberry filling evenly in the shell. Bake the pie in the bottom third of the oven for 15 minutes. Cover loosely with foil and bake for 10 minutes longer.

5. Uncover and spread the pie evenly with the reserved almond-oat topping. Reduce the heat to 350° and bake for 20 to 25 minutes longer, until bubbly. (If the topping begins to get too dark, cover loosely with foil.) Let cool on a rack.

—Ken Haedrich

• • •

OATMEAL-ALMOND DOUGH

Makes a Single 9-Inch Crust

¾ cup all-purpose flour
½ cup oat flour* or ⅔ cup old-fashioned rolled oats, ground in a blender
¼ cup finely ground almonds
½ teaspoon salt
⅓ cup cold vegetable shortening
3 tablespoons ice water
****Available at health food stores***

1. In a large bowl, combine the all-purpose flour, oat flour, ground almonds and salt; stir well. Cut in the shortening until the mixture resembles coarse meal.

2. Sprinkle on the ice water, 1 tablespoon at a time, tossing with a fork after each addition. Gather the dough into a ball and flatten into a ½-inch-thick disk. Cover with plastic wrap and refrigerate for 30 to 45 minutes.

—Ken Haedrich

• • •

APPLE-QUINCE PIE

On a very still Napa afternoon in November, it was a shortage of apples that sent me out to the quince tree. The slices of amber fruit, scattered among the slices of apple, made a pie tasting of autumn as none other I can remember.

8 to 10 Servings

4 tart green apples—peeled, cored and cut into ½-inch slices
2 ripe quinces—peeled, cored and cut into ⅛-inch slices
Grated zest and juice of 1 medium lemon
¾ cup sugar
1 tablespoon all-purpose flour
Flaky Pie Dough (recipe follows)
3 tablespoons unsalted butter, cut into ½-inch dice

1. Preheat the oven to 400°. In a large bowl, toss together the apples, quinces, lemon zest, lemon juice, sugar and flour.

2. On a lightly floured surface, roll out one disk of dough about ⅛ inch to a 12-inch circle. Fit the pastry into a 9-inch (23-centimeter) glass pie plate. Roll out the top crust in the same manner.

3. Mound the fruit mixture in the lined pie plate and dot with the butter. Moisten the rim of the pie shell with water and lay the top crust over the fruit.

4. Using scissors, trim the edges of the dough so that they extend no more than ¾ inch beyond the rim of the plate. Roll the dough under and crimp to make an attractive border. Cut at least 5 steam vents in the top crust.

5. Bake the pie in the lower third of the oven for 25 minutes. Reduce the oven temperature to 350° and bake for 35 to 40 minutes longer, or until the crust is golden brown and the fruit is tender. Let cool for at least 2 hours before serving.

—Michael James

• • •

FLAKY PIE DOUGH

Makes Two 9-Inch Crusts

2¼ cups all-purpose flour
¾ teaspoon salt
¾ cup cold vegetable shortening
5 to 6 tablespoons ice water

1. In a large bowl, combine the flour and salt. Cut in the shortening until the mixture resembles very coarse meal with some pieces of shortening the size of corn kernels still visible.

2. Sprinkle 5 tablespoons of the ice water over the mixture, tossing to moisten evenly. Gather the dough into a ball, adding up to 1 tablespoon more ice water if the dough is too dry.

3. Handling the dough as little as possible, divide it in half and pat each piece into a 6-inch disk. Wrap separately in plastic wrap and refrigerate for at least 30 minutes.

—Michael James

• • •

DOUBLE-CRUST PLUM PIE

With very few exceptions, my rule on blending different fruits in one pie is: don't do it. Here the tart sweetness of plums makes a straightforward and delicious fruit pie.

8 to 10 Servings

2 pounds plums, preferably Italian prune plums, halved and pitted, or quartered if very large
½ to ¾ cup sugar, depending on the sweetness of the fruit
¼ cup all-purpose flour
Flaky Pie Dough (above)
3 tablespoons unsalted butter, cut into small pieces

1. Preheat the oven to 400°. Place the plums in a large bowl and toss with the sugar and flour.

2. On a lightly floured surface, roll out one disk of the dough about ⅛ inch thick to a 12-inch circle. Fit the dough into a 9-inch (23-centimeter) glass pie plate without stretching. Turn the fruit into the pie shell and dot with the butter.

3. Roll out the dough for the top crust about ⅛ inch thick to a 12-inch circle. Using a pastry brush, moisten the dough around the rim of the pie shell with cold water. Center the dough for the top crust over the fruit. Using scissors, trim the edges of the dough together so that they extend no more than ¾ inch beyond the rim of the dish. Roll the dough under and crimp the edge to make an attractive border. Cut 5 steam vents in the top crust.

4. Bake the pie in the lower third of the oven for 20 minutes. Reduce the oven temperature to 350° and continue baking for another 35 to 40 minutes, or until the crust is golden brown. Let cool for at least 2 hours before serving.

—Michael James

• • •

RASPBERRY AND FRESH FIG PIE

If you can't get fresh figs, use five cups of raspberries for a heavenly raspberry pie.

—8 to 10 Servings—

4 cups fresh raspberries
1 cup diced (½ inch) fresh figs
¾ to 1 cup sugar, depending on the sweetness of the fruit
2 tablespoons all-purpose flour
Flaky Pie Dough (p. 193)
3 tablespoons unsalted butter, cut into small pieces

1. Preheat the oven to 400°. In a medium bowl, toss the raspberries and figs with the sugar and flour.

2. On a lightly floured surface, roll out one disk of the dough about ⅛ inch thick to a 12-inch circle. Fit the pastry into a 9-inch (23-centimeter) heatproof glass pie plate. Roll out the second disk in the same manner.

3. Turn the tossed fruit into the pie shell and dot with the butter. Moisten the rim of the bottom pastry with water and lay the top crust over the fruit.

4. Using scissors, trim the edges of the dough so that they extend no more than ¾ inch beyond the rim of the plate. Roll the dough under and crimp to make an attractive border. Cut at least 5 steam vents in the top crust.

5. Bake the pie in the lower third of the oven for 20 minutes. Reduce the oven temperature to 350° and bake for 30 to 35 minutes, until the crust is golden. Let cool for at least 2 hours before serving.

—Michael James

• • •

GINGERED PEAR PIE IN A SPICED WHOLE WHEAT CRUST

This pie's very tender crust is especially nice with fruit fillings. It is tawny and fragrant with a pronounced wheaty flavor.

—8 Servings—

6 large firm-ripe pears (about 3 pounds)—peeled, cored and quartered
2 tablespoons fresh lemon juice
½ cup sugar
1½ tablespoons quick-cooking tapioca
1 teaspoon ground ginger
Pinch of salt
Spiced Whole Wheat Dough (recipe follows)
2 tablespoons unsalted butter

1. Slice the pears ⅛ to ¼ inch thick and place in a bowl. Sprinkle with the lemon juice, sugar, tapioca, ginger and salt; toss gently to combine.

2. Preheat the oven to 425°. On a lightly floured surface, roll the larger disk of dough into an 11-inch circle, ⅛ inch thick. Fit the dough into a 9-inch pie pan without stretching.

3. Roll the remaining dough into a 10-inch circle, ⅛ inch thick. Spoon the pears into the shell and smooth the surface. Dot with the butter. Moisten the dough rim and place the lid on top; press gently all around the rim to seal. Trim the dough with scissors, leaving a ¼-inch overhang.

4. Fold the rim under to form an even ridge. Prick several steam vents in the lid with a fork and bake the pie in the middle of the oven for 25 minutes. Reduce the heat to 375° and bake for 20 to 25 minutes longer, until thick syrup bubbles through the vents. Let cool on a rack.

—Ken Haedrich

• • •

SPICED WHOLE WHEAT DOUGH

—Makes a Double 9-Inch Crust—

1¼ cups whole wheat flour
1¼ cups all-purpose flour
1 teaspoon cinnamon
1 teaspoon freshly grated nutmeg
½ teaspoon salt
¾ cup cold vegetable shortening
2 tablespoons cold unsalted butter, cut into ¼-inch slices
4 to 5 tablespoons ice water

1. In a large bowl, combine the whole wheat and all-purpose flours with the cinnamon, nutmeg and salt; stir well. Cut in the shortening and butter until the mixture resembles coarse meal.

2. Sprinkle on the ice water, 1 tablespoon at a time, tossing with a fork after each addition. When the dough begins to mass together, form into 2 balls, one slightly larger than the other. Flatten each into a ½-inch-thick disk. Cover with plastic wrap and refrigerate for at least 30 minutes before rolling out.

—Ken Haedrich

• • •

MEATLESS MINCE PIE WITH BOURBON

This is actually a kind of spiked apple pie. It is delicate and fruity, and it contains brown butter, a flavor that is very appealing with pies that have restrained amounts of spice.

8 to 10 Servings

Flaky Pie Dough (p. 193)
2/3 cup golden raisins
1/3 cup currants
1/4 cup bourbon
1/4 cup apple juice or cider
1 pound tart green apples, peeled and cored
3 tablespoons fresh lemon juice
1 navel orange, unpeeled, coarsely chopped
2/3 cup sugar
1/2 teaspoon salt
1/2 teaspoon cinnamon
1/2 teaspoon mace
1/4 teaspoon ground cloves
1/4 teaspoon ground ginger
2 tablespoons unsulphured molasses
1 tablespoon all-purpose flour
4 tablespoons unsalted butter

1. On a lightly floured surface, roll out one disk of the dough about 1/8 inch thick to a 12-inch circle. Fit the dough without stretching into a 9-inch (23-centimeter) glass pie plate. Fold the edge of the dough under and crimp it to form a fluted rim. Refrigerate the pastry shell for at least 30 minutes.

2. Meanwhile, preheat the oven to 400°. In a large bowl, combine the raisins, currants, bourbon and apple juice.

3. In a food processor, very finely chop the apples. Add the apples and lemon juice to the raisin mixture; toss to mix.

4. Without rinsing the bowl, process the coarsely chopped unpeeled orange until it is a fine pulp. Add the orange to the raisin mixture along with the sugar, salt, cinnamon, mace, cloves, ginger, molasses and flour. Mix the mincemeat mixture to blend well.

5. In a small skillet, melt the butter over low heat. Cook until it becomes light brown, about 5 minutes. Stir the browned butter into the mincemeat and pour the filling into the chilled pie shell.

6. Roll out the remaining disk of dough about 1/8 inch thick to a 12-inch circle. Using a crimped dough cutter, cut the pastry into 1/2- to 3/4-inch wide strips. Moisten the edge of the pie shell with water and with the strips of pastry, weave a lattice top. Press the strips to the moistened rim of the dough to seal the ends.

7. Place the pie on a baking sheet and bake in the lower third of the oven for 25 minutes. Reduce the oven temperature to 350° and bake for 45 minutes longer, or until the crust is golden brown and the filling is bubbling. Let cool completely before serving.

—Michael James

• • •

SWEET POTATO PIE

This pie is lightened by beaten egg whites and, compared to many sweet potato pies, is delicately spiced.

8 to 10 Servings

3/4 pound sweet potatoes
1 cup milk
2 eggs, separated
1/3 cup plus 2 tablespoons sugar
2 tablespoons maple syrup
1/2 teaspoon vanilla extract
1/4 teaspoon cinnamon
1/4 teaspoon freshly grated nutmeg
Salt
1 stick (4 ounces) unsalted butter
Cornmeal Crust (recipe follows), partially baked
1 teaspoon confectioners' sugar
Sweetened whipped cream

1. Preheat the oven to 350°. Bake the sweet potatoes until tender when pierced with a fork, about 1 hour. Let cool; then peel and cut the sweet potatoes into large dice. *(The recipe can be prepared to this point up to 1 day ahead.)*

2. Preheat the oven to 400°. In a food processor or blender, puree the sweet potatoes, gradually adding the milk to make a smooth mixture.

3. Add the egg yolks, 1/3 cup of the sugar, the maple syrup, vanilla, cinnamon, nutmeg and 1/4 teaspoon salt. Mix until well blended, about 1 minute.

4. In a small saucepan, cook the butter over low heat until nut brown, about 5 minutes. Pour the butter into the sweet potato puree, discarding any dark residue at the bottom of the pan; mix well.

5. Beat the egg whites with a pinch of salt until they form soft peaks. Gradually beat in the remaining 2 tablespoons sugar, 1 teaspoon at a time, until firm peaks form. Fold the sweet potato puree into the beaten egg whites.

6. Pour the filling into the partially baked Cornmeal Crust. Bake the pie for 20 minutes. Reduce the oven temperature to 350° and bake for 20 minutes longer, or until the pie filling is set and the crust is nicely browned.

7. Let the pie cool. Lightly dust the crust with the confectioners' sugar. Serve with sweetened whipped cream.

—Michael James

• • •

CORNMEAL CRUST

—Makes a Single 9-Inch Crust—

1 cup plus 2 tablespoons all-purpose flour
1/4 cup finely ground yellow cornmeal
1/2 teaspoon salt
6 tablespoons cold vegetable shortening
About 1/4 cup ice water

1. In a medium bowl, combine the flour, cornmeal and salt. Cut the shortening into the flour until the mixture resembles oatmeal with some pieces of shortening the size of corn kernels still visible; do not overmix. Sprinkle the ice water over the flour mixture and toss to combine. Squeeze the dough into a ball, adding a few more drops of water if necessary.

2. Handling the dough as little as possible, shape it into a 6-inch disk. Wrap the dough in plastic wrap and refrigerate for at least 30 minutes.

3. On a lightly floured surface, roll out the dough about 1/8 inch thick to a 12-inch circle. Fit the pastry, without stretching, into a 9-inch (23-centimeter) glass pie plate. Fold under the edge of the pastry until it is flush with the rim and crimp the edge. With a fork, prick the dough all over. Freeze the pastry shell for 30 minutes. Meanwhile, preheat the oven to 450°.

4. *For a partially baked pie shell,* line the crust with a sheet of aluminum foil and fill with pie weights or dried beans. Bake in the lower third of the oven for 10 minutes, or until the pie shell is very lightly browned. Remove the foil and weights.

For a fully baked pie shell, follow the instructions for a partially baked shell above, then reduce the oven temperature to 400° and bake the empty pie shell for 15 minutes, or until the shell is golden brown.

—Michael James

• • •

MAPLE SQUASH PIE IN A POPPY SEED-CORN CRUST

The poppy seed-cornmeal crust provides a toothsome contrast of textures—smooth against crunchy. I prefer to use freshly ground whole cornmeal because it has a better flavor and coarser texture than the packaged variety.

—8 Servings—

Poppy Seed-Corn Dough (recipe follows)
1 1/2 cups cooked and well-drained winter squash or canned pumpkin
3/4 cup maple syrup
3 eggs, lightly beaten
3/4 cup heavy cream
1 teaspoon cinnamon
1/2 teaspoon allspice
1/2 teaspoon ground ginger
1/2 teaspoon ground cloves
1/4 teaspoon salt

1. Roll the dough into an 11-inch circle, 1/8 inch thick. Fit the dough into a 9-inch pie pan, without stretching. Form the edge into an even ridge and flute. Freeze the shell for 15 minutes.

2. Meanwhile, preheat the oven to 450°. In a food processor, puree the squash and maple syrup. Add the eggs, cream, cinnamon, allspice, ginger, cloves and salt; process until blended.

3. Pour the filling into the partially frozen shell and bake in the lower third of the oven for 10 minutes. Reduce the heat to 325° and bake for 45 to 50 minutes, until all but the very center of the pie is set. (The center will firm up as the pie cools.) Let cool on a rack.

—Ken Haedrich

• • •

POPPY SEED-CORN DOUGH

—Makes a Single 9-Inch Crust—

3/4 cup all-purpose flour
1/2 cup stone-ground cornmeal
2 tablespoons poppy seeds
1/2 teaspoon salt
1/4 cup cold vegetable shortening
2 tablespoons cold unsalted butter
2 1/2 to 3 1/2 tablespoons ice water

1. In a large bowl, combine the flour, cornmeal, poppy seeds and salt; stir well. Cut in the shortening and butter until the mixture resembles coarse meal.

2. Sprinkle on the ice water, 1 tablespoon at a time, tossing with a fork after each addition. Gather the dough into a ball and flatten into a 1/2-inch-thick disk. Cover with plastic wrap and refrigerate for 30 minutes.

—Ken Haedrich

• • •

PUMPKIN-PECAN PIE

Associate Test Kitchen Director Marcia Kiesel has combined the Thanksgiving season's favorite pies into one.

—6 to 8 Servings—

2 cups chopped pecans
1/4 cup plus 2 tablespoons (packed) light brown sugar
3 tablespoons unsalted butter, melted
1 1/3 cups canned unsweetened solid-pack pumpkin
1 1/2 teaspoons ground ginger
1 1/2 teaspoons cinnamon
1 teaspoon allspice
3 eggs, lightly beaten
1/3 cup unsulphured molasses
2 tablespoons granulated sugar
1 cup sour cream
1/2 cup heavy cream
Pie Pastry (recipe follows)
Whipped cream, as accompaniment

1. Preheat the oven to 350°. In a medium bowl, toss together the pecans, brown sugar and melted butter; set aside.

2. In a large bowl, combine the pumpkin, ginger, cinnamon, allspice and eggs. Whisk to blend well. Mix in the molasses, granulated sugar, sour cream and heavy cream until thoroughly blended.

3. Roll out the Pie Pastry to a 12-inch circle about ⅛ inch thick. Fit the dough loosely into a 10-inch pie dish, preferably glass. Trim the edge, leaving an extra ½ inch all around. Fold the edge under itself and flute if desired.

4. Pour in the pumpkin filling and bake for 15 minutes. Sprinkle the reserved pecan mixture evenly over the pie and bake for about 30 minutes longer, until the top is brown and crusty and the filling is set. Let the pie cool for at least 2 hours before serving, with a bowl of whipped cream on the side. *(The pie can be made up to 6 hours in advance and refrigerated.)*

—Marcia Kiesel

• • •

PIE PASTRY

—Makes a Single 10-Inch Crust—

1¼ cups all-purpose flour
¼ teaspoon baking powder
¼ teaspoon salt
6 tablespoons cold butter, cut into small pieces
2 tablespoons vegetable shortening
1 egg, lightly beaten

In a large bowl, stir together the flour, baking powder and salt. Cut in the butter and then, using your fingertips, work in the shortening until the mixture resembles coarse meal. Stir in the egg and gather the dough into a ball. Flatten the dough into a 6-inch disk, wrap in plastic wrap and refrigerate for at least 30 minutes before rolling out.

—Marcia Kiesel

• • •

BANANA-MACADAMIA NUT PIE WITH HOT FUDGE SAUCE

Stephan Pyles of the Routh Street Café in Dallas updated this old-fashioned dessert with macadamia nuts and dressed it with a dark, rich chocolate sauce.

—8 to 10 Servings—

2¾ cups milk
¼ cup banana liqueur
½ vanilla bean, split lengthwise
4 eggs, separated
⅔ cup plus 6 tablespoons sugar
½ cup all-purpose flour
2 bananas, cut into ¼-inch slices
1 cup chopped unsalted macadamia nuts
Pie Pastry (at left), prebaked
Pinch of salt
Hot Fudge Sauce (p. 258)

1. In a medium saucepan, combine the milk, banana liqueur and vanilla bean. Bring to a boil, remove from the heat, cover and let steep while you prepare the egg custard.

2. In a medium bowl, lightly beat the egg yolks. Gradually whisk in ⅔ cup of the sugar. Beat until thickened and pale yellow, about 2 minutes. Sift in the flour and beat until blended, about 30 seconds.

3. Strain the vanilla milk and gradually whisk it into the egg yolk mixture. Pour the vanilla cream into a heavy medium saucepan and bring to a boil over moderate heat, whisking constantly. Boil, stirring, for 2 to 3 minutes, until thickened and smooth. Remove from the heat.

4. Spread half the banana slices and half the macadamia nuts in the bottom of the Prebaked Pie Shell. Pour in half of the vanilla cream. Cover with the remaining bananas and nuts and top with the remaining vanilla cream.

5. Place a sheet of plastic wrap directly onto the surface of the pie and refrigerate until the cream is cool and set, about 2 hours.

6. Preheat the oven to 400°. Beat the egg whites and salt with an electric mixer on high speed until soft peaks form. Gradually beat in the remaining 6 tablespoons sugar, 1 tablespoon at a time, until the meringue stands in stiff peaks.

7. Spoon the meringue on top of the pie, swirling it decoratively and spreading it all the way to the inside edges of the crust. Bake the pie for 3 to 5 minutes, or until the meringue is lightly browned. Serve warm or chilled, accompanied with Hot Fudge Sauce.

—Stephan Pyles,
Routh Street Café, Dallas

• • •

MAPLE PECAN PIE

For this pie, a made-from-scratch caramel mixture of cream, sugar and maple syrup takes the place of the usual cloying corn syrup.

—8 Servings—

1½ cups heavy cream
¾ cup sugar
¾ cup maple syrup
2 eggs, lightly beaten
2 teaspoons vanilla extract
2 cups pecan halves
Cornmeal Crust (p. 196), partially baked
Lightly sweetened whipped cream, as accompaniment

1. Preheat the oven to 400°. In a large heavy saucepan, bring the heavy cream and sugar to a simmer over moderate heat. Simmer for 25 minutes, whisking occasionally, until the mixture slightly caramelizes to a light brown.

2. Remove from the heat and whisk in the maple syrup, eggs and vanilla. Stir in the pecans. Pour the mixture into the partially baked Cornmeal Crust.

3. Bake the pie in the lower third of the oven for 25 to 30 minutes, or until the custard is nearly set and the top is richly browned. Let cool completely. Serve with lightly sweetened whipped cream.

—Michael James

• • •

COCONUT CREAM PIE WITH HOT WATER CRUST

The crust recipe for this pie comes from Ruth Cashdollar. It's delicious and easy.

6 to 8 Servings

2 cups milk
¾ cup sweetened cream of coconut, such as Coco Lopez
¼ cup cornstarch
¼ teaspoon salt
3 eggs, separated, at room temperature
1 teaspoon vanilla extract
1 tablespoon unsalted butter
1¼ cups sweetened shredded coconut
Hot Water Crust (recipe follows)
¼ teaspoon cream of tartar
⅓ cup sugar

1. In a medium saucepan, whisk the milk, cream of coconut, cornstarch and ⅛ teaspoon of the salt. Cook over moderate heat, stirring constantly, until the filling thickens slightly and just begins to boil, about 8 minutes.

2. In a medium bowl, lightly whisk the egg yolks. Whisk in a little of the hot coconut milk to warm them; then whisk the yolks into the remaining coconut milk. Cook over moderate heat, stirring constantly, until thick and smooth, about 1 minute.

3. Remove from the heat and stir in the vanilla, butter and 1 cup of the coconut. Place a round of waxed paper directly on the surface of the custard to prevent a skin from forming. Let cool completely. Spread the mixture in the cooled Hot Water Crust.

4. Preheat the oven to 325°. In a medium bowl, beat the egg whites with an electric mixer until foamy. Add the cream of tartar and the remaining ⅛ teaspoon salt and beat until soft peaks form. Gradually add the sugar and beat until stiff.

5. Spread the meringue evenly over the coconut cream, to cover the filling completely. Swirl the meringue with the back of a spoon. Sprinkle the remaining ¼ cup coconut over the top and bake for 12 to 15 minutes, until the meringue is set and golden brown. Let cool on a rack. Serve slightly warm, at room temperature, or refrigerate for up to 2 hours.

—Lee Bailey

• • •

HOT WATER CRUST

Makes a Single 9-Inch Crust

½ cup vegetable shortening
2½ tablespoons boiling water
2 teaspoons milk
¼ teaspoon salt
1⅓ cups sifted all-purpose flour

1. In a medium bowl, beat the shortening and boiling water with an electric mixer on medium speed until well blended, 2 to 3 minutes. Add the milk and salt and beat until smooth. Gradually add the flour, beating on low speed until the mixture begins to form a ball, about 2 minutes. Knead into a ball and then pat into a 6-inch disk, cover with plastic wrap and refrigerate until firm, about 1 hour.

2. Preheat the oven to 450°. On a lightly floured surface, roll out the dough ⅛ to ¼ inch thick. Fit the dough into a 9-inch metal pie pan. Trim off any excess dough. Press with the back of a fork to decorate the edge. (To maintain the best shape, cover the dough with plastic wrap and freeze for 15 minutes before baking.) Line the dough with foil and fill with pie weights or dried beans.

3. Bake for 10 minutes, until almost golden. Remove the foil and continue baking for 8 to 10 minutes, or until lightly browned. Let cool before filling.

—Lee Bailey

• • •

COFFEE CREAM PIE IN A BUCKWHEAT COCOA CRUST

8 Servings

¾ cup (lightly packed) light brown sugar
¼ cup plus 1 teaspoon cornstarch
¼ teaspoon salt
3 cups milk
2 tablespoons plus 2 teaspoons instant coffee granules
4 egg yolks, lightly beaten
2 tablespoons unsalted butter, softened to room temperature
½ teaspoon vanilla extract
Buckwheat Cocoa Crust, baked (recipe follows)

1. In a large saucepan, whisk the brown sugar, cornstarch and salt. Place over moderate heat and gradually whisk in the milk. Heat until lukewarm; whisk in the instant coffee and egg yolks.

2. Whisking constantly, cook the mixture until it comes to a boil, about 10 minutes. Boil for 30 seconds, then reduce the heat to moderately low and simmer for 2 minutes, whisking constantly. Remove from the heat and whisk in the butter and vanilla. Place a piece of plastic wrap directly over the filling and set aside for 10 minutes.

3. Remove the plastic wrap and pour the filling into the baked crust. Let cool to room temperature on a rack, then cover loosely with plastic wrap and refrigerate for at least 2 hours before serving.

—Ken Haedrich

• • •

BUCKWHEAT COCOA CRUST

If you want a very intense buckwheat flavor, roast the buckwheat flour in a dry, heavy skillet over moderate heat, stirring constantly, until it darkens a shade or two. Remove from the pan and let cool to room temperature before proceeding.

—Makes a Single 9-Inch Crust—

3/4 cup buckwheat flour
1/2 cup all-purpose flour
1 tablespoon sugar
2 teaspoons sifted unsweetened cocoa
1/4 teaspoon salt
3 tablespoons cold vegetable shortening
3 tablespoons cold unsalted butter, cut into 1/4-inch pieces
3 1/2 tablespoons ice water

1. In a large bowl, combine the buckwheat and all-purpose flours with the sugar, cocoa and salt, stir well. Cut in the shortening and butter until the mixture resembles coarse meal.

2. Add the ice water, 1 tablespoon at a time, tossing with a fork. Gather the dough into a ball and flatten to form a 1/2-inch-thick disk. Cover with plastic wrap and refrigerate for 45 to 60 minutes.

3. Roll out the dough to form an 11-inch circle, 1/8 inch thick. Fit the dough into a 9-inch pie pan without stretching. Shape the edge into an even ridge and freeze the shell for at least 30 minutes.

4. Meanwhile, preheat the oven to 425°. Bake the shell in the bottom third of the oven for 20 minutes. Transfer to a rack and let cool completely.

—Ken Haedrich

• • •

APPLE AND PRUNE COBBLER WITH BUTTERMILK BISCUIT CRUST

Really a pie with no bottom crust, this apple and prune cobbler is a perfect way to combine fruit and pastry quickly and easily. Although prunes enter into few American desserts, they are common in France and in Eastern Europe. The prunes and apples marry well, sharing a slight tartness and a melting texture after baking. The buttermilk biscuit crust is thick and buttery—a perfect complement to the tart juices of the prune and apple filling.

Try the cobbler in the summer, substituting peaches or apricots for apples and raspberries or cherries for the prunes.

—8 to 10 Servings—

2 pounds firm cooking apples, such as Golden Delicious
1 cup pitted prunes (about 8 ounces)
1/2 cup walnut pieces, coarsely chopped
1/2 cup plus 1 tablespoon sugar
1/2 teaspoon cinnamon
2 tablespoons all-purpose flour
2 tablespoons fresh lemon juice
2 tablespoons unsalted butter
Buttermilk Biscuit Dough (recipe follows)
1 tablespoon milk or buttermilk

1. Peel, halve and core the apples. Slice each half into 5 or 6 wedges, from stem to blossom end. Slice each prune into 3 or 4 strips. In a large bowl combine the apples, prunes and chopped walnuts.

2. Preheat the oven to 375°. In a bowl, combine 1/2 cup of the sugar, the cinnamon and the flour. Toss with the fruit and nut mixture. Pour the filling into a 1 1/2-quart shallow baking dish, sprinkle on the lemon juice and dot with the butter.

3. On a lightly floured surface, roll the Buttermilk Biscuit Dough a little less than 1/4 inch thick, slightly larger than the baking dish. Transfer the dough to the top of the filling and trim any overhang even with the rim of the dish. Flute the edge of the dough at the rim. Slash 4 or 5 vent holes about 1 inch long in the center of the crust. Paint the dough with the milk and sprinkle with the remaining 1 tablespoon sugar.

4. Bake the cobbler for 30 minutes, or until the dough is baked through and deep golden and the filling is beginning to bubble. Let the cobbler cool on a rack. Serve warm or at room temperature.

—Nicholas Malgieri

• • •

BUTTERMILK BISCUIT DOUGH

Don't be alarmed if the biscuit dough is soft; if it is too firm, the crust will be tough. Just flour the work surface and the dough well before rolling the dough out. Support the dough with a tart pan bottom or thin, flexible cookie sheet to transfer it to the top of the filling. Unlike flaky pastry, baking powder biscuit dough is rolled out immediately after it is made.

This recipe also makes excellent biscuits for shortcake. For these, roll out the dough ½ inch thick. Cut with a 3-inch round cutter and bake at 400° for 12 to 15 minutes.

Makes Enough for a Single 9-Inch Crust

¾ cup unbleached all-purpose flour
¾ cup cake flour
1½ teaspoons baking powder
½ teaspoon salt
4 tablespoons cold unsalted butter
¾ cup buttermilk or milk

1. Combine the all-purpose flour, cake flour, baking powder and salt. Sift into a mixing bowl.

2. Cut the butter into 8 or 10 pieces and add to the dry ingredients. Rub the butter in with your fingertips until the mixture resembles coarse meal.

3. Make a well in the center and add the buttermilk. Toss with a fork to moisten evenly. Let the dough stand in the bowl for 1 minute to absorb the liquid. Turn out onto a floured work surface. Fold the dough over on itself 2 or 3 times until it is smooth and less sticky.

—Nicholas Malgieri

• • •

ORANGE-ZESTED NECTARINE COBBLER

Orange zest in the topping provides a lively counterpoint to the lushness of ripe nectarines. Fresh peaches also work beautifully in this recipe.

12 Servings

3½ pounds nectarines—peeled, quartered and each quarter cut crosswise into fourths
¾ cup plus 2 tablespoons sugar
1½ cups cake flour
2 teaspoons baking soda
1 teaspoon cream of tartar
⅛ teaspoon salt
1 stick (4 ounces) unsalted butter, softened to room temperature
1 egg, lightly beaten
½ cup buttermilk, slightly warmed
2 tablespoons grated orange zest

1. Preheat the oven to 375°. In a 2½-quart shallow baking dish, toss the nectarines with 2 tablespoons of the sugar.

2. In a medium bowl, combine the cake flour, baking soda, cream of tartar and salt.

3. In a large mixer bowl, beat the butter and remaining ¾ cup sugar with an electric mixer on medium-high speed until fluffy and light in color, 5 to 10 minutes. Add the egg and beat until well blended.

4. On low speed, slowly beat in one-third of the flour mixture; mix until smooth. Beat in half of the buttermilk and then half of the remaining flour. Repeat once more with the remaining buttermilk and flour, beating until the batter is smooth and light. Stir in the orange zest.

5. Using a large spoon, gently dollop the batter all over the surface of the fruit to within 1 inch of the edge. (Do not spread the batter evenly.) Bake for 35 to 40 minutes, until golden brown.

—Jim Dodge, Stanford Court, San Francisco

• • •

CRANBERRY CRUMB TART

A tender crunchy topping and fresh cranberries with just the right amount of sugar make this colorful tart a treat for any occasion.

10 Servings

1¼ cups all-purpose flour
2½ cups sugar
1½ sticks (6 ounces) cold unsalted butter, cut into 1-inch cubes
½ teaspoon salt
6 cups fresh cranberries (about two 12-ounce bags)
Prebaked Tart Shell (recipe follows)

1. Preheat the oven to 375°. In a large bowl, combine the flour and 1¾ cups of the sugar. Cut in the butter until the mixture resembles coarse meal. Continue cutting until the mixture forms nickel-sized clumps that crumble easily.

2. In a medium bowl, combine the remaining ¾ cup sugar with the salt. Add the cranberries and toss to coat well.

3. Spoon the cranberries into the Prebaked Tart Shell, mounding them slightly in the center. Using your fingers, lightly squeeze pieces of the crumb topping and drop them gently over the berries. (Do not press the topping into the fruit.)

4. Bake until the topping is golden brown and the fruit is bubbling around the edge, about 40 minutes. Serve at room temperature. The tart will keep for up to 3 days in the refrigerator.

—Jim Dodge, Stanford Court, San Francisco

• • •

PREBAKED TART SHELL

— Makes a Single 9-Inch Crust —

1 cup plus 2 tablespoons all-purpose flour
1 stick (4 ounces) cold unsalted butter, cut into ½-inch pieces
1½ teaspoons sugar
⅛ teaspoon salt
¼ cup ice water

1. Put the flour in a medium bowl. Cut in the butter until the mixture resembles coarse meal. In a small bowl, dissolve the sugar and salt in the water. Sprinkle over the flour mixture, tossing until the dough begins to mass together.

2. Turn the dough out onto a floured surface and form it into a ball. Wrap in plastic wrap and flatten into a 6-inch disk. Refrigerate for at least 30 minutes.

3. On a lightly floured surface, roll out the dough into a large round, ⅛ to ¼ inch thick. Trim to a 13-inch circle. Dust the dough lightly with flour and fold into quarters. Place it, with the point in the center, in a 9½- or 10-inch tart pan, about 1 inch high, with a removable bottom. Open up the pastry and fit into the pan, folding down the excess to reinforce the sides. Press the pastry against the fluted sides of the pan; trim off any excess dough. Cover with plastic wrap and refrigerate for at least 1 hour, or overnight.

4. Preheat the oven to 425°. Line the pastry with foil and fill with pie weights or dried beans. Bake for 20 to 25 minutes, or until the pastry is almost dry. Remove the foil and weights, prick the bottom and sides all over with a fork and continue baking for 5 to 8 minutes, or until the crust is golden brown.

—Jim Dodge, Stanford Court, San Francisco

• • •

TANGY LIME TART

The tart lime curd contrasts nicely with the sweet buttery crust, and a dollop of whipped cream adds the final touch to this luscious dessert. Briefly soaking the limes in boiling water removes bitterness from the zest (the colored part of the skin), as well as wax or impurities, and releases more juice when the limes are squeezed. The tart can be prepared one day ahead.

— 8 to 10 Servings —

5 large juicy limes
1 cup plus 2 tablespoons granulated sugar
2 whole eggs
4 egg yolks
2 sticks (8 ounces) unsalted butter, cut into tablespoons
1½ cups all-purpose flour
½ cup confectioners' sugar
Strips of lime zest, for garnish
Lightly sweetened whipped cream, as accompaniment

1. In a medium heatproof bowl, cover the limes with boiling water and let steep for 2 minutes. Drain the limes and pat dry. Let cool.

2. Finely grate enough zest from the limes to yield 4 teaspoons; do not include any of the bitter white pith. Squeeze ⅔ cup of juice from the limes.

3. In a heavy, medium nonreactive saucepan, combine the zest, juice and granulated sugar. Stir to partially dissolve the sugar.

4. In a small bowl, lightly whisk the whole eggs and egg yolks to blend.

5. Set the saucepan of lime juice over moderate heat and whisk in the eggs. Continue whisking until the mixture is very hot and slightly thickened, about 5 minutes; do not let boil.

6. Remove the pan from the heat and quickly whisk in 6 tablespoons of the butter. Strain the lime curd into a small bowl. Cover the surface with a circle of waxed paper to prevent a skin from forming. Let cool to room temperature. *(The curd can be prepared up to 3 days ahead and refrigerated.)*

7. Preheat the oven to 350°. In a medium bowl, stir together the flour and confectioners' sugar. Cut or rub in the remaining 1 stick plus 2 tablespoons butter until the dough can be squeezed into a ball. Flatten the dough into an 8-inch disk and transfer it to a 9-by-1-inch fluted tart pan with a removable bottom. Press the dough evenly over the bottom and up the sides of the pan. Prick the dough all over with a fork.

8. Place the pan on a baking sheet and bake on the lower shelf of the oven for 30 to 35 minutes, or until the crust is golden brown. Transfer to a rack and let cool to room temperature.

9. Unmold the tart shell and place it on a serving platter. Spread the lime curd evenly over the tart shell, cover loosely with foil and refrigerate until chilled, about 1 hour or overnight.

10. Garnish the tart with twisted strips of lime zest and some of the whipped cream. Pass the remaining whipped cream separately.

—Diana Sturgis

• • •

GRAPE TART WITH RED CURRANT GLAZE

Seedless red grapes are the best kind to use for this tart.

—6 to 8 Servings—

1 cup all-purpose flour
1/3 cup confectioners' sugar
1 stick (4 ounces) unsalted butter, softened
2 tablespoons granulated sugar
1 egg, lightly beaten
3/4 cup sour cream
2 cups (about 1 pound) seedless red grapes
1 tablespoon fresh lemon juice
1/2 cup red currant jelly
Whipped cream, as accompaniment

1. Preheat the oven to 350°. In a medium bowl, combine the flour and confectioners' sugar; mix well. Using your fingers, work in the butter until it resembles coarse meal. Gather into a stiff dough. Press and pat into an 8-inch tart pan with a removable bottom. Bake for 30 minutes, until golden brown. Let cool in the pan on a rack.

2. In a medium bowl, combine the granulated sugar, egg and sour cream. Whisk to blend well. Pour the custard into the pastry shell. Arrange the grapes in an even layer on top. Sprinkle with the lemon juice. Bake for 25 minutes, or until the custard is set. Let cool for about 10 minutes before removing the outer rim of the pan.

3. In a small saucepan, melt the jelly over low heat, stirring frequently. Brush over the tart to glaze. Serve with chilled whipped cream if desired. *(The tart can be prepared 1 day ahead.)*

—Lee Bailey

• • •

RASPBERRY CHEESE TART

Make this tart with any individually quick-frozen berries or stone fruit. These berries and fruit, with no sugar added, come in 12-ounce bags, which yield two cups of fruit—just the right amount for this recipe. Be careful to leave the fruit frozen until ready to arrange in the tart so that it won't defrost and become difficult to handle. Later, when fresh berries are plentiful, use two cupfuls.

—8 Servings—

Sweet Pastry Dough (p. 205)
1/2 pound cream cheese, preferably fresh
1/3 cup sugar
1/2 cup sour cream or heavy cream
3 eggs
1 teaspoon grated orange zest
1 bag (12 ounces) individually quick-frozen raspberries

1. Preheat the oven to 350°. On a lightly floured surface, roll out the Sweet Pastry Dough into a 12- to 13-inch round. Fit the dough without stretching into a 10-inch tart pan with a removable bottom and trim away the excess dough at the edge by pressing the rolling pin over it.

2. In a mixer bowl, beat the cream cheese until softened, then beat in the sugar. Beat in the sour cream and then the eggs and orange zest, scraping down the sides of the bowl occasionally.

3. Arrange the frozen berries over the tart shell in an even layer. Pour the cheese batter over the berries and shake the pan gently so that the batter reaches to the edge of the crust and the berries are evenly immersed.

4. Bake the tart on a rack in the bottom third of the oven for 40 to 50 minutes, until the batter is set and very light golden and the crust is dry and lightly browned. Let the tart cool slightly on a rack before unmolding.

—Nicholas Malgieri

• • •

PLUM AND APRICOT MARZIPAN TART

This tart can be made with all plums or apricots or with a mixture of the two. The marzipan called for here, sometimes also referred to as almond paste, is available at most supermarkets. It adds a deep-flavored, satisfying richness to open fruit tarts and marries particularly well with the fruits I've selected. I like to serve this dessert in small wedges with a cup of fine tea, such as Earl Grey.

🍷 This rich, sweet dessert is full of flavors that find their echo in a heady, fragrant muscat dessert wine, such as 1986 Muscat de Beaumes de Venise or 1987 Robert Pecota Moscato di Andrea.

—6 to 8 Servings—

1 1/4 cups all-purpose flour
Pinch of salt
5 tablespoons cold unsalted butter, cut into pieces, plus 2 tablespoons melted butter
1 egg, lightly beaten
1 package (7 ounces) marzipan, at room temperature
3/4 pound small red plums (6 to 7), halved lengthwise and pitted
1/2 pound apricots (3 to 4), halved lengthwise and pitted
1 tablespoon sugar (optional)

1. Preheat the oven to 400°. Butter a 9½-by-1-inch tart pan with a removable bottom.

2. In a medium bowl, combine the flour and salt. Add the cold butter and rub or cut it into the flour until the mixture resembles fine bread crumbs. Stir in the beaten egg and gather the dough into a smooth ball.

3. On a lightly floured surface, roll out the dough into an 11-inch circle. Fit the dough into the prepared pan without stretching. Trim the pastry level with the rim of the pan by gently rolling your pin across the top.

4. Roll the marzipan into a ball and then, on a lightly floured surface, roll it out to form a 9-inch circle. Gently press the marzipan onto the dough in the pan.

5. Cut each of the plum and apricot halves into 3 lengthwise wedges. Arrange the plum and apricot wedges in the pan, skin-side down, in alternating concentric circles. *(The tart can be prepared to this point and refrigerated, covered, for up to 12 hours before baking.)*

6. Brush the fruit with the melted butter. If the fruit is tart, sprinkle with up to 1 tablespoon sugar. Set the tart on a cookie sheet and bake in the middle of the oven until the fruit is tender and the pastry crisp and nicely browned, about 45 minutes. Let the tart cool to room temperature on a rack. Unmold onto a flat platter before serving.

—Diana Sturgis

• • •

APPLE TART WITH ALMOND CUSTARD

French housewives use Reinette apples for this tart, but in the States I suggest Golden Russet, Jonathan or Golden Delicious. The apples will caramelize faster if sautéed in a cast-iron skillet.

🍷 Apple and almond flavors pair especially well with Late-Harvest Riesling. Try a West Coast example, such as 1982 Joseph Phelps Special Select Late Harvest, which is spectacular, or the less intense 1984 Chateau Ste. Michelle Late Harvest Hahn Hill Vineyard.

—8 to 10 Servings—

4 tablespoons unsalted butter
¼ cup dark rum
2¼ pounds firm cooking apples, such as Jonathan, Golden Delicious or Golden Russet—peeled, cored and cut into 1-inch cubes
⅓ cup plus ½ cup sugar
Prebaked Butter-Crust Tart Shell (recipe follows)
½ cup crème fraîche
2 eggs
¾ cup ground almonds
Crème fraîche or whipped cream, as accompaniment

1. In a large heavy nonreactive skillet, combine the butter, rum, apples and ⅓ cup of the sugar. Cook over moderate heat, tossing, until the apples are golden brown, 10 to 15 minutes. Let cool slightly. Pour the apples into the baked tart shell.

2. Preheat the oven to 400°. In a medium bowl, stir together the crème fraîche, eggs, almonds and remaining ½ cup sugar. Pour the mixture over the apples in the tart shell.

3. Set the tart on a cookie sheet and bake for 25 to 30 minutes or until golden brown. Serve warm, with additional crème fraîche if desired.

—Lydie Marshall

• • •

PREBAKED BUTTER-CRUST TART SHELL

—Makes One 11-Inch Tart Shell—

1½ cups unbleached all-purpose flour
1½ sticks (6 ounces) cold unsalted butter, cut into small pieces
1 tablespoon sugar
⅛ teaspoon salt
3 to 4 tablespoons cold water

1. In a food processor, combine the flour, butter, sugar and salt. Process until the mixture resembles coarse meal, about 10 seconds. Add the water and process, turning the machine on and off, until the mixture resembles small peas, about 5 seconds; do not mix until it forms a ball.

2. Turn the dough out onto a lightly floured work surface and knead lightly, just until the dough holds together. Flatten the pastry into a 6-inch disk, wrap it in plastic wrap and refrigerate for at least 15 minutes.

3. On a generously floured surface, roll out the dough into a 15-inch circle. Transfer to an 11-inch tart pan and fit the pastry into the pan without stretching. Press the pastry against the fluted side of the pan and trim off any excess. Prick the bottom of the pastry, cover with plastic wrap and freeze for about 30 minutes before baking.

4. Meanwhile, preheat the oven to 400°. Remove the plastic wrap from the pie shell. Line the pastry with foil and fill it with pie weights or dried beans, making sure they are pushed well against the sides.

5. Bake for 20 minutes, or until the pastry is almost dry. Remove the foil and weights and bake for 5 to 8 minutes longer, or until the crust is lightly browned.

—Lydie Marshall

• • •

ORANGE TART

Bavarian cream, flavored with orange liqueur, forms a cool, creamy base for the orange sections that garnish this tart.

🍷 A fine young Sauternes will beautifully complement the orange and vanilla flavors of this dessert. The 1982 Château Suduiraut or a California equivalent such as the 1985 Chateau St. Jean Sémillon d'Or Select Late Harvest would be good choices.

—8 Servings—

4 egg yolks
½ cup sugar
1 envelope (¼ ounce) unflavored gelatin
1 cup warm milk
1½ tablespoons Grand Marnier
½ cup heavy cream, chilled
Sweet Tart Shell (recipe follows)
6 large navel oranges
1 tablespoon apricot preserves, strained

1. In a small heavy saucepan, whisk together the egg yolks, sugar and gelatin. Gradually whisk in the warm milk. Cook over moderately low heat, stirring constantly, until the custard thickens enough to coat the back of a spoon, about 6 minutes; do not boil. Strain into a chilled bowl set over a larger bowl of ice and water. Stir in the Grand Marnier and stir frequently until the custard is chilled and just beginning to thicken.

2. Meanwhile, in a medium bowl, beat the cream until soft peaks form. Lightly fold the cream into the custard until blended. Spread the Bavarian cream in the cooled tart shell and refrigerate.

3. Using a vegetable peeler or a sharp knife, strip the zest from 2 of the oranges. Cut the zest into fine julienne strips and measure out 3 tablespoons. Blanch the julienned zest in boiling water for 2 minutes; drain, rinse and set aside.

4. With a knife, peel all 6 oranges, cutting off all the bitter white pith. Working over a bowl, cut in between the membranes to release the sections. Squeeze the membranes to extract 2 tablespoons juice and set aside.

5. Arrange the orange sections over the Bavarian cream in concentric circles. In a small bowl, combine the apricot preserves with the reserved orange juice. Brush the orange sections with this glaze and garnish the tart with the julienned orange zest.

—André Soltner, Lutèce, New York City

• • •

SWEET TART SHELL

—Makes One 11-Inch Tart Shell—

1½ cups all-purpose flour
⅓ cup sugar
½ teaspoon salt
1 stick (4 ounces) cold unsalted butter, cut into small pieces
1 egg, lightly beaten
1 to 2 tablespoons ice water

1. In a medium bowl, mix together the flour, sugar and salt. Cut in the butter until the mixture resembles coarse meal. Stir in the egg and 1 tablespoon of the ice water and gather the dough into a smooth ball. Add the remaining ice water if the mixture seems dry. Flatten the dough into a 6-inch disk, cover with plastic wrap and refrigerate for at least 1 hour.

2. Preheat the oven to 375°. Roll out the pastry to a 13-inch circle. Without stretching, fit the pastry into an an 11-inch tart pan with a removable bottom. Trim away any excess dough. Prick the pastry all over with a fork. Cover with plastic wrap and freeze for 15 minutes.

3. Line the pastry with foil and fill with pie weights or dried beans. Bake for 30 minutes, until the sides are golden brown. Remove the pie weights and continue baking until the bottom is golden, about 5 minutes longer. Let cool completely on a rack before filling.

—André Soltner, Lutèce, New York City

• • •

BANANA WALNUT TART

I first made this dessert two years ago while planning a tart class that was to take place during the winter when the usual stone fruits and berries would not be available. Since then it has become one of my favorites. When the bananas bake between the walnut filling and the tart crust, they acquire the consistency of preserves, and their moist texture is in perfect contrast to the crumbly crust and the dense walnut filling.

—8 Servings—

Sweet Pastry Dough (recipe follows)
3 ripe bananas
1½ cups walnut pieces (about 6 ounces)
½ cup (packed) light brown sugar
4 tablespoons unsalted butter, softened to room temperature
2 eggs

3 tablespoons unbleached all-purpose flour
¼ teaspoon cinnamon
1 tablespoon dark rum

1. Preheat the oven to 350°. On a lightly floured work surface, roll the Sweet Pastry Dough into a 12- to 13-inch disk, ⅛ to ¼ inch thick. Fit the dough into a 10-inch tart pan with a removable bottom and trim the excess dough even with the edge.

2. Cut the bananas into ½-inch-thick slices. Cover the bottom of the dough with the banana slices, fitting them tightly together.

3. In a food processor, coarsely chop the walnuts. Remove ½ cup of the chopped walnuts and set aside. Add the brown sugar to the work bowl and process until the walnuts are very finely ground. Add the butter and process until mixed. Add the eggs, 1 at a time, processing only until the mixture is smooth and scraping down the sides of the bowl occasionally. Add the flour and cinnamon and process until blended.

4. Spread the walnut filling evenly over the bananas, covering as much of the surface as possible. Scatter the reserved chopped walnuts over the top.

5. Bake the tart on the bottom rack of the oven for 40 minutes, or until the pastry is baked through and the walnut filling is set and a deep golden color. Remove the tart from the oven to a rack and immediately sprinkle the rum over the top.

—Nicholas Malgieri

• • •

SWEET PASTRY DOUGH

Use this dough for any pie or tart with a raw or liquid filling. The presence of the baking powder makes the dough expand slightly during baking so that it maintains a constant contact with the hot bottom of the pan and bakes through evenly, eliminating raw and soggy bottoms.

—Makes One 10-Inch Tart Shell—

1 cup unbleached all-purpose flour
¼ cup sugar
½ teaspoon baking powder
Pinch of salt
4 tablespoons unsalted butter
1 egg, lightly beaten

In a bowl, combine the flour, sugar, baking powder and salt. Rub in the butter with your fingertips until the mixture resembles coarse meal. Stir the egg into the dough with a fork to moisten evenly. Press the dough together in the bowl and turn out onto a lightly floured surface. Knead lightly 2 or 3 times, press into a 6-inch disk and wrap in plastic wrap. Refrigerate until firm, about 1 hour.

—Nicholas Malgieri

• • •

SIX-NUT TART

Bradley Ogden of Campton Place in San Francisco takes pecan pie six steps forward.

—8 Servings—

½ cup plus 2 tablespoons blanched almonds
½ cup plus 2 tablespoons hazelnuts (filberts)
½ cup confectioners' sugar
1 stick (4 ounces) unsalted butter, softened to room temperature
⅔ cup cake flour
1 egg yolk
2 tablespoons pecan halves
2 tablespoons walnut halves
2 tablespoons unsalted macadamia nuts
2 tablespoons unsalted pistachio nuts
1 cup (packed) dark brown sugar
⅓ cup light corn syrup
3 whole eggs
1 tablespoon brandy
½ teaspoon vanilla extract
Unsweetened whipped cream, as accompaniment

1. In a food processor, combine ½ cup each of the almonds and filberts. Add the confectioners' sugar and process until the nuts are finely ground.

2. In a medium bowl, cream 4 tablespoons of the butter until light and fluffy. Stir in the flour and the ground nuts. Add the egg yolk and beat with an electric mixer on medium speed until the dough begins to form a ball, about 2 minutes. Press into a 9-inch tart pan with a removable bottom: trim off any excess dough. Cover with plastic wrap and refrigerate for at least 30 minutes.

3. Preheat the oven to 350°. In separate sections on a cookie sheet, spread out the pecans, walnuts, macadamia nuts and pistachios and the remaining 2 tablespoons each almonds and filberts. Bake until golden brown and toasted, about 12 minutes; set the nuts aside to cool. Wrap the warm filberts in a kitchen towel and rub to remove most of the dark brown skins. Mix all of the nuts together. Meanwhile, increase the oven temperature to 375°.

4. In a medium bowl, beat the remaining 4 tablespoons butter with the brown sugar and corn syrup until smooth and well blended, about 2 minutes. Beat in the whole eggs 1 at a time, then add the brandy and vanilla.

5. Spread ½ cup of the mixed toasted nuts in the bottom of the tart shell. Pour the filling over the nuts and sprinkle the remaining nuts on top.

6. Bake in the lower third of the oven for 20 minutes. Reduce the oven temperature to 350° and bake until the filling is set and the crust is crisp and golden brown, about 20 minutes longer. Let cool to room temperature before serving. Accompany with a dollop of whipped cream.

—Bradley Ogden, Campton Place, San Francisco

• • •

CARAMELIZED ALMOND TART

🍷 Rather than matching this extremely rich dessert with an equally rich wine, serve it with café filtre.

8 Servings

2½ cups whole blanched almonds
1¼ cups sugar
1 stick (4 ounces) unsalted butter, softened to room temperature
2 eggs
2 tablespoons all-purpose flour
¼ teaspoon almond extract
Dessert Tart Shell (recipe follows)
1 tablespoon corn syrup
¼ cup heavy cream

1. Preheat the oven to 350°. Place ½ cup of the almonds and ½ cup of the sugar in a food processor and process until the nuts are finely ground, about 1 minute. Add 4 tablespoons of the butter, the eggs, flour and almond extract and process until well blended, about 30 seconds. Spread the filling over the cooled Dessert Tart Shell and bake until lightly browned, about 30 minutes. Let cool.

2. Place the remaining 2 cups of almonds on a baking sheet and toast until lightly browned, 12 to 15 minutes. Coarsely chop the nuts and set aside.

3. In a heavy medium saucepan, combine the remaining ¾ cup sugar with the corn syrup and 2 tablespoons of water. Cook over moderately low heat, stirring, until the sugar dissolves, about 3 minutes. Increase the heat to moderately high and boil without stirring until golden brown, about 2 minutes. Immediately remove from the heat.

4. Using a wooden spoon, stir in the remaining 4 tablespoons butter, cream and the chopped toasted almonds. Immediately spoon the caramel nut topping over the tart and smooth the surface. (Do not refrigerate; the tart will keep at room temperature for up to 2 days.)

—Mary Risley

• • •

DESSERT TART SHELL

Makes One 9-Inch Tart Shell

1¼ cups all-purpose flour
2½ tablespoons sugar
⅛ teaspoon salt
1 stick (4 ounces) cold unsalted butter, cut into small pieces
1 egg yolk
½ teaspoon vanilla extract

1. Preheat the oven to 375°. In a food processor, place the flour, sugar, salt and butter. Process until the mixture resembles coarse meal, about 30 seconds. With the machine on, add the egg yolk and vanilla. Process, turning the machine quickly on and off, just until the pastry begins to mass together. Pat the pastry into a 6-inch disk, wrap in plastic wrap and refrigerate for at least 15 minutes.

2. On a lightly floured surface, roll out the dough to a 12-inch circle about ⅛ inch thick. Line a 9-inch tart pan with a removable bottom with the dough, cut off any excess at the rim and freeze for 15 minutes before baking.

3. Line the pastry with foil and fill with pie weights or dried beans, making sure they are pushed up well against the sides.

4. Bake for 20 minutes. Remove the foil and weights and continue baking for 5 to 8 minutes, or until the pastry is lightly browned. Let cool.

—Mary Risley

• • •

CARAMELIZED UPSIDE-DOWN PLUM TART

Beginning in mid-August, there is an abundance of plums in all French markets. My favorite variety is the mirabelle plum; it makes fabulous preserves and a wonderful liquor. When I'm in the States, I love the small Italian prune plums and use them for this recipe.

8 to 10 Servings

4 tablespoons unsalted butter
¾ cup sugar
1 pound dark Italian prune plums, halved (or quartered if large) and pitted
Pâte Brisée (recipe follows)
2 tablespoons heavy cream
1 cup crème fraîche or sour cream
1 teaspoon kirsch

1. In a 9-inch skillet with an ovenproof handle, melt the butter over moderate heat. Stir in ½ cup of the sugar. Arrange the plums, cut-side up, in concentric circles and cook until the sugar begins to caramelize, 15 to 20 minutes. Let stand until completely cool.

2. On a generously floured surface, roll the Pâte Brisée into a 12-inch circle. Drape the dough over a rolling pin and flip it over the caramelized plums. Trim off the excess dough. Roll the edges down so that the crust lies flat on top of the fruit but reaches the edges of the pan. Refrigerate, covered, for 30 minutes.

3. Preheat the oven to 425°. In a small bowl, combine the heavy cream with 1 tablespoon of the sugar. Brush this glaze over the dough. Using a fork, prick the dough in several places and bake for 20 to 25 minutes or until golden brown.

4. In a small bowl, combine the crème fraîche, kirsch and remaining 3 tablespoons sugar.

5. Immediately invert the tart onto a large platter. Serve warm or cold with the flavored crème fraîche.

—Lydie Marshall

• • •

PATE BRISEE

Unlike French housewives, we in America frequently use food processors. When making a *pâte brisée*, or buttery tart dough, don't process the flour, butter and water until it forms a ball; stop when the mixture resembles small peas. Pinch a small amount of dough between your fingers; if it holds together without any trouble, it's time to proceed to Step 2, as explained in the following recipe.

One more important note—the amount of water added to the dough will depend on the weather. The more humid it is, the less water is used and vice versa. During the summer months, I have made *pâte brisée* with only two tablespoons of water, sometimes less. Keep your flour in the freezer during the summer months; it will be easier to handle.

—Makes One 9-Inch Tart Shell—

1 cup unbleached all-purpose flour
1 stick (4 ounces) cold unsalted butter, cut into small pieces
2 tablespoons sugar
Pinch of salt
2 to 3 tablespoons cold water

1. In a food processor, combine the flour, butter, sugar and salt. Process until the mixture resembles coarse meal, about 8 seconds. Add the water and process, turning the machine on and off, until the mixture resembles small peas, about 5 seconds.

2. Turn the dough out onto a lightly floured surface and knead lightly, just until the dough holds together. Flatten the pastry into a 6-inch disk. Wrap in plastic wrap and refrigerate for at least 15 minutes or up to 3 days before using.

—Lydie Marshall

• • •

BITTERSWEET CHOCOLATE TRUFFLE TART

A dollop of whipped cream cuts the intensity of this rich, chocolatey tart.

🍷 No wine could cope with the intensity of the chocolate here, but an espresso or café filtre would provide a rich contrast to this truffle tart.

—20 Servings—

6 tablespoons unsalted butter, softened to room temperature
½ cup sugar
⅛ teaspoon salt
¾ teaspoon vanilla extract
¼ cup plus 3 tablespoons Dutch-process unsweetened cocoa powder
¾ cup all-purpose flour
10 ounces bittersweet chocolate, chopped
1¼ cups heavy cream

1. In a food processor, combine the butter, sugar and salt; process until creamy. Add the vanilla and 6 tablespoons of the cocoa. Process, scraping the bowl occasionally, until the mixture forms a smooth paste, about 1 minute. Add the flour and turn the machine on and off until just blended. Turn the dough out onto a piece of plastic wrap and press it into an 8-inch disk. Wrap and chill the dough until firm, about 40 minutes.

2. Roll out the dough between 2 sheets of plastic wrap into an 11-inch round about ⅛ inch thick. Peel off the top sheet of plastic and invert the pastry into a 9½-inch tart pan with a removable bottom. Press the pastry gently against the fluted sides of the pan. (If the dough becomes too soft, refrigerate for 5 to 10 minutes before continuing.) Peel away the plastic wrap and trim the dough even with the top of the pan. Refrigerate until firm, at least 30 minutes or overnight.

3. Preheat the oven to 375°. Prick the bottom of the tart shell with a fork. Bake for 12 to 14 minutes, or until the pastry is dry. Let cool in the pan on a rack.

4. Place the chocolate in a medium heatproof bowl. In a small saucepan, bring the cream to a simmer over moderate heat. Pour the hot cream over the chocolate and let stand for 30 seconds. Stir until the chocolate is melted and smooth. Strain the chocolate cream into the cooled tart shell and spread to form a smooth even layer. Refrigerate until chilled and set, 3 to 5 hours. As soon as the chocolate is firm, cover the tart with plastic wrap. *(The recipe can be made to this point up to 3 days in advance. Cover and refrigerate until ready to use.)*

5. Meanwhile, cut a decorative stencil from a piece of light, thin cardboard or use a doily. Center the stencil over the tart and, using a fine strainer, sift the remaining 1 tablespoon cocoa over the top. Carefully lift off the stencil; it will leave a decorative pattern on the tart.

6. For best texture and appearance, remove the truffle tart from the refrigerator about 30 minutes before serving.

—Alice Medrich

• • •

GINGERBREAD TARTLET SHELLS

I have to confess that I hate creaming butter. Either I forget to take the butter out of the refrigerator in time, or I don't feel like cleaning my electric mixer. So I was delighted to discover the method used below in *Marion Harland's Complete Cook Book*, published in 1903; adding the butter to warm molasses works just as well as creaming.

These shells are delicious with ice cream, a chocolate or fruit mousse, or with whipped cream and berries. Fill just before serving so that the shell remains crisp.

Makes 24 Tartlet Shells

1 teaspoon ground ginger
1 teaspoon cinnamon
½ teaspoon salt
¼ teaspoon freshly grated nutmeg
¼ teaspoon ground cloves
⅓ cup light unsulphured molasses
1 stick (4 ounces) unsalted butter, at room temperature
⅓ cup (packed) light brown sugar
1 egg
2 cups all-purpose flour

1. In a bowl, combine the ginger, cinnamon, salt, nutmeg and cloves.

2. In a small saucepan, heat the molasses over low heat until bubbles begin to form around the sides. Remove from the heat and stir in the butter, 1 tablespoon at a time, until completely blended.

3. Scrape the molasses into a large mixer bowl and stir in the spice mixture and brown sugar. Add the egg and beat until well blended. Add the flour in 3 batches, stirring until smooth after each addition. Pat the dough into a 6-inch disk, cover with plastic wrap and refrigerate until cold, about 2 hours. *(The dough can be refrigerated for up to 1 week or frozen for up to 1 month.)*

4. Preheat the oven to 350°. Invert twelve ½-cup muffin tins and butter the outside of the cups.

5. Roll out one-fourth of the dough ⅛ inch thick. (Keep the rest of the dough wrapped and chilled until ready to roll out.) Stamp out six 4-inch rounds. Drape the rounds over the buttered muffin cups and pleat to fit snugly. Repeat with another one-fourth of the dough.

6. Bake the tart shells for 10 minutes, until firm and golden brown. Unmold and let cool completely on a wire rack before filling. Repeat Step 5 with the remaining dough. The tartlet shells can be stored, wrapped in foil and at room temperature, for up to 2 days.

—Linda Merinoff

• • •

DESSERTS

FLOATING ISLANDS

This original interpretation of the classic *oeufs à la neige* is from Madame Pozzetto, who combined her skills with those of her Italian cook, Isola Bella. Instead of poaching the egg whites whipped with sugar, they substituted Italian meringue, a soft, creamy version made by beating egg whites with sugar syrup boiled to the soft-ball stage, which needs no further cooking.

If you don't use a candy thermometer, the best method for checking when the syrup has reached the soft-ball stage is to scoop out a bit and immediately immerse it in a bowl of cold water. Then plunge your fingers into the water and try to pinch the syrup into a small soft ball. If it dissolves, cook the syrup a little longer. If it hardens to a crackle, add more boiling water to the syrup and begin the procedure again. As soon as the syrup has reached the soft-ball stage, act quickly and begin pouring it into the half-beaten egg whites.

8 Servings

6 egg whites
1 cup plus 2 tablespoons superfine sugar
Custard Sauce (p. 257), chilled
1 tablespoon unsalted butter
½ cup chopped blanched almonds

1. In a large bowl, beat the egg whites with an electric mixer on high speed until frothy, about 1 minute.

2. In a small heavy saucepan, combine 1 cup of the sugar with 3 tablespoons of water. Bring to a boil over moderate heat and cook to the soft-ball stage (240° on a candy thermometer), about 8 minutes.

3. Gradually beat the syrup into the egg whites in a thin steady stream; continue beating until the egg whites form very stiff peaks, about 6 minutes.

4. Pour the chilled Custard Sauce into a large shallow serving bowl. Using a large spoon dipped in cold water, scoop out 8 large egg shapes from the meringue and float them in the custard sauce. Refrigerate for at least 1 hour before serving.

5. In a small skillet, melt the butter over moderate heat. Add the almonds and remaining 2 tablespoons sugar and sauté until the nuts are lightly browned, about 2 minutes. Let cool. Just before serving, sprinkle 1 tablespoon of the nuts over each meringue egg.

—Lydie Marshall

• • •

PAVLOVA

This ethereal dessert from New Zealand is composed of crunchy meringue with a soft center of whipped cream and tart fresh fruit. The meringue base can be made up to two days ahead if stored in an airtight container, but the Pavlova must be served within two hours of assembly; otherwise the meringue will lose its light crunch. To assure success, choose a day that's not humid for meringue making.

8 Servings

6 egg whites, at room temperature
¼ teaspoon cream of tartar
1⅓ cups superfine sugar
1 teaspoon lemon juice
½ cup plus 1 tablespoon confectioners' sugar, sifted
2 cups heavy cream, chilled
2 teaspoons vanilla extract
½ small pineapple—peeled, cored and cut into 1-inch chunks
2½ cups raspberries
4 ripe kiwis, peeled and sliced
Sprigs of fresh mint, for garnish

1. Preheat the oven to 250°. Draw a 9-inch circle on a sheet of parchment paper and place it on a large cookie sheet.

2. In a large mixer bowl, beat the egg whites with the cream of tartar on low speed until foamy. Increase the speed to high and beat until soft peaks form.

3. Gradually beat in the superfine sugar, 1 tablespoon at a time, beating for about 10 seconds after each addition to be sure the sugar dissolves. Beat in the lemon juice. The whites will be stiff, dense and glossy at this point.

4. Sprinkle ½ cup of the confectioners' sugar over the beaten egg whites. Using a large rubber spatula, gently fold the sugar into the whites until thoroughly blended.

5. Scoop the meringue onto the parchment paper and spread to form a 9-inch round. Hollow the center slightly to make a nest, leaving the meringue at least 1 inch thick at the base and 1½ inches high around the sides.

6. Bake the meringue in the middle of the oven for 1 hour. Reduce the oven temperature to 200° and bake for 1 hour longer. Turn off the heat and leave the meringue in the warm oven with the door closed for 1½ hours or overnight, until crisp and dry throughout. (Purists prefer an absolutely white meringue, but I like the flavor and color of a pale beige one, so don't worry if the heat colors the meringue slightly.) When the meringue is completely cool, peel off the paper. Place the meringue on a flat serving platter.

7. In a large bowl, beat the cream with the remaining 1 tablespoon confectioners' sugar and the vanilla until stiff peaks form. Spread half the cream in the meringue shell and sprinkle with half of the pineapple and raspberries. Mound the rest of the cream on top and cover with the remaining pineapple and raspberries. Overlap the kiwi slices around the inner rim of the Pavlova and garnish with the mint springs.

—Diana Sturgis

• • •

TANGERINE MOUSSE

A few tangerine slices placed on top of each mousse make an attractive garnish.

6 Servings

1 envelope (1/4 ounce) unflavored gelatin
3/4 cup frozen tangerine juice concentrate, thawed but not diluted (orange juice can be substituted)
1/2 cup sugar
Pinch of salt
1 tablespoon fresh lemon juice
2 cups heavy cream, chilled

1. Pour 1/4 cup of cold water into a small bowl. Sprinkle the gelatin over the water and let soften, about 5 minutes.

2. In a small nonreactive saucepan, combine the tangerine juice with the sugar, salt, lemon juice and softened gelatin. Simmer over moderate heat until the gelatin dissolves completely and the mixture is clear, about 3 minutes. Remove the pan from the heat and let stand until the mixture is cool and slightly thickened, about 20 minutes.

3. In a large mixer bowl, beat the heavy cream until soft peaks form.

4. In a small bowl, place 3/4 cup of the whipped cream and fold 2 tablespoons of the tangerine liquid into it; set the tangerine cream aside.

5. Fold the remaining tangerine liquid into the remaining whipped cream in the larger bowl. Divide this mousse evenly among 6 individual dessert bowls.

6. Cover the top of each with a thin layer of the reserved tangerine cream and refrigerate until chilled and set, about 1 hour. *(The mousse can be covered and chilled overnight if desired.)*

—Lee Bailey

• • •

MOLDED RICOTTA AND MASCARPONE WITH STRAWBERRIES

This dessert is particularly pretty when molded in a heart-shaped form, such as a *coeur à la crème* mold.

6 Servings

1 envelope (1/4 ounce) unflavored gelatin
1/3 cup plus 3 tablespoons orange liqueur
1/2 pound ricotta cheese, preferably fresh
1/2 pound mascarpone*
1/2 cup confectioners' sugar, sifted
1 teaspoon vanilla extract
1 tablespoon plus 1 teaspoon fresh lemon juice
Pinch of salt
1/2 cup heavy cream
1 pint strawberries, sliced
1/4 cup raspberry jam
Whole strawberries and fresh mint leaves, for garnish
****Available at Italian markets and select cheese shops***

1. In a small saucepan, combine the gelatin with 1/3 cup of the orange liqueur and let stand until softened, about 5 minutes. Set the saucepan over low heat and stir until the gelatin dissolves, 2 to 3 minutes. Set aside to cool slightly.

2. In a large bowl, beat the ricotta and mascarpone with an electric mixer. Beat in the confectioners' sugar, vanilla, 1 teaspoon of the lemon juice and the salt; then beat in the cooled gelatin mixture.

3. In another bowl, beat the cream until stiff peaks form. Fold the whipped cream into the cheese mixture and pour into a 4-cup mold or bowl lined with plastic wrap. Smooth the top and refrigerate until chilled and set, about 3 hours.

4. In a blender or food processor, combine 1/2 cup of the sliced strawberries with raspberry jam. Puree until smooth. Strain the sauce to remove the seeds and stir in the remaining 1 tablespoon lemon juice and 3 tablespoons orange liqueur. Add the remaining sliced berries.

5. Unmold the cheese dessert onto a serving plate and surround it with the strawberry sauce. Decorate with whole strawberries and mint leaves.

—Nancy Verde Barr

• • •

STRAWBERRIES POMPIDOU

This elaborate-looking cake is surprisingly simple to make.

8 Servings

4 egg whites, at room temperature
1/8 teaspoon cream of tartar
1/2 cup plus 3 tablespoons sugar
1 cup finely ground almonds
6 tablespoons unsalted butter, melted and cooled slightly

¼ teaspoon almond extract
3½ to 4 pints ripe strawberries
¾ cup heavy cream
1 cup crème fraîche
¼ cup strained apricot or strawberry preserves
2 tablespoons finely chopped unsalted pistachio nuts

1. Preheat the oven to 400°. Butter and flour the bottom of an 8-by-3-inch springform pan.

2. In a large bowl, beat the egg whites with the cream of tartar until soft peaks form. Gradually beat in ½ cup of the sugar, 1 tablespoon at a time, until stiff peaks form.

3. Using a spatula, fold in the almonds, butter and almond extract. Turn the mixture into the prepared pan and spread evenly. Bake for 20 minutes, or until browned. Let the torte cool in the pan on a rack, about 30 minutes.

4. Run a knife around the side of the torte and remove the sides of the springform pan. Run a spatula underneath the torte to free it from the pan. Wash and dry the springform pan and reassemble it. Replace the torte in the pan.

5. Choose about 10 berries of equal height. Cut them in half vertically and arrange them, pointed-ends up, with the cut sides pressed against the sides of the pan. Leave the remaining berries whole and arrange them, pointed-ends up, over the torte. (The berry tops should reach ⅛ inch below the pan rim; trim from the stem ends if necessary.)

6. In a medium bowl, whip the cream until it begins to thicken. Gradually beat in the remaining 3 tablespoons sugar and continue beating until stiff peaks form.

7. In a medium bowl, beat the crème fraîche until stiff peaks form. Fold in the sweetened whipped cream.

8. Spread the cream over the berries, filling in all the gaps and making sure the cream touches the sides of the pan between the cut berries. Smooth the top even with the rim of the pan. Cover and refrigerate until set, at least 2 hours and up to 4 hours.

9. Wrap the pan briefly in a hot wet kitchen towel and carefully remove the sides of the pan.

10. In a small saucepan, warm the preserves over low heat, stirring until melted. (If necessary, thin the glaze with 1 to 2 teaspoons of water.)

11. Brush the sides of the torte with the glaze. Press the chopped pistachios against the lower rim of the torte. Refrigerate until ready to serve.

—Alice Medrich

• • •

CHOCOLATE PATE WITH PISTACHIO SAUCE

An intense chocolate experience shaded with the sophistication of pistachio custard sauce.

10 to 12 Servings

15 ounces bittersweet chocolate, such as Tobler Extra Bittersweet, broken into pieces
1 cup heavy cream
4 tablespoons unsalted butter, cut into tablespoons
4 egg yolks
1 cup confectioners' sugar, sifted
½ cup Myers dark rum
Pistachio Sauce (p. 258)
Sprigs of fresh mint and chopped toasted peeled pistachios, for garnish

1. In a double boiler or in a medium bowl set over simmering water, combine the chocolate, cream and butter. Cook over low heat, stirring occasionally, until the chocolate is melted and the mixture is smooth, about 10 minutes. Remove from the heat.

2. One at a time, whisk the egg yolks into the chocolate until well blended. Gradually whisk in the confectioners' sugar and then the rum.

3. Line the bottom and sides of a 3-cup loaf pan with a sheet of plastic wrap. Pour the hot chocolate mixture into the pan. Let cool to room temperature, then cover and refrigerate overnight.

4. Invert the pâté onto a platter to unmold and peel away the plastic wrap. Refrigerate until ready to serve. Cut with a cold knife or a wire cheese cutter into ½-inch slices. Serve each slice with a couple of tablespoons of Pistachio Sauce and garnish with mint sprigs and chopped pistachios.

—Jimmy Schmidt, The Rattlesnake Club, Denver

• • •

CHOCOLATE FUDGE SHEBA

A brazen chocolate indulgence for sweets fanciers of all ages, from Ella Brennan of Commander's Palace in New Orleans.

12 to 16 Servings

1¼ pounds semisweet chocolate, broken into pieces
6 egg yolks
1½ sticks (6 ounces) unsalted butter, at room temperature
7 egg whites
½ cup sugar
1 cup chopped pecans
Unsweetened whipped cream or vanilla custard sauce, as accompaniment

1. Butter a 9-inch springform pan. Melt the chocolate in a double boiler over simmering water, stirring until smooth. Set aside to cool.

2. In a medium bowl over simmering water, whisk the egg yolks until warm and lighter in color, about 2 minutes. Remove from the heat and whisk until cool, about 1 minute.

3. In a large bowl, beat the butter until light and fluffy. Fold in the cooled melted chocolate and then the egg yolks.

4. In a large bowl, beat the egg whites until soft peaks begin to form. Gradually beat in the sugar, 1 tablespoon at a time, until the meringue forms stiff peaks. Fold the meringue into the chocolate mixture and pour into the buttered pan.

5. Sprinkle the chopped pecans over the top and lightly press them into the chocolate. Cover with plastic wrap and refrigerate until set, at least 3 hours. Remove the sides of the springform, cut into slices and serve with whipped cream or custard sauce.

—Commander's Palace, New Orleans

• • •

ESPRESSO BAVARIAN CREAM

This not-too-sweet ethereal dessert combines billows of coffee cream with semisweet chocolate.

2 Servings

3/4 teaspoon unflavored gelatin
2 egg yolks
1/3 cup sugar
1/2 cup milk
1 tablespoon instant espresso
1/2 cup heavy cream
1/2 teaspoon vanilla extract
1 ounce semisweet chocolate
1 teaspoon brandy

1. In a small bowl, sprinkle the gelatin over 2 tablespoons of cold water. Set aside until softened, about 5 minutes.

2. In a medium bowl, whisk the egg yolks with the sugar until pale and fluffy, about 3 minutes.

3. In a medium saucepan, bring the milk to a simmer over moderate heat. Stir in the coffee and softened gelatin until thoroughly dissolved. Slowly whisk the hot coffee mixture into the egg yolks and sugar. Set the bowl over a saucepan of simmering water and stir until the mixture thickens enough to coat the back of a spoon, 1½ to 2 minutes.

4. Strain the coffee custard into a bowl and let cool in the refrigerator, stirring from time to time. Alternatively, set the bowl over a larger bowl of ice and water and stir constantly until well chilled.

5. In another bowl, beat the cream with the vanilla until stiff peaks form. Beat ¼ cup of the whipped cream into the custard, then fold in the remaining cream until no streaks of white remain. Pour the custard into 2 long-stemmed glasses and refrigerate until set, 2 to 3 hours.

6. In a small saucepan, combine the chocolate with the brandy and 1 tablespoon of water. Stir over very low heat until the chocolate melts and the mixture is smooth. Drizzle the chocolate over the surface of the set custard in a decorative pattern. *(The recipe can be prepared up to 2 days ahead. Cover and refrigerate until 1/2 hour before serving.)*

—Bob Chambers

• • •

RICE PUDDING WITH ORANGE AND BAY

Basmati rice adds a delicious, nutty flavor to this pudding, and the whipped cream that is folded in at the last moment makes this traditional dessert uncommonly light. Serve the pudding plain or with the Blueberry-Bay Compote (p. 226).

6 Servings

1 cup basmati rice
4 bay leaves
Pinch of salt
3 cups milk
3/4 cup sugar
1 teaspoon grated orange zest
1 teaspoon vanilla extract
1/3 cup heavy cream
2 tablespoons confectioners' sugar

1. In a large saucepan, combine the rice with 2½ cups of water. Add the bay leaves and salt and bring to a boil over high heat. Reduce the heat to low, cover and cook, without removing the lid, for 20 minutes. Remove from the heat and keep covered for 10 minutes longer.

2. Stir the milk and sugar into the rice and simmer over low heat, stirring occasionally, until the mixture is thick and creamy and the rice is very soft, about 45 minutes.

3. Spoon the pudding into a bowl and stir in the orange zest and vanilla. Keep the bay leaves in the pudding and cool to room temperature, stirring occasionally. Place plastic wrap directly over the pudding and refrigerate overnight.

4. Place a stainless steel bowl and beaters in the freezer for about 10 minutes. Place the cream and confectioners' sugar in the bowl and beat until stiff peaks form. Remove the bay leaves from the pudding and fold in the whipped cream. Serve slightly chilled.

—Marcia Kiesel

• • •

KIRSCH CUSTARDS

Lindsey Shere's custards are deliciously rich. At Chez Panisse, they are served in ramekins, either warm or at room temperature, with fresh berries.

10 Servings

3 cups heavy cream
1/2 cup sugar
6 egg yolks
2 tablespoons kirsch
Fresh strawberries or raspberries, as accompaniment

1. Preheat the oven to 325°. In a medium saucepan, bring the cream and sugar just to a boil over moderately high heat. Remove from the heat and let cool slightly, about 5 minutes.

2. In a medium bowl, whisk the egg yolks just to break them up. Stirring constantly, pour in the hot sweetened cream. Stir in the kirsch.

3. Strain the custard into ten 4-ounce ramekins or custard cups. Set the ramekins in a baking pan and fill the pan with enough warm water to reach halfway up the sides of the ramekins. Cover the pan loosely with foil and bake for 25 to 30 minutes, until the custards are set around the edges but still soft in the center.

4. Using tongs, transfer the ramekins to a rack to cool. Serve the custards warm, at room temperature or chilled, with fresh berries if desired.

—Lindsey Shere, Chez Panisse, Berkeley, California

• • •

CHOCOLATE PECAN PUDDING WITH BOURBON SAUCE

Midway between a chocolate cake and a soufflé, this pudding can be served right from the oven or allowed to cool slightly. Although it sinks a bit when fully cooled, it is still delicious and moist.

6 to 8 Servings

4 ounces semisweet chocolate, chopped
1 1/2 cups pecan pieces (about 5 1/2 ounces)
1/3 cup sugar
1/4 cup dry bread crumbs
1/4 teaspoon cinnamon
1 stick (4 ounces) unsalted butter, softened to room temperature
1 tablespoon bourbon
5 eggs, separated
Pinch of salt
Bourbon Sauce (p. 257)

1. Preheat the oven to 350°. Place the chocolate in a small heatproof bowl. Add 3 tablespoons of hot water and set the bowl over a pan of hot but not simmering water. Stir with a whisk until the chocolate is melted and smooth. Remove the bowl from the water and let the chocolate cool to room temperature.

2. Coarsely chop the pecan pieces in a food processor. Remove 1/2 cup of the pecans and set aside. Add 1 tablespoon of the sugar to the remaining nuts and grind to a fine powder. Combine the finely ground pecans, bread crumbs and cinnamon in a bowl; mix well and set the mixture aside.

3. In a large mixer bowl, beat the butter with half the remaining sugar until soft and light. Beat in the cooled chocolate and then the bourbon. Add the egg yolks, 1 at a time, beating until smooth. Stir in the pecan-bread crumb mixture.

4. In a large bowl, beat the egg whites with the salt until they form very soft peaks. Gradually beat in the remaining sugar in a slow stream and continue beating until the egg whites hold soft peaks. Stir one-fourth of the beaten egg whites into the chocolate batter, then gently fold in the remaining egg whites.

5. Pour the batter into a buttered 1 1/2-quart baking dish or 8-inch square baking pan. Smooth the top. Scatter the reserved chopped pecans evenly over the surface of the batter. Place the baking dish in a larger pan and pour hot tap water into the larger pan to reach halfway up the sides of the baking dish. Bake the pudding in the middle of the oven for 30 to 35 minutes, until the pudding puffs and feels slightly firm when pressed with the palm of the hand; do not overbake.

6. To serve, spoon the warm chocolate pecan pudding onto dessert plates. Ladle 2 or 3 tablespoons of the Bourbon Sauce over or around the pudding. Pass the remaining sauce separately.

—Nicholas Malgieri

• • •

ORANGE AND HONEY BREAD PUDDING

If you like, peel and slice the oranges after using their zest to flavor the pudding. Sprinkle them with a little sugar and orange liqueur and serve them along with the pudding.

8 Servings

1 stick (4 ounces) unsalted butter
24 to 30 slices of French bread, 1 1/2 inches in diameter, cut 1/8 to 1/4 inch thick
2 cups milk
1 cup heavy cream
2/3 cup honey, preferably orange blossom
3 navel oranges
5 eggs

1. Preheat the oven to 325°. Melt the butter and let cool slightly. Dip one side of each bread slice into the butter and arrange the bread, buttered-side up, overlapping slightly in a shallow 1½-quart baking dish.

2. In a medium saucepan, combine the milk, cream and honey. Strip the colored zest from the oranges with a swivel-bladed vegetable peeler and add to the pan. Bring to a boil over moderate heat, remove from the heat and let stand for 5 minutes.

3. In a large mixing bowl, whisk the eggs until liquefied. Gradually whisk in the hot milk and cream mixture. Do not overbeat, or the custard will have a great deal of foam on the surface. Strain the custard back into the pan and skim off the foam with a large spoon. Pour the custard evenly over the bread in the dish; the bread will rise to the top.

4. Place the baking dish in a larger pan and pour warm water into the pan to reach halfway up the side of the baking dish. Bake the bread pudding for 45 minutes, or until the custard is set and the bread is an even golden brown.

—Nicholas Malgieri

• • •

INDIAN PUDDING

This sweet, dense pudding from Managing Editor Warren Picower is a traditional New England dessert. It can be made a day ahead and served slightly warm, with Brandy Butter Sauce, whipped cream or vanilla ice cream.

6 to 8 Servings

6 cups milk
1 cup yellow cornmeal
2 eggs
½ cup dark unsulphured molasses
4 tablespoons unsalted butter, at room temperature
¼ cup sugar
1½ teaspoons cinnamon
1½ teaspoons freshly grated nutmeg
½ teaspoon salt
¼ teaspoon baking powder
Brandy Butter Sauce (p. 258)

1. Preheat the oven to 300°. Butter a 1½- to 2-quart casserole.

2. In a large heavy saucepan, scald the milk over moderately high heat. In a medium bowl, combine the cornmeal, eggs, molasses, butter, sugar, cinnamon, nutmeg, salt and baking powder. Stir to blend well. Gradually whisk in all of the scalded milk. Pour the pudding mixture back into the saucepan and cook over moderate heat, stirring until it just begins to boil, about 2 minutes. Pour into the buttered casserole.

3. Set a roasting pan on the bottom shelf of the oven and fill with warm water. Place the pudding on the middle shelf and bake until set, 3½ to 4 hours. Replenish the water in the roasting pan if necessary during cooking. Serve the pudding warm. Pass the Brandy Butter Sauce separately. *(The pudding can be prepared up to 1 day ahead. Let the pudding cool, then cover and refrigerate. Reheat in a 350° oven until warmed through, about 20 minutes.)*

—Warren Picower

• • •

BEIGNETS WITH GINGER CREAM

A French housewife will always make *pâte à choux* by hand; therefore, I kept the recipe that way. Eggs are not always the same size even when they come from the same carton, so I suggest you measure the volume of eggs for this recipe.

8 to 12 Servings

½ teaspoon salt
7 tablespoons unsalted butter, cut into small pieces
⅓ cup plus 1 teaspoon granulated sugar
1 cup plus 1½ tablespoons all-purpose flour
5 eggs (1 cup)
4 cups corn oil, for deep-frying
4 ounces cream cheese, at room temperature
1 cup heavy cream
1 tablespoon minced crystallized ginger
Confectioners' sugar, for garnish
½ cup warm apricot preserves

1. In a medium saucepan, combine the salt, butter, 1 teaspoon of the granulated sugar and 1 cup plus 2 tablespoons of water. Bring just to a boil, over moderate heat. Remove from the heat. Immediately add all the flour and stir into a mass with a wooden spoon. Cook briefly over low heat until the mixture cleans the pan and forms a smooth ball.

2. Remove from the heat and stir for 30 seconds to cool slightly. Add the eggs, 1 at a time, beating well with a wooden spoon after each addition. Continue beating until the dough becomes glossy and light, 3 to 5 minutes.

3. In a medium heavy saucepan or deep-fat fryer, heat the oil to 325°. Drop the dough by teaspoonfuls, 5 to 6 at a time, into the hot oil. Fry the beignets, turning once, until puffed and golden brown, 8 to 10 minutes. Using a slotted spoon, remove the beignets, blot on paper towels and cool on a rack.

4. In a medium mixer bowl, beat the cream cheese on medium speed until light and fluffy, 1 to 2 minutes. Gradually beat in the heavy cream and the remaining ⅓ cup granulated sugar. Beat until thickened, about 2 minutes. Fold in the ginger.

5. Cut the beignets halfway through and fill them generously with the ginger cream. Sprinkle with the confectioners' sugar and serve 2 to 3 per person. Pass the preserves separately for dipping.

—Lydie Marshall

• • •

CANNOLI SICILIANI

Cindy Pawlcyn serves these chocolatey cannoli at Tra Vigne. The dough is quite soft and should be kept as cool as possible during shaping and rolling.

Makes About 20

2 cups all-purpose flour
½ cup plus 3 tablespoons unsweetened cocoa powder
1½ cups granulated sugar
4 tablespoons unsalted butter, softened to room temperature
1 cup Marsala
4 cups vegetable oil, for deep-frying
1 egg, beaten with 1 teaspoon water
1 cup heavy cream
⅔ cup plus 1 tablespoon ricotta
⅔ cup raisins, chopped
3½ ounces unsalted shelled pistachios, toasted and finely chopped
3½ ounces semisweet chocolate, finely chopped
Confectioners' sugar, for garnish

1. In a large bowl, combine the flour, cocoa powder and 6 tablespoons plus 2 teaspoons of the granulated sugar. Add the butter and Marsala and stir with a wooden spoon until a soft dough forms. Cover and refrigerate for 15 minutes. *(The recipe can be prepared to this point up to 1 day ahead.)*

2. On a well-floured surface, sprinkle one-third of the dough with flour and roll out ¼ inch thick. Stamp out 3½-inch circles and set the scraps aside. Roll the circles into oval shapes; transfer to a cookie sheet and refrigerate until ready to mold. Repeat with the remaining dough; then repeat with all the scraps.

3. In a medium saucepan, heat the oil to 350°. Wrap the ovals around cannoli forms, sealing the edges with the beaten egg wash. Fry the cannoli shells in batches for 2 minutes. Transfer to a rack to cool slightly, then remove the cannoli forms. Wrap and fry the remaining cannoli shells in the same fashion.

4. In a medium bowl, beat the cream until stiff. In another bowl, blend the ricotta with the remaining granulated sugar. Stir in the raisins, pistachios and chocolate, then fold in the whipped cream. Cover and refrigerate until ready to use.

5. Using a piping bag or a small spoon, fill the cannoli shells with the ricotta cream mixture. Just before serving, sprinkle with confectioners' sugar.

—*Cindy Pawlcyn, Tra Vigne, St. Helena, California*

• • •

CREPES FILLED WITH LEMON SOUFFLE

I remember making crêpes with my mother on Mardi Gras every year. It was a special treat because I grew up in the Forties, when eggs and butter were scarce. The best crêpes are eaten as soon as they're made, and in France they are usually served as a late-afternoon snack.

8 Servings

½ cup all-purpose flour
¾ cup plus 1 teaspoon granulated sugar
9 eggs
1 cup milk
1 tablespoon dark rum
3 to 4 tablespoons clarified butter
Pinch of salt
2 tablespoons grated lemon zest
¼ cup fresh lemon juice
3 tablespoons confectioners' sugar
⅓ cup Cointreau or framboise (optional)

1. In a large bowl, whisk together the flour and 1 teaspoon of the granulated sugar. Make a well in the center and add 3 of the eggs. Whisk the eggs and gradually mix in the flour until smooth. Stir in the milk and rum. Strain through a sieve and stir in 2 tablespoons of the clarified butter. Let the batter rest at room temperature for 30 minutes.

2. Heat 2 crêpe pans or well-seasoned 7-inch skillets over moderately high heat; brush lightly with some of the remaining clarified butter. Pour 2 to 3 tablespoons of crêpe batter into each pan and swirl the batter around to coat the bottom evenly. Cook until the crêpes are lightly browned and golden around the edges, 1 to 1½ minutes. Flip the crêpes or turn with a spatula and cook until spotted brown on the second side, 20 to 30 seconds longer. Stack the crêpes on a plate.

3. Preheat the oven to 400°. Butter 2 large ovenproof platters.

4. Separate the remaining 6 eggs. In a large bowl, preferably copper, beat the egg whites with the salt until stiff but not dry, about 2 minutes.

5. In another large bowl, beat the egg yolks with the remaining ¾ cup granulated sugar until the mixture is pale and dissolves in a ribbon when the beaters are lifted, about 5 minutes. Beat in the lemon zest and juice. Fold one-fourth of the egg whites into the lemon mixture to lighten it, then gently fold the mixture into the remaining egg whites.

6. Spoon about ¼ cup of the soufflé mixture onto one side of each crêpe; fold the other half of the crêpe over to cover the soufflé. Arrange the stuffed crêpes on the prepared platters. *(The crêpes can be refrigerated and covered for up to 1 hour before baking.)*

7. Bake the filled crêpes until the soufflé mixture is puffed and set, about 7 minutes. Dust the crêpes with the confectioners' sugar and drizzle with Cointreau or framboise, or flambé if desired.

—*Lydie Marshall*

• • •

PEAR BUTTERSCOTCH PECAN STRIPS

If you are assembling this dessert to serve right away, place a dollop of whipped cream right in the middle of the tart strips and top with a pecan half. Otherwise, top the strips with the pecans and serve the whipped cream on the side. To save yourself a step, you can leave the skin on the pears.

18 Servings

CRUST:

2 cups all-purpose flour
1/2 cup granulated sugar
1/2 cup ground pecans
2 sticks (8 ounces) cold unsalted butter, cut into small pieces
1/4 teaspoon salt

TOPPING:

18 pecan halves, for garnish
1/2 cup all-purpose flour
1/8 teaspoon salt
1 stick (4 ounces) unsalted butter, softened to room temperature
3/4 cup (packed) dark brown sugar
4 eggs, at room temperature
1/3 cup Poire Williams (pear eau-de-vie) or bourbon
1 teaspoon vanilla extract
1 1/2 cups heavy cream
4 large firm-ripe pears, preferably Bosc
1/3 cup apple jelly
1 tablespoon confectioners' sugar

1. *Prepare the crust:* Preheat the oven to 350°. Combine all of the crust ingredients in a food processor and process, turning the machine on and off, until the mixture resembles small peas. Pat the dough into a 15-by-10½-inch jelly-roll pan. Bake for 12 to 15 minutes, or until lightly browned. Let cool. Leave the oven on.

2. *Make the topping:* Spread the pecans on a baking sheet and bake for 12 minutes, or until crisp and toasted.

3. In a medium bowl, stir together the flour and salt.

4. In a large mixer bowl, beat the butter until light and fluffy. Gradually beat in the brown sugar. Add the eggs, 1 at a time, beating thoroughly after each addition. Beat in ¼ cup of the Poire Williams and the vanilla.

5. On low speed, beat in half the flour until well blended. Add ½ cup of the cream and mix thoroughly. Repeat with the remaining flour and another ½ cup of cream. Set the batter aside.

6. Peel the pears. Cut off 1 inch from the tapered end of each pear. Halve the pears lengthwise and use a melon baller to scoop out the cores. Slice the pear halves crosswise ⅛ inch thick, keeping the pear form.

7. Using a metal spatula, transfer the pears to the cooked crust and press lightly to fan them lengthwise into 3 even rows. Spread the batter evenly over the crust and the pears. Bake for 35 to 40 minutes, until the batter is puffed and golden brown. The pears will show through. Let cool completely. *(The recipe can be prepared to this point up to 1 day ahead. Cover and refrigerate. Let return to room temperature before serving.)*

8. In a small saucepan, melt the apple jelly over moderately low heat. Remove from the heat and stir in 1 tablespoon of the Poire Williams. Brush over the top of the tart. Using a sharp knife, cut the tart into 3 even lengthwise strips, then cut each strip crosswise into 6 strips. Top each piece with a toasted pecan half.

9. In a bowl, beat the remaining ½ cup cream and 1 teaspoon Poire Williams with the confectioners' sugar until stiff. Serve alongside the pear tart strips or dolloped on top.

—Mimi Ruth Brodeur

• • •

CHOCOLATE TRIFLE

Here is a variation of my favorite messy dessert.

8 Servings

4 cups plus 2 tablespoons heavy cream, chilled
1 cup milk
4 ounces semisweet chocolate, grated
5 eggs
1/2 cup plus 2 tablespoons sugar
1 teaspoon cornstarch
1 teaspoon vanilla extract
3 ounces white chocolate, grated
Chocolate Loaf Cake (recipe follows)
2/3 cup strawberry jam
1/4 cup brandy
1/3 cup dry sherry
1/3 cup slivered almonds
Fresh strawberries or grated semisweet chocolate, for garnish

1. In a heavy medium saucepan, combine 2 cups of the cream with the milk. Bring just to a boil over moderate heat. Remove from the heat and stir in the semisweet chocolate until melted.

2. In a medium mixer bowl, beat the eggs until foamy. Beat in ½ cup of the sugar and the cornstarch until thoroughly mixed, about 1 minute. Gradually stir the chocolate cream into the eggs until well blended. Pour into a heavy medium saucepan and cook, stirring constantly, until thick and creamy, about 10 minutes; do not let boil. Remove from the heat and stir in the vanilla. Cover the chocolate custard with plastic wrap and let cool to room temperature.

3. In a small heavy saucepan, combine 2 tablespoons of the heavy cream with the remaining 2 tablespoons sugar. Cook over moderately low heat, stirring until dissolved. Remove from the heat and stir in the white chocolate until melted. Set aside to cool at room temperature.

4. In a large mixer bowl, beat the remaining 2 cups cream until soft peaks form. Fold in the cooled white chocolate mixture.

5. Trim the crusts from the Chocolate Loaf Cake; cut in half lengthwise and then into ½-inch-thick slices. Line the bottom of a 4-quart glass serving bowl with half of the slices, trimming if necessary. Spread half the jam over the cake slices in the bowl.

6. In a small bowl, mix the brandy and sherry. Pour half over the cake and sprinkle with half of the almonds.

7. Using a rubber spatula, pour half the semisweet chocolate custard over the first layer of cake in the bowl. Arrange the remaining slices of cake on top and spread with the remaining ⅓ cup jam. Sprinkle the remaining liquor and almonds over the jam and cover with the last of the semisweet chocolate custard. Top with the white chocolate whipped cream and cover with plastic wrap. Refrigerate the trifle for at least several hours, or overnight, before serving. Decorate the top with fresh strawberries or grated semisweet chocolate if desired.

—Lee Bailey

• • •

CHOCOLATE LOAF CAKE

—Makes a 7½-Inch Loaf Cake—

4 tablespoons unsalted butter, softened to room temperature
½ cup sugar
2 ounces semisweet chocolate, melted
½ teaspoon vanilla extract
2 eggs
1 cup all-purpose flour
1 teaspoon baking powder

1. Preheat the oven to 325°. Butter a 7½-by-3½-inch loaf pan.

2. In a large mixer bowl, beat together the butter and sugar until light and fluffy, about 5 minutes. Add the melted chocolate and vanilla and mix until well blended. Beat in the eggs 1 at a time, beating well after each addition.

3. In a medium bowl, sift together the flour and baking powder. Fold half of the flour mixture into the batter and mix well. Repeat with the remaining flour. Turn into the prepared pan and spread evenly.

4. Bake the cake for 1 hour, or until a cake tester inserted in the center comes out clean. Let stand for about 5 minutes before inverting onto a rack to cool.

—Lee Bailey

• • •

CHARLOTTE WITH SUMMER FRUIT

The name of this dessert, *charlotte aux fruits d'été* in French, comes from the mold in which it is prepared. It is a versatile baking dish, which can also be used to make soufflés. This recipe is very simple, but you must remember to boil down the syrup to the perfect consistency, as it holds the fruit together and prevents the dessert from collapsing.

Most pastry shops in France sell delicious ladyfingers; thus, few French cooks make their own. In case they are difficult to find, however, I am including a simple sponge cake recipe.

🍷 A fruity sparkling wine, such as the Korbel Rosé from California or the grapey, delicate 1985 Moscato d'Asti (Vietti) from Italy will complement the berries, while the effervescence will contrast nicely with the dessert's soft texture.

—10 Servings—

2 pints (6½ cups) fresh blueberries or about 2 pounds frozen unsweetened blueberries
¾ cup sugar
2 pints (6½ cups) raspberries
Sponge Cake (p. 167) or 12 to 16 storebought ladyfingers
Fresh raspberries, for garnish
1 pint plain yogurt, sweetened to taste

1. In a large nonreactive skillet, stir together the blueberries, sugar and 1½ cups of water. Bring to a boil over moderate heat and cook until the berries begin to swell, 1 to 2 minutes. Using a slotted spoon, transfer the berries to a fine-mesh strainer set over a medium bowl.

2. Add 3 cups of the raspberries to the simmering liquid and poach for 30 seconds. Transfer the raspberries to the strainer with the blueberries, pressing gently to extract some of their juice. Transfer the berries to a bowl. Repeat with the remaining 3 cups raspberries. Add the drained berry juice to the poaching liquid in the skillet.

3. Boil the poaching liquid over moderately high heat until slightly thickened and reduced to 1¼ cups, about 15 minutes. Set aside to cool or chill over a bowl of ice. *(The recipe can be made to this point up to 3 days ahead. Cover and refrigerate the berries and syrup separately until ready to use.)*

4. If using the Sponge Cake, cut it into 12 "ladyfingers" 4 inches long and 1½ inches wide. If using ladyfingers, trim the ends so that they will fit tightly in the mold.

5. Butter a 6-cup charlotte mold or glass soufflé dish. Line the bottom with waxed paper; butter the paper. Line the sides of the pan with 10 of the ladyfingers, pressing them upright around the sides. Reserve the remaining ladyfingers.

6. Pack half the poached berries into the ladyfinger-lined mold and pour ½ cup of the cooled syrup over them. Add the remaining poached fruit and ½ cup of the

syrup. Cover the top of the fruit with the 2 reserved ladyfingers and pour the remaining 1/4 cup syrup over the charlotte. Cover and refrigerate overnight.

7. Unmold the charlotte and garnish with fresh raspberries. Serve with the sweetened yogurt.

—Lydie Marshall

• • •

COFFEE ALMOND BAKED ALASKA

This is actually a double meringue version of the classic dessert. A nutty meringue replaces the cake on the bottom and provides a crisp contrast to the billowy meringue on the top. The meringue topping can be spread free-form or, for a more delicate presentation, piped with a bag fitted with a large star tip.

20 Servings

10 egg whites
1/4 teaspoon cream of tartar
2 cups superfine sugar
1/4 cup confectioners' sugar, sifted
3/4 cup finely ground blanched almonds
3 pints coffee ice cream
1/4 cup sliced blanched almonds

1. Preheat the oven to 200°. Butter and flour a large heavy cookie sheet and mark out a 12-by-7-inch oval.

2. In a mixer bowl, beat 4 of the egg whites until foamy. Add 1/8 teaspoon of the cream of tartar and beat until soft peaks form. Gradually beat in 3/4 cup of the superfine sugar and continue beating until stiff peaks form. Fold in the confectioners' sugar and the ground almonds until well blended.

3. Using a spatula, evenly spread the almond meringue within the outline of the oval. Bake for 2 hours, or until the meringue is completely dry. Let cool completely. Set the meringue on a large ovenproof platter.

4. Let the ice cream soften slightly. Spread the ice cream over the baked meringue in an even layer. Cover with plastic wrap and freeze for 1 hour, or overnight.

5. In a large mixer bowl, beat the remaining 6 egg whites with the remaining 1/8 teaspoon cream of tartar until soft peaks form. Gradually beat in the remaining 1 1/4 cups superfine sugar, 2 tablespoons at a time, beating until stiff. Spoon the meringue onto the ice cream and smooth to completely cover the ice cream and the baked meringue base evenly. Sprinkle the sliced almonds over the top. Freeze the assembled Alaska, uncovered, until the meringue is hard, then cover with plastic wrap. *(The recipe can be prepared to this point up to 1 month in advance.)*

6. Preheat the broiler. Just before serving, remove the plastic and broil the Alaska 4 inches from the heat until golden brown, about 50 seconds.

—Mimi Ruth Brodeur

• • •

APRICOT EARL GREY ICE CREAM

The bergamot flavoring of Earl Grey tea gives a floral accent to this rich, dense ice cream.

Makes About 1 Quart

1 cup dried apricots (about 6 ounces)
1/3 cup plus 2 tablespoons sugar
1 1/2 cups milk
2 tablespoons Earl Grey tea leaves
1 1/2 cups heavy cream
Pinch of salt
4 egg yolks
1 tablespoon apricot brandy or orange liqueur

1. In a small heavy saucepan, combine the apricots, 2 tablespoons of the sugar and 2/3 cup of water. Bring to a boil over moderate heat. Reduce the heat to moderately low and simmer, uncovered, until the apricots are tender, 10 to 12 minutes.

2. Transfer the apricots and any remaining liquid to a food processor and puree until smooth, scraping down the sides of the bowl once or twice. Set aside.

3. In a heavy medium saucepan, combine the milk and tea leaves. Warm over low heat until the milk is hot. Remove from the heat and let steep for 5 minutes. Strain the milk through a fine-meshed strainer.

4. Return the milk to the saucepan and add the heavy cream, remaining 1/3 cup sugar and salt. Cook over moderate heat, stirring frequently with a wooden spoon, until the sugar is completely dissolved and the mixture is hot, 5 to 6 minutes. Remove from the heat.

5. In a medium bowl, whisk the egg yolks until blended. Gradually whisk in one-third of the hot cream in a thin stream, then whisk the mixture back into the remaining cream in the saucepan.

6. Cook over moderately low heat, stirring constantly, until the custard lightly coats the back of the spoon, 5 to 7 minutes; do not let boil.

7. Immediately remove from the heat and strain the custard into a medium bowl. Set the bowl in a larger bowl of ice and water. Let the custard cool to room temperature, stirring occasionally. Whisk in the reserved apricot puree and the brandy until blended. Cover and refrigerate until cold, at least 6 hours or overnight.

8. Pour the custard into an ice cream maker and freeze according to the manufacturer's instructions.

—Ceri E. Hadda

• • •

LAVENDER ICE CREAM

Just about everyone who has ever eaten at Les Bories, just outside Gordes, comes back raving about the lavender ice cream. The secret to this flower-infused treat is a homemade mix of ground lavender and sugar. The lavender powder can be made in advance and frozen for up to three weeks in an airtight container.

8 Servings

1¼ cups plus 2 tablespoons sugar
1 tablespoon plus 2 teaspoons lavender flowers*
3 cups milk
3 tablespoons crème fraîche or heavy cream
1 vanilla bean, split lengthwise
6 egg yolks
****Available at specialty food and spice shops***

1. In a small heavy saucepan, combine 2 tablespoons of the sugar, 1½ tablespoons of the lavender and 1½ teaspoons of water. Cook over moderate heat, stirring constantly, until the sugar dissolves and the mixture forms a dry mass, 2 to 3 minutes. Transfer to a plate to cool, then grind to a fine powder in a spice grinder; set aside.

2. In a large heavy saucepan, combine the milk, crème fraîche, vanilla bean and remaining 1¼ cups sugar and ½ teaspoon lavender. Cook over moderate heat, stirring frequently, until the sugar dissolves and the mixture is hot, about 8 minutes. Remove from the heat, cover and let steep for 15 minutes. Strain the milk through a fine-mesh sieve and return to the saucepan.

3. In a large bowl, whisk the egg yolks until blended. Gradually whisk in one-third of the warmed milk mixture in a thin stream, then whisk the mixture back into the remaining milk in the saucepan. Stir in the reserved lavender powder.

4. Cook over moderately low heat, stirring constantly, until the custard lightly coats the back of a spoon, 5 to 7 minutes. Do not let boil.

5. Immediately remove from the heat and strain the custard into a medium bowl. Set the bowl in a larger bowl of ice and water and let cool to room temperature, stirring occasionally. Cover and refrigerate until cold, at least 2 hours or overnight.

6. Pour the custard into an ice cream maker and freeze according to the manufacturer's instructions.

—*Gabriel Rousselet, Les Bories, Gordes, France*

• • •

CRANBERRY-RASPBERRY SORBET

Beautifully colored and packing a lively flavor wallop, the raspberry taste predominates in this refreshing sorbet from Test Kitchen Director Diana Sturgis.

8 Servings

1 bag (12 ounces) fresh or frozen cranberries
1½ cups sugar
1 bag (12 ounces) frozen unsweetened raspberries

1. Put the cranberries in a medium nonreactive saucepan, add 1 cup of water and bring to a boil. Reduce the heat and simmer until the berries burst, about 5 minutes.

2. Stir in the sugar and then the raspberries and cook, stirring until the sugar dissolves, about 1 minute. Pour into a bowl, stir in ½ cup of cold water and refrigerate until chilled. *(The recipe can be prepared ahead to this point up to 1 day ahead.*

3. Strain the fruit mixture in batches, pressing hard on the solids with a wooden spoon. Pour into an ice cream maker and freeze according to the manufacturer's instructions. Transfer the sorbet to a chilled container and freeze, covered, for 2 hours, or for up to 3 days before serving.

—*Diana Sturgis*

• • •

APPLE SORBET

Refreshing and delicious, this apple sorbet gets a zesty flavor from the addition of apple brandy. However, it's just as good without it. Serve it garnished with thin slices of apple.

6 Servings

4 tart apples, preferably Granny Smith—peeled, cored and quartered
⅔ cup sugar
2 teaspoons fresh lemon juice
Calvados or other apple brandy (optional)

1. In a medium nonreactive saucepan, combine the apples, sugar, lemon juice and 1 cup of water. Bring to a simmer over moderate heat. Cook until the apples are tender, about 10 minutes.

2. Transfer the apple mixture to a food processor and puree. Let cool.

3. Pour into an ice cream maker and freeze according to the manufacturer's instructions.

4. Serve in dessert glasses. To add a powerful, pungent flavor to the sorbet, make an indentation with the back of a spoon on the top of each sorbet and fill with 1 tablespoon apple brandy.

—*Lee Bailey*

• • •

Gratin of Fresh Fruit (p. 243).

Above, Pecan Cake with Chocolate Cream (p. 175). Near right, Orange and Honey Bread Pudding (p. 214). Far right, Cranberry-Raspberry Sorbet (p. 220).

FRUIT SMOOTHY POPS

Make these frozen fruit pops in your favorite funny paper cups.

Makes 8

2 cups chilled assorted fruit, such as bananas, figs and strawberries
1½ cups milk
1 cup plain yogurt
⅓ cup honey or maple syrup
1 teaspoon vanilla extract
½ teaspoon freshly grated nutmeg

1. Place all ingredients in a blender. Blend until thick and smooth, about 30 seconds.

2. Pour equal amounts of the fruit mixture into eight 4-ounce paper cups and place in the freezer until partially frozen, about 1 hour. Insert a popsicle stick into the center of each pop and freeze until firm. Tear off the paper and serve, or cover with plastic wrap and store in the freezer for up to 3 days.

—Marcia Kiesel

• • •

POMEGRANATE ICE

A wonderfully tart, slightly bitter taste and stunning color make this refreshing ice the perfect interlude for a sumptuous meal. If you like, the ice can be sprinkled with a few jewel-like whole pomegranate seeds before serving.

2 to 4 Servings

6 medium pomegranates
7 tablespoons sugar
¼ cup fresh lemon juice

1. Halve the pomegranates crosswise. Using a manual citrus reamer, squeeze the juice from the pomegranates; strain the juice through a fine-mesh sieve.

2. In a medium nonreactive saucepan, combine the sugar with ¼ cup of water and bring to a boil over moderate heat. Cook just until the sugar dissolves, then remove from the heat and let cool completely.

3. Stir the pomegranate juice and lemon juice into the cooled syrup. Pour the syrup into an ice cream maker and freeze according to the manufacturer's instructions. *(The ice will keep in the freezer for up to 2 days.)* Serve the ice in well-chilled stemmed glasses.

—Bob Chambers

• • •

MELON SORBET

Makes About 5 Cups

1 cup sugar
1 medium honeydew melon
1 teaspoon fresh lemon juice

1. In a saucepan, bring the sugar and 1⅓ cups of water to a boil over high heat. Cook, stirring, until the sugar dissolves, about 1 minute. Remove from the heat and let cool to room temperature.

2. Cut the melon in half, discard the seeds and scoop out the flesh. Place the melon in a food processor and puree until smooth, about 2 minutes.

3. In a medium bowl, stir together the sugar syrup, melon puree and lemon juice. Pour into an ice cream maker and freeze according to the manufacturer's instructions.

—Jim Dodge, Stanford Court,
San Francisco

• • •

EXOTIC FRUITS IN PHYLLO PURSES

Gary Hansen, of New York City's Prunelle restaurant, uses the heady La Grande Passion liqueur in the sauce for these purses, but you can substitute two tablespoons of Armagnac, Cognac or rum and add an additional tablespoon of poaching liquid.

6 Servings

½ cup plus 1 tablespoon granulated sugar
2 mangoes, peeled and cut into ½-inch dice
2 kiwis, peeled and cut into ½-inch dice
5 passion fruits
6 tablespoons unsalted butter
2 teaspoons light brown sugar
1 large banana, halved lengthwise and sliced ¼ inch thick
2 tablespoons dark rum
3 tablespoons passion fruit liqueur
9 sheets of phyllo dough
1 tablespoon minced fresh chervil or ½ teaspoon minced fresh tarragon

1. In a nonreactive saucepan, combine 1 cup of water with ½ cup of the granulated sugar and bring to a boil over moderately high heat, stirring to dissolve the sugar. Add half the mango and the kiwis and poach for 30 seconds. Remove from the heat. Using a slotted spoon, transfer the fruit to a plate to drain. Reserve the poaching liquid.

2. Cut the tops off 2 of the passion fruits. In a medium skillet, melt 1 tablespoon of the butter over moderate heat. Add the brown sugar and cook, stirring, until melted, about 30 seconds. Scoop the passion fruit pulp into the skillet and add the poached fruit, banana and rum. Toss until well blended. Spoon the fruit into a wide dish and let cool.

Espresso Crème Brûlée (p. 242).

3. Cut the tops off the remaining 3 passion fruits, scoop out the pulp and press through a sieve set over a small nonreactive saucepan. Add the remaining mango, passion fruit liqueur, 2 tablespoons of the butter and ¼ cup of the reserved poaching liquid. Bring to a boil and cook over moderately high heat until the mango is very soft. Transfer the sauce to a food processor or blender and puree until smooth. *(The sauce can be prepared up to 1 day ahead. Cover and refrigerate overnight.)*

4. Preheat the oven to 350°. In a small saucepan, melt the remaining 3 tablespoons butter; let cool.

5. Cut the phyllo sheets in half crosswise. Brush 1 of the half sheets lightly with melted butter. Place another half on top, at right angles, and brush lightly with butter. Place a third half, again at right angles, on top of the phyllo; brush lightly with butter. Place one-sixth of the fruit mixture on the stack of buttered phyllo. Gather up the edges of the dough and twist into a pouch. Roll down the top edges of the phyllo around the topknot to secure the packet. Gently brush with butter and sprinkle with ½ teaspoon of the remaining granulated sugar. Set the "purse" on a nonstick baking sheet. Repeat with the remaining phyllo dough, butter, fruit and granulated sugar.

6. Bake the pouches for 12 minutes, or until the pastry is golden. Transfer to 6 individual serving plates.

7. Meanwhile, reheat the sauce; stir in the chervil. Spoon the sauce evenly around the pouches and serve.

—Gary Hansen, Prunelle, New York City

• • •

PEPPERMINT PEARS

Should it appeal to you, add a few pink peppercorns to the syrup. The pears will then have a little extra bite.

6 Servings

2 cups sugar
6 medium, firm-ripe Bosc pears—peeled, halved and cored
6 sprigs of fresh mint or ¼ teaspoon peppermint extract, or more to taste
¾ cup crème fraîche
Grated semisweet chocolate, for garnish

1. In a heavy medium saucepan, combine the sugar with 2 cups of water. Stir over moderate heat until the sugar dissolves, 1 to 2 minutes. Increase the heat to high and bring to a boil.

2. Add the pears and mint and simmer, uncovered, turning the pears once or twice, 10 to 15 minutes, or until tender but firm. Remove from the heat and let the pears cool in the liquid.

3. Place the pears in a glass bowl and pour the syrup over them. Cover and refrigerate until chilled, about 1 hour. *(The recipe can be prepared to this point up to 1 day ahead.)*

4. Garnish each pear with a spoonful of crème fraîche and grated chocolate.

—Lee Bailey

• • •

BLUEBERRY-BAY COMPOTE

Serve this compote with ice cream, pound cake or rice pudding.

Makes About 3 Cups

2 cups fresh orange juice
½ cup sugar
2 bay leaves, broken in half
1 pint fresh blueberries

In a medium nonreactive saucepan, combine the orange juice, sugar and bay leaves. Bring to a boil over high heat until reduced to about ⅔ cup, about 15 minutes. Stir in the blueberries and remove from the heat. Serve warm or cold.

—Marcia Kiesel

• • •

WINTRY FRUIT SALAD

Here's a contemporary finish to a rich meal—especially appealing to the weight conscious. For heartier appetites, serve the salad with Lemon-Cardamom Pound Cake (p. 167) or Pear Butterscotch Pecan Strips (p. 217).

16 Servings

3 kiwis—peeled, quartered and sliced ¼ inch thick
2 apples—peeled, quartered, cored and sliced ¼ inch thick
1 firm-ripe pear—peeled, quartered, cored and sliced ¼ inch thick
1 cantaloupe—halved, seeded and scooped into little balls with a melon baller
1 honeydew melon—halved, seeded and scooped into little balls with a melon baller
1 papaya—peeled, halved, seeded and cut into 2-by-¼-inch strips
1 pint fresh raspberries or strawberries

¼ cup sugar
3 tablespoons fresh lemon juice

In a large glass bowl, combine all the fruit. Sprinkle on the sugar and lemon juice and toss gently. Cover with plastic wrap and refrigerate for 2 hours, or overnight, before serving.

—Mimi Ruth Brodeur

• • •

HONEYDEW IN JALAPENO SYRUP WITH MELON SORBET

Here is a perfect example of how the unlikely but refreshing pairing of sweet and cold with spicy hot can expand the boundaries of what we consider dessert.

8 Servings

2 cups sugar
2 medium serrano or jalapeño chiles—seeded and minced
1 honeydew melon (about 4 pounds), cut into 1½-inch pieces
2 teaspoons grated lime zest
3 tablespoons fresh lime juice
Melon Sorbet (p. 225)
1 lime, thinly sliced

1. In a medium saucepan, bring 3 cups of water and the sugar to a boil over high heat and cook, stirring, until the sugar dissolves, about 2 minutes. Remove the syrup from the heat and add the minced chiles. Let cool to room temperature; refrigerate until well chilled.

2. Meanwhile, place the melon in a large bowl, add the lime zest and juice and toss. Cover and chill for at least 3 hours.

3. Pour the chilled syrup over the cold melon and divide the mixture among 8 dessert dishes. Place a scoop of Melon Sorbet on one side of each bowl and garnish with the lime slices.

—Jim Dodge, Stanford Court, San Francisco

• • •

AMBROSIA CRUMBLE

An especially good dessert for a lazy weekend lunch, this is a cross between the classic fruit salad called ambrosia and a baked fruit crisp.

6 Servings

1½ cups shredded sweetened coconut
1 cup all-purpose flour
1 cup granulated sugar
½ cup (packed) brown sugar
1 stick (4 ounces) unsalted butter, softened to room temperature
½ large ripe pineapple, cut into 1-inch cubes
3 large navel oranges, peeled and sectioned
3 ripe bananas, cut into ½-inch slices
2 tablespoons fresh lemon juice
1 pint vanilla ice cream

1. Preheat the oven to 350°. Generously butter a shallow, 3-quart baking dish. In a medium bowl, combine 1 cup of the coconut, the flour, ¾ cup of the granulated sugar and all the brown sugar. Using your hands, pinch the butter into the flour mixture to form coarse crumbs.

2. In another medium bowl, toss together the pineapple, oranges and bananas with the remaining ½ cup coconut, ¼ cup sugar and the lemon juice. Place the fruit in the baking dish and sprinkle the topping evenly over all.

3. Bake for 45 minutes, or until the top is golden brown. Serve with a scoop of vanilla ice cream.

—Lee Bailey

• • •

CHINESE APPLE PEAR COMPOTE WITH CANDIED GINGER

Serve this compote of Chinese apple pears with vanilla ice cream.

🍷 The striking combination of sweet and spicy flavors in this dessert needs an equally striking wine to bridge the varied tastes. A well chilled glass of scented, intensely flavored Muscat Beaumes-de-Venise, such as the 1985 Paul Jaboulet Ainé, would be perfect.

4 Servings

½ cup plus 2 tablespoons sugar
1 vanilla bean, split lengthwise
2 pounds Chinese apple pears or firm pears—peeled, cored and sliced
1 tablespoon fresh lemon juice
3 tablespoons unsalted butter, cut into small pieces
2 tablespoons finely chopped candied ginger
1 pint vanilla ice cream (optional)

1. Put 2 tablespoons of the sugar in a small bowl. Scrape the seeds of the vanilla bean into the sugar. Stir to mix. Set the vanilla sugar aside.

2. In a large skillet, bring the vanilla pod, the remaining ½ cup sugar and 1 cup of water to a boil over moderately high heat, stirring to dissolve the sugar. Boil until the syrup is reduced by one-third, about 5 minutes.

3. Add the apple pears, vanilla sugar and lemon juice and simmer until just tender, about 5 minutes. Stir in the butter and candied ginger. Serve warm or let cool completely. *(The recipe can be prepared ahead to this point and refrigerated overnight.)*

4. Serve the apple pears with a few spoonfuls of the syrup and a scoop of vanilla ice cream on the side if desired.

—Ken Hom

• • •

MAPLE-POACHED PINEAPPLE WITH WHITE CHOCOLATE

Maple syrup creates a beautiful, crystallized coating on the fruit. The maple, pineapple and white chocolate flavors are a perfect match.

Makes About 20 Wedges

¼ cup maple syrup
3 tablespoons dark rum
1 medium pineapple—peeled, quartered lengthwise, cored and cut into twenty 2-inch wedges
3 ounces white chocolate

1. In a medium nonreactive saucepan, combine the maple syrup and rum. Bring to a boil over moderately high heat. Add half the pineapple wedges and cook for 2 minutes. Turn and continue cooking until the pineapple is tender, 2 to 3 minutes longer. Using a slotted spoon, transfer the pineapple to a baking sheet, spacing the pieces ½ inch apart. Let cool. Repeat with the remaining pineapple.

2. Place the pineapple in the freezer until firm, about 20 minutes.

3. Put the white chocolate in a small stainless steel bowl and heat over a pan of simmering water, stirring occasionally, until melted. Remove the chocolate from the water and stir to cool slightly.

4. Dip half of each pineapple wedge into the melted white chocolate; allow any excess chocolate to drip off. Arrange the pineapple on a baking sheet lined with waxed paper. Freeze until solid, about 30 minutes. Cover with plastic wrap and freeze for up to 2 weeks.

—Marcia Kiesel

• • •

HAZELNUT CREAM-FILLED FIGS

Fresh figs are made even more sensual when filled with this voluptuous cream. This recipe transforms figs into an irresistible frozen sweet. Serve these bonbons at a lavish summer party.

Makes 12

⅓ cup plus 1 tablespoon heavy cream
2 teaspoons confectioners' sugar
1½ tablespoons hazelnut paste,* at room temperature
Pinch of cinnamon
1½ ounces semisweet chocolate
12 small ripe green figs
****Available at specialty food shops***

1. In a chilled medium stainless steel bowl, whip ⅓ cup of the heavy cream and the sugar until stiff peaks form.

2. Place the hazelnut paste in a small bowl and stir in the remaining 1 tablespoon heavy cream until smooth. Fold the hazelnut paste and the cinnamon into the whipped cream. Place the mixture in a pastry bag fitted with a #4 star tip and refrigerate, or cover the bowl with plastic wrap and refrigerate until ready to use.

3. Put the chocolate in a small stainless steel bowl. Set over a pan of simmering water. Heat, stirring occasionally, until melted. Remove from the water and cover to keep warm.

4. Cut about one-third off the top of each fig. Using a small spoon, scoop out enough of the fruit to make a ½-inch indentation.

5. Dip each fig, cut-side down, into the melted chocolate to create a ring around the top. Arrange the figs on a baking sheet lined with waxed paper to set.

6. Pipe or spoon equal amounts of hazelnut cream into each fig. Freeze until hard, about 30 minutes. Cover with plastic wrap and freeze for up to 2 weeks. Serve frozen or partially thawed.

—Marcia Kiesel

• • •

PECAN BRITTLE

I like to break this brittle into small chunks (you can do this in a food processor) and sprinkle over individual portions of vanilla or coffee ice cream.

Makes 1¼ Pounds

2 cups pecans, broken into small pieces
1 cup sugar
1 cup light corn syrup
1 tablespoon baking soda, sifted

1. Butter a large baking sheet; set aside. In a large saucepan, combine the pecans, sugar and corn syrup. Bring to a boil over moderate heat, stirring constantly. Continue to boil without stirring until the syrup reaches the hard-crack stage (300° on a candy thermometer), about 15 minutes.

2. Immediately remove from the heat and quickly stir in the baking soda (the caramel mixture will start to foam). Pour the brittle onto the buttered baking sheet and let stand until cool enough to handle.

3. With a spatula, stretch the candy out to fill the sheet, making it as thin as possible. Let cool completely until hard; then break into small pieces. (The brittle can be stored in an airtight container for up to 1 month.)

—Lee Bailey

• • •

LOW-CALORIE DISHES

OYSTERS AU GRATIN

These oysters could certainly be served by themselves, but they're even better paired with Corn Bread-Stuffed Artichokes (p. 231). Together they weigh in at 355 calories per serving.

4 Servings
——160 Calories per Serving——

32 oysters—shucked, 32 shell halves scrubbed and dried and ½ cup liquor reserved
1 cup milk
1 garlic clove, minced
¼ teaspoon freshly grated nutmeg
¼ cup all-purpose flour
½ teaspoon hot pepper sauce
2 tablespoons freshly grated Parmesan cheese (½ ounce)
4 small limes, cut into wedges, for garnish

1. In a large heavy skillet, bring ¼ inch of water to a simmer over moderate heat. Add the oysters in 2 or 3 batches and poach until the edges just begin to curl, about 1 minute. Remove with a skimmer or slotted spoon; drain on paper towels.

2. Preheat the broiler. In a medium saucepan, combine the milk, the reserved oyster liquor, garlic and nutmeg. Hold a sieve over the pan and add the flour to the sieve. Gently tap the sieve and gradually whisk the flour into the liquid. Set over moderate heat and bring to a boil. Boil, whisking constantly, for 3 minutes. Remove from the heat and stir in the hot pepper sauce. Set the sauce aside.

3. Return the oysters to their half-shells and place on 2 baking sheets that will fit under the broiler (or do in 2 batches). Coat each oyster with about 2 teaspoons of the sauce and a generous pinch of the Parmesan cheese. Broil the oysters about 4 inches from the heat until the sauce is bubbly and speckled brown, 2 to 3 minutes. Serve hot, with lime wedges on the side.

—Jim Fobel

• • •

CRAYFISH RAGOUT

The crayfish stock, crayfish and vegetables can be prepared a day in advance, making it possible to assemble the ragout at the last minute.

🍷 This richly satisfying dish needs a wine with enveloping flavor and depth of character. A round, fruity California Chardonnay, such as 1985 Gundlach-Bundschu or 1985 Domaine Laurier, is just the ticket. A single four-ounce glass will enhance the elegance of the menu at a cost of only about 100 calories.

4 Servings
——248 Calories per Serving——

1 large carrot, chopped (½ cup)
1 large onion, chopped (1 cup)
1 leek (white and tender green), chopped (¾ cup)
1 sprig of fresh thyme or ½ teaspoon dried
1 bay leaf
3 sprigs of parsley
2 cups dry white wine
1¼ teaspoons salt
1 large red bell pepper
1 large yellow bell pepper
½ pound asparagus, trimmed and cut into ½-inch pieces
5 pounds live crayfish or 1¼ pounds medium shrimp (see Note)
1 teaspoon olive oil
4 large shallots, minced (½ cup)
Small pinch of saffron threads
¾ cup drained and chopped canned Italian peeled tomatoes
¼ cup heavy cream
½ teaspoon freshly ground black pepper
2 tablespoons minced fresh chives, chervil or parsley

1. In a large saucepan, combine the carrot, onion, leek, thyme, bay leaf, parsley, white wine, salt and 8 cups of water. Bring to a boil over high heat. Reduce the heat to low and simmer the court bouillon for 30 minutes.

2. Meanwhile, roast the red and yellow bell peppers directly over a gas flame or under the broiler as close to the heat as possible, turning, until charred all over. Place the peppers in a bag to steam for 10 minutes. Peel the peppers and remove the cores, seeds and membranes. Cut the peppers into ½-inch dice.

3. In a medium saucepan of boiling salted water, cook the asparagus for 2 minutes. Drain and rinse under cold running water; drain well and set aside.

A SLIMMING AND SATISFYING MEAL

Although the recipes in this menu from Sally Schneider require a bit of work, the results are well worth the effort and most of this can be prepared a day in advance. 624 Calories per Person/Serves 4.

Crayfish Ragout (p. 230)

Spiced Onion Pan Bread (p. 239)

Greens with Orange Dressing (p. 241)

Grapefruit Cassis Sorbet (p. 244)

4. Return the court bouillon to a boil over high heat. Add one-fourth of the crayfish and cook 5 minutes; remove the crayfish with a slotted spoon and transfer to a large bowl. Return the liquid to a boil and repeat with the remaining crayfish in 3 more batches. Set the crayfish aside to cool. Boil the court bouillon over high heat until reduced to 4 cups, about 10 minutes. Cover to keep warm.

5. Remove the crayfish shells by twisting the tails from the heads and breaking off the end flippers. Using small kitchen scissors, cut down the middle of the inside tail shell. Grasp the sides of the tail shell between the index finger and thumb of each hand and break away from the meat. Place the tail meat in a bowl and cover with plastic wrap. Reserve the shells.

6. In a food processor, grind the shells in 2 batches. Return all the ground shells to the bowl of the food processor and add 1 cup of the hot court bouillon. Process until the mixture becomes reddish in color, about 3 minutes. Scrape the mixture into the remaining court bouillon and simmer over low heat for 20 minutes. Strain through a fine sieve (lined with cheesecloth if necessary), pressing down on the shells with the back of a wooden spoon to extract all the liquid. Discard the shells and vegetables.

7. In a medium saucepan, combine the olive oil and 2 teaspoons of water. Add the shallots and cook, covered, until soft and translucent, about 5 minutes.

8. Add the saffron and tomatoes and cook, stirring 1 minute. Stir in the crayfish stock and cream and bring to a boil over high heat. Reduce the heat to low and add the crayfish tails, red and yellow bell peppers and asparagus. Cook until heated through, about 3 minutes. Season with the black pepper. Divide the ragout among 4 warm soup bowls. Garnish each serving with the minced fresh herbs.

NOTE: If live crayfish are not available, substitute 1¼ pounds medium shrimp and use only 5 cups of water for the court bouillon. In Step 4, cook the shrimp in one batch until opaque, about 5 minutes. Peel and devein the shrimp and grind the shells in one batch for about 2 minutes. Cut the cooked shrimp into bite-size pieces and add to the ragout in Step 7.

—Sally Schneider

• • •

CORN BREAD-STUFFED ARTICHOKES WITH OYSTERS AU GRATIN

Oysters on the half shell are lightly coated with a creamy sauce and sprinkled with Parmesan cheese before broiling. Tasso—the spicy smoked ham from New Orleans—flavors a moist corn bread stuffing for artichokes.

🍷 Artichokes have a tendency to alter the taste of wine, but the oysters here are the dominant flavor. A crisp California Fumé Blanc would stand up to the dish best; try the 1986 Robert Mondavi or Dry Creek.

4 Servings
—355 Calories per Serving—

¼ cup yellow cornmeal
¼ cup all-purpose flour
1 teaspoon sugar
1 teaspoon baking powder
Pinch of salt
1 egg white
¼ cup milk
1 teaspoon vegetable oil
4 medium artichokes (about 10 ounces each)
½ lemon
1 teaspoon unsalted butter
⅓ cup finely chopped onion
⅓ cup finely chopped green bell pepper
⅓ cup finely chopped celery
⅓ cup minced tasso* or Black Forest ham (2 ounces)
⅓ cup chicken stock or canned broth
1 teaspoon Worcestershire sauce
Oysters au Gratin (p. 230)
****Available at some specialty food shops and by mail order***

1. Preheat the oven to 400°. Lightly coat a 6- to 7-inch ovenproof skillet, preferably cast iron, with nonstick vegetable spray, or oil very lightly.

2. In a medium bowl, stir together the cornmeal, flour, sugar, baking powder and salt. In another bowl, whisk together the egg white, milk and vegetable oil. Pour the liquid all at once over the dry ingredients and stir just until blended.

3. Turn the batter into the prepared skillet and bake until a tester inserted in the center comes out clean, about 15 minutes. Turn out and let cool on a rack. Crumble the corn bread and set aside.

4. Meanwhile, trim the artichokes: Cut off the stems and about 1 inch of the tops. Rub with the cut lemon. With scissors, snip off the prickly points on the leaves and pull off any tough outer leaves. Drop into a large saucepan of water, add the lemon half, cover and bring to a boil. Boil, partially covered, until barely tender, about 15 minutes. Drain the artichokes upside down.

5. Melt the butter in a medium skillet over moderate heat. Add the onion, bell pepper and celery. Sauté until softened, 3 to 5 minutes. Add the ham and cook for 1 minute. Remove from the heat and stir in the crumbled corn bread, chicken broth and Worcestershire sauce.

6. Spread the leaves of each artichoke and with a small spoon, scoop out the fuzzy chokes. Spoon about ¼ cup of the corn bread stuffing into the center of each artichoke; spoon the rest between the 2 outer rows of leaves. *(The recipe can be prepared ahead to this point. Wrap and* *refrigerate the stuffed artichokes. Let return to room temperature before baking.)*

7. Preheat the oven to 375°. Place the artichokes in an 8-inch-square baking pan and cover with aluminum foil. Bake for 10 to 15 minutes. Remove the foil and bake until the artichokes are tender, about 10 minutes longer.

8. Serve each stuffed artichoke in the center of a large plate, surrounded by 8 Oysters au Gratin.

—Jim Fobel

• • •

BROILED MARINATED CHICKEN WITH VEGETABLES

The wonderful, slightly charred flavor of grilled vegetables is achieved in the broiler with little fuss or mess. The flavors improve if the vegetables are cooked several hours ahead, leaving just the marinated chicken to be broiled at dinnertime. The chicken should marinate for at least 12 hours.

🍷 A mild-flavored fruity wine, such as 1987 J. Pedroncelli or Grand Cru Chenin Blanc, would set off the tart yet mild flavors of the chicken.

4 Servings

289 Calories per Serving

5 large garlic cloves, unpeeled
½ teaspoon salt
1 teaspoon freshly ground black pepper
½ teaspoon oregano
½ teaspoon ground cumin
⅛ teaspoon ground cloves
2 tablespoons fresh lime juice
4 small skinless, boneless chicken breast halves (4 ounces each)
2 medium green bell peppers (6 ounces each)
4 medium zucchini (6 ounces each), halved lengthwise
4 small eggplants (4 ounces each), halved lengthwise
4 small onions (2 ounces each), halved crosswise, plus ½ cup finely chopped onion
4 small plum tomatoes (3 ounces each), halved lengthwise
1 tablespoon vegetable oil
2 teaspoons all-purpose flour
1 cup chicken stock or canned broth
¼ cup dry white wine
¼ cup chopped parsley

1. Place the garlic cloves on a heavy griddle or in a cast-iron skillet over moderate heat and toast, turning frequently, until spotted dark brown on the outside and soft inside, 15 to 20 minutes. Let cool slightly. Peel and chop on a cutting board. Add the salt and work into a paste.

2. Scrape the garlic paste into a small bowl and stir in the black pepper, oregano, cumin and cloves. Gradually stir in the lime juice. Spread this seasoned paste all over the chicken breast halves, wrap tightly and refrigerate for 12 to 24 hours.

3. Roast the green peppers directly over a gas flame or under the broiler as close to the heat as possible, turning, until charred all over. Place in a bag and let steam for 5 minutes. Peel the peppers under gently running warm water. Remove the cores and seeds; cut the peppers into ½-inch strips.

4. Preheat the broiler. Deeply score the cut sides of the zucchini and the eggplants in diagonal lines about ½ inch apart. Working in 2 batches, if necessary, arrange the zucchini, eggplants, halved onions and tomatoes in a single layer on a foil-lined broiler pan. Brush the zucchini, eggplants, onions and tomatoes with 2 teaspoons of the oil. Broil about 4 inches from the heat until the vegetables are slightly blackened on top and soft and tender inside, 5 to 7 minutes. Remove, cover with foil and set aside.

5. Let the chicken return to room temperature before broiling. Remove the chicken from the marinade; reserve the marinade for the sauce. Broil the chicken on a foil-lined broiler pan until speckled dark brown, about 3 minutes on top. Turn and broil until just cooked through, 1 to 2 minutes longer. Wrap in foil to keep warm and pour any drippings into the reserved marinade.

6. Put the remaining 1 teaspoon vegetable oil in a small heavy skillet, preferably nonstick. Add the chopped onion and sauté over moderate heat until lightly colored, about 3 minutes. Add the flour and cook, stirring, for 1 minute. Whisk in the reserved marinade, the chicken stock and the wine. Bring to a boil, whisking, until thickened slightly. Simmer, stirring frequently, until reduced to 1 cup, about 5 minutes. Remove from the heat and stir in the parsley. Season with salt to taste.

7. To serve, thinly slice the chicken breasts across the grain and fan in the center of each dinner plate; divide the vegetables among the plates and drizzle the sauce over the chicken and vegetables. Serve warm or at room temperature.

—Jim Fobel

• • •

DEVILED BLUEFISH WITH CORN AND TOMATO SALSA

🍷 The assertiveness of the fish and the spicy salsa would be best matched by the attractive bitter hoppiness of a fine lager beer, such as Harp or Carlsberg.

6 Servings

236 Calories per Serving

¼ cup grainy Dijon-style mustard
2 teaspoons extra-virgin olive oil
¼ cup chopped fresh basil
½ teaspoon freshly ground black pepper
¼ teaspoon cayenne pepper
2 pounds bluefish fillets, 1 inch thick
1 tablespoon vegetable oil

½ teaspoon salt
Fresh Corn and Tomato Salsa (recipe follows)

1. In a medium bowl, stir together the mustard, olive oil, basil, black pepper and cayenne until well blended. Spread the mixture over the fish. Cover and set aside at room temperature for 1 hour.

2. Light a charcoal grill or preheat the broiler. Brush the grill rack or broiler pan with the vegetable oil and cook the fish about 4 inches from the heat, turning once, until opaque throughout, 3 to 5 minutes on each side.

3. Arrange the fillets on a serving platter and season with the salt. Spoon the Fresh Corn and Tomato Salsa around the fish and serve.

—Phillip Stephen Schulz

• • •

FRESH CORN AND TOMATO SALSA

Makes About 3½ Cups

1 medium ear of fresh corn
1 large tomato—peeled, seeded and finely diced
1 small cucumber—peeled, seeded and finely diced
1 small celery rib, finely diced
1 small onion, finely chopped
1 large garlic clove, minced
1 jalapeño pepper—seeded and minced
3 tablespoons fresh lime juice
½ teaspoon ground cumin
½ teaspoon salt
3 tablespoons chopped fresh coriander

1. Bring a saucepan of salted water to a boil over high heat. Add the corn and cook until tender, 2 to 4 minutes. Drain and rinse under cold running water; drain. Scrape the kernels from the cob.

2. In a medium bowl, stir together the corn, tomato, cucumber, celery, onion, garlic, jalapeño pepper, lime juice, cumin, salt and coriander until well blended. Cover and refrigerate until ready to serve.

—Phillip Stephen Schulz

• • •

SHRIMP AND SCALLION PANCAKES WITH CHINESE BLACK BEAN SAUCE

Tender, juicy shrimp, crunchy vegetables and tasty Chinese black bean sauce turn scallion pancakes into a main course. Serve with an assortment of freshly steamed vegetables, such as broccoli florets, carrot slices and julienned red pepper, sprinkled with soy sauce and lemon juice. Allow four ounces of steamed vegetables per person (about 35 calories) and ½ cup cooked rice (112 calories), for a sumptuous Chinese dinner at only about 300 calories.

🍷 The spiciness and bite of this dish are best contrasted with a round, tart, fruity white, such as 1987 Freemark Abbey or 1986 Covey Run Johannisberg Riesling.

4 Servings
155 Calories per Serving

About ⅓ cup shredded fresh ginger
2 whole eggs
1 egg white
1 teaspoon Oriental sesame oil
½ teaspoon minced garlic
½ teaspoon salt
¼ teaspoon freshly ground pepper
½ pound shelled and deveined shrimp, cut into ½-inch pieces
1 cup thinly sliced scallions
1 cup fresh bean sprouts, coarsely chopped
½ cup diced (¼-inch) celery
½ cup diced (¼-inch) mushrooms (about 2 ounces)
1½ teaspoons vegetable oil
Chinese Black Bean Sauce (recipe and calories follow)

1. Put the ginger in a double layer of cheesecloth and squeeze over a bowl to wring out 1 tablespoon ginger juice.

2. Add the whole eggs, egg white, sesame oil, garlic, salt and pepper. Blend well. Stir in the shrimp, scallions, bean sprouts, celery and mushrooms.

3. Heat a large nonstick skillet over moderately high heat. Brush with ½ teaspoon of the vegetable oil. Using a ¼-cup measure, ladle in 4 pancakes and spread out the vegetables slightly to distribute evenly. Reduce the heat to moderate and cook until lightly browned on the bottom, 1 to 2 minutes. Turn and cook until lightly browned on the second side, about 1 minute longer. Transfer to a warm platter and cover with foil to keep warm. Wipe the skillet clean with a paper towel and repeat twice, using ½ teaspoon oil for each batch. Pour the warm Chinese Black Bean Sauce over the pancakes and serve.

—Jim Fobel

• • •

CHINESE BLACK BEAN SAUCE

Makes About 1¼ Cups
32 Calories per ¼ Cup

1 tablespoon cornstarch
1 cup beef stock or canned broth
1 tablespoon dry sherry
1 tablespoon soy sauce
1 teaspoon distilled white vinegar
1 teaspoon sugar
1 tablespoon Chinese salted black beans
1 teaspoon Oriental sesame oil

In a small heavy saucepan, combine the cornstarch and broth; stir until smooth. Stir in the sherry, soy sauce, vinegar and sugar. Bring just to a boil over moderate heat, stirring constantly, until thickened and translucent, about 2 minutes. Remove from the heat and stir in the black beans and sesame oil, pressing against the beans with a fork to mash slightly. Serve warm.

—Jim Fobel

• • •

GRILLED TUNA WITH ANCHO CHILE GUACAMOLE

🍷 Tuna is one of the few fish rich enough to match with a red. The use of grilling and the spicy accompaniments point to one that can be served cool, such as 1985 Carneros Creek or Alexander Valley Vineyards Pinot Noir.

4 Servings

358 Calories per Serving

4 tuna steaks, 1 inch thick (about ½ pound each)
¼ cup fresh lemon juice
½ cup extra-virgin olive oil
1 small garlic clove, minced
⅛ teaspoon crumbled oregano
½ teaspoon finely grated lemon zest
¼ teaspoon salt
¼ teaspoon freshly ground pepper
Ancho Chile Guacamole (recipe follows)

1. Place the tuna steaks in a shallow glass or ceramic dish. In a small bowl, combine the lemon juice, olive oil, garlic, oregano, lemon zest, salt and pepper. Pour the marinade over the fish. Cover and let stand for 30 to 45 minutes.

2. Meanwhile, light a charcoal grill or preheat the broiler. Brush the grill rack or broiler pan lightly with vegetable oil and cook the fish steaks about 4 inches from the heat, turning once and basting occasionally with the marinade, until opaque throughout, 3 to 5 minutes on each side. Serve with the Ancho Chile Guacamole.

—Phillip Stephen Schulz

• • •

ANCHO CHILE GUACAMOLE

Although this was designed to go with grilled tuna (at left), it would make a lovely dish all by itself.

Makes 1¾ Cups

117 Calories per ¼ Cup

1 ancho chile, stemmed and seeded
2 tablespoons minced yellow onion
1 small jalapeño pepper, seeded and minced
1 tablespoon minced fresh coriander
½ teaspoon salt
2 medium avocados, preferably Hass
¼ cup chopped, seeded tomato
2 tablespoons minced red onion
1 tablespoon extra-virgin olive oil
2 tablespoons fresh lime juice

1. Put the chile in a small saucepan and add enough cold water to barely cover. Bring to a boil, reduce the heat to low and simmer until tender, 15 to 20 minutes. Drain, pat dry and finely chop.

2. In a medium bowl, combine the yellow onion, jalapeño, 1½ teaspoons of the coriander and the salt. Using the back of a spoon, mash the mixture together until a fairly smooth paste forms.

3. Cut the avocados in half lengthwise; remove the pits and reserve. Scoop out the flesh and mash the avocados into the onion/pepper paste until smooth. Stir in the tomato, reserved chopped ancho chile, red onion, olive oil and remaining 1½ teaspoons coriander.

4. Transfer the mixture to a bowl, press the reserved avocado pits into the top and sprinkle with 1 tablespoon of the lime juice. Cover and refrigerate, until ready to serve. Just before serving, remove the avocado pits and stir in the remaining 1 tablespoon lime juice.

—Phillip Stephen Schulz

• • •

SAUTEED CODFISH CAKES

Golden, crisp fried fish cakes on a diet? Yes, when you follow this streamlined recipe. The cod cakes are hearty and satisfying, especially when accompanied with Low-Cal Coleslaw (p. 240).

🍷 The rustic, hearty flavors of this dish—not to mention the tartness of the coleslaw—call for a direct-flavored white, such as 1986 Bollini Pinot Grigio or 1985 Beringer Dry French Colombard.

4 Servings

328 Calories per Serving

1 pound fresh cod fillets, skinned
1 large baking potato (½ pound), peeled and cut into 1-inch chunks
1 whole egg
1 egg white
¼ cup milk
1 tablespoon fresh lemon juice
1 tablespoon vegetable oil
1 cup finely chopped onion
1 garlic clove, minced
3 tablespoons minced fresh dill
½ teaspoon salt
¼ teaspoon freshly ground pepper
½ teaspoon grated lemon zest
1 teaspoon Worcestershire sauce
¼ teaspoon hot pepper sauce
½ cup thinly sliced scallions
¾ cup finely crushed saltine crackers (about 32 crackers)
2 teaspoons unsalted butter
1 tablespoon plus 1 teaspoon chopped parsley
Lemon wedges, for garnish

1. Place the cod fillets in a steamer and steam, covered, over moderate heat until the fillets are opaque throughout and the edges flake easily with a fork, about 6 minutes. Let cool, then flake the fish into small pieces.

2. Put the potato chunks in a small saucepan and cover with cold water. Bring to a boil over moderately high heat.

Cook until tender, 10 to 12 minutes; drain well. Transfer the potato to a medium bowl and mash with a fork until smooth. Stir in the whole egg, egg white, milk and lemon juice.

3. In a small skillet, preferably nonstick, heat 1 teaspoon of the oil. Add the onion and sauté over moderate heat until softened, 3 to 5 minutes. Add the garlic and cook for 1 minute longer. Remove from the heat and let cool slightly.

4. Stir the sautéed onion, dill, salt, pepper, lemon zest, Worcestershire sauce, hot sauce, scallions, flaked cod and half of the cracker crumbs into the potato mixture; blend well. Cover and refrigerate until firm, about 1 hour. *(The codfish mixture can be prepared up to 1 day in advance.)*

5. Place 3 tablespoons of the remaining cracker crumbs on a sheet of waxed paper. Divide the fish mixture in half. Using a ¼-cup measure, scoop out 6 codfish cakes and drop them onto the cracker crumbs; turn to coat both sides with crumbs as you shape into 2½-inch cakes. Repeat with the remaining 3 tablespoons crumbs and cod mixture to make 6 more fish cakes.

6. In a large heavy skillet, melt 1 teaspoon of the butter in 1½ teaspoons of the vegetable oil over moderately high heat. Add half the codfish cakes, reduce the heat to moderate and fry until crusty and golden brown on the bottom, 8 to 10 minutes. Turn and cook until golden on the second side, about 5 minutes longer. Repeat with the remaining oil, butter and codfish cakes. Serve 3 per person. Sprinkle each serving with 1 teaspoon of the parsley and serve with a lemon wedge.

—Jim Fobel

• • •

MANGO-TINGED SCALLOP-AND-SHRIMP KEBABS

When buying the scallops and shrimp, tell the fishmonger they are to be skewered, so he will not give you any broken specimens. If you use wooden skewers, soak them in water for at least two hours before assembling the kebabs.

🍷 This mild, slightly sweet dish would best be set off by a simple, straightforward white, such as Trefethen Eshcol White or 1986 Tyrrell's Long Flat White.

4 Servings

——263 Calories per Serving——

1 large ripe mango—peeled and cut into 1-inch chunks
2 tablespoons extra-virgin olive oil
2½ tablespoons fresh lime juice
¼ teaspoon salt
⅛ teaspoon freshly ground white pepper
¾ pound sea scallops
½ pound large shrimp, shelled and deveined
24 snow peas (about 2 ounces)
1 tablespoon vegetable oil

1. In a food processor or blender, puree the mango until smooth, about 40 seconds. Add the olive oil and lime juice and process until well blended. Season with the salt and white pepper.

2. In a medium bowl, combine the scallops and ¼ cup of the mango sauce. In a small bowl, combine ¼ cup of the remaining mango sauce and the shrimp. Let the seafood marinate at room temperature for 1 hour.

3. Bring a medium saucepan of salted water to a boil over high heat. Add the snow peas and cook until crisp-tender, about 30 seconds. Drain and rinse under cold running water; drain well.

4. Light a charcoal grill or preheat the broiler. Remove the seafood from the marinade. Thread the scallops, alternating with the shrimp and snow peas, on 4 metal skewers.

5. Brush the grill rack or broiler pan lightly with the vegetable oil and cook the kebabs about 4 inches from the heat, turning, until the scallops and shrimp are opaque throughout, about 1½ minutes on each side. Serve the remaining mango sauce on the side.

—Phillip Stephen Schulz

• • •

GRILLED GINGERED SWORDFISH

Mako shark makes the perfect stand-in for swordfish, but grouper and mahimahi can also be used.

4 Servings

——304 Calories per Serving——

4 swordfish steaks, 1 inch thick (about ½ pound each)
⅔ cup soy sauce
¼ cup dry sherry
1 small carrot, minced
1 garlic clove, minced
1 tablespoon minced red bell pepper
1½ teaspoons minced fresh ginger
2 small scallions, finely chopped
1 teaspoon grated lemon zest
2 tablespoons extra-virgin olive oil

1. Place the swordfish steaks in a shallow glass or ceramic dish.

2. In a small bowl, combine the soy sauce, sherry, carrot, garlic, red pepper, ginger, scallions and lemon zest. Pour the marinade over the fish steaks. Cover and set aside at room temperature for 1 hour. Meanwhile, light a charcoal grill or preheat the broiler.

3. Remove the fish from the marinade, pat dry and brush with the olive oil. Brush the grill rack or broiler pan lightly with vegetable oil and cook the fish steaks about 4 inches from the heat, turning once and basting occasionally with the remaining marinade, until the fish is opaque throughout, 4 to 5 minutes on each side.

—Phillip Stephen Schulz

• • •

BEEF ENCHILADA PIE

This has great south-of-the-border flavor with only a small portion of the usual calories. The corn tortillas are layered with beef, corn, green chiles and cheese to make a light but filling entrée, which is also good reheated the next day. If you can afford the extra calories, serve with Spanish Rice Timbales (p. 238) for a fiesta that still slides in at under 400 calories.

4 Servings
280 Calories per Serving

6 ounces extra-lean ground beef
1 garlic clove, minced
1/2 teaspoon oregano
1/2 teaspoon ground cumin
1/4 teaspoon salt
1/8 teaspoon freshly ground pepper
1/3 cup corn kernels—fresh, frozen or canned
1/3 cup sliced scallions
2 tablespoons chopped fresh coriander
1 cup chicken stock or canned broth
1 tablespoon all-purpose flour
1 can (4 ounces) diced or chopped mild green chiles, drained
4 ounces corn tortillas (4 to 6), 6 inches in diameter
2 teaspoons vegetable oil
1/2 cup (2 ounces) shredded Longhorn or mild Cheddar cheese
1/4 teaspoon paprika
Sprigs of fresh coriander, for garnish

1. Preheat the oven to 450°. Crumble the ground beef into a heavy medium skillet. Add the garlic, oregano, 1/4 teaspoon of the cumin, the salt and the pepper. Cook, stirring, until the meat is no longer pink, about 3 minutes. Drain off any fat.

2. Reserve 2 tablespoons of the corn kernels for garnish; add the remainder to the beef. Remove from the heat and stir in the scallions and coriander.

3. Pour the stock into a small heavy saucepan. Place the flour in a sieve over the pan. Gently tap the sieve and gradually whisk the flour into the stock. Stir in the remaining 1/4 teaspoon cumin. Cook over moderate heat, whisking constantly, until the sauce boils and thickens. Reduce the heat to moderately low. Add the chiles and simmer, stirring, for 2 minutes. Remove the sauce from the heat.

4. Lightly brush both sides of the tortillas with the oil. Place a heavy medium skillet or griddle, preferably nonstick, over moderate heat. Working quickly, cook the tortillas, one at a time, turning once or twice until softened, 1 to 2 minutes. Stack them on a cutting board and cut into 6 wedges each.

5. Arrange half of the tortilla wedges in an 8-inch-square baking pan and top with all of the meat filling. Spoon half of the sauce and half of the cheese over the meat. Layer the remaining tortilla wedges over the cheese, followed by the remaining sauce and cheese. Sprinkle the top with the paprika and the reserved 2 tablespoons corn.

6. Bake until hot and lightly browned, about 20 minutes. Let stand for 5 to 10 minutes before serving. Garnish with the coriander sprigs.

—Jim Fobel

• • •

VEGETARIAN CHILI

Rich, tasty and nutritious too, this chili is terra-cotta color, accented with a topping of Cheddar cheese, sliced scallions and sour cream. Make the chili a day before you want to serve it. It improves upon standing.

For chopping vegetables in this quantity, I strongly recommend using a food processor.

8 Servings
342 Calories per Serving

8 ounces (1/2 package) dried small red beans, rinsed and picked over or 3 cups drained and rinsed canned red beans
1 tablespoon vegetable oil
3 medium onions (about 1 pound), chopped
3 large celery ribs, cut into 1/4-inch dice
1/4 cup minced garlic
3 large carrots, finely chopped (2 cups)
2 cups (packed) finely chopped cabbage (about 1/2 pound)
1/2 pound mushrooms, finely chopped (2 cups)
2 medium red bell peppers (8 ounces total), finely chopped (2 cups)
2 medium green bell peppers (8 ounces total), finely chopped (2 cups)
1/3 cup chili powder (1 1/2 ounces)
1 tablespoon unsweetened cocoa powder
1 tablespoon sugar
1 tablespoon cumin seeds
1 tablespoon plus 1/4 teaspoon oregano
2 teaspoons fennel seeds
1 teaspoon thyme
1/2 teaspoon cayenne pepper
1/2 teaspoon cinnamon
1 tablespoon salt
1/2 teaspoon freshly ground black pepper

1 can (28 ounces) Italian peeled tomatoes, with their liquid
2 tablespoons soy sauce
2 tablespoons dry sherry
1 teaspoon hot pepper sauce
¾ cup sour cream
1½ cups sliced scallions (about 4 scallions)
¼ pound Cheddar cheese, shredded

1. Put the beans in a medium bowl and add enough water to cover by 3 inches. Let soak overnight; drain. Alternatively, place the beans in a medium saucepan and add enough cold water to cover by 2 inches. Bring to a boil and cook for 1 minute. Remove from the heat, cover and let stand for 1 hour; drain.

2. Place the beans in a medium saucepan, add enough cold water to cover by 3 inches and bring to a boil over high heat. Reduce the heat and simmer until tender, about 1 hour; drain.

3. In a large flameproof casserole, heat the oil over moderate heat. Add the onions and celery and sauté until the onions are softened and translucent, 6 to 8 minutes. Add the garlic and cook for 1 minute longer.

4. Add the carrots, cabbage and mushrooms to the casserole and cook, stirring occasionally, until the vegetables are tender, about 10 minutes. Add the red and green peppers and cook until softened, 5 to 8 minutes.

5. Stir in the chili powder, cocoa, sugar, cumin seeds, 1 tablespoon of the oregano, the fennel seeds, thyme, cayenne, cinnamon, salt and ¼ teaspoon of the black pepper. Stir in the tomatoes and their liquid; break the tomatoes up with a spoon. Add the beans (see Note) and 4 cups of water. Simmer over low heat, stirring occasionally, until thick and rich tasting, about 2 hours. Remove from the heat and let cool to room temperature. Cover and refrigerate overnight.

6. Reheat the chili over low heat. Add the reserved ¼ teaspoon each oregano and black pepper. Remove from the heat and stir in the soy sauce, sherry and hot sauce. Serve the chili hot in 1½-cup portions, topped with 1 heaping tablespoon sour cream, 3 tablespoons sliced scallions and 2 tablespoons shredded Cheddar cheese.

NOTE: If using canned beans, add when the chili is removed from the heat.

—Jim Fobel

• • •

LIGHT AND LUSCIOUS BUFFET

This easygoing menu for an outdoor gathering from Bob Chambers is filled with a selection of dishes with light, fresh, true flavors. The sauces and dressings don't weigh down the ingredients or mask tastes; they feature fruits, yogurt and vinaigrette instead of cream, butter and mayonnaise. Serves 12.

Salmon Salad with Fennel and Radish Vinaigrette (p. 238)

Herbed Veal Roast Stuffed with Sweet Peppers (p. 237)

Summer Fresh Fruit Chutney (p. 244)

Indian Cucumber Salad with Yogurt and Pistachios (p. 241)

Green Bean and Tomato Salad with Basil-Shallot Vinaigrette (p. 240)

Orzo Salad with Carrots and Parsley (p. 240)

Seeded Breadsticks (p. 239)

🍷 Gewürztraminer and Chianti Classico

Poached Peaches in Red Wine and Raspberry Sauce (p. 243)

Hazelnut Bran Biscotti (p. 242)

HERBED VEAL ROAST STUFFED WITH SWEET PEPPERS

Roasted peppers, thyme and Worcestershire sauce flavor this cold roast shoulder of veal. The meat can be cooked one day ahead and refrigerated. It is easiest to slice when cold, and the flavors are at their best at room temperature.

12 Servings
339 Calories per Serving

4½-pound boned and butterflied veal shoulder
¼ cup Worcestershire sauce
1 tablespoon fresh thyme or 1 teaspoon dried
1 teaspoon crushed hot pepper
½ teaspoon coarsely cracked black pepper
2 large yellow bell peppers
2 large red bell peppers
1 cup fresh bread crumbs
2 tablespoons olive oil

1. In a large nonreactive baking dish, lay the veal out flat and brush with half of the Worcestershire sauce. Sprinkle with half of the thyme, hot pepper and cracked black pepper. Turn the meat over and repeat with the remaining Worcestershire sauce and seasonings. Cover with plastic wrap and let marinate in the refrigerator for 2 to 3 hours, or overnight.

2. Roast the yellow and red bell peppers directly over a gas flame or under the broiler as close to the heat as possible, turning, until charred all over. Place the peppers in a bag and let steam for 10 minutes. Peel the peppers and discard the cores, seeds and ribs. Cut the peppers into 1½-inch-thick strips.

3. When you are ready to cook the veal, remove it from the baking dish and place on a work surface, skin-side down. Evenly distribute ½ cup of the bread crumbs over the meat. Arrange alternating strips of the yellow and red peppers in a single layer over the bread crumbs and sprinkle with the remaining ½ cup bread crumbs. Carefully roll up the veal to form a neat package. Tie the roast securely with kitchen string.

4. Preheat the oven to 450°. In a large heavy ovenproof skillet, preferably cast-iron, heat the olive oil until it just begins to smoke. Add the veal and place in the oven. Roast the meat, turning every 10 minutes, until evenly browned all over, about 40 minutes.

5. Reduce the oven temperature to 350°. Continue to cook for another 40 to 50 minutes, until an instant-reading thermometer inserted in the center of the meat measures 150°. Let the roast cool completely on a rack. *(The meat can be prepared to this point and refrigerated overnight.)*

6. Remove the strings and thinly slice the meat. Serve at room temperature.

—*Bob Chambers*

• • •

SALMON SALAD WITH FENNEL AND RADISH VINAIGRETTE

The salmon in this salad is lightly steamed over fragrant fennel stems. The tangy vinaigrette makes a tart counterpart to the anise crunch of the fennel and the mild bite of the radishes.

12 Servings

307 Calories per Serving

½ cup fresh lemon juice
⅓ cup minced shallots
1 teaspoon fennel seeds
½ teaspoon thyme
1 teaspoon salt
¾ teaspoon freshly ground black pepper
⅛ teaspoon cayenne pepper
3 pounds center-cut skinless salmon fillet, cut into 1-inch cubes
¾ cup extra-virgin olive oil
4 pounds fennel bulbs—trimmed, cored and thinly sliced, stems and some green tops reserved
2 large bunches of radishes, thinly sliced
½ cup chopped Italian flat-leaf parsley
¼ cup capers

1. In a large bowl, combine the lemon juice, shallots, fennel seeds, thyme, ½ teaspoon each of the salt and black pepper and the cayenne. Place the cubes of salmon in a medium bowl and pour on half of the marinade. Toss well to coat. Cover and refrigerate for 2 to 3 hours, tossing occasionally.

2. Whisk the olive oil into the remaining marinade. Add the sliced fennel, radishes and parsley and toss well.

3. Coarsely chop the fennel stems and place them in the bottom of a large pot with 2 inches of water. Bring to a boil. Arrange the marinated salmon cubes in a steamer basket and sprinkle with the remaining ½ teaspoon salt and ¼ teaspoon pepper. Steam the salmon over the fennel until just opaque throughout, about 4 minutes. Let the salmon cool slightly; discard the fennel stems.

4. Add the salmon to the fennel and radish salad and toss gently; let cool completely. *(The salad can be prepared to this point up to 1 day ahead, covered with plastic wrap and refrigerated.)*

5. Transfer the salad to a serving bowl and toss gently. Sprinkle with the capers and garnish with fennel greens.

—*Bob Chambers*

• • •

SPANISH RICE TIMBALES

Low on calories does not mean short on taste or elegance. Packing this tomato-and-chili-tinged rice into a timbale to give it shape adds a touch of class to a controlled-portion side dish. Serve these timbales with Beef Enchilada Pie (p. 236).

4 Servings

119 Calories per Serving

1 teaspoon vegetable oil
½ cup long-grain converted white rice
½ cup chopped onion
1 garlic clove, minced
½ cup diced tomato
1 cup chicken stock or canned broth
½ teaspoon chili powder
¼ teaspoon oregano
¼ teaspoon salt
Pinch of freshly ground pepper

1. In a small heavy saucepan, cook the oil and rice over moderately high heat, stirring constantly, until the rice is golden, 3 to 4 minutes.

2. Add the onion and garlic and cook, stirring constantly, for 1 minute. Add the tomato and cook until heated through, about 1 minute. Add the stock, chili powder, oregano, salt and pepper and bring to a boil. Reduce the heat to moderate, cover tightly and simmer until the rice is tender and the liquid is absorbed, about 15 minutes.

3. Fluff the rice with a fork and let stand, covered, for 10 to 15 minutes before serving. *(The rice can be made up to 3 hours ahead. Set aside at room temperature. If necessary, reheat over low heat.)*

4. For each timbale, pack one-fourth of the rice into a ½-cup measure or timbale and turn out onto a dinner plate.

—*Jim Fobel*

• • •

SPICED ONION PAN BREAD

Prepared pizza dough is available frozen in supermarkets, or ask for it at your neighborhood pizza parlor. Commercial bread dough, available in the dairy case of most supermarkets, also works well.

4 Servings

—220 Calories per Serving—

1 cup thinly sliced red onion
1 tablespoon plus 2 teaspoons extra-virgin olive oil
Pinch of salt
Pinch of sugar
½ teaspoon peppercorns
½ teaspoon coriander seeds
¼ teaspoon fennel seeds
¼ teaspoon coarse (kosher) salt
½ pound pizza dough or French bread dough
About 1 teaspoon cornmeal

1. Preheat the oven to 500°. In a medium skillet, combine the red onion, oil, salt and sugar. Cover and cook over low heat until the onions are softened and translucent, about 10 minutes.

2. Using a spice grinder, grind the peppercorns, coriander seeds, fennel seeds and kosher salt to a coarse powder.

3. Cut the dough into 4 equal pieces. Sprinkle ¼ teaspoon of the seasoned salt over each piece of dough and knead 2 or 3 times to work into the dough. Sprinkle tiny amounts of cornmeal on the work surface to keep the dough from sticking if necessary. Shape each portion of dough into a flat disk 4½ to 5 inches in diameter. *(The recipe can be prepared to this point up to 6 hours in advance. Place the shaped dough on a cookie sheet, cover with plastic wrap and refrigerate.)*

4. Place a 12-inch cast-iron skillet or pizza stone in the oven to heat, about 10 minutes. Arrange the dough in the hot skillet. Spoon one-fourth of the onion mixture onto each piece, leaving a ½-inch border around the edge. Bake for 7 to 9 minutes, or until golden brown. Serve at once.

—*Sally Schneider*

• • •

SEEDED BREADSTICKS

Each of the various seeds gives its own character to the breadsticks when they are baked. If you like the ends of your breadsticks uniform, trim them before baking.

Makes 30

—126 Calories per Breadstick—

1 envelope (¼ ounce) active dry yeast
1 tablespoon sugar
4 eggs, at room temperature
4¼ to 4¾ cups all-purpose flour
½ cup olive oil
1½ teaspoons salt
2 tablespoons fennel seeds
2 tablespoons poppy seeds
2 tablespoons sesame seeds
2 tablespoons caraway seeds

1. In a large bowl, combine the yeast, sugar and ½ cup of warm water. Set aside in a warm place for 10 to 15 minutes to foam.

2. Whisk 3 of the eggs into the yeast mixture. Sprinkle on 1 cup of the flour and whisk until blended. Cover this batter with plastic wrap and set aside in a warm place for 1 hour.

3. Add the olive oil, salt and 3¼ cups of the remaining flour to the bowl. Stir well, then turn the dough out onto a lightly floured surface and knead until smooth and easy to handle, 10 to 12 minutes. Add more flour if the dough feels sticky. Transfer the dough to an oiled bowl, cover with plastic wrap and let rise until doubled in volume, about 1½ hours.

4. Divide the dough into 30 pieces. Roll each piece into an oval, then gently roll the dough, extending it thinner and thinner and applying steady pressure toward the ends, until it is 10 to 12 inches long and ½ inch thick.

5. Preheat the oven to 425°. When all the breadsticks have been rolled, place the fennel, poppy, sesame and caraway seeds on separate pieces of waxed paper. Beat the remaining egg with 2 teaspoons of water. Brush the sticks with the beaten egg, divide them into 4 groups and roll each group in one of the 4 types of seeds.

6. Place the seeded breadsticks ½ inch apart on lightly oiled baking sheets. Let rest for 5 minutes, then bake for 12 to 15 minutes, until the breadsticks are nicely browned. Let cool completely on a rack. Store the breadsticks in an airtight container for up to 4 days.

—*Bob Chambers*

• • •

LOW-CAL COLESLAW

Sautéed Codfish Cakes (p. 234) served with this low-calorie version of the classic side dish is comfort food of the highest order.

4 Servings
27 Calories per Serving

¼ cup plain yogurt
2 teaspoons Dijon-style mustard
½ teaspoon dry mustard
½ teaspoon prepared white horseradish, drained
1 teaspoon sugar
¼ teaspoon celery seed
½ teaspoon salt
¼ teaspoon freshly ground pepper
1½ tablespoons fresh lemon juice
2 cups (packed) finely shredded green cabbage (about 6 ounces)

In a medium bowl, stir together the yogurt, Dijon-style mustard, dry mustard, horseradish, sugar, celery seed, salt, pepper and lemon juice. Add the cabbage and toss to coat. Refrigerate, stirring occasionally, for 2 to 3 hours.

—Jim Fobel

• • •

ORZO SALAD WITH CARROTS AND PARSLEY

Orzo bears a striking resemblance to rice when it is cooked. Here, the pearly grains of pasta are turned bright yellow by the saffron.

12 Servings
241 Calories per Serving

2½ teaspoons salt
½ teaspoon saffron threads
1 box (16 ounces) orzo
1 pound carrots, cut into 2- to 3-inch lengths and then into fine julienne strips
3 tablespoons Dijon-style mustard
2 tablespoons white wine vinegar
1 teaspoon freshly ground pepper
½ teaspoon thyme
½ cup extra-virgin olive oil
2 bunches of parsley, finely chopped (about 1 cup)

1. In a large saucepan or flameproof casserole, bring 3 quarts of water to a boil. Add 2 teaspoons of the salt and the saffron. Remove from the heat, cover and set aside for 10 minutes.

2. Return the saffron water to a simmer. Add the orzo and cook for 7 minutes, stirring frequently. Add the carrots and continue to cook until the orzo and carrots are tender but firm to the bite, about 2 minutes longer. Drain and rinse under cold running water. Drain well.

3. In a large bowl, whisk together the mustard, vinegar, pepper, thyme and remaining ½ teaspoon salt. Whisk in the olive oil. Add the drained orzo and carrots and toss well. *(The salad can be prepared to this point up to 3 days ahead and refrigerated, covered. Let return to room temperature.)* Stir in the parsley shortly before serving.

—Bob Chambers

• • •

COMFORTING LOW-CAL LUNCH

Comfort food can also be low in calories, and if you don't believe it, try this streamlined version of crispy fried fish cakes. 585 Calories per Person/Serves 4.

Sautéed Codfish Cakes (p. 234)
Low-Cal Coleslaw (p. 240)

Gratin of Fresh Fruit (p. 243)

GREEN BEAN AND TOMATO SALAD WITH BASIL-SHALLOT VINAIGRETTE

These thin green beans form a cozy nest for a mound of bright red and yellow cherry tomatoes.

12 Servings
110 Calories per Serving

2 large shallots, thinly sliced
¼ cup red wine vinegar
1 tablespoon Dijon-style mustard
¼ teaspoon salt
1 teaspoon freshly ground pepper
½ cup extra-virgin olive oil
1½ pounds thin green beans, trimmed
½ cup finely shredded fresh basil
3 pints red and yellow cherry or pear tomatoes, halved lengthwise

1. In a medium bowl, cover the shallots with the vinegar and let macerate for 2 to 3 hours, or overnight.

2. Whisk in the mustard, salt and pepper. Gradually whisk in the olive oil.

3. In a large pot of boiling salted water, cook the green beans until tender but still firm to the bite, 1½ to 2 minutes after the water returns to a boil. Drain, rinse under cold running water and drain well. *(The recipe can be prepared to this point up to 2 days ahead. Cover and refrigerate the dressing and beans separately.)*

4. Stir the basil into the dressing. In a bowl, toss the beans with half the dressing. Arrange them around the rim of a large platter. Toss the tomatoes with the remaining dressing and mound them in the center of the beans.

—Bob Chambers

• • •

GREENS WITH ORANGE DRESSING

4 Servings

21 Calories per Serving

1½ teaspoons balsamic vinegar
1½ teaspoons finely slivered orange zest
Pinch of salt
¼ teaspoon freshly ground pepper
1¼ teaspoons hazelnut oil
2 Belgian endive (4 ounces), leaves separated
1 large bunch of watercress (4 ounces), tough stems removed

1. In a small bowl, whisk together the vinegar, orange zest, 1 teaspoon of water, the salt and the pepper. Slowly whisk in the oil. Let the dressing stand at room temperature for 15 minutes.

2. In a large bowl, combine the endive and watercress. Drizzle the dressing over the leaves and toss to coat. Divide equally among 4 salad plates and serve.

—Sally Schneider

• • •

COMPOSED SALAD OF TOMATOES, PEPPERS AND GOAT CHEESE WITH SHALLOT VINAIGRETTE

I double the ingredients and serve this salad on two large platters to brighten both ends of a buffet table.

8 Servings

216 Calories per Serving

11-ounce log of Montrachet or other mild goat cheese, thinly sliced
2 pounds beefsteak tomatoes, halved and sliced
Shallot Vinaigrette (recipe follows)
2 bunches of arugula, tough stems removed
1 head of Bibb lettuce, torn into pieces
2 red bell peppers, cut into thin strips
2 yellow bell peppers, cut into thin strips

1. Arrange the goat cheese, overlapping the slices, in the center of a large platter. Surround the cheese with the tomatoes. Drizzle the cheese and tomatoes with half of the Shallot Vinaigrette.

2. In a large bowl, combine the arugula, lettuce and red and yellow pepper strips. Add the remaining vinaigrette and toss to coat. Arrange the tossed salad around the tomato slices.

—Diana Sturgis

• • •

SHALLOT VINAIGRETTE

Associate Test Kitchen Director Marcia Kiesel created this lively dressing.

Makes ½ Cup

63 Calories per Tablespoon

1 large shallot, minced
1 small garlic clove, minced
1 tablespoon chopped fresh parsley
1½ tablespoons red wine vinegar
1 teaspoon Dijon-style mustard
½ teaspoon salt
½ teaspoon freshly ground pepper
¼ cup extra-virgin olive oil

In a small jar, combine the shallot, garlic, parsley, vinegar, mustard, salt and pepper. Cover with a tight lid and shake to blend well. Add the oil, shake again and set aside for at least 30 minutes.

—Marcia Kiesel

• • •

INDIAN CUCUMBER SALAD WITH YOGURT AND PISTACHIOS

Many of the spices that are used to make a curry are combined here to flavor a cool yogurt dressing for cucumbers.

12 Servings

104 Calories per Serving

1½ teaspoons ground cumin
½ teaspoon celery seeds
½ teaspoon mustard seeds
½ teaspoon ground coriander
½ teaspoon ground cardamom
¼ teaspoon cayenne pepper
2 cups plain yogurt
1 teaspoon salt
3 European seedless cucumbers
½ cup finely chopped parsley
½ cup sliced scallions, cut on the diagonal
1 cup shelled unsalted pistachio nuts (5 ounces), very coarsely chopped

1. In a small dry skillet, combine the cumin, celery seeds, mustard seeds, coriander, cardamom and cayenne. Toast over moderate heat, stirring, until the spices are fragrant and beginning to smoke slightly, 2 to 3 minutes. Pour into a small bowl and let cool.

2. In a medium bowl, combine the yogurt with the toasted spices and ½ teaspoon of the salt. Stir well. *(The recipe can be prepared to this point up to 2 days ahead. Cover and refrigerate the seasoned yogurt.)*

3. Halve the cucumbers lengthwise, then cut each half into 4 lengthwise strips. Cut the strips into 1-inch pieces.

4. In a large colander set over a bowl, toss the cucumbers with the remaining ½ teaspoon salt; set aside for 1 hour to drain. Pat dry.

5. To serve, toss the cucumbers with the parsley, ¼ cup of the scallions and the seasoned yogurt. Transfer to a large bowl or platter. Sprinkle with the remaining ¼ cup scallions and the pistachios.

—*Bob Chambers*

• • •

ESPRESSO CREME BRULEE

At last count, a serving of crème brûlée weighed in at an extraordinary 570 calories worth of cream, egg yolks and sugar. This lightened version gives the illusion of richness at little more than half the calories.

6 Servings
290 Calories per Serving

¼ cup plus 2 tablespoons (packed) dark brown sugar
2½ cups milk
½ cup freshly ground espresso
1 vanilla bean, split lengthwise
2 whole eggs
3 egg yolks
¼ cup plus 2 tablespoons granulated sugar
¼ cup plus 2 tablespoons heavy cream

1. Preheat the oven to 200°. Spread the brown sugar on a baking sheet and bake until dry, about 12 minutes. Let the sugar cool slightly, then press through a sieve into a small bowl. Increase the oven temperature to 300°.

2. In a medium saucepan, bring the milk to a boil over moderately high heat. Remove from the heat and stir in the espresso and the vanilla bean. Cover and let steep for 10 minutes.

3. Line a fine sieve with a double thickness of dampened paper towel and set over a bowl. Remove the vanilla bean and slowly pour the milk through the strainer, stirring up the coffee grounds with a wooden spoon so the milk will filter through. Fold the edges of the towel over the coffee grounds and press to extract all the milk. Scrape the seeds from the vanilla bean into the milk.

4. In a medium bowl, stir together the whole eggs, eggs yolks, granulated sugar and cream until blended. Stir in the infused milk and strain the mixture into a pitcher or large measuring cup. Skim any bubbles from the surface.

5. Place six ½-cup ramekins in a baking pan and fill with the custard. Place the baking pan in the oven and pour in enough warm water to reach halfway up the sides of the ramekins. Cover the ramekins loosely with foil and bake for 1 hour, or until the custards are firm around the edges; they may still wobble in the center but will set when chilled.

6. Remove the ramekins from the water bath and let cool. Cover and refrigerate until cold, at least 3 hours. (*The custards can be prepared to this point up to 2 days ahead. Cover with plastic and refrigerate. If moisture collects on top, blot with paper towels before proceeding.*)

7. Preheat the broiler. Set the ramekins on a baking sheet. Sprinkle 1 tablespoon of the sieved brown sugar over the top of each custard in an even layer. Broil the custards as close to the heat as possible until the sugar is caramelized, 30 seconds to 2 minutes. Let cool and serve immediately or refrigerate, uncovered, for up to 3 hours.

—*Sally Schneider*

• • •

HAZELNUT BRAN BISCOTTI

This is a variation of a *biscotti* recipe that was given to me by an Italian contessa. I've used hazelnuts instead of almonds and added bran. The crunch of these cookies is the perfect foil for cool poached peaches.

Makes About 4 Dozen Biscotti
100 Calories per Cookie

2 cups hazelnuts (filberts)
1 stick (4 ounces) unsalted butter, at room temperature
1 cup sugar
1 teaspoon vanilla extract
3 eggs
2⅔ cups all-purpose flour
1 teaspoon baking powder
½ teaspoon salt
1 cup unprocessed bran*
¼ cup confectioners' sugar
****Available at health food stores***

1. Preheat the oven to 375°. Spread the hazelnuts on a baking sheet and toast them until their dark brown skins crack and they begin to color, about 12 minutes. While the nuts are still hot, rub them together vigorously in a kitchen towel to remove most of their skins. Let cool to room temperature. Reduce the oven temperature to 350°.

2. Place the nuts in a food processor. Turn the machine on and off about 25 times until the nuts are coarsely chopped.

3. In a mixer bowl, cream the butter with the sugar. Add the vanilla. Beat in the eggs, 1 at a time, beating well after each addition. Continue beating until the mixture is light and fluffy, 2 to 3 minutes.

4. Sift the flour with the baking powder and the salt. Combine the flour mixture with the bran and fold into the egg mixture until blended. Add the hazelnuts and stir gently until evenly distributed.

5. Sprinkle a work surface with the confectioners' sugar. Turn the dough out onto the sugar and form it into a ball. Divide the dough in half. Roll each half into a log about 1 inch in diameter. Set the logs 3 or 4 inches apart on a well-buttered cookie sheet and bake for 25 to 30 minutes, until golden brown and firm. Let cool for 10 minutes.

6. Using a serrated knife, carefully cut the logs in half crosswise. Transfer the logs to a cutting board. Cut the logs into ½-inch-thick slices. Return to the cookie sheet and bake for 25 minutes. Turn and cook for 5 minutes longer, or until nicely browned on both sides. Transfer to a rack to cool.

—Bob Chambers

• • •

POACHED PEACHES IN RED WINE AND RASPBERRY SAUCE

These lightly spiced, wine-poached peaches, with their raspberry-scented sauce, make a light and spirited finish to any summer meal.

12 Servings
—165 Calories per Serving—

Zest from 1 lemon, cut into strips
2 packages (10 ounces each) frozen raspberries in syrup, thawed
6 cups dry red wine
¾ cup sugar
6 whole cloves
15 peppercorns
12 firm-ripe freestone peaches
1 tablespoon arrowroot

1. In a small saucepan, blanch the lemon zest in boiling water for 1 minute. Drain and rinse well.

2. In a large nonreactive saucepan, combine the raspberries with their syrup, the wine, sugar, cloves, peppercorns and lemon zest. Bring to a boil, reduce the heat and simmer for 2 minutes, stirring to dissolve the sugar.

3. Add the peaches to the saucepan and cover with a circle of parchment or waxed paper. Return the liquid to a boil and immediately reduce to a simmer. Cook over low heat for 7 minutes. Remove the parchment and turn the peaches so that they cook evenly. Continue cooking for 5 minutes; if the skins still adhere to the peaches, cook for 5 minutes longer. Remove the saucepan from the heat and let the peaches cool to room temperature in the syrup.

4. When the peaches are cool, remove the parchment and lift them out with a slotted spoon. Peel the peaches and set them on a plate, stem ends down. Cover tightly with plastic wrap and refrigerate.

5. Return the poaching liquid to a boil and boil over moderately high heat until reduced by half, about 15 minutes.

6. Dissolve the arrowroot in 2 tablespoons cold water and whisk into the syrup until blended. Return to a boil to thicken; remove from the heat and strain the syrup. Let cool to room temperature, then cover tightly and refrigerate. *(The recipe can be prepared to this point up to 2 days in advance.)*

7. To serve, set the peaches on a deep platter or in individual stemmed goblets, stem ends down. Spoon 2 to 3 tablespoons of the raspberry-wine syrup over each one.

—Bob Chambers

• • •

GRATIN OF FRESH FRUIT

This fresh fruit gratin topped with a warm sabayon was inspired by a dessert at Roger Vergé's restaurant in the south of France, Le Moulin de Mougins.

4 Servings
—230 Calories per Serving—

1 medium navel orange
3 egg yolks
3 tablespoons sugar
2 tablespoons heavy cream
3 cups of any of the following fresh fruits: orange sections, strawberries, raspberries, sliced kiwis, sliced fresh pineapple

1. Using a swivel-bladed vegetable peeler, remove the zest from half the orange. Cut into very fine strips.

2. In a small saucepan, put the julienned zest in ½ cup of cold water and bring to a boil. Boil for 30 seconds, then rinse under cold water; drain well.

3. Squeeze the juice from the orange and strain to remove pulp. Measure out ¼ cup plus 1 teaspoon of the orange juice.

4. Preheat the broiler. In a small bowl set over a pan of simmering water, whisk together the egg yolks, sugar, orange juice and cream. Continue whisking over low heat until the mixture is frothy and thick enough to coat the back of a spoon. Remove from the heat and stir in the julienned orange zest. Set aside to cool.

5. Arrange ¾ cup of the fruit in each of four 4-inch gratin or ovenproof dishes. Spoon about 3 tablespoons of the sauce evenly over each. Place the dishes on a baking sheet and broil about 3 inches from the heat for 30 seconds, or until the sabayon is lightly browned. Do not overcook, or the sauce will separate.

—Sally Schneider

• • •

GRAPEFRUIT CASSIS SORBET

Each helping of sorbet may be served with one small plain cookie (about ¼ ounce), such as an Amaretti Di Saronno or a gingersnap.

Several black currant syrups are available, but I recommend Cassis Vedrenne Père & Fils, which is available in specialty food shops. Note that this is not *crème de cassis*, which is black currant liqueur.

4 Servings
—135 Calories per Serving—

3 cups fresh pink grapefruit juice
¼ cup plus 1 tablespoon black currant syrup (cassis)
12 fine slivers of lemon zest
About 8 candied violets or lilacs (optional)

1. Place the grapefruit and black currant syrup in an ice cream maker and freeze according to the manufacturer's instructions. *(The recipe can be prepared to this point up to 2 days in advance. Place the sorbet in a bowl, cover and freeze until ready to serve.)*

2. To serve, spoon equal amounts of sorbet into 4 ice cream glasses or dessert bowls. Garnish each with a few slivers of lemon zest and 2 candied violets or lilacs. (If the sorbet is too hard to serve, it can be softened briefly in a food processor.)

—Sally Schneider

• • •

SUMMER FRESH FRUIT CHUTNEY

This tart and refreshing mixture of savory and sweet is delicious with veal roast. If fresh tomatillos are hard to come by, green tomatoes would make a fine substitute in this chutney.

Makes About 4 Cups
—65 Calories per ¼-Cup Serving—

½ cup herb vinegar or white wine vinegar
¼ cup currants
¼ cup golden raisins
1 small hot red pepper, fresh or dried
2 tablespoons olive oil
2 medium onions, minced
2 garlic cloves, crushed through a press
¼ cup sugar
1½ pounds fresh tomatillos—husked, rinsed and quartered
1 tablespoon fresh lemon juice
1 cup blueberries
1 cup raspberries

1. In a small nonreactive saucepan, combine the herb vinegar with ¼ cup of water and bring to a boil over high heat. Add the currants, raisins and hot pepper. Reduce the heat to moderately low and simmer for 1 minute. Remove from the heat and set aside.

2. In a large nonreactive skillet, heat the olive oil. Add the onions and cook over moderate heat, stirring occasionally, until softened and translucent, about 5 minutes. Add the garlic, cover and cook for 2 minutes longer.

3. Add the sugar and increase the heat to high. Stir in the reserved currants, raisins, hot pepper and liquid. Boil, stirring, until the liquid thickens, 2 to 3 minutes. Add the tomatillos and cook over moderately high heat, stirring frequently, until very tender, 5 to 7 minutes. Stir in the lemon juice and remove from the heat. Let the chutney cool for about 10 minutes, then remove and discard the hot pepper.

4. Fold in the blueberries and raspberries and let cool to room temperature. Cover tightly and refrigerate for up to 3 days before serving. Remove from the refrigerator 30 minutes before serving time.

—Bob Chambers

• • •

STOCKS, SAUCES & CONDIMENTS

BROWN STOCK

Deep amber, flavorful brown stock forms the basis for many sauces.

Makes 4 to 5 Quarts

6 pounds beef shin with bones
6 pounds veal bones
6 carrots, cut into 2-inch lengths
3 onions—unpeeled, halved and each half stuck with 1 whole clove
3 leeks (white part only), split lengthwise, plus 1 leek (including green top), quartered
2 celery ribs with leaves, cut into 2-inch lengths
1 small white turnip
2 cups coarsely chopped tomatoes, canned or fresh
Bouquet garni: 6 sprigs of parsley, 1 teaspoon thyme, 1 large bay leaf, 7 peppercorns and 2 unpeeled garlic cloves tied in a double thickness of cheesecloth

1. Preheat the oven to 450°. Place the meat and bones in a large roasting pan in 1 or 2 layers, or in 2 roasting pans if necessary. Bake, uncovered, for 30 minutes. Add the carrots and onions and bake, turning occasionally, until the bones are deep brown but not charred, 30 to 60 minutes longer.

2. Transfer the bones and vegetables to a large stockpot. Pour off and discard any fat from the roasting pan. Add 2 to 3 cups of cold water to the pan and deglaze over medium heat, scraping up any browned particles that cling to the bottom. Pour the liquid into the stockpot, add enough additional cold water to cover the bones—about 4 quarts—and bring the water slowly to a simmer over low heat; to insure a clear stock, this slow heating should take about 1 hour. Skim off all the scum that rises to the surface.

3. Add the leeks, celery, turnip, tomatoes, bouquet garni and enough additional water to cover. Simmer, partially covered, over low heat for 5 to 8 hours, skimming the surface occasionally. Add additional water to cover as necessary.

4. Carefully ladle the stock into a large bowl through a colander lined with several thicknesses of dampened cheesecloth. Do not press on the bones and vegetables, or the resulting stock will be cloudy. Refrigerate, uncovered, overnight; then remove any fat from the surface. The stock may be refrigerated for 3 to 4 days, then reboiled, or frozen for several months.

—F&W

• • •

QUICK CHICKEN STOCK

This stock can be made ahead and stored in the refrigerator for up to three days or in the freezer for up to two months.

Makes About 2 Quarts

3 pounds chicken wings
1 large onion, chopped
8 garlic cloves, unpeeled
2 medium celery ribs, chopped
2 medium carrots, chopped
3 sprigs of fresh thyme or ½ teaspoon dried
1 bay leaf

In a large heavy saucepan or flameproof casserole, combine the chicken, onion, garlic, celery, carrots, thyme and bay leaf. Add 12 cups of cold water and bring to a boil over high heat. Reduce the heat to low and simmer, skimming occasionally, for 2 hours. Strain the stock through a colander into a large bowl.

—Marcia Kiesel

• • •

RICH CHICKEN STOCK

Although this deliciously rich stock calls for two whole chickens in addition to chicken parts, the whole birds are removed as soon as they are cooked, so you can eat them as is or use the meat for other dishes, salads or sandwiches. You may substitute additional chicken parts for the whole chickens. Use this stock as a base for soups or sauces.

Makes About 3 Quarts

4 pounds chicken backs, necks and/or wings
2 whole chickens (about 3 pounds each), including necks and gizzards
3 large carrots, sliced
2 large onions, sliced
4 medium leeks—split lengthwise, rinsed and sliced crosswise (or substitute 1 extra onion)
2 celery ribs with leaves, sliced
Bouquet garni: 8 sprigs of parsley, 1 teaspoon thyme, 1 bay leaf, ½ teaspoon peppercorns and 3 whole cloves tied in a double thickness of cheesecloth

1. Place the chicken parts in a large, heavy stockpot; place the whole chickens on top. Add 6 quarts of cold water and place over low heat. Heat to simmering without stirring; for a clear stock, this should take about 1 hour. While the water is heating, skim off any scum that rises to the surface.

2. Add the carrots, onions, leeks, celery and bouquet garni. Simmer, partially covered, without stirring, for about 45 minutes. Remove both chickens. Continue simmering the stock, without stirring, for about 4 hours, skimming occasionally. (The meat can be removed from the two chickens as soon as they are cool enough to handle and the bones returned to the pot.)

3. Ladle the stock carefully through a colander lined with several layers of dampened cheesecloth. Strain a second time, if desired, for an even clearer stock. Let cool to room temperature; then cover and refrigerate. Remove the congealed fat from the top. If using the hot stock immediately, remove the fat by first skimming and then blotting the surface with paper towels, or use a degreasing utensil designed for that purpose.

—*F&W*

• • •

BROWN CHICKEN STOCK

Makes 3 Cups

3 to 4 pounds chicken backs, wings and/or necks
1 medium onion, unpeeled and quartered
1 celery rib, thickly sliced
1½ cups dry white wine
2 medium tomatoes, quartered
1 sprig of fresh thyme or ¼ teaspoon dried
½ imported bay leaf
½ teaspoon black peppercorns

1. Preheat the oven to 500°. Place the chicken, onion and celery in a roasting pan and roast, turning the bones once or twice, until they are a dark golden brown, about 30 minutes.

2. Transfer the chicken and vegetables to a stockpot. Pour off any fat from the roasting pan and place it on top of the stove. Add the wine to the pan and bring to a boil, scraping up any browned bits from the pan. Pour into the stockpot.

3. Add the tomatoes, thyme, bay leaf, peppercorns and 2½ quarts of water. Bring to a boil over high heat, reduce the heat to moderately low and simmer, uncovered, for 3 hours, skimming off the foam and fat occasionally.

4. Strain the stock into a large saucepan. Skim off any fat. Boil over high heat until the stock is reduced to 3 cups.

—*F&W*

• • •

TURKEY STOCK

Makes About 3¼ Cups

Turkey neck, gizzard and heart
1 medium onion, chopped
1 large celery rib with leaves, chopped
1 large carrot, unpeeled and chopped
3 sprigs of parsley

1. Preheat the oven to 350°. In a small roasting pan, toss the neck and giblets with the onion and roast, stirring occasionally, until browned all over, about 1 hour. Transfer the browned ingredients to a medium saucepan.

2. Place the roasting pan over high heat. Pour in 1 cup of water and bring to a boil, scraping up the browned bits from the bottom of the pan. Pour this liquid into the saucepan and add the celery, carrot, parsley and 3 cups of water. Bring to a boil over high heat. Reduce the heat to low and simmer until reduced to 3¼ cups, about 1½ hours. Strain the stock before using.

—*Stephan Pyles, Routh Street Cafe, Dallas*

• • •

WHITE VEAL STOCK

Use this clear, delicate stock to create sauces for veal, chicken or fish dishes.

Makes 2 to 3 Quarts

4½ pounds veal bones
3 pounds veal stew meat, such as shank, breast, neck
2 leeks (white part only), cut into 2-inch lengths
2 medium onions, quartered
2 celery ribs with leaves, cut into 2-inch lengths
2 carrots, cut into 2-inch lengths
Bouquet garni: 6 sprigs of parsley, ½ teaspoon thyme, 1 bay leaf, 2 unpeeled garlic cloves, 3 whole cloves and 4 peppercorns tied in a double thickness of cheesecloth

1. Place the veal bones and meat in a large stockpot. Add enough cold water to cover, about 3 quarts. Cover the pot and bring to a boil over high heat. Lower the heat to moderate and boil gently for 5 minutes. Drain, discarding the water, and rinse the bones under cold running water. Rinse out the pot. Return the bones and meat to the stockpot and add enough cold water to cover. Bring to a simmer over low heat and skim off any scum that rises to the surface. Add 1 cup cold water and when the liquid has returned to a simmer, skim again. Repeat the cold water-skimming process until the liquid is clear.

2. Add the leeks, onions, celery, carrots and bouquet garni. Simmer, partially covered, for 4 to 5 hours, adding water to cover as necessary.

3. When the stock is ready, carefully ladle it through a colander lined with several thicknesses of dampened cheesecloth into a large bowl. Allow to cool. Cover and refrigerate. After the stock has jelled, remove any fat that has accumulated on the surface.

—*F&W*

• • •

FISH STOCK

When cleaning whole fish, save the heads and frames for stock; or, inquire at your local fish market. Use this stock for a variety of sauces.

Makes About 2 Quarts

4 pounds fish bones and trimmings (heads, tails, skin)
3 tablespoons vegetable oil
1 medium onion, cut into eighths
1 large celery rib, cut into 1-inch lengths
1 large carrot, cut into 1-inch lengths
Bouquet garni: 3 sprigs of parsley, ½ teaspoon thyme, 1 bay leaf and 8 to 10 peppercorns tied in a double thickness of cheesecloth

1. Rinse the fish bones and trimmings under cold running water to remove any blood; drain.

2. Heat the oil in a large, heavy stockpot. Add the fish bones and trimmings and sauté over moderate heat for 5 minutes, breaking them up occasionally with a wooden spoon. Cook, partially covered, for 5 minutes longer.

3. Add the onion, celery, carrot and bouquet garni. Pour in 3 quarts of cold water. Bring the mixture to a boil over high heat, skimming off any foam from the surface. Reduce the heat to low and simmer, uncovered, for 30 minutes. Strain through a fine sieve lined with several layers of dampened cheesecloth.

—F&W

• • •

SAFFRON FISH STOCK

With the addition of a little seafood, this stock can be transformed into a Mediterranean fish soup. It is the base for my bouillabaisse.

Makes About 2 Quarts

⅓ cup extra-virgin olive oil
2 medium onions, sliced
2 medium leeks (white and tender green), chopped
½ fennel bulb, chopped, or 1 teaspoon fennel seeds
12 to 15 sprigs of parsley
5 garlic cloves, lightly crushed
3 pounds tomatoes, diced
3 large pinches of saffron threads
1 imported bay leaf
5 sprigs of fresh thyme or ½ teaspoon dried
Zest of 1 orange
5 pounds non-oily fish heads and bones, soaked in ice water for at least 20 minutes
2 cups dry white wine
½ teaspoon salt
¼ teaspoon freshly ground pepper

1. In a large nonreactive stockpot, heat the oil over moderate heat. Add the onions, leeks, fennel or fennel seeds and parsley. Sauté, stirring occasionally, until the leeks are softened but not browned, about 5 minutes.

2. Stir in the garlic, tomatoes, saffron, bay leaf, thyme and orange zest. Add the fish heads and bones, wine, salt, pepper and 6 cups of water. Bring to a boil over moderate heat and continue to boil for 20 minutes.

3. Strain the stock through a fine-mesh sieve, pressing on the solids to extract as much liquid as possible. Let cool, then cover and refrigerate. *(The stock can be made up to 3 days in advance and refrigerated, or frozen for up to 1 month.)*

—Richard Grausman

• • •

VEGETABLE STOCK

Makes About 1½ Quarts

3 celery ribs, cut into 2-inch lengths
2 large carrots, cut into 2-inch lengths
2 small onions, unpeeled and quartered
1 large boiling potato, cut into 1-inch slices
½ pound mushrooms, roughly chopped
4 small leeks (white part only), split lengthwise
2 small white turnips, peeled and quartered
6 garlic cloves, unpeeled
1½ teaspoons salt
1½ teaspoons Hungarian sweet paprika
Bouquet garni: 10 sprigs of parsley, 1½ teaspoons marjoram, 2 bay leaves and 8 peppercorns tied in a double thickness of cheesecloth

1. Place all the vegetables in a stockpot. Add the garlic, salt, paprika, bouquet garni and 3 quarts of water and bring to a boil over moderate heat.

2. Reduce the heat to low and simmer the stock, partially covered, until reduced by half, about 1½ hours.

3. Strain through a double thickness of dampened cheesecloth, pressing lightly on the vegetables with the back of a spoon.

—F&W

• • •

LAMB GLAZE

This light reduction sauce is powered with flavor. It can be prepared up to two days ahead and kept in the refrigerator.

Makes About 3/4 Cup

1 pound lamb bones and trimmings
3 tablespoons vegetable oil
1 medium onion, coarsely chopped
1 celery rib, coarsely chopped
2 small garlic cloves, coarsely chopped
1 small carrot, coarsely chopped
1/2 pound mushrooms
1 can (8 ounces) peeled tomatoes, with their juice
2 tablespoons tomato paste
1/2 cup dry red wine
1 can (13 3/4 ounces) unsalted chicken stock
1 imported bay leaf
4 peppercorns
8 parsley stems
Salt and freshly ground pepper

1. Preheat the oven to 450°. In a medium roasting pan, toss the lamb bones with 1 tablespoon of the oil. Roast the bones until well browned, 30 to 40 minutes. Transfer the bones to a baking sheet lined with paper towels to remove excess fat.

2. In a medium nonreactive saucepan, heat the remaining 2 tablespoons oil. Add the onion, celery and garlic and cook over moderately high heat until softened, about 2 minutes. Stir in the carrot and mushrooms and cook, stirring occasionally, until the vegetables are golden brown, about 8 minutes.

3. Add the lamb bones along with the tomatoes and their juice, tomato paste, wine, stock, bay leaf, peppercorns and parsley stems. Bring to a boil, reduce the heat to moderate and simmer until the liquid reduces by three-fourths, 30 to 40 minutes.

4. Discard the bones and the bay leaf. Strain the glaze through a fine-mesh sieve, pressing hard on the vegetables to extract all the liquid. Scrape any puree from the underside of the sieve into the sauce. Let cool, then refrigerate overnight. Skim the fat off the surface before reheating the sauce. Season with salt and pepper to taste before serving.

—Bob Chambers

• • •

CREME FRAICHE

Makes About 2 1/4 Cups

2 cups heavy cream
1/3 cup active-culture buttermilk

1. In a small saucepan, gently heat the cream and buttermilk to just under 100° (higher will kill the culture).

2. Pour into a clean glass jar, cover and place in a saucepan filled with warm (100°) water; or put in a thermos bottle. Allow to stand for 8 to 36 hours, or until thickened, replenishing the warm water from time to time. The longer you culture the cream, the tangier it will become.

3. Refrigerate until chilled. Crème fraîche will keep in the refrigerator for a week to 10 days.

—F&W

• • •

FINES HERBES BUTTER

This all-purpose butter goes with almost anything, from meats and fish to vegetables and shellfish, notably oysters.

Makes 1/2 Pound

2 sticks (8 ounces) unsalted butter, at room temperature
2 tablespoons minced fresh tarragon
2 tablespoons minced fresh chives
2 tablespoons minced fresh chervil or parsley
1/2 teaspoon freshly ground white pepper
1/2 teaspoon salt

1. In a food processor, combine the butter, tarragon, chives, chervil, white pepper and salt. Process, scraping down the sides once, until thoroughly blended, about 30 seconds.

2. Scrape the butter onto a large sheet of plastic wrap, parchment or waxed paper. With a rubber spatula, smooth the butter into a cylinder shape about 1½ inches in diameter. Roll up, twisting both ends to seal. Label, date and store in the freezer for up to 2 months.

—Malcolm Hudson

• • •

DILL BUTTER

This is a good butter to have on hand, as it will enhance a wide range of dishes, including seafood (especially scallops), chicken (a few slices of the butter slipped under the breast skin before roasting does wonders), veal and vegetables.

Makes 1/2 Pound

2 sticks (8 ounces) unsalted butter, at room temperature
1/4 cup minced fresh dill
1 teaspoon minced dillseed
3 tablespoons fresh lemon juice
1/2 teaspoon freshly ground white pepper

1. In a food processor, combine the butter, dill, dillseed, lemon juice and white pepper. Process, scraping down the sides once, until thoroughly blended, about 30 seconds.

2. Scrape the butter onto a large sheet of plastic wrap, parchment or waxed paper. With a rubber spatula, smooth the butter into a cylinder shape about 1½ inches in diameter. Roll up, twisting both ends to seal. Label, date and store in the freezer for up to 2 months.

—Malcolm Hudson

• • •

CHIVE BUTTER

A wonderful butter to have on hand for its versatility. Quickly sauté chicken or fillet of turkey breast, deglaze with a little dry vermouth or white wine, whisk in some chive butter, and there you have it. In less than 10 minutes you have a dish worthy of anyone. Use this butter with vegetables (particularly good on a baked potato), poultry, fish and veal.

Makes ½ Pound

2 sticks (8 ounces) unsalted butter, at room temperature
½ cup minced fresh chives
2 tablespoons fresh lemon juice
½ teaspoon salt

1. In a food processor, combine the butter, chives, lemon juice and salt. Process, scraping down the sides once, until thoroughly blended, about 30 seconds.

2. Scrape the butter onto a large sheet of plastic wrap, parchment or waxed paper. With a rubber spatula, smooth the butter into a cylinder shape about 1½ inches in diameter. Roll up, twisting both ends to seal. Label and date the butter and store in the freezer for up to 2 months.

—Malcolm Hudson

• • •

SHALLOT BUTTER

Shallot butter produces a fine sauce with a minimum of effort, using only the pan juices and a little wine. Serve it with fish, shellfish, meats and vegetables.

Makes ½ Pound

8 shallots, minced
1 garlic clove, minced
¼ cup dry white wine
2 sticks (8 ounces) unsalted butter, at room temperature
2 tablespoons minced parsley
½ teaspoon freshly ground white pepper
½ teaspoon salt

1. In a small nonreactive saucepan, combine the shallots, garlic and white wine. Boil over high heat until the liquid is reduced to 1 tablespoon, about 3 minutes. Let cool.

2. Pour the cooled liquid into a food processor. Add the butter, parsley, white pepper and salt. Process, scraping down the sides once, until thoroughly blended, about 30 seconds.

3. Scrape the butter onto a large sheet of plastic wrap, parchment or waxed paper. With a rubber spatula, smooth the butter into a cylinder shape about 1½ inches in diameter. Roll up, twisting both ends to seal. Label, date and store in the freezer for up to 2 months.

—Malcolm Hudson

• • •

RED WINE AND HERBES DE PROVENCE BUTTER

Well suited for finishing a quick sauce, basting a roast or accompanying a rare steak, *herbes de Provence* butter is quick and easy to make.

Makes ½ Pound

¼ cup plus 2 tablespoons dry red wine
4 shallots, minced
1 garlic clove, minced
2 tablespoons herbes de Provence*
2 sticks (8 ounces)unsalted butter, at room temperature
¼ teaspoon salt
½ teaspoon freshly ground pepper
****Available at spice shops and specialty food stores***

1. In a small nonreactive saucepan, combine the red wine, shallots, garlic and *herbes de Provence*. Boil over high heat until the liquid is reduced to 1 tablespoon, about 3 minutes. Let cool.

2. Pour the cooled liquid into a food processor. Add the butter, salt and pepper. Process, scraping down the sides once, until thoroughly blended, about 30 seconds.

3. Scrape the butter onto a large sheet of plastic wrap, parchment or waxed paper. With a rubber spatula, smooth the butter into a cylinder shape about 1½ inches in diameter. Roll up, twisting both ends to seal. Label, date and store in the freezer for up to 2 months.

—Malcolm Hudson

• • •

HERB BUTTER FOR FISH

This is a fine seasoning for grilled, poached or fried fish.

Makes ½ Pound

3 shallots, minced
3 tablespoons dry white wine
2 sticks (8 ounces) unsalted butter, at room temperature
1 tablespoon minced fresh tarragon
1 tablespoon minced fresh chives
1 tablespoon minced fresh chervil or parsley
½ teaspon salt

1. In a small nonreactive saucepan, combine the shallots and white wine. Boil

over high heat until the wine is reduced to 1 tablespoon, about 2 minutes. Let cool.

2. Pour the cooled liquid into a food processor. Add the butter, tarragon, chives, chervil and salt. Process, scraping down the sides once, until thoroughly blended, about 30 seconds.

3. Scrape the butter onto a large sheet of plastic wrap, parchment or waxed paper. With a rubber spatula, smooth the butter into a cylinder shape about 1½ inches in diameter. Roll up, twisting both ends to seal. Label, date and store in the freezer for up to 2 months.

—Malcolm Hudson

• • •

GARLIC BUTTER

This should be a mainstay in any kitchen. It is excellent with roast birds, lamb, beef, game or pork, and it may be used in combination with another herb butter.

Makes ½ Pound

4 large garlic cloves, minced
2 shallots, minced
3 tablespoons dry white wine
2 sticks (8 ounces) unsalted butter, at room temperature
2 tablespoons minced parsley
½ teaspoon salt
½ teaspoon freshly ground white pepper

1. In a small nonreactive saucepan, combine the garlic, shallots and white wine. Boil over high heat until the wine is reduced to 1 tablespoon, about 2 minutes. Let cool.

2. Pour the cooled liquid into a food processor. Add the butter, parsley, salt and white pepper. Process, scraping down the sides once, until thoroughly blended, about 30 seconds.

3. Scrape the butter onto a large sheet of plastic wrap, parchment or waxed paper. With a rubber spatula, smooth the butter into a cylinder shape about 1½ inches in diameter. Roll up, twisting both ends to seal. Label, date and store in the freezer for up to 2 months.

—Malcolm Hudson

• • •

BASIL BUTTER

This butter, which can be made with any of the many varieties of basil, will enhance numerous dishes, including pastas, soups and vegetables.

Makes ½ Pound

2 sticks (8 ounces) unsalted butter, at room temperature
¼ cup plus 2 tablespoons minced fresh basil
1 garlic clove, minced
1 tablespoon fresh lemon juice
½ teaspoon salt

1. In a food processor, combine the butter, basil, garlic, lemon juice and salt. Process, scraping down the sides once, until the mixture is thoroughly blended, about 30 seconds.

2. Scrape the butter onto a large sheet of plastic wrap, parchment or waxed paper. With a rubber spatula, smooth the butter into a cylinder shape about 1½ inches in diameter. Roll up, twisting both ends to seal. Label, date and store in the freezer for up to 2 months.

—Malcolm Hudson

• • •

ROSEMARY BUTTER

This is superb with roasts of all kinds, especially lamb and pork. It may also be used to baste grilled fish; monkfish, marlin, mackerel and swordfish can handle its dominant flavor.

Makes ½ Pound

1 tablespoon minced fresh rosemary
1 shallot, minced
1 garlic clove, minced
2 sticks (8 ounces) unsalted butter, at room temperature
2 tablespoons minced parsley
¼ teaspoon salt
½ teaspoon freshly ground white pepper

1. Bring a small saucepan of water to a boil. Place the rosemary, shallot and garlic in the boiling water and poach for 1 minute. Strain through a fine-mesh sieve and let the rosemary mixture cool.

2. In a food processor, combine the rosemary mixture, butter, parsley, salt and white pepper. Process, scraping down the sides once, until thoroughly blended, about 30 seconds.

3. Scrape the butter onto a large sheet of plastic wrap, parchment or waxed paper. With a rubber spatula, smooth the butter into a cylinder shape about 1½ inches in diameter. Roll up, twisting both ends to seal. Label, date and store in the freezer for up to 2 months.

—Malcolm Hudson

• • •

CILANTRO AND CUMIN BUTTER

A perfect accompaniment to grilled steak, pork and chicken, this spicy butter should be used with discretion.

Makes ½ Pound

2 sticks (8 ounces) unsalted butter, at room temperature
3 tablespoons minced fresh coriander (cilantro)

3 tablespoons minced parsley
½ teaspoon ground cumin
2 small dried hot red peppers with seeds, chopped
½ teaspoon salt

1. In a food processor, combine the butter, fresh coriander, parsley, cumin, hot peppers and salt. Process, scraping down the sides once, until thoroughly blended, about 30 seconds.

2. Scrape the butter onto a large sheet of plastic wrap, parchment or waxed paper. With a rubber spatula, smooth the butter into a cylinder shape about 1½ inches in diameter. Roll up, twisting both ends to seal. Label, date and store in the freezer for up to 2 months.

—Malcolm Hudson

• • •

CILANTRO AND PEPPER BUTTER

Here is a fiery butter with a southwestern flavor.

Makes ½ Pound

2 sticks (8 ounces) unsalted butter, at room temperature
¼ cup plus 2 tablespoons minced fresh coriander (cilantro)
¼ cup minced parsley
2 small jalapeño peppers, minced, with some seeds
1 small green bell pepper, minced
2 garlic cloves, minced
½ teaspoon salt

1. In a food processor, combine the butter, fresh coriander, parsley, jalapeño peppers with seeds, bell pepper, garlic and salt. Process, scraping down the sides once, until thoroughly blended, about 30 seconds.

2. Scrape the butter onto a large sheet of plastic wrap, parchment or waxed paper. With a rubber spatula, smooth the butter into a cylinder shape about 1½ inches in diameter. Roll up, twisting both ends to seal. Label, date and store in the freezer for up to 2 months.

—Malcolm Hudson

• • •

TARRAGON BUTTER

A butter with many uses in the kitchen, it is excellent with chicken, seafood and veal, as well as vegetables.

Makes ½ Pound

2 shallots, minced
¼ cup dry white wine
6 tablespoons minced fresh tarragon
2 sticks (8 ounces) unsalted butter, at room temperature
½ teaspoon salt

1. In a small nonreactive saucepan, combine the garlic, shallots and white wine. Boil over high heat until the wine is reduced to 1 tablespoon, about 2 minutes. Let cool.

2. Place the tarragon in a fine strainer and pour 2 cups of boiling water over it. Rinse under cold running water and press to remove as much liquid as possible.

3. Pour the cooled shallots and wine into a food processor. Add the butter, tarragon and salt. Process, scraping down the sides once, until blended, about 30 seconds.

4. Scrape the butter onto a large sheet of plastic wrap, parchment or waxed paper. With a rubber spatula, smooth the butter into a cylinder shape about 1½ inches in diameter. Roll up, twisting both ends to seal. Label, date and store in the freezer for up to 2 months.

—Malcolm Hudson

• • •

ORANGE, ANISE AND GINGER BUTTER

This butter matches well with most crustaceans, especially lobster, as well as with carrots, chicken and pork.

Makes ½ Pound

2 sticks (8 ounces) unsalted butter, at room temperature
½ teaspoon finely chopped or ground aniseed
2 teaspoons grated orange zest
2 teaspoons grated fresh ginger
½ teaspoon salt

1. In a food processor, combine the butter, aniseed, orange zest, ginger and salt. Process, scraping down the sides once, until thoroughly blended, about 30 seconds.

2. Scrape the butter onto a large sheet of plastic wrap, parchment or waxed paper. With a rubber spatula, smooth the butter into a cylinder shape about 1½ inches in diameter. Roll up, twisting both ends to seal. Label, date and store in the freezer for up to 2 months.

—Malcolm Hudson

• • •

MAITRE D'HOTEL BUTTER

A culinary classic, this is a fine accompaniment to grilled meat and fish.

Makes ½ Pound

2 sticks (8 ounces) unsalted butter, at room temperature
3 tablespoons minced parsley
1 teaspoon fresh lemon juice
½ teaspoon salt
½ teaspoon freshly ground white pepper

1. In a food processor, combine the butter, parsley, lemon juice, salt and pepper. Process, scraping down the sides once, until thoroughly blended, about 30 seconds.

2. Scrape the butter onto a large sheet of plastic wrap, parchment or waxed paper. With a rubber spatula, smooth the butter into a cylinder shape about 1½ inches in diameter. Roll up, twisting both ends to seal. Label, date and store in the freezer for up to 2 months.

—Malcolm Hudson

• • •

LIME-CORIANDER BUTTER

I like this butter best when it is spread over hot corn on the cob. Try it also with grilled fish, chicken and steak.

Makes ½ Pound

2 sticks (8 ounces) unsalted butter, at room temperature
½ cup finely chopped fresh coriander
2 tablespoons fresh lime juice
1 teaspoon grated lime zest
½ teaspoon salt

1. In a medium bowl, combine the butter, coriander, lime juice, lime zest and salt. Beat together with a wooden spoon until well blended.

2. Divide the mixture in half. Using 2 sheets of plastic wrap, shape the butter into two 8-inch logs; wrap tightly and refrigerate until chilled. *(The butter can be refrigerated for up to 3 days or frozen for up to 2 months.)*

—Diana Sturgis

• • •

HOLLANDAISE SAUCE WITH CHIVES

This classic *sauce hollandaise*, an emulsion of egg yolks and butter flavored with lemon, is a perfect match for fish. To keep the egg yolks from curdling, this sauce is often made in a double boiler, a technique that is tedious and results in a sauce that is quite heavy. When made by the following method, however, the sauce is more quickly prepared and is lighter.

It is important to get the egg yolks thick and fluffy enough to support the quantity of butter used. This is done by whisking the yolks in a small heavy saucepan over moderately high heat. The higher the heat, the more important the quality of your pan becomes—a core of aluminum or copper is best—and the faster you need to whisk to prevent the eggs from overcooking and curdling.

Makes About 1¼ Cups

1½ sticks (6 ounces) unsalted butter
2 egg yolks
¼ teaspoon salt
2 teaspoons fresh lemon juice
3 tablespoons minced chives

1. Place the butter in a small saucepan and warm over low heat until almost completely melted, about 5 minutes. Remove from the heat and let melt completely; set aside.

2. In a small heavy nonreactive saucepan, whisk the egg yolks with 2 tablespoons of water over moderate to moderately high heat until fluffy and thickened enough so that you see the bottom of the pan while whisking, 2 to 3 minutes.

3. Remove the pan from the heat and continue whisking for several seconds to cool slightly. The mixture should be thick enough to cling to your whisk. Let cool for 1 minute.

4. Gradually whisk the melted butter into the egg yolks in a thin, slow stream, as you would for a mayonnaise. Add the salt and lemon juice. Stir in the minced chives. The hollandaise sauce can be held in a double boiler over warm water for up to 1 hour, whisking occasionally.

—Richard Grausman

• • •

BEARNAISE SAUCE

A béarnaise sauce is essentially a hollandaise flavored with a reduction of tarragon, chervil, shallots, pepper, wine and vinegar. Once the reduction is made, the technique for the sauce is the same as that used for hollandaise. Classically, only vinegar was used in the reduction, and when using fresh herbs, nothing else is needed. The convenience of dried herbs, however, requires that additional moisture be added, and the white wine in the recipe serves this purpose.

Makes About 1¼ Cups

1½ sticks (6 ounces) unsalted butter
2 shallots, finely chopped
1 teaspoon dried tarragon
1 teaspoon dried chervil
¼ teaspoon freshly ground pepper
2 tablespoons tarragon vinegar
2 tablespoons dry white wine
2 egg yolks
Salt

1. Place the butter in a small saucepan and warm over low heat until almost completely melted, about 5 minutes. Remove from the heat and let melt completely; set aside.

2. In a small, heavy nonreactive saucepan, combine the shallots, tarragon, chervil, pepper, vinegar and wine. Boil over moderately high heat until the liquid is reduced to 1 teaspoon, about 2 minutes.

3. Add the egg yolks and 2 tablespoons of water to the reduction and whisk constantly over moderate to moderately high heat until thick and fluffy, 2 to 3 minutes. As soon as the sauce thickens enough so that you see the bottom of the pan while whisking, remove from the heat. Continue whisking off the heat for several seconds. The sauce should be thick enough to cling to your whisk.

4. Let the egg yolk mixture cool for a minute before slowly adding the melted butter, which should be no hotter than the egg yolks. Whisk continually while adding the butter, as you would for a mayonnaise. Season with salt to taste. Keep the sauce warm in a double boiler over warm water for up to 1 hour before serving.

—Richard Grausman

• • •

BASIC MAYONNAISE

Mayonnaise works best if all the ingredients are at room temperature before you begin. The emulsion (the suspension of the particles of oil within the yolk) will not form if the oil or the yolks are too cold. On a chilly day, warm the bowl and whisk in hot water, then dry well before starting.

Makes About 1½ Cups

3 egg yolks, at room temperature
1 teaspoon Dijon-style mustard
½ teaspoon salt
Pinch of white pepper
1 tablespoon fresh lemon juice
½ cup olive oil mixed with ½ cup light vegetable oil (see Note)
1 tablespoon white wine vinegar
1 tablespoon boiling water

1. In a medium bowl, whisk the egg yolks until they lighten in color and begin to thicken. Beat in the mustard, salt, pepper and lemon juice and continue whisking until the mixture thickens enough to leave a trail when the whisk is drawn across the bottom of the bowl.

2. Very gradually, begin whisking in the oil by droplets. The emulsion will not form if the oil is added too quickly at this stage.

3. Once the emulsion forms and the mayonnaise begins to thicken, you can add the oil more rapidly, but never faster than in a thin stream.

4. After all the oil has been incorporated, whisk in the vinegar and the boiling water. (The vinegar will lighten and flavor the sauce, the boiling water will help stabilize it.) Taste the mayonnaise and adjust the seasonings according to your taste and the planned use. Cover and refrigerate for up to 5 days.

NOTE: We find this combination of oils produces the perfect balance of flavor and lightness for an all-purpose mayonnaise. You can adjust the proportions according to your taste and particular use.

—F&W

• • •

GREEN MAYONNAISE

This delicate, light green sauce is flavored and colored with the juices of chopped parsley, spinach and watercress.

Makes About 2¼ Cups

2 egg yolks, at room temperature
1 teaspoon Dijon-style mustard
1 tablespoon white wine vinegar
½ teaspoon salt
¼ teaspoon freshly ground white pepper
2 cups sunflower or safflower oil
1 tablespoon hot water
1 cup (packed) parsley sprigs
1 cup (packed) stemmed spinach leaves
1 cup (packed) watercress

1. In a medium bowl, whisk together the egg yolks, mustard, vinegar, salt and pepper. Very gradually whisk in the oil, drop by drop at first and then in a thin stream, until thickened. Whisk in the hot water.

2. Place the parsley, spinach and watercress in a food processor and process until minced. Scrape the minced greens onto a clean kitchen towel and squeeze over a small bowl to extract the juices. Stir the juices into the mayonnaise.

—André Soltner, Lutèce, New York City

• • •

AIOLI

This is an authentic Provençal aioli, which needs fresh, juicy garlic cloves. If you do not have a large mortar and pestle, you can crush the garlic and salt together to a paste with the flat side of a knife and make the aioli with a whisk or an electric hand mixer.

Makes About 1¼ Cups

6 garlic cloves, halved lengthwise
½ teaspoon salt
2 egg yolks, at room temperature
1 cup extra-virgin olive oil

1. Remove the green sprouting "germ" that runs through the center of the garlic if there is one. Coarsely chop the garlic.

2. Pour boiling water into a large mortar to warm it; discard the water and dry the mortar. Add the garlic and salt and mash together to form a paste. Slowly add the egg yolks one at a time, stirring and pressing slowly and evenly with the pestle in the same direction to thoroughly blend the garlic and egg yolks.

3. Very slowly work in the oil, drop by drop, until the mixture thickens. Gradually whisk in the remaining oil in a slow, thin stream until the sauce is thickened to a mayonnaise consistency.

—Hôtel Jules-César, Arles, France

• • •

ROUILLE

Aioli, also known as *beurre de Provence*, is a strongly flavored garlic mayonnaise made with olive oil and lemon juice, which is used extensively in the south of France. With the addition of crushed fresh hot red chile pepper, aioli becomes, in effect, a *rouille*, the traditional accompaniment to the Mediterranean fish soup and bouillabaisse.

6 Servings

1 egg yolk
1/2 teaspoon salt
5 garlic cloves, crushed through a press
3/4 cup extra-virgin olive oil
2 tablespoons fresh lemon juice
1 small fresh hot red pepper, finely minced, or cayenne pepper to taste

In a small bowl, whisk the egg yolk with a pinch of the salt. Add the garlic. Gradually beat in the oil, drop by drop at first, until the mixture thickens. Continue whisking, adding the oil in a slow, thin stream until the sauce is thick. Thin with 1 tablespoon of the lemon juice. Then beat in the remaining oil. Season with the rest of the salt, the remaining 1 tablespoon lemon juice and hot pepper to taste.

—Richard Grausman

• • •

SOY SESAME SAUCE

Use this as a dipping sauce for Flower Dumplings (p. 20) or Pot Stickers (p. 19).

Makes About 1/2 Cup

1 1/2 tablespoons chicken broth or water
1 tablespoon dark soy sauce
1 tablespoon light soy sauce
1 tablespoon distilled white vinegar
1 tablespoon Oriental sesame oil
1 1/2 teaspoons crushed hot pepper
1 tablespoon thinly sliced scallions

Combine all the ingredients in a small bowl and mix well. Let stand for about 30 minutes to let the flavors blend.

—Eileen Yin-Fei Lo

• • •

SWEET AND SOUR SAUCE

Dip egg rolls or spring rolls, such as Vegetarian Spring Roll (p. 17), in this tart-sweet sauce.

Makes About 1 3/4 Cups

1/2 cup red wine vinegar
1/3 cup sugar
1 can (8 ounces) tomato sauce
1/8 teaspoon salt
2 tablespoons cornstarch mixed with 2 teaspoons cold water
2 tablespoons minced green bell pepper
2 teaspoons minced fresh coriander (optional)

In a small nonreactive saucepan, combine the vinegar, sugar, tomato sauce, salt and dissolved cornstarch. Bring to a boil over moderately high heat, stirring frequently. Boil for 1 minute. Add the bell pepper and coriander. Pour into a bowl and serve warm or at room temperature.

—Eileen Yin-Fei Lo

• • •

CHILI SOY SAUCE

Along with Sweet and Sour Sauce (above), this makes a nice dipping sauce for Vegetarian Spring Roll (p. 17).

Makes About 1/2 Cup

1 tablespoon dark soy sauce
1 tablespoon light soy sauce
1 1/4 teaspoons minced fresh hot red chiles, or 1/2 teaspoon crushed hot pepper
1 tablespoon distilled white vinegar
3 tablespoons chicken broth or water
1/2 teaspoon sugar
2 teaspoons Oriental sesame oil
1 1/2 teaspoons minced garlic
1 1/2 teaspoons minced fresh ginger
1 tablespoon thinly sliced scallions

In a small bowl, combine all the ingredients. Let stand for 30 minutes and serve at room temperature.

—Eileen Yin-Fei Lo

• • •

TOMATILLO-SERRANO CHILE VINAIGRETTE

This is a chunky vinaigrette; take care to cut the vegetables into small dice, but not too fine. Fearing also serves this vinaigrette with grilled swordfish.

Makes About 2 1/2 Cups

4 fresh tomatillos, husked, rinsed and cut into small dice
1/3 cup diced jicama
1 1/2 tablespoons diced red bell pepper
1 1/2 tablespoons diced yellow bell pepper
1/2 mango, peeled and cut into small dice
1 serrano chile, seeded and finely diced
1/3 cup peanut oil
2 tablespoons olive oil
2 tablespoons white wine vinegar
1 1/2 tablespoons balsamic vinegar
1 tablespoon fresh lime juice
1 tablespoon fresh lemon juice
1 small garlic clove, minced
1 to 2 tablespoons minced fresh coriander
Salt

1. In a bowl, combine the tomatillos, jicama, red and yellow bell peppers, mango and serrano chile; toss to mix.

2. In a small bowl, combine the peanut oil, olive oil, white wine vinegar, balsamic vinegar, lime juice, lemon juice, garlic and coriander. Whisk to blend well.

3. Pour the dressing over the diced vegetables and stir lightly to mix. Season with salt to taste.

—Dean Fearing, The Mansion on Turtle Creek, Dallas

• • •

COFFEE BARBECUE SAUCE

This excellent sauce goes well with full-flavored meats: ribs and pork chops, squab, quail and duck. Use it to baste barbecue meats during the last 15 minutes of cooking.

Makes About 1½ Cups

2 tablespoons olive oil
3 tablespoons finely chopped onion
½ teaspoon minced garlic
3½ tablespoons tomato paste
3 tablespoons light unsulphured molasses
3 tablespoons strongly brewed espresso
2½ tablespoons dry Madeira
1½ tablespoons balsamic vinegar
1 tablespoon fresh lemon juice
1 teaspoon grated fresh ginger
½ teaspoon Worcestershire sauce
½ teaspoon dry mustard
¼ teaspoon ground coriander
¼ teaspoon cayenne pepper

1. In a small skillet, heat 1 tablespoon of the oil. Add the onion and cook over moderately low heat until softened but not browned, about 4 minutes. Transfer to a medium bowl.

2. In the same skillet, heat the remaining 1 tablespoon oil. Add the garlic and cook over moderately low heat until golden, about 2 minutes. Add the garlic to the onion.

3. Add the remaining ingredients to the bowl and stir until well mixed. Let the sauce stand for at least 1 hour to develop the flavors.

—Barbara Figueroa, Sorrento Hotel, Seattle

• • •

YELLOW PEPPER SAUCE

The hot pepper vinegar gives this colorful yellow pepper sauce a wonderful bite. Serve it as a dipping sauce with Pork Empanaditas (p. 21).

Makes About 2 Cups

4 medium yellow bell peppers, cut into 1-inch-wide strips
⅓ cup plus 2 tablespoons olive oil
½ teaspoon coarse (kosher) salt
½ teaspoon freshly ground black pepper
3 tablespoons hot pepper vinegar (see Note)

1. Preheat the oven to 350°. Toss the pepper strips with 2 tablespoons of the olive oil and season with ¼ teaspoon each of the salt and black pepper. Place the strips in a baking dish and cover tightly with foil. Bake for 30 to 45 minutes, until softened. Uncover and let cool.

2. Puree the peppers in a food processor or blender; strain to remove the skins.

3. In a small saucepan, cook the puree over moderate heat, stirring, until hot but not boiling. Whisk in the vinegar and then gradually add the remaining ⅓ cup olive oil, whisking until blended. Season with the remaining ¼ teaspoon each salt and pepper.

NOTE: Hot pepper vinegar can be purchased in specialty food shops. Brendan Walsh makes his own by soaking fresh serrano chiles in rice wine vinegar for 3 days to 2 weeks; it will get hotter as it stands.

—Brendan Walsh, Arizona 206, New York City

• • •

CHERRY TOMATO SALSA

Serve this salsa as a dip with tortilla chips or as an accompaniment to enchiladas.

Makes About 2 Cups

2 pints cherry tomatoes
1 large shallot, minced
1 large garlic clove, minced
2 tablespoons minced fresh coriander
1 tablespoon Champagne vinegar or white wine vinegar
2 serrano chiles, seeded and minced
2 teaspoons fresh lime juice
¼ teaspoon salt

1. In a food processor, coarsely chop the tomatoes, turning the machine on and off. Do not puree.

2. In a medium bowl, combine the chopped tomatoes and their juices with the shallot, garlic, coriander, vinegar, chiles, lime juice and salt. Stir well. Cover with plastic wrap and set aside for at least 2 hours to blend the flavors.

—Dean Fearing, The Mansion on Turtle Creek, Dallas

• • •

CREOJA SAUCE

This fresh salsa tastes delicious with broiled or grilled fish and was designed to go with Marinated and Grilled Swordfish Medallions (p. 56).

Makes About 1 Cup

3 tablespoons sherry wine vinegar
⅛ teaspoon salt
⅛ teaspoon freshly ground black pepper
½ cup extra-virgin olive oil

1 tablespoon finely chopped red onion
1 tablespoon finely chopped celery
1 tablespoon finely chopped carrot
1 tablespoon finely chopped green bell pepper
2 tablespoons finely chopped, peeled and seeded tomato
1 tablespoon finely chopped fresh chives
1 tablespoon finely chopped fresh coriander
1 tablespoons finely chopped parsley

1. In a small mixing bowl, combine the vinegar, salt and black pepper. Slowly whisk in the olive oil to form an emulsion.

2. Stir in the finely chopped vegetables and herbs. Cover the sauce and set it aside at room temperature for the flavors to blend for at least 1 hour before serving.

—Hubert Keller, Fleur de Lys, San Francisco

• • •

SOUTHWEST SALSA

Makes About 3 Cups

1 large onion, chopped
1 tablespoon minced and seeded jalapeño pepper
1½ teaspoons minced garlic
2 tablespoons olive oil
2 large tomatoes, peeled and finely chopped
1 can (8 ounces) tomato sauce
¾ teaspoon salt
1 tablespoon chopped fresh coriander

1. In a medium nonreactive saucepan, combine the onion, jalapeño, garlic and oil. Sauté over moderately high heat until the onion is softened and translucent, about 3 minutes.

2. Add the tomatoes and cook for 2 minutes. Add the tomato sauce and salt. Cover the pan, reduce the heat to moderately low and simmer for 5 minutes. Remove from the heat, stir in the coriander and serve hot or at room temperature.

—Eileen Yin-Fei Lo

• • •

BOURBON SAUCE

Custard sauces are so versatile that you can flavor them to your taste. Other variations can be created by substituting a favorite liquor or liqueur. Or omit the alcohol and double the vanilla.

Makes About 2 Cups

1½ cups milk
⅓ cup sugar
4 egg yolks
2 tablespoons bourbon
1 teaspoon vanilla extract

1. In a medium nonreactive saucepan, combine the milk and sugar. Bring to a boil over moderate heat.

2. Beat the egg yolks in a small bowl until liquefied. When the milk boils, gradually whisk ⅓ of it into the yolks. Return the remaining milk to a boil over low heat and whisk in the yolk mixture. Cook, whisking constantly, until the sauce thickens, 1 to 1½ minutes; do not let boil. Immediately remove from the heat.

3. Whisk the sauce constantly for 1 minute to cool. Strain through a fine sieve into a bowl and whisk for 30 seconds. Stir in the bourbon and vanilla. Serve the sauce warm (see Note).

NOTE: If it is necessary to reheat the sauce, pour it into a heatproof bowl and whisk over a pan of simmering water until just warm, about 2 minutes.

—Nicholas Malgieri

• • •

CUSTARD SAUCE

Makes About 3½ Cups

6 egg yolks
1 cup sugar
3 cups milk
1 tablespoon vanilla extract
1 tablespoon dark rum

1. In a heavy medium saucepan, beat the egg yolks and sugar until the mixture is pale and thick and slowly dissolves in a ribbon when the beaters are lifted.

2. In a medium saucepan, warm the milk over moderate heat until it just begins to boil, about 8 minutes. Gradually whisk the hot milk into the egg yolk mixture.

3. Cook over low heat, stirring constantly, until the custard is thick enough to coat the back of a spoon lightly, about 10 minutes; do not let boil.

4. Immediately strain the custard sauce into a bowl and let cool, about 15 minutes. Stir in the vanilla and dark rum. Cover and refrigerate until chilled, about 1 hour. *(The custard sauce can be prepared to this point up to 3 days ahead.)*

—Lydie Marshall

• • •

PISTACHIO SAUCE

Toasted pistachios and nut liqueur (pistachio or hazelnut) add a wonderful dimension to this dessert sauce. It is especially good with anything made with chocolate—mousse, pound cake or Chocolate Pâté (p. 212).

Makes About 2 Cups

3/4 cup unsalted shelled pistachio nuts (about 4 ounces)
1 3/4 cups half-and-half, scalded
5 egg yolks, at room temperature
1/4 cup sugar
1/4 teaspoon vanilla extract
Pinch of salt
2 tablespoons pistachio liqueur or Frangelico (hazelnut liqueur)

1. Place the pistachios in a small heatproof bowl and cover them with boiling water. Drain the nuts and slip off their skins. Place the peeled pistachios in a medium skillet and cook over moderately high heat, tossing, until lightly toasted, 2 to 3 minutes.

2. In a blender or food processor, combine the toasted pistachios and 1 cup of the half-and-half. Blend until the nuts are coarsely chopped. Add the remaining 3/4 cup half-and-half and process for 30 seconds. Let cool completely.

3. Strain the nut cream through a fine-mesh sieve into a heavy-bottomed saucepan, pressing on the nuts to extract as much liquid as possible; discard the nuts. Bring the pistachio-flavored half-and-half to a boil.

4. In a medium heatproof bowl, combine the egg yolks, sugar, vanilla and salt. Whisk briefly to blend. Gradually whisk in the hot half-and-half. Return the mixture to the saucepan and cook over moderate heat, stirring constantly, until the custard thickens enough to coat the back of a spoon lightly, 2 to 3 minutes; do not let boil. Remove the sauce from the heat and whisk until it is slightly cooled, about 2 minutes.

5. Strain the sauce into a medium bowl. Stir in the pistachio liqueur. Let the sauce cool to room temperature, then cover and refrigerate until cold. *(The sauce can be prepared 1 day ahead.)*

—Jimmy Schmidt, The Rattlesnake Club, Denver

• • •

HOT FUDGE SAUCE

This sauce can be made up to five days in advance and refrigerated in a covered jar. Warm over low heat or in a microwave oven before serving.

Makes About 1 1/2 Cups

1/4 cup unsweetened cocoa powder
3/4 cup sugar
1/3 cup light corn syrup
2 ounces unsweetened chocolate, coarsely chopped
2 tablespoons unsalted butter
1/3 cup heavy cream

1. Sift together the cocoa and sugar. In a small saucepan, boil the corn syrup over moderate heat for 2 minutes. Stir in 1/4 cup of water. Return to a boil and add the cocoa and sugar. Reduce the heat to low and simmer, stirring constantly, until the sugar dissolves, 3 to 5 minutes.

2. Add the unsweetened chocolate and the butter and bring to a boil, stirring until smooth. Add the cream and return to a boil. Remove from the heat.

—Stephan Pyles, Routh Street Café, Dallas

• • •

BRANDY BUTTER SAUCE

This is a wonderfully rich and creamy hard sauce. Serve it with Indian Pudding (p. 215).

Makes About 1 1/2 Cups

1 stick (4 ounces) unsalted butter, at room temperature
1/4 teaspoon salt
2 cups confectioners' sugar
2 tablespoons heavy cream
2 tablespoons Cognac

In a small bowl, cream the butter with the salt until light and fluffy. Add the sugar, 1 tablespoon at a time, alternating with the cream and Cognac; beat until smooth. The sauce will be creamy. (If not using right away, cover and refrigerate for up to 3 days.) Let return to room temperature before serving.

—Warren Picower

• • •

ROSEMARY OIL WITH RED CHILES

You can substitute this oil in any dish calling for olive oil when you want to add an extra kick.

Makes 1 Quart

5 large, thick branches of rosemary
2 dried red chiles
1 quart extra-virgin olive oil

Rub the rosemary branches between your fingers to bruise them. Using a knife, bruise the chiles, then put them and the rosemary in a jar with a tight-fitting lid. Pour the olive oil into the jar, seal and let stand at room temperature for 10 days. Strain the oil through a fine-mesh sieve and return to the jar. This oil will keep for up to 2 months.

—Marcia Kiesel

• • •

GERMAN-STYLE MUSTARD

You can serve this hot-and-sweet mustard with other meat, add it to salad dressing, use it in deviled eggs or brush it on meat or poultry before grilling. If you like really hot mustard, stir in some freshly grated or well-drained prepared horseradish, half a teaspoon at a time, tasting constantly. You can also doctor store-bought mustards by adding a small amount of crushed mustard seeds, horseradish, honey, beer, wine, minced garlic or fresh herbs.

Makes About 1½ Cups

¼ cup plus 2 tablespoons mustard seed, preferably black but yellow acceptable
½ cup dry mustard
½ cup pale German beer or dry white wine
¼ cup cider vinegar or white wine vinegar
¼ cup (packed) light brown sugar
2 medium garlic cloves, minced
1 teaspoon salt
⅛ teaspoon ground allspice
⅛ teaspoon ground cloves
½ teaspoon minced fresh tarragon or ¼ teaspoon dried
1 tablespoon honey

1. Place the mustard seeds and dry mustard in a food processor or blender. In a small saucepan, combine ¼ cup of the beer or wine with the vinegar, brown sugar, garlic, salt, allspice, cloves, tarragon and ½ cup water. Bring to a boil over high heat. Immediately pour the liquid into the processor or blender and process for 1 minute. Set aside for 3 hours to allow the flavors to blend.

2. Add the honey and the remaining ¼ cup beer or wine. Process or blend the mustard until the desired consistency is reached; I prefer it just slightly grainy. The mustard can be stored in a covered glass jar in the refrigerator for 2 to 3 months. If it becomes dry, stir in a little beer or wine to moisten it.

—Linda Merinoff

• • •

ROASTED GARLIC PUREE

I find this puree to be an indispensable ingredient. The sweet, mellow flavor makes it a delicious addition to salad dressings, baked vegetables, soups, stews and sauces. This recipe can be doubled or tripled and will keep for up to two weeks in the refrigerator.

Makes ¼ Cup

2 large heads of garlic (about ½ pound)
1 teaspoon salt
1 teaspoon freshly ground pepper
2 tablespoons extra-virgin olive oil

1. Preheat the oven to 350°. Cut the heads of garlic in half horizontally, being careful that the cloves remain intact. Season the cut surfaces with the salt and pepper and drizzle on the olive oil. Reassemble the heads, set them in a small roasting pan and bake until the cloves are soft and golden, about 1 hour. Remove and let cool to room temperature.

2. Strain the roasted garlic through a fine-mesh sieve over a bowl; discard any skin that remains. Scrape any paste from the back of the sieve and add to the paste in the bowl. *(To store, scrape the garlic paste into a glass jar, cover the surface with olive oil and refrigerate.)*

—Bob Chambers

• • •

HOT DOG RELISH

Relishes were created hundreds of years ago to preserve vegetables for long, barren winters. This relish was served with cold meats or used as a stuffing for baked ham. Although we have refrigeration today, the texture and vinegary taste of the vegetables are still very appealing.

Makes About 8½ Cups

1½ cups cider vinegar
⅔ cup sugar
¼ cup coarse (kosher) salt
2 tablespoons yellow mustard seeds
1 tablespoon whole allspice berries
3 green bell peppers, finely diced
2 red bell peppers, finely diced
2 medium onions, chopped
2 cups shredded green cabbage
1 cup tiny cauliflower florets
1 can (16 ounces) whole corn kernels, drained
1 cup finely diced dill pickles
1 cup finely diced bread-and-butter pickles
1 tablespoon prepared mustard

1. In a large nonreactive saucepan, combine the vinegar, sugar, salt, mustard seeds and allspice berries. Stir in the green and red bell peppers, onions, cabbage, cauliflower and corn. Bring to a boil over high heat. Reduce the heat to low and simmer, uncovered, for 10 minutes.

2. Remove from the heat and stir in the dill pickles, bread-and-butter pickles and mustard. Let cool, then spoon the relish into jars, cover and refrigerate. This relish will keep in the refrigerator for at least 2 months.

—Linda Merinoff

• • •

JICAMA-ORANGE RELISH

This fresh relish is a wonderful blend of soft, sweet and crisp. Serve it with Grilled Quail with Sweet Potato Pancakes (p. 89).

Makes About 1½ Cups

½ pound jicama, peeled and cut into ¼-inch dice
½ small ripe mango, cut into ¼-inch dice
1 large navel orange—peeled, sectioned and cut into ¼-inch dice
3 tablespoons fresh orange juice
2 tablespoons finely diced, peeled and seeded cucumber
1 tablespoon finely diced red bell pepper
1 tablespoon finely diced yellow bell pepper
1 tablespoon chopped onion
½ serrano chile, seeded and minced
1 teaspoon chopped fresh mint
2 tablespoons fresh lime juice
Pinch of salt

In a medium bowl, combine all the ingredients. Toss well and season with additional salt to taste. Cover and let marinate for 1 hour at cool room temperature or for up to 4 hours in the refrigerator before serving.

—Stephan Pyles, Routh Street Cafe, Dallas

• • •

CRANBERRY RELISH

Test Kitchen Director Diana Sturgis's fresh-tasting, no-cook relish combines the tang and crunch of cranberries and walnuts with unpeeled orange and pear. A meat grinder or food processor makes preparation a snap. This relish is refreshing at any time of year, and if you want to make it in the summer, when cranberries are in season, freeze them in double plastic bags. The relish can then be prepared while the berries are still frozen.

Makes About 3 Cups

1 juice orange—scrubbed, halved, seeded and coarsely chopped
1 small bosc pear—cored and coarsely chopped
2¼ cups (½ pound) fresh cranberries
½ cup walnut halves
½ cup sugar

Pass the orange, pear, cranberries and walnuts through a meat grinder or coarsely chop in a food processor, turning the machine on and off for 20 to 30 seconds; do not overprocess. Scrape this mixture into a bowl and stir in the sugar. The relish can be stored in the refrigerator in a covered jar for up to 5 days.

—Diana Sturgis

• • •

CANDIED MINT LEAVES

Use these sugared leaves to garnish desserts of every variety. They can be stored in an airtight container for up to two months.

Makes 40 to 50 Loaves

1 egg white, lightly beaten
1 cup sifted superfine sugar
40 to 50 mint leaves, washed and dried

Put the egg white in a small bowl and the sugar in a shallow dish. Brush each mint leaf with the egg white and place it face down in the sugar. Cover the entire leaf with sugar, pressing down to coat both sides evenly. Carefully shake the leaves to remove any excess sugar and place them on a wire rack to dry completely for 3 to 5 days, depending on the humidity level.

—Marcia Kiesel

• • •

CANDIED ORANGE PEEL

I know that candied orange peel is sold in supermarkets and specialty stores, but it is simply not the same as homemade. Candied orange peel is not only a wonderful addition to chocolate or fruit cakes, but also a fine accompaniment to an after-dinner espresso. It will keep for up to three months in an airtight container at room temperature.

Makes About ¾ Cup

1 large navel orange
¼ cup plus 2 tablespoons granulated sugar
2 tablespoons crystal sugar (optional)

1. Preheat the oven to 250°. Cut the bottom and top off the orange and discard. Using a sharp knife, slit the skin of the orange into quarters from top to bottom; peel the orange. Stack the peels and cut them lengthwise into ⅛-inch-thick julienne strips.

2. In a small saucepan, place the orange peel and enough cold water to cover. Bring to a rolling boil over high heat and boil for 5 minutes. Drain, rinse under cold running water and repeat the procedure twice more.

3. Return the peels to the saucepan and add the granulated sugar and ¼ cup of water. Bring to a boil over moderate heat. Reduce the heat and simmer until the liquid evaporates and the sugar glazes the rinds, about 30 minutes. Drain on a rack set on a cookie sheet. Separate the peels.

4. Place the peels on the rack in the oven and bake until almost dry, about 20 minutes. (If you are using crystal sugar, roll the rinds in it at this point.) Store in an airtight container.

—Lydie Marshall

• • •

INDEX

A

B

C

D-E

F

G-H

I-J-K

L

M

N-O

P

Q-R

S

T-U-V

W-X-Y-Z

CONTRIBUTORS

Jean Anderson is a food writer and photographer, newspaper food columnist and the author of, most recently, *The Food of Portugal* (William Morrow). She is currently working, with Elaine Hanna, on a microwave cookbook for Doubleday.
Lee Bailey is a designer, cookbook author and the author of the *Entertaining with Lee Bailey* column in *Food & Wine.* He is currently working on *Southern Food and Plantation Houses* to be published in fall of 1990 by Clarkson Potter.
Nancy Verde Barr is a food writer and cooking teacher currently working on a book on the foods of southern Italy.
Lidia Bastianich is chef/owner of Felidia Ristorante in New York City and is working on a cookbook tentatively titled *Lidia's Kitchen.*
Daniel Boulud is executive chef of Le Cirque in New York City and the publisher of a newsletter entitled "Easy Cooking with Great Chefs."
Antoine Bouterin is executive chef at Le Périgord in New York City.
Mimi Ruth Brodeur is a former Associate Test Kitchen Director of *Food & Wine.*
Ed Brown is a cooking teacher, the author of *The Tassajara Bread Book, Tassajara Cooking, The Tassajara Recipe Book* (all from Shambhala) and co-author of *The Greens Cookbook* (Bantam).
James W. Brown, Jr. is author of *Food & Wine*'s monthly menus page.
Hugh Carpenter is executive chef at Chopstix Dimsum Cafe in Hollywood, California, a cooking teacher and the author of *Pacific Flavors: Oriental Recipes for a Contemporary Kitchen* (Stewart, Tabori & Chang).
Bob Chambers is a New York-based chef and food stylist.
Laura Chenel is owner of Laura Chenel's Chèvre in Santa Rosa, California.
Nancy Christy is a cook and freelance writer.
John Clancy is chef/owner of John Clancy's Restaurant in New York City.
Peggy Cullen is a New York-based pastry chef and freelance writer.
Marion Cunningham is a cooking teacher, consultant, food writer and the author of, most recently, *The Breakfast Book* (Knopf).
Robert Del Grande is chef/owner of Cafe Annie in Houston.
François Dionot is the director of L'Académie de Cuisine in Bethesda, Maryland.
Jim Dodge is pastry chef at the Stanford Court Hotel in San Francisco.
Myra Dorros is a newspaper food columnist, professional chef, recipe developer and cooking teacher in Milwaukee.
Clive du Val III is chef/owner of Tila's in Houston and its sister restaurant in Washington, D.C.
Franco Dunn is chef at Jordan Vineyard in Healdsburg, California.
Dean Fearing is executive chef at The Mansion on Turtle Creek in Dallas and the author of *The Mansion on Turtle Creek Cookbook* (Weidenfeld & Nicolson).
Carol Field is a food journalist and the author of *The Italian Baker* (Harper & Row) and an upcoming book on Italian cuisine.
Barbara Figueroa is executive chef of the Sorrento Hotel in Seattle.
Jim Fobel is a food journalist, artist and the author of, most recently, *Jim Fobel's Old-Fashioned Baking Book* (Ballantine). He is currently working on a book about hearty diet dishes for Doubleday.
Margaret Fox is chef/owner of Café Beaujolais in Mendocino, California, and is working on a sequel to her cookbook *Café Beaujolais* (Ten Speed Press).
André Gaillard is executive chef of La Réserve in New York City.
Joyce Goldstein is chef/owner of Square One in San Francisco and author of the upcoming *Tastes of the Mediterranean* (William Morrow).
Richard Grausman is a cooking teacher and the author of the upcoming *At Home with the French Classics* (Workman).
Dorie Greenspan is a food writer currently at work on a dessert cookbook to be published by William Morrow in 1990.
Ceri E. Hadda is a freelance food writer, editor and recipe developer.
Ken Haedrich is a food writer, magazine food columnist and the author of, most recently, *The Maple Syrup Cookbook* (Garden Way).
Gary Hansen is chef at Prunelle in New York City.
Bruce Healy is a cooking teacher (Healy-Lucullus School of French Cooking in Boulder, Colorado) and the co-author, with Paul Bugat, of *Mastering the Art of French Pastry* (Barron's).
Ken Hom is a Chinese cooking authority and cookbook author currently working on a number of books for future publication: *Asian Vegetarian Feast* (William Morrow), *The Fragrant Harbor Taste: Hong Kong's New Chinese Cooking* and *The Taste of China* (both from Simon and Schuster).
Monique Hooker is a cooking teacher and chef/owner of Monique's Café in Chicago.
Malcolm Hudson is a chef who was named to *Food & Wine*'s "Honor Roll of Chefs" in 1983.
Michael James is a chef, food writer and cookbook author currently working on a book entitled *American Pie.*
Evan Jones is the author of *American Food: The Gastronomic Story* (Vintage) and co-author, with **Judith Jones**—Senior Editor at Alfred A. Knopf, Inc.—of *The L.L. Bean Book of New New England Cookery* (Random House).
Barbara Kafka is a cooking teacher, food and restaurant columnist and the author of, most recently, *Microwave Gourmet* (William Morrow). She is currently working on *MicroSlim Gourmet* for William Morrow.
Hubert Keller is executive chef and co-owner of Fleur de Lys in San Francisco.
Marcia Kiesel is Associate Test Kitchen Director of *Food & Wine.*
Laure Cantor Kimpton is a cook and freelance writer.
Peter Kump is the owner of Peter Kump's New York Cooking School in New York City. He is currently working on *The New York Cooking School Cookbook* for publication in 1990.
Gilbert Le Coze is executive chef/owner of Le Bernardin in New York City.
Sarabeth Levine is founder of Sarabeth's Kitchen in New York City.
David Liederman is chef/owner of Chez Louis Restaurant in New York City and the founder of David's Specialty Foods, Inc.
Eileen Yin-Fei Lo is a cooking teacher (China Institute in America, New York City), food writer and the author of, most recently, *Eileen Yin-Fei Lo's New Cantonese Cooking* (Viking).
Michael and Wendy London are the owners of Mrs. London's Bakeshop in Saratoga Springs, New York.
Nicholas Malgieri is a pastry chef, cooking teacher (at Peter Kump's New York Cooking School), consultant and author of the forthcoming *Nick Malgieri's Perfect Pastry* (1989, Macmillan) and *Italian Pastry and Dessert Book* (1989, Little, Brown).
Lydie Marshall is a cooking teacher (A La Bonne Cocotte, New York City), the author of *Cooking with Lydie Marshall* (Knopf) and co-author (with Pierre Moulin and Pierre Levecq) of an upcoming (1990) cookbook tentatively titled *Pierre Deux.*
John Robert Massie is a food stylist and recipe developer.
Elin McCoy & John Frederick Walker are contributing wines and spirits editors for *Food & Wine* and the co-authors of the forthcoming *Rethinking Wine* (Simon and Schuster).
Robert McGrath is executive chef at the Four Seasons Hotel in Dallas.
Michael McLaughlin is a food writer and cookbook author currently working on the upcoming *The New American Kitchen* (Simon and Schuster).

Alice Medrich is owner of Cocolat in Berkeley, California.
Linda Merinoff is a food writer and author of *The Glorious Noodle* (Poseidon Press), *The Savory Sausage* (Poseidon Press) and the upcoming *Gingerbread* (Fireside Press).
Roger Michel is the executive chef at the Hyatt Regency Sarasota in Sarasota, Florida.
Roland Muller is chef at Sonoma Mission Inn & Spa in Sonoma, California.
David Munn is a chef at the New York Restaurant School and the author of *The Joy of Pastry* (Barron's) and the forthcoming *The Professional Baker* (1989, Van Nostrand Reinhold).
Rick O'Connell is executive chef of RAF and Rosalies in San Francisco.
Bradley Ogden is executive chef of Campton Place Hotel in San Francisco and is working on *Breakfast, Lunch and Dinner with Bradley Ogden* to be published by Random House in late 1989.
Philippe Padovani is corporate chef at the Halekulani Hotel in Honolulu.
Jean-Louis Palladin is chef/owner of Jean-Louis in Washington, D.C.
Gérard Pangaud is executive chef at Aurora in New York City.
Jean-Paul Passédat is executive chef and owner of Le Petit Nice in Marseilles, France.
Cindy Pawlcyn is chef/owner of Mustards Grill in Yountville, California, and of Tra Vigne in St. Helena, California.
Georges Perrier is chef/owner of Le Bec-Fin in Philadephia.
Warren Picower is Managing Editor of *Food & Wine*.
Christian Planchon is the executive chef at Down Under in Fort Lauderdale, Florida.
Walter Plendner is executive chef at the Vista International Hotel in New York.
W. Peter Prestcott is *Food & Wine*'s Entertaining and Special Projects Editor.
Stephan Pyles is chef/owner of Routh Street Cafe in Dallas.
Jean Reynolds is sous-chef at Jordan Vineyard in Healdsburg, California.
Felipe Rojas-Lombardi is chef/owner of The Ballroom Restaurant and Tapas Bar in New York City and the author of the upcoming *Chef Felipe's South American Cooking* (1989, Atheneum).
Michael Romano is executive chef at La Caravelle in New York City.
Anne Rosenzweig is chef/owner of Arcadia in New York City and the author of *The Arcadia Seasonal Mural & Cookbook* (Harry N. Abrams).
Gabriel Rousselet, now retired, was the chef/owner of Les Bories in Gordes, France.
Julie Sahni is a chef, consultant, cooking teacher (Julie Sahni's Indian Cooking School in New York City) and cookbook author currently working on *Indian Microwave Cooking* to be published by William Morrow in mid-1989.
Jimmy Schmidt is chef/owner of The Rattlesnake Club in Denver, as well as two new branches of the restaurant in Detroit and Washington, D.C. He is currently working on *Cook for All Seasons* tentatively scheduled for publication in 1990.
Sally Schneider, food writer, consultant, food stylist and the author of the *Low-Calorie Cooking* column for *Food & Wine*, is currently working on a book on low-calorie cooking to be published by Stewart, Tabori & Chang in the fall of 1990.
Phillip Stephen Schulz is a cooking teacher, food writer and the author of *Cooking with Fire & Smoke* (Simon and Schuster) and *Better By the Dozen*, due out from Simon and Schuster in the fall of 1989.
Guenter Seeger is executive chef at The Ritz-Carlton Buckhead in Atlanta.
Lindsey Shere is pastry chef and part owner of Chez Panisse in Berkeley, California, and part owner of Downtown Bakery and Creamery in Healdsburg, California. She is also the author of *Chez Panisse Desserts* (Random House).
André Soltner is the chef/owner of Lutèce in New York City.
Frank Stitt is the executive chef and owner of Highlands Bar & Grill in Birmingham, Alabama.
Diana Sturgis is the Test Kitchen Director of *Food & Wine*.
Mary Taylor is a food writer and stylist, cooking teacher and co-author of *The Cholerestol Connection* to be published in mid-1989.
Elizabeth Terry is chef/owner of Elizabeth on 37th in Savannah.
Philippe Thème is chef/owner of La Riboto de Taven in Les Baux-de-Provence, France.
Tina Ujlaki is an Associate Editor of *Food & Wine*.
Jean-Georges Vongerichten is chef at Restaurant Lafayette in New York City.
Brendan Walsh is executive chef at Arizona 206 in New York City.
David Waltuck is chef/owner of Chanterelle in New York City.
Patricia Wells is the restaurant critic for *The International Herald Tribune* and the author of *The Food Lover's Guide to Paris* and *The Food Lover's Guide to France* (both from Workman) and, to be published by Workman in 1989, *The French Bistro Cookbook*.
Gayle Henderson Wilson is a food writer and consultant and the author of a forthcoming book tentatively titled *Cooking for Pleasure* (Price/Stern/Sloan).
Susan Wyler is Food Editor of *Food & Wine*.

We would also like to thank the following restaurants and individuals for their contributions to *Food & Wine* and to this cookbook:
Ella and Dick Brennan, Commander's Palace in New Orleans; **Ruth Brodeur**; **The Four Seasons** in New York City; **Gaylord India**; **Hugo's** in West Hollywood, California; **Hôtel Jules-César** in Arles, France; **Emeril Lagasse,** Commander's Palace in New Orleans; **Manhattan Ocean Club** in New York City; **O. Ottomanelli & Sons** in New York City; **Joseph Phelps Vineyards** in St. Helena, California; **Quartorze** in New York City; **Gordon Sinclair,** Gordon Restaurant in Chicago; **Taxi** in San Francisco; **Irene Woodson**.

PHOTO CREDITS
Cover: Jerry Simpson. **Page 33:** Michael Skott. **Page 34:** Michael Skott. **Page 35:** Jerry Simpson. **Page 36:** Dennis Galante. **Page 69:** Constance Hansen. **Page 70:** Michael Skott. **Page 71:** Michael Skott. **Page 72:** Dennis Galante. **Pages 72-73:** Michael Skott. **Pages 74-75:** Constance Hansen. **Page 75:** Charles Purvis. **Page 76:** Lisa Charles. **Page 109:** Lisa Charles. **Pages 110-111:** Jerry Simpson. **Page 111:** Jerry Simpson. **Page 112:** Jerry Simpson. **Page 145:** Mark Thomas. **Page 146:** Elizabeth Watt. **Pages 146-147:** Jerry Simpson. **Page 148:** Jerry Simpson. **Page 181:** Dennis Galante. **Page 182:** Jerry Simpson. **Page 183:** Jerry Simpson. **Page 184:** Steven Mark Needham. **Pages 184-185:** Jerry Simpson. **Pages 186-187:** Jerry Simpson. **Page 187:** Dennis Galante. **Page 188:** Chris Baker. **Page 221:** Dennis Galante. **Page 222 top:** Joshua Greene. **Page 222 bottom:** Jerry Simpson. **Page 223:** Michael Skott. **Page 224:** Dennis Galante.